MARRIAGES
of
DAVIDSON COUNTY, TENNESSEE

1789-1847

MARRIAGES of DAVIDSON COUNTY, TENNESSEE

1789-1847

Compiled by
EDYTHE RUCKER WHITLEY

With an Index by Patti Matulonis

Baltimore
GENEALOGICAL PUBLISHING CO., INC.
1981

Genealogical Publishing Co., Inc.
Baltimore, Maryland

Library of Congress Catalogue Card Number 80-84320
International Standard Book Number 0-8063-0919-9
Made in the United States of America

Introduction

DAVIDSON COUNTY, Tennessee was created by an act of the Legislature of North Carolina on October 6, 1783. It originally included most of the territory west of the Cumberland Mountains now making up Middle Tennessee. It was named for General William Lea Davidson, who was killed at Cowan's Fort, North Carolina, on February 1, 1781 while resisting the advance of British troops.

When Davidson County was formed the county seat was named Nashborough, honoring General Francis Nash of North Carolina, who was killed in the Battle of Germantown. The name was changed to Nashville by an act of the North Carolina Legislature in 1784. In this year the first courthouse was built. It was constructed of hewn logs and was eighteen feet square, with a lean-to of twelve feet. It has been replaced several times to meet the requirements of the city and county.

All of the early Davidson County marriage bonds and licenses were destroyed by fire, but the first two volumes of marriage registers, compiled from the original bonds and licenses, are intact, although both are fragile and worn with age. The records published herein have been transcribed from these two volumes, the first of which covers the period from January 1789 to December 1837, the second the period from January 1838 to December 1847.

The reader should note that marriage bonds were frequently issued the same day as licenses, but the marriage itself was usually—though not always—solemnized at a later date. If no date of marriage, or solemnization (abbreviated *Sol.*), is given, then the single date provided refers to the date of issue of either the bond or the license.

Edythe Rucker Whitley
Nashville, Tennessee
May 1980

DAVIDSON COUNTY, TENNESSEE

Marriage Book I, 1789-1837

Page 1
Haythorn, William to Mary Kelley, Jan. 11, 1793.
Courtney, Nehemiah to Elizabeth Johnston, Oct. 14, 1790.
Buchanan, Andrew to Jane McKinney, Oct. 22, 1798.
Rounswell, Amos to Elizabeth Thomas, Sep. 10, 1794.
Rutherford, James to Elizabeth Cartwright, Jan. 7, 1791.
Dunham, John to Polly Waller, Nov. 2, 1793.
Flynn, William to Hannah Ramsy, May 8, 1793.
Crow, Jacob to Nancy Crow, July 5, 1793.
Lewis, Seth to Nancy Hardiman, April 5, 1793.
Bosley, Beal to Margery Shute, Dec. 24, 1794.

Page 2
Heaton, Thomas to Mary Stuart, July 19, 1794.
Downey, Benjamin to Mary Hollis, March 22, 1794.
Dean, James to Polly Dickinson, Sep. 24, 1794.
Bodie, William to Jennie Lane, June 14, 1790.
Walker, George to Rachel Caffrey, Aug. 9, 1790.
Snyder, Charles to Elizabeth Savier, --- 18, 1790.
Glasgow, Cornelius to Lucia Merida, Nov. 16, 1793.
Ewing, Finis to Peggy Davidson, Jan. 12, 1793.
Willocks, Thomas to Mary Bryant, Sep. 12, 1792.
Brown, Thomas to Mary Love, June 27, 1791.

Page 3
Champ, John to Polly Mayfield, Dec. 21, 1796.
Neily, William to Jennie Buchanan, April 20, 1791.
Reader, Jacob to Polly Allen, July 2, 1792.
Hooper, William to Sarah Hollis, March 4, 1789.
Slayton, Seward to Nancy Williams, July 8, 1789.
Guice, Jacob to Elizabeth Bickly, Feb. 2, 1789.
Harlin, Joshua to Mary Smith, Nov. 17, 1789.
Kirkpatrick, Jno. to Martha Buchanan, Sep. 6, 1789.
Heaton, Enoch to Ruth Topp, Oct. 20, 1789.
Nelson, Robert to Elizabeth Bell, Sep. 1, 1789.

Page 4
Hollis, Joshua to Mary Wilheim, Aug. 19, 1789.
Payne, Josiah to Mary Barnett, May 4, 1789.
Mitchell, Robert to Drusila Everett, June 1, 1789.
Harrington, Abijah to Sarah Marrs, Nov. 19, 1789.
Barnett, Robert to Margaret Young, July 31, 1789.
Rogers, Simon to Elizabeth Mitchell, March 7, 1789.
Hudson, Wm. to Elizabeth Dunn, Oct. 15, 1789.
Rordine, Francis to Rebecca Cashaw, March 9, 1790.
Murry, Wm. to Margaret Boyd, March 31, 1790.

Oneal, Mitchel to Delilah Martin, March 5, 1790.

Page 5
Hightower, Richard to Nancy Smith, Oct. 17, 1791.
Fleming, Ralph to Hannah Boyd, April 13, 1791.
Brewer, Elisha to Mary Renolds, May 17, 1791.
Whitsett, James to Jennie Menees, Dec. 10, 1792.
Green, Henry to Jennie Davidson, July 4, 1791.
Caffrey, Peter to --------, Jan. 5, 1791.
Dunham, Joseph to Nancy Bronson, Nov. 24, 1793.
Oneal, Mitchell to Judith Hughes, March 19, 1793.
Chiles, Henry to Sallie Sugg, Sep. 11, 1793.
Wilson, John to Nancy McKnight, Sep. 10, 1791.

Page 6
Pratt, Ephriam to Sarah Buchanan, June 28, 1790.
Shaffer, David to Jane Bowlin, Jan. 23, 1792.
Boyd, John to Mary Boyd, Sep. 1, 1790.
Hart, Joseph to Anna Sugg, Aug. 21, 1791.
Black, Mitchell to Eva Raimer, Oct. 3, 1791.
Shaffer, Richard to Elizabeth Gambal, Oct. 21, 1789.
Pipkin, Phillip to Margaret Brown, --- 8, 1792.
Latimer, Witheral to Margaret Anderson, March 21, 1793.
McCance, Matthew to Anna Walker, March 24, 1794.
Jackson, Andrew to Rachel Donelson, Jan. 17, 1794.

Page 7
Baker, Zacheus to Elsee Rhods, Oct. 24, 1794.
Boyd, Abraham to Nancy Lyon, April 1, 1794.
McClich, William to Jennie Johnston, Nov. 10, 1794.
Squires, Michael to Martha Turner, July 7, 1792.
Campbell, Chas. to Ann Nowland, May 4, 1791.
Smith, William to Phoebe Denton, Sep. 4, 1792.
Berryal, Lewis to Jean Benton, ----------.
Evans, Daniel to Belizabeth Courtney, Feb. 8, 1794.
Buchanan, John to Hannah Buchanan, June 6, 1794.
Moore, Wm. to Palifina Castleman, Dec. 7, 1791.

Page 8
Raimer, Adam to Mary Carihan, May 30, 1791.
Topp, John to Comfort Everitt, July 26, 1794.
Murry, William to Elizabeth Pillow, July 16, 1795.
Edwards, Jacob to Elizabeth Hah, April 3, 1795.
Bleakley, James to Nancy Wilkison, Dec. 19, 1795.
Robertson, James to Mary Bradshaw, Dec. 15, 1795.
Roseberry, Robert to Susannah McFaugh, Jan. 3, 1795.
Alston, John to Sinah Hooper, June 3, 1795.
Payne, William to Elizabeth Payne, June 10, 1796.
Hixon, Elijah to Polly Moore, Aug. 22, 1796.

Page 9
Young, David to Sarah Phillips, Dec. 27, 1796.
Evans, John to Polly Thomas, Aug. 24, 1796.
Donelson, Wm. to Charity Dickinson, Aug. 9, 1796.

Hilton, Daniel to Elizabeth Lancaster, July 26, 1796.
Dillahunty, Wm. to Sarah Johnston, Oct. 10, 1796.
Perry, Hugh to Jane Kendrick, Nov. 4, 1796.
Walker, Joseph to Sarah Carothers, Jan. 18, 1796.
Witherspoon, John to Elizabeth Shute, Jan. 31, 1796.
Shute, John to Nancy Childress, Dec. 5, 1796.
Harris, John to Elizabeth Lucas, Jan. 20, 1796.

Page 10
Ralston, Joseph to Jane Walker, April 25, 1796.
Ward, Frederick to Mary Bosley, May 26, 1796.
Holland, Darden to Charlotte Crawford, Nov. 14, 1796.
Buchanan, Thomas to Jennie Neely, June 6, 1796.
Hooper, Eneas to Anne Young, March 10, 1796.
Brown, Joseph to Sarah Thomas, --- 18, 1796.
McBride, Sam to Elizabeth Howell, April 9, 1796.
Johnston, John to Elizabeth Baker, Jan. 4, 1796.
Harrod, Barnebeth to Polly Williams, May 4, 1795.
Loftin, Jeremiah to Hannah Dillihunt, June 4, 1796.

Page 11
Watkins, Noel to Sallie Smith, Sep. 11, 1797.
Walker, David to Phoebe Finley, Sep. 25, 1797.
Small, Daniel to Mary Hutchens, Nov. 27, 1797.
Hodge, James to Nancy Becton, Jan. 25, 1797.
Stuart, James to Sallie Hooper, Feb. 4, 1797.
Balance, Joshua to Mary D. Roberts, Oct. 10, 1797.
Smith, Moses to Ruth Smith, Dec. 30, 1797.
Thomas, Jesse to Mary Drusilla Tracy, Dec. 1, 1797.
Parrish, Joel to Hannah Smith, Dec. 3, 1797.
Hampton, Anthony to Polly Williams, Dec. 20, 1797.

Page 12
McQuerry, Pleasant to Nancy Smith, Sep. 27, 1797.
Huddleston, Baldwin to Rebecca Henderson, June 14, 1797.
Miles, Daniel to Susanna Frensly, Oct. 17, 1797.
Lancaster, Thomas to Anna Walker, Dec. 13, 1797.
Smith, Robert to Mary T. Donelson, Nov. 30, 1798.
Walker, Abraham to Martha Patton, March 31, 1798.
McAlister, John to Nettie Bearden, March 9, 1798.
Fairless, James to Mary Armstrong, Jan. 4, 1798.
Wiggin, Permot to Rachel Wendel, March 9, 1798.
Hill, James to Mary S. Hunt, Dec. 18, 1798.

Page 13
Mullen, Wm. to Mary E. Becton, Nov. 29, 1798.
Moore, Alexander to Mary Cloyd, Feb. 22, 1798.
Phenix, Henry to Nancy Todd, Feb. 11, 1798.
Castleman, David to Mary Campbell, March 22, 1798.
Fly, Jeremiah to Mary Z. Pipkins, June 16, 1798.
Rutherford, Thos. to Mary Woodard, March 3, 1798.
Davidson, John to Betsy Caffrey, Jan. 18, 1799.
Ross, Daniel to Martha C. Napier, Jan. 12, 1799.
Smith, Wm. to Polly Heaton, Jan. 9, 1798.

Campbell, Jno. to Nellie Boren, Oct. 10, 1799.

Page 14
Walker, John to Marie Enochs, Jan. 12, 1803.
Benjamin, Thomas to Amelia Thomas, Sep. 23, 1800.
Reaves, James to Polly Gower, July 8, 1800.
Clark, Richard to Elizabeth Farman, March 23, 1796.
Dowlen, Harris, to Susannah Hartgrave, --- 16, 1799.
Nolen, Abram to Elizabeth Blithe, May 5, 1797.
Long, John to Winnie Watts, Jan. 7, 1797.
Parker, Isom S. to Peggy Curtis, March 27, 1797.
Allison, Hugh to Lidia Harrison, March 24, 1797.
Miller, John to Prudence Gower, March 20, 1797.

Page 15
Smith, Roberts to Martha McNight, Oct. 14, 1799.
Chambers, Alexander to Darky Tracy, March 25, 1797.
Searoy, Bennett to Nancy Cross, Dec. 17, 1796.
Wegle, Henry to Ruth Logue, -----, 1796.
Anderson, Cornelius to Mary Scott, Dec. 2, 1796.
Neely, James to Eleanor Phillips, -----, 1796.
James, Thomas to Elizabeth Duke, April 15, 1797.
Shannon, George to Mary McNight, May 2, 1797.
Bingham,Alexander to Winefred Reeves, Feb. 2, 1797.
Gleaves, Thomas to Sallie Smith, March 13, 1797.

Page 16
Johnston, Joseph to Rachel Dellahunty, Sep. 1, 1796.
Johnston, John to Isabell Reaves, April 29, 1797.
McNight, Sam to Sally Smith, Feb. 28, 1796.
Weakley, Isaac to Sarah McGaugh, March 10, 1797.
Porter, John to Lucy Hopkins, Jan. 7, 1797.
Koen, David to Patsy Winstead, Sep. 21, 1800.
Elliston, Joseph T. to Louisa Mullen, Aug. 20, 1800.
Felen, Smith to Sallie Webb, June 28, 1800.
Oliver, Frederick to Rosanna Oliver, July 16, 1800.
Chapman, Wm. to Sallie Oglesby, June 26, 1800.

Page 17
Brady, Jonathon to Elizabeth Hanes, June 28, 1800.
Tarkington, Joshua to Polly Berry, Sep. 15, 1800.
Williams, Claiborne to Miss Shumate, Sep. 25, 1800.
Mathes, Allen to Lenora Perry, Oct. 27, 1800.
Whitehead, Benjamin to Sally Hargrove, Sep. 16, 1800.
Laremore, Thomas to Elizabeth Atkins, Aug. 9, 1800.
Low, Marvel to Mary Harris, Aug. 25, 1800.
Fielder, John to Mary J. McCutchen, July 19, 1800.
Bellemney, Elisha to Hannah Stansberry, Oct. 28, 1800.
Morriss, Simeon to Nancy Haile, Dec. 9, 1800.

Page 18
James, McAlister to Jennie Mills, July 10, 1800.
Sharlock, John to Marry J. Williamson, Sep. 22, 1800.
Hardeman, Eleazer to Elizabeth Foster, Aug. 20, 1800.

Stockell, Samuel to Bettie Johnston, Aug. 18, 1800.
Edwards, Joseph to Patsy Rodgers, Sep. 2, 1800.
Smith, William to Nancy Powell, Jan. 20, 1801.
Crossy, Nichols to Ann Cole, July 14, 1801.
Lynn, Charles to Nancy Payne, June 25, 1801.
Dange, Enoch to Margaret Average, March 4, 1801.
Shute, William to Olive Collinsworth, Jan. 7, 1801.

Page 19
Jackson, John to Jovis Kren, Feb. 21, 1801.
Shouse, John to Sallie Collins, May 4, 1801.
Koen, Daniel to Rachel Jackson, Sep. 16, 1801.
Williams, Richard to Tabitha Topp, Jan. 27, 1801.
Koen, Samuel to Lelia Hooper, Feb. 21, 1801.
Claiborne, Thos. A. to Sarah T. Lewis, April 20, 1801.
Bowers, Jno. to Elizabeth Foster, Jan. 7, 1801.
Parker, William to Sally Tettleton, July 14, 1801.
Green, Abraham to Patsy Caffrey, Jan. 7, 1801.
Duke, Philemon to Sally Heaton, June 9, 1801.

Page 20
Lightfoot, Thos. to Sallie Allen, April 10, 1801.
Simmons, Charles to Polly Thompson, April 6, 1801.
Buckler, Joseph to Elizabeth Hampton, Sep. 15, 1801.
Simpson, Thomas to Drusilla Verra, April 6, 1801.
Thomas, John to Sallie Eatherly, Feb. 7, 1801.
Lunn, David to Nancy Leek, May 9, 1801.
Roach, Spirus to Margaret Curry, June 30, 1801.
Bradberry, George to Mary Taylor, April 21, 1801.
Gulleford, James to Susannah Eatherly, Feb. 27, 1801.
Hunt, Sion to Rebecca Dunham, Feb. 11, 1801.

Page 21
Davis, Isaac to Nancy Quilling, April 29, 1801.
Noble, Mark to Anne Jackson, Feb. 28, 1801.
Ratcliff, Benjamin to Anna Davis, Dec. 29, 1804.
Boyd, Richard to Rachel Horton, Nov. 22, 1804.
Stephenson, Alex. W. to Patty Robertson, Feb. 7, 1805.
Buchanan, John to Peggy Sample, Sep. 18, 1805.
Brown, James to Polly Lucas, Dec. 27, 1805.
Hemphill, William (no name given), Feb. 13, 1805.
Miller, William R. to Elizabeth Overall, Dec. 31, 1805.
Young, John L. to Nancy Boyd, April 12, 1805.

Page 22
Walker, Philip to Abagail Eager, Feb. 13, 1805.
Sargent, William to Frances Hope, Jan. 16, 1805.
Crawford, James to Mary Siecrist, Feb. 1, 1805.
Cavender, Stephen to Elizabeth McCormick, Dec. 30, 1805.
May, John to Nancy Greer, Feb. 6, 1805.
Green, James to Jane Trimble, Jan. 8, 1806.
Hill, Thomas to Betsy Seat, May 24, 1806.
Baker, Wm. to Alsee Baker, Jan. 28, 1806.
Harwood, Wm. to Sallie Grizzard, Jan. 4, 1806.

Leak, John to Sallie Mitchell, April 19, 1806.

Page 23
McCarty, John to Margaret McElleya, March 14, 1806.
Green, Asa to Sukey Brooks, Jan. 15, 1806.
Walls, George to Catherine Segar, March 1, 1806.
Scott, Abraham to Jenny Price, March 24, 1806.
Bassford, John to Sally Hamlet, May 5, 1806.
Hupp, Philip to Sophia Wooden, May 25, 1806.
Cook, William to Polly Earthman, Jan. 21, 1806.
Richardson, William to Peggy Howell; May 16, 1806.
Childress, Nathan G. to Sally Harris, April 16, 1806.
Johnston, Abraham to Rachel Eakins, April 9, 1806.

Page 24
Forehand, Allen to Ephey Rodes, March 16, 1806.
Ezell, Wm. to Peggy Buchanan, May 10, 1806.
Hall, George to Harriet Blackamore, March 25, 1806.
Cropper, Wm. to Abigail Ellis, March 7, 1806.
Taylor, Robert to Eliza Branch, April 4, 1806.
Mitchell, John to Sally Payne, March 15, 1806.
Haney, Samuel to Nancy Overall, April 26, 1806.
McCutchen, John to Anne Modrill, March 5, 1806.
Crow, Elisha to Elizabeth Gibson, Feb. 25, 1806.
Garrett, Morris to Polly Cooper, Feb. 5, 1806.

Page 25
Gray, Joseph to Matilda Scruggs, April 19, 1806.
Wisiner, Wm. to Patsy Due, March 25, 1806.
Childress, Henry to Elizabeth C. Smith, March 15, 1806.
Douglas, John to Sally Killam, Feb. 22, 1806.
Morgan, John to Elizabeth Morris, March 1, 1806.
Dear, John to Rebecca Bowen, Jan. 11, 1806.
Burnett, Brocking to Tempy Seat, Jan. 27, 1806.
Williams, William to Rebecca Burnett, March 24, 1806.
McKay, Alexander to Rebecca Lamaster, Dec. 21, 1806.
Fisk, Isaac to Elizabeth Johnston, Jan. 31, 1806.

Page 26
Murrey, Thomas to Hannah Bushart, Oct. 12, 1790.
Tilly, John to Jennie Blair, Nov. 5, 1791.
Bay, Kennedy to Jennie Reed, March 22, 1791.
McLaughlin, Henry to Ann Harkin, Dec. 3, 1791.
Rece, Elisha to Anna Collier, May 20, 1791.
Billingsley, John to Martha Blair, Aug. 14, 1792.
Payne, Matthew to Amelia Cooper, June 17, 1791
Shannon, Joseph to Mary Billingsley, Nov. 24, 1792.
Oneal, Mitchell to Judith Hughes, March 18, 1793.
Desaque, Joseph to Elizabeth Bennett, March 12, 1793.

Page 27
Stuart, Peter B. to Senath Lucas, July 24, 1793.
Brient, James to Mary Lee, June 17, 1793.
Neely, William to Esther Walker, March 18, 1793.

Anderson, John to Hannah Sutton, May 29, 1793.
Porter, Joseph to Elizabeth Thomas, July 21, 1794.
Collinsworth, James to Jennie Brown, July 26, 1794.
Lane, Henry to Margaret Moore, July 28, 1794.
Parks, Reuben to Charity Johnston, Jan. 20, 1794.
Boltor, Nicholas to Nancy Johnston, Jan. 2, 1794.
Perry, John to Charity Baker, Jan. 7, 1794.

Page 28
Gorham, Thomas to Sallie W. Suggs, Oct. 5, 1795.
Skinner, Henry to Jane Hays, Jan. 11, 1792.
Lancaster, Richard to Jane Vernon, April 25, 1795.
Sutton, Malachiah to Hannah Moore, Sep. 13, 1792.
Carpenter, John to Mary Fisher, Dec. 18, 1795.
Collinsworth, Edmond to Alice Thompson, Dec. 14, 1795.
Ervin, William to Nancy Lucas, Jan. 26, 1795.
Edmondson, John to Mary Buchanan, Sep. 6, 1796.
Kennedy, John to Louisa Simpson, Aug. 6, 1796.
Gowen, William to Martha Rains, Dec. 3, 1797.

Page 29
McGaugh, John to Nancy Parker, June 26, 1793.
Hunt, Matthew to Nancy Kimbro, Nov. 13, 1797.
O'Dair, Stephen to Susannah Thomas, July 26, 1797.
McKnight, John to Patsy Hughes, Sep. 27, 1797.
Hinton, Jeremiah to Sarah Boyd, Oct. 18, 1797.
Sugg, Josiah to Elizabeth Johns, Aug. 14, 1797.
Beardon, Winn to Mary McAlister, Dec. 30, 1797.
Hayes, Chas. to Anna Blackman, June 17, 1797.
Evans, Robert to Betsy Robertson, Sep. 21, 1797.
Olifant, James to Polly Compton, Sep. 1, 1797.

Page 30
Gullage, Wm. to Tempo Jones, Dec. 22, 1797.
Adams, Tobias to Isabella Gibson, Jan. 7, 1791.
Gray, Deliverance to Parmer Halstead, June 29, 1791.
Bell, Samuel to Margaret Edmondson, June 14, 1791.
Choat, Squire to Rebecca Smith, Sep. 11, 1792.
Robertson, James to Sallie Ridley, May 5, 1792.
McCutchen, Samuel to Catherine Bell, Aug. 6, 1791.
Nancanon, John to Rebecca Hogan, Sep. 19, 1791.
Buchanan, John to Jane Patterson, Dec. 31, 1792.
Morris, John J. to Sarah Shoat, April 5, 1792.

Page 31
Everett, James to Lettie Ridley, May 5, 1792.
Frenleyson, Richard to Elizabeth Black, May 18, 1793.
Turney, Hy to Martha Lancaster, Dec. 13, 1788.
Moore, Jeremich to Nancy Slaton, May 30, 1796.
Mishler, Jno. L. to Mary Cassellman, Dec. 17, 1791.
Hamilton, John to Sarah Lucas, April 10, 1794.
Moore, Amos to Margaret Neely, Sep. 17, 1791.
McCutchen, James to Elizabeth Dean, April 23, 1792.
McLane, George to Parmelia Davidson, July 20, 1789.

McCutchen, Patrick to Hannah Marshall, March 24, 1789.

Page 32
White, Robert to Nancy Hayes, Jan. 7, 1789.
Ray, William to Mary Menoes, July 20, 1791.
Nash, William to Polly Evans, June 5, 1790.
Gower, Elijah to Prudence Coon, Dec. 22, 1790.
Smith, David to Beauty Fort, -----, 1791.
Carmack, Aquilla to Eunice Williams, June 25, 1791.
Edmiston, Samuel to Nellie Dean, May 23, 1791.
Anderson, Luke to Elizabeth Shaffer, Aug. 1, 1794.
Tracy, Evan to -------- Taylor, Aug. 6, 1794.
Robertson, Henry to Margaret Bradshaw, April 3, 1793.

Page 33
Rains, William to Urcella Pillow, Sep. 9, 1795.
Williams, Oliver to Betsy Hickman, Dec. 16, 1795.
Titus, James to Rebecca Buchanan, June 10, 1795.
Estis, John to Lenora Bayles, Sep. 15, 1795.
Rogers, Isom to Margaret Mitchell, July 5, 1795.
Castilio, John to Elenor Low, Aug. 3, 1795.
Bell, Robert to Gazzel McCutchen, April 29, 1794.
Donelson, Samuel to Mary Smith, June 20, 1796.
Osborn, Ichabod to Sarah Graham, June 28, 1796.
Edney, Allison to Polly Dunham, Oct. 26, 1791.

Page 34
Stars, Henry to Elizabeth Chism, March 12, 1796.
Woodward, Henry to Mary Wilson, Feb. 13, 1796.
Mitchell, John to Sarah Watts, Feb. 3, 1796.
Hudson, Adam B. to Prissie Thomas, Oct. 11, 1797.
Patterson, John to Elenor Wilson, Dec. 27, 1797.
Hoggatt, William to Mary Bell, May 26, 1798.
Dupree, James to Nancy Nichols, Dec. 12, 1798.
Walker, John to Hepsęe Hudson, Nov. 20, 1798.
Woodward, Pitts to Elizabeth Smith, Nov. 16, 1795.
McAfee, Moses to Sarah Chamberlin, Nov. 23, 1798.

Page 35
Malugent, Joseph to Polly Mitchell, Nov. 28, 1798.
Malugent, William to Polly Gee, July 25, 1798.
Gambull, John to Sarah Kimbro, Nov. 1, 1798.
Davis, John to Mary D. Gleaves, Aug. 4, 1798.
Gatlin, Richard to Susannah Gatlin, April 12, 1798.
Jones, Aquilla to Lettie Cooke, April 16, 1798.
Armstrong, Frances to Elizabeth Jones, July 9, 1798.
McKinney, John, Jr. to Elizabeth Buchanan, Oct. 29, 1798.
Higdon, James to Sallie Thomas, July 9, 1798.
Harness, Richard to Clary Elliott, July 7, 1798.

Page 36
Fowler, William to Deborah Liles, Oct. --, 1798.
Harmon, Thomas to Elizabeth White, April 29, 1798.
Garner, John to Margaret Carothers, Dec. 20, 1798.

Crawford, John to Margaret Buchanan, Aug. 6, 1798.
Brown, Robert to Jane Robertson, Dec. 24, 1798.
McClure, William to Polly Lynn, Dec. 25, 1798.
Searcy, Bennett to Polly Wendel, Aug. 29, 1798.
Boyd, John to Elizabeth Daley, May 24, 1798.
Duke, Josiah G. to Sallie Hargrove, Sep. 21, 1798.
Miles, Hartwell to Polly Pillow, May 13, 1798.

Page 37
Lassitor, Frederick to Rachel Rhodes, Nov. 23, 1798.
White, James to Polly Gardner, April 28, 1798.
Woodrum, Jacob to Jane Williamson, Dec. 11, 1798.
Smith, Alexander to Sally Leiper, Nov. 21, 1798.
Lisle, George W. to Sallie Evans, Dec. 12, 1798.
Farmbaugh, Stuart to Susanna Topp, May 21, 1798.
Drew, Benjamin to Nancy Buchanan, Jan. 14, 1799.
Cummins, James to Elenor Waller, Jan. 13, 1799.
Everett, John to Sallie Davis, Jan. 19, 1799.
Berry, Isaac to Polly Johnston, Jan. 13, 1803.

Page 38
Gregory, John to Susannah Corbett, Dec. 23, 1801.
Gowen, John to Lydia Shute, Oct. 30, 1801.
Joslin, Gabriel to Elizabeth Hooper, Dec. 18, 1801.
Buford, Henry to Margaret Branch, Dec. 12, 1801.
Curtis, William to Polly Drake, Dec. 16, 1801.
Magness, Robert to Lydia Gamble, Oct. 20, 1801.
Peyton, George Y. to Frances Morris, May 28, 1801.
Youree, Joseph to Anne McSpadden, Dec. 16, 1801.
Robertson, David to Elizabeth Hooper, Dec. 19, 1801.
Gamble, Aaron to Elizabeth Kennedy, Nov. 27, 1801.

Page 39
Truett, Henry M. to Sally Clampett, Dec. 13, 1801.
Duke, Macasah to Anne Brooks, Dec. 2, 1801.
Wolf, Philip to Elizabeth Barnes, Dec. 29, 1801.
Copeland, Samuel to Polly White, Dec. 29, 1801.
Binkley, Joseph to Catherine Carpenter, June 2, 1800.
Stump, John to Rebecca Hyde, May 16, 1801.
Patton, Isaac to Phoebe Thomas, Oct. 5, 1801.
Liles, Malachi to Betsy Parker, April 10, 1801.
Caldwell, Joseph to Sidney Becton, Dec. 23, 1801.
Dunn, M. C. to Elizabeth Rains, Sep. 26, 1801.

Page 40
Sender, Thomas to Elizabeth Balim, Jan. 1, 1801.
Billens, Harding to Katy Hargrove, Oct. 28, 1801.
Allsup, John to Sally Robertson, July 1, 1802.
Payne, John to Polly Cane, Aug. 5, 1802.
Morris, Matthews to Hannah Lucas, July 8, 1802.
Burnham, John to Betsy Jackson, Aug. 28, 1802.
King, James to Sallie Lewis, July 14, 1802.
Hooper, Ennis to Elizabeth Thomas, Aug. 30, 1802.
Keeling, Lenard to Patsy Sugg, Dec. 23, 1802.

Wilson, William to Sally Patterson, Dec. 18, 1802.

Page 41
Galbraith, John to Mary Smothers, Dec. 21, 1802.
Turner, William to Martha Mulloy, Dec. 25, 1802.
Brown, Shadrack to Polly C. Tatum, Dec. 18, 1802.
Averett, Aaron to Nancy Gatlin, Dec. 22, 1802.
Desha, James to Lucy Lockett, Oct. 26, 1802.
Porter, David to Margaret R. Crawford, Dec. 15, 1802.
Martin, James to Sally Mitchell, Nov. 29, 1802.
Whitford, Martin to Polly Clark, Sep. 17, 1802.
Wood, John H. to Patsy Benge, Oct. 21, 1802.
Smith, William to Sally Robertson, Oct. 29, 1802.

Page 42
Evans, John to Rachel Harman, May 13, 1802.
Walker, Tandy to Elizabeth Grant, Sep. 16, 1802.
Curtis, James to Sally Herculus, Oct. 21, 1802.
Ogilsvie, Wm. to Nancy Phelps, Dec. 15, 1802.
Scott, David to Nancy Lamaster, May 21, 1802.
Joy, William to Sally Ballame, April 25, 1802.
Crawford, William to Rachel Titus, April 29, 1802.
Gillespie, John to Nancy McFerrin, July 20, 1802.
Bromley, Neely to Elizabeth Morgan, July 6, 1802.
Cartwright, Vincent to Thone Koen, Sep. 7, 1802.

Page 43
Travers, William to Jane Andrews, July 27, 1802.
Dyer, Joel to Sally Jones Christmas, July 16, 1802.
Norton, Joseph to Elizabeth Shappel, Feb. 23, 1802.
Dorris, William to Rebecca Nesbit, Jan. 9, 1802.
Bowen, Wm. to Elizabeth Allison, Feb. 22, 1802.
Mayfield, Isaac to Nancy Mitchell, -----, 1802.
Gower, William to Charlotte Garland, July 15, 1802.
Garrett, Jacob to Charity Taylor, March 12, 1802.
Biter, John to Mary Cocks, Feb. 6, 1802.
Hamilton, James D. to Ann Ury, March 1, 1803.

Page 44
Jones, Shadrack to Celia Dowlin, April 4, 1803.
Heaton, Enoch to Polly Hyde, Jan. 19, 1803.
Davis, John to Sally Pace, Feb. 28, 1803.
McKay, John to Anna Lamaster, Jan. 27, 1803.
Smith, Bartholomew to Dolly Everitt, March 12, 1803.
Linch, James to Elizabeth McMorn, Jan. 3, 1803.
Hayes, James to Mary Thompson, March 21, 1803.
Green, Littleton to Nancy Morris, Jan. 3, 1803.
Hicks, William to Betsy Mulherin, Oct. 7, 1802.
Cates, Thomas to Anna Thomas, Oct. 7, 1802.

Page 45
May, John to Sally West, Dec. 11, 1802.
DeVault, Jno. to Catherine Cain, Sep. 11, 1802.
Williams, Thomas to Nancy Gilliland, Sep. 15, 1802

Johnston, Matthew to Patsy Harding, Nov. 27, 1802.
Parker, Thomas to Sally Topp, Oct. 27, 1802.
Tilford, William to Elizabeth Edwards, March 27, 1802.
Pillow, Gideon, to Anne Payne, Jan. 22, 1803.
Smothers, Jno. to Catherine Sherwood, --- 4, 1803.
Lambert, Thomas to Lucy Syms, Jan. 20, 1803.
Powell, James to Sally Drake, Jan. 1, 1803.

Page 46
Porter, David to Nancy Reid, Oct. 15, 1804.
Holstead, Samuel to Nancy Burnham, July 9, 1805.
Marr, Geo. W. T. to Jane Hickman, Oct. 14, 1805.
Washington, Gray to Elizabeth Everitt, Oct. 5, 1805.
Gray, Young A. to Elizabeth Dyer, July 30, 1805.
Castleman, David to Polly Heckling, May 1, 1805.
Lile, Daniel to Sally Cooper, June 18, 1805.
Ridley, Thomas to Peggy Harwood, July 6, 1805.
Hooper, Enas to Anne Young, March 10, 1796.
Alston, John to Sinah Hooper, June 3, 1795.

Page 47
McGaugh, John to Nancy Parker, June 26, 1793.
Russell, Thomas to Engley Gower, Nov. 13, 1789.
Morgan, Isaac to Judith Smith, July 29, 1789.
Hoggett, James to Grizzel Nesset, Sep. 8, 1790.
Baker, Humphrey to Sally Hyde, July 26, 1803.
Baxter, David to Nancy Reed, Oct. 15, 1804.
Edmondson, Wm. to Polly Edmonson, Sep. 24, 1804.
Merritt, Shennie to Polly Seat, Sep. 29, 1804.
Hope, Adam to Rebecca V. Clark, Sep. 4, 1805.
Childress, Thomas to Patsy Curtis, Feb. 23, 1805.

Page 48
McGaugh, Thomas to Catherine Sumner, Feb. 28, 1805.
Payne, Squire to Sallie Hannah, March 16, 1805.
Castleman, Benjamin to Polly Gatlin, June 3, 1805.
Ivy, Frederick to Polly Linton, April 8, 1805.
Roads, Samuel to Mary Burnham, July 5, 1805.
Felts, Drury to Nellie Berry, Sep. 21, 1805.
Hayes, Charles to Mourning Enochs, April 3, 1805.
May, John to Jennie Martin, Aug. 24, 1805.
Jackson, Thomas to Elizabeth Davy, Feb. 21, 1805.
Orr, John to Elizabeth Davis, Sep. 2, 1805.

Page 49
Smith, Ebenezer to Jane Porter, Oct. 8, 1805.
Kellum, William to Susannah Hannah, Sep. 26, 1805.
McCreary, Andrew to Milberry Dickenson, Sep. 28, 1805.
Russell, William to Polly Kellum, Sep. 13, 1805.
Evan, Lewis to Sallie Roland, May 27, 1805.
Knox, John to Polly Caffrey, Sep. 11, 1805.
Steel, Samuel to Patience Shane, June 19, 1805.
Ezell, John to Rebecca Van Barthow, Aug. 6, 1805.
Ridley, Thomas to Peggy Harwood, July 6, 1805.

Doty, Edmond to Betsy Vick, July 6, 1806.

Page 50
Carney, Elijah to Elizabeth C. Goldsberry, May 22, 1806.
Clark, Thomas to Elvira Mornan, June 7, 1806.
Murrell, William to Willie Cato, March 19, 1806.
Thomas, Phinehus to Polly Chisholm, May 31, 1806.
Boyles, James to Frances Wood, Dec. 3, 1806.
Cole, Edward to Ursula Johnson, Dec. 20, 1806.
Doudge, Peter to Tozzy Hooper, May 2, 1806.
Murray, William to Rebecca McKay, May 8, 1806.
White, Thomas to Polly McCormack, Dec. 27, 1806.
McConnell, Jno. P. to Patsy Kennedy, June 7, 1806.

Page 51
Bainbridge, Peter to Lidia Goodman, May 11, 1806.
Williams, John to Mary Myers, July 1, 1806.
Webb, James to Michael Harris, Aug. 5, 1806.
Mann, Robert to Mary Bryant, Nov. 7, 1806.
Scruggs, John to Peggy Bishop, Dec. 13, 1806.
Whitesides, Samuel to Cynthia Farris, Oct. 23, 1806.
McKay, David to Sally Harris, Dec. 12, 1806.
Williams, John to Nancy Dawson, Nov. 12, 1806.
Trim, Elisha to Margery Nicholson, --- 14, 1806.
Harrison, John to Polly Gibson, Nov. 11, 1806.

Page 52
Watson, John to Martha Edmunds, Dec. 20, 1806.
Brackin, James to Jane Sharp, Nov. 18, 1806.
Carroll, Samuel to Huldah Davy, Dec. 20, 1806.
Cato, Michael to Sallie Swift, Jan. 12, 1807.
Bentley, Richard to Celia Hayes, Dec. 29, 1806.
Porter, Thomas to Jane McCann, May 30, 1807.
Wray, John to Jenny Ray, Dec. 7, 1807.
Morton, James to Nancy Newsom, Nov. 26, 1806.
Wilson, James to Nancy Tucker, Dec. 16, 1807.
McAdams, James to Rachel McFarland, Dec. 19, 1807.

Page 53
Reese, Henry to Amelia Clark, Nov. 21, 1807.
Coon, James to Betsy Pinkley, Dec. 21, 1807.
Eakin, Robert H. to Rosannah Johnston, Dec. 29, 1807.
Tate, John to Hannah Bryant, Dec. 31, 1807.
Reaves, Jonathon to Elizabeth Ridge, Jan. 30, 1807.
Taylor, Abraham to Sally Sawyers, Dec. 26, 1807.
Jackson, Wm. to Nancy Eubanks, Oct. 6, 1807.
Rudd, James to Kessy Richardson, Dec. 21, 1807.
Clark, Solomon to Sally Watkins, March 2, 1807.
Walker, Matthew P. to Agnes Hope, March 16, 1807.

Page 54
Beaty, Wm. to Penny Bird, Jan. 21, 1807.
Barr, Hugh to Sally Cooper, Jan. 28, 1807.
Stewart, James to Sally Heaton, Jan. 24, 1807.

Miles, Byrd to Nancy Cartwright, Feb. 11, 1807.
Robertson, Wm. B. to Ledicia Erwin, April 2, 1807.
Robertson, Christopher to Nancy Demoss, Oct. 6, 1807.
Andrews, Gray to Rebecca Walker, March 16, 1807.
Hackney, William to Christian Booth, March 10, 1807.
Hopper, Wm. to Mickie Cobler, May 22, 1807.
Castleman, Henry to Elizabeth Gillaspey, Jan. 31, 1807.

Page 55
Myers, Adam to Elinor Gabriel, June 15, 1807.
Reaves, Edmund to Polly Harding, June 11, 1807.
Gower, Samuel to Celia Koen, Jan. 30, 1807.
Walker, Wesley to Fanny Lovitt, July 4, 1807.
Moss, Benjamin to Nancy Gower, Aug. 6, 1806.
Sexton, Jesse to Polly Long, April 11, 1807.
McAlister, -------- to Sally Sager, March 29, 1807.
Tygert, James to Sally Lamaster, Dec. 16, 1805.
Kelly, James to Sally Pigg, June 28, 1806.
Scott, Samuel to Susannah Cunningham, Aug. 16, 1806.

Page 56
Turner, Elisha E. to Catey Billings, Oct. 3, 1806.
Rogers, Peter to Sally Pirtle, Aug. 9, 1806.
Wheaton, Calvin to Jane Wheaton, June 12, 1806.
Murphy, Wm. to Anna Williams, Oct. 1, 1806.
Nelson, William to Nancy Lake, July 22, 1806.
Perkins, James to Pricilla Brewer, Sep. 9, 1806.
Woolridge, Josiah to Keziah Nichols, Aug. 12, 1806.
Thornhill, Reubin to Polly Gray, Sep. 18, 1806.
Harrison, Thomas to Polly Corbitt, June 25, 1806.
Mouldings, James to Sally Harrison, Sep. 22, 1806.

Page 57
Davis, Nathan to Sally Davis, July 10, 1806.
Quimby, Burwell to Susannah Rains, Aug. 9, 1806.
Clements, Curtis to Nancy Kennedy, Aug. 18, 1806.
Rawlings, Jas. S. to Rachel D. Hutchings, Aug. 1, 1806.
Lester, Alexander to Susannah Smith, Oct. 8, 1806.
Blackman, Bennett to Anna Clinton, June 10, 1806.
Harding, John to Susannah Shute, Aug. 1, 1806.
Smith, Wm. to Elizabeth Singletary, Oct. 13, 1806.
Mason, Isaac to Sallie T. Rice, Oct. 11, 1806.
Perkins, Samuel to Sally Perkins, Aug. 6, 1806.

Page 58
Wall, Burgess to Polly Holt, Oct. 4, 1806.
Hogg, Samuel to Polly Tolbot, March 31, 1806.
Bellamy, Isaac to Sarah McWright, Oct. 3, 1806.
Graham, James to Courtney Spence, Sep. 23, 1806.
Roper, George to Agness Harris, Oct. 13, 1806.
Rigion, James to Nancy Skelly, Aug. 8, 1806.
Cole, William to Ann Arnett, Sep. 27, 1806.
Furnival, Henry L. to Polly Perry, July 2, 1806.
Criddle, John to Hannah Drake, Sep. 4, 1806.

Ward, Pleasant to Sally East, Nov. 7, 1807.

Page 59
Nelson, Humphrey to Sally Jackson, July 31, 1809.
Viser, Jno. L. to Polly B. Dillihunty, March 1, 1810.
Harris, Willie to June Lucas, Nov. 13, 1810.
Walker, Nicholas to Nancy Key, Oct. 20, 1810.
Brahan, John to Polly Weakley, July 24, 1810.
Gower, Elishua to Jemima Patterson, May 5, 1810.
Hutton, Charles to Frances Coleman, Feb. 19, 1810.
Hudson, Wesley to Priscilla Price, Feb. 7, 1810.
Ware, John to Polly Gingery, July 12, 1810.
Caldwell, Samuel to Polly Harding, June 4, 1810.

Page 60
Snow, Davie to Hannah Gleason, May 13, 1810.
Young, Dannie to Paggy Branch, Aug. 26, 1810.
Hay, David P. to Barbara Gingrick, Nov. 7, 1810.
Hooper, Jeptha to Sally Russell, April 18, 1810.
Wright, John M. to Sally Thompson, Jan. 8, 1810.
Elmore, Christopher to Patsy Holt, July 10, 1810.
Vest, Gabriel to Phoebe Carter, Sep. 25, 1810.
Cason, Lewis to Sarah Paradise, June 27, 1806.
Ballentine, David to Margaret James, Sep. 22, 1810.
Compton, Richard to Peggy Charter, Dec. 21, 1810.

Page 61
Pipkin, Phillip to Susannah Morris, Oct. 11, 1810.
McRea, Duncan to Elizabeth Vinson, Jan. 15, 1810.
McGavock, James to Lucinda Ewing, Dec. 16, 1810
Waugh, John to Mary P. Brunaugh, Dec. 13, 1810.
Reaves, William to Lucy Garland, Nov. 10, 1810.
Clampitt, Wm. to Polly Jackson, Sep. 27, 1810
Jackson, Wm. to Patsy Bradshaw, Sep. 27, 1810.
Bond, Shadrack to Achsah Bond, Nov. 22, 1810.
Hughes, Champness to Elizabeth Laughlin, Sep. 26, 1810.
Waggoner, Daniell to Rebecca Site, Aug. 12, 1810.

Page 62
Howell, Willie to Tabitha Hobdy, Aug. 13, 1810.
Bass, Benjamin J. to Francis Smith, March 10, 1810.
Harrin, Abimelech to Sally McWhirter, Aug. 18, 1810.
Edmondson, William to Betsy Burge, Feb. 14, 1810.
Bratton, Thomas to Polly Wilson, Feb. 20, 1810.
Vaughn, Johnson to Nancy Love, Oct. 25, 1810.
Richard, Horn to Sally Earthman, Sep. 15, 1810.
Buford, James to Polly Hope, April 6, 1810.
Johnson, Exum to Rebecca Rivers, Nov. 14, 1810.
May, Nathaniel to Sally Hays, Dec. 24, 1810.

Page 63
Capps, Benjamin to Sally Moulton, March 30, 1810.
Spence, Elisha to Jane Bell, Oct. 25, 1810.
Orton, Joseph to Polly Bryan, Nov. 6, 1810.

Cowden, Henry to Sally Ward, Oct. 10, 1810.
Jones, Wm. to Ruth Fleming, Aug. 29, 1810.
Owen, Frederick to Polly Bibb, Oct. 12, 1810.
Seat, Joseph to Polly Sanders, Aug. 25, 1810.
Burland, Thomas to Sarah Cockrill, Oct. 5, 1810.
Heard, Stephen to Delila Wilcox, May 22, 1810.
Allen, Lewis to Lucy Phelts, Nov. 10, 1810.

Page 64
Everitt, Thomas H. to Elizabeth Buchanan, Oct. 30, 1810.
Rogers, William to Juliet D. Merryman, Aug. 27, 1810.
Owen, William to Esther Singletary, Dec. 24, 1810.
Zimiman, Ferdinand to Susannah Rule, Dec. 16, 1810.
Moore, James to Sally Alford, April 25, 1810.
Grizzard, William to Polly Powell, May 2, 1810.
Abernathy, John to Catherine Tapley, June 12, 1810.
Thomas, William to Eliza Bass, April 7, 1810.
Johnston, Matthew to Nelly Rush, Oct. 26, 1810.
Cannon, Minos to Polly Thompson, June 9, 1810.

Page 65
Patterson, Martin to Elizabeth Russell, Feb. 20, 1810.
Russell, William to Tabitha Hall, Feb. 15, 1810.
Smith, Edwin to Tansy Salsberry, March 25, 1810.
Biggs, Reuben to Elizabeth Vick, Dec. 24, 1810.
Earthman, Lewis to Judith Holt, Sep. 27, 1810.
Branch, John to Peggy Taylor, Sep. 15, 1810.
Sims, James to Sally Earthman, Oct. 25, 1810.
Fry, Thomas to Rachel Bailey, Sep. 24, 1810.
Walker, Patterson to Prissilla Shaw, May 31, 1810.
Sneed, William to Nancy Keeling, May 7, 1810.

Page 66
Barker, Sutton to Esther Vick, Feb. 24, 1810.
Martin, Alexander to Sarah Thomas, Feb. 1, 1810.
Reid, George to Nancy Carter, Sep. 21, 1810.
Landrum, Shepherd to Polly Anderson, Oct. 18, 1810.
Payne, Reubin to Cindarilla Hudson, Oct. 18, 1810.
Harris, Thomas K. to Polly Moore, Oct. 23, 1810.
McAllister, James to Mary Shaw, Jan. 10, 1810.
Lane, Thomas to Joanna Ensley, Aug. 6, 1810.
Boyd, William to Susannah Simmons, March 1, 1810.
Osmar, Wm. to Elizabeth Marks, April 6, 1810.

Page 67
Carter, Wm. L. to Rhody Scott, Oct. 15, 1810.
Lucas, Robert to Betsy Levy, March 2, 1810.
Dukird, Jacob to Nancy Keel, April 4, 1810.
Cooper, James to Rachel I. West, April 3, 1810.
McCrory, Hugh to Amy Mays, Aug. 14, 1810.
Waters, George W. to Peggy Walker, Sep. 5, 1810.
Sadler, Thomas to Jennie Smith, April 7, 1810.
Wright, William to Elizabeth Bland, July 3, 1810.
Kellum, Gustus to Elizabeth Kaspberry, March 28, 1810.

Buchanan, James to Lucinda East, April 24, 1810.

Page 68
Underwood, John to Clarissa Kook, Feb. 27, 1810.
Bartow, John to Elizabeth Jones, Dec. 3, 1810.
Todd, Samuel to Nancy Newton, July 25, 1810.
Hobdy, William to Betsy Scruggs, Dec. 20, 1810.
Park, Benjamin to Elizabeth Garland, June 2, 1810.
Anderson, Levi to Polly Landrum, Sep. 17, 1810.
Hooper, Joseph to Catherine Whayling, Sep. 17, 1810.
Wright, Peter to Jenette Edmondson, Sep. 15, 1810.
Stratton, Calvin to Gabriella Johnston, Dec. 10, 1810.
Feland, James to Jemima Patterson, April 28, 1810.

Page 69
Seat, James to Chaney Sullivan, Dec. 27, 1810.
Cagle, Charles to Polly Demumbry, Aug. 11, 1810.
Lanier, Buchanan to Nancy Earthman, March 13, 1810.
Walker, Enos to Elizabeth Neely, Dec. 25, 1810.
Bell, John to Sally Bell, March 8, 1810.
Pinkerton, David to Jenny Bryan, Oct. 22, 1810.
Nelson, Chas. B. to Celia Newell, Jan. 18, 1810.
Campbell, Phillip to Sally Thompson, April 2, 1813.
Carney, William to Rebecca Gullage, March 22, 1802.
Miller, Simion to Lucinda Rucker, April 26, 1802.

Page 70
Mayfield, Samuel to Dicy Rhodes, Sep. 1, 1801.
Crouch, David to Rhody Gowen, Aug. 22, 1799.
Enochs, Robert to Mary Ann Walker, June 15, 1802.
Buchanan, Robert to Rachel Legate, Nov. 30, 1802.
Davis, John to Sally Edmondson, June 12, 1802.
Reardon, Thomas to Sally Adams, Aug. 18, 1802.
Cranshaw, Nicholas to Margeret Kinnison, April 2, 1802.
Allison, James to Hannah Anderson, June 2, 1802.
Conner, John to Susannah Piles, June 3, 1802.
Cassellman, Sylvanus to Betsy Lucas, Aug. 19, 1803.

Page 71
Clampett, Nathan to Susannah Graves, Sep. 1, 1803.
Williams, Simon to Martha Sumner, Dec. 11, 1803.
Witherspoon, John to Polly McNight, Sep. 8, 1803.
Thompson, Reubin to Elizabeth Williams, Aug. 6, 1803.
Harris, Isaac to Rhoady Parker, May 29, 1803.
Patton, Wm. to Margaret Wright, Jan. 24, 1804.
Blackburn, Edward to Patsy Carney, Oct. 29, 1803.
Gatlin, Nathan to Obedience Lucas, Feb. 16, 1803.
Penington, Graves to Franky Graves, Aug. 11, 1803.
Foster, James to Sarah Williamson, Aug. 9, 1803.

Page 72
Richard, Tate to Jenny Wilson, Aug. 1, 1803.
Williamson, Thomas to Peggy Williamson, April 30, 1803.
Davis, Daniel to Betsy Davidson, Dec. 9, 1803.

Davis, Blakemon to Judith Harding, Nov. 2, 1803.
Bean, Robert to Sally Miller, June 6, 1803.
Martin, Thomas to Margeret Miller, Feb. 22, 1803.
Cockrill, John to Betsy Underwood, Oct. 20, 1803.
Biter, Nicholas to Mary Hugle, Aug. 31, 1803.
Walker, James to Sally Patton, Dec. 8, 1803.
Quesenbury, Wm. M. to Betsy Bean, June 6, 1803.

Page 73
Bass, Lawrence to Nancy Patton, Oct. 15, 1803.
James, Amos to June McAllister, Oct. 20, 1803.
Nevins, Isaac to Anne Matthews, Oct. 7, 1803.
Doak, John to Sally Shaw, Nov. 1, 1803.
Allen, George to Ferbe Russell, Nov. 21, 1803.
Hunter, David to Sarah Horn, Feb. 19, 1803.
Gower, Alexander to Eddy Evans, Sep. 23, 1803.
Span, William to Mary Tarber, Oct. 24, 1803.
Laughlin, Wm. to Polly Edward, Aug. 4, 1803.
Meek, Moses to Elizabeth Miller, Dec. 11, 1803.

Page 74
Jennings, William to Winnifred Adams, Feb. 5, 1803.
Davidson, Robert to Jane Brown Crawford, April 25, 1803.
Kelly, Matthews to Elizabeth Bellow, Nov. 24, 1803.
Cartwright, Jacob to Patience Hobdy, Nov. 23, 1803.
Liles, Robert to Mary Walker, March 19, 1803.
Davis, Absolom to Jane McClening, Dec. 20, 1803.
Danly, John to Elizabeth Inman, Feb. 19, 1803.
Tyler, Thomas to Elizabeth Ship, Feb. 12, 1803.
Linn, Joseph to Elizabeth Joslin, July 6, 1803.
Earthman, John to Polly Cooke, Aug. 7, 1803.

Page 75
May, James to Sally Moon, June 20, 1802.
Wilson, William to Elizabeth Cravens, Aug. 17, 1803.
Nash, Thomas to Hannah West, May 28, 1803.
Cash, John to Sally McQuary, July 13, 1803.
Warmack, Wm. to Nancy Griffin, Dec. 5, 1803.
Moore, Robert to Elizabeth Pierce, Dec. 21, 1803.
Carter, James to Susannah Dukey, May 10, 1803.
McRice, John to Nelly Smothers, Oct. 6, 1803.
Martin, George to Margaret Kennedy, Aug. 31, 1803.
Matthews, Dudly to Alice Newman, Dec. 23, 1803.

Page 76
Whitson, George to Mary Davis, Dec. 17, 1803
Jenkins, Hiram to Deborah Allison, May 31, 1803.
Ramond, Nicholas to Sallie Wisner, Oct. 11, 1803.
Lyons, Andrew G. to Rebecca Holt, Oct. 10, 1803.
Bennett, James to Elizabeth Clark, Feb. 17, 1803.
Gamble, James to Esther Bidwell, Feb. 9, 1803.
Jameson, James to Sallie Tate, Sep. 28, 1803.
Shivers, James to Peggy Crutcher, June 30, 1803.
Foster, Wm. to Margaret Dorris, July 20, 1803.

Harding, Giles to Martha Donelly, Jan. 31, 1804.

Page 77
Petway, William to Sarah Adkins, July 9, 1803.
Mulherrin, Chas. to Abigail Rickey, July 30, 1804.
Morris, Micajah to Wilhelmina Holt, March 1, 1804.
Lannom, Wm. to Nancy Nelson, May 31, 1804.
Davis, John to Elizabeth Williams, Jan. --, 1804.
Scott, Thomas to Annie Hannah, March 17, 1804.
Green, Thomas to Celia Morris, Oct. 11, 1804.
Sneed, William to Mary Delvah, Jan. 21, 1804.
Brown, Henry to Susan Harwood, July 28, 1804.
Pomprey, Jonathan to Ann Bowers, Feb. 20, 1804.

Page 78
Cash, William to Mary Hobbs, May 5, 1804.
Allen, George to Polly Oglesby, March 24, 1804.
Hay, Joseph W. to Betsy Young, March 16, 1804.
Pipkin, Enas to Betsy Die, Aug. 18, 1804.
Henderson, Robert to Judith Hogan, Feb. 13, 1804.
Gibson, Robert to Elizabeth Armstrong, Jan. 7, 1804.
Hodge, Robert to Nancy Lucas, Sep. 14, 1804.
Smith, Joshua to Panky Sally, Dec. 28, 1804.
Garner, Joseph to Betsy Williams, Dec. 24, 1804.
Allen, Zachariah to Elizabeth Law, Dec. 11, 1804.

Page 79
Prim, Abraham to Judith Jones, Nov. 28, 1804.
Jackson, James to Frawny Brown, Dec. 12, 1804.
Sullivan, Wm. to Patsy Sullivan, Oct. 10, 1804.
Bryant, Nathan to Nelly Wisner, July 16, 1804.
James, Thomas to Pricilla Inman, July 9, 1804.
Campbell, Cornelius to Betsy Lennox, March 23, 1804.
Hannum, Washington L. to Patsy Robertson, June 28, 1804.
Clopton, Anthony to Rhoady Hoggett, May 23, 1804.
Dun, Stephen to Mary Harvey, March 31, 1804.
Saunders, Philip to Penelope Adams, April 14, 1804.

Page 80
McCaslin, Andrew to Elizabeth Johnston, April 19, 1804.
Eakin, William to Ann Bishop, April 17, 1804.
Waggoner, John to Elizabeth Keagle, Feb. 26, 1804.
Kemp, Holland to Jenny Murry, June 19, 1804.
Bradshaw, William to Sallie Evans, July 3, 1804.
Binkley, Frederick to Adeline Shackleford, Dec. 12, 1804.
Morris, William to Polly Thompson, April 11, 1804.
McCain, John to Elizabeth Johnston, Aug. 24, 1804.
Owen, Nathan to Anne Reaves, Aug. 2, 1804.
Rickman, Joshua to Jennette Beaty, July 1, 1804.

Page 81
Davis, John to Betsy Carroll, Aug. 6, 1804.
Bradshaw, Samuel to Nancy Rhodes, Dec. 27, 1804.
Bumpass, Wm. to Betsy Billings, June 28, 1804.

Ivey, John to Nancy Pritchitt, Nov. 3, 1804.
Melungin, James to Sally Connelly, Jan. 24, 1804.
Gatlin, Thomas to Nancy May, June 16, 1804.
Dickenson, Jacob to Patsy Bond, Dec. 14, 1805.
Dew, Luther to Susannah Harris, Dec. 19, 1805.
Riggs, Wm. to Sally Whitford, Nov. 13, 1805.
Stewart, David to Nancy Singletary, Dec. 4, 1805.

Page 82
Thomas, Philip to Nancy Thomas, July 6, 1805.
Cooper, John to Jane Campbell, July 29, 1805.
Mayfield, Linas to Courtney Kennedy, May 13, 1805.
Sudgarth, John to Nancy Rowland, Aug. 17, 1805.
Vick, Henry to Meda Thornton, Dec. 6, 1805.
Reams, Rowland to Elizabeth McCoy, Dec. 4, 1805.
Loftin, Thomas to Rebecca Gilliam, Jan. 25, 1805.
McFerrin, James to Nancy Vanderville, Jan. 2, 1805.
Hays, Balaam to Lucy Hays, Nov. 13, 1805.
Kingston, Paul to Peggy Newsom, Dec. 24, 1805.

Page 83
Payne, Greenwood to Patsy Payne, Dec. 14, 1805.
Hardin, Wm. to Elizabeth Pirtle, July 12, 1805.
Johns, John to Polly Durham, Nov. 13, 1805.
Richardson, Daniel to June Stinson, Nov. 5, 1805.
Davis, John to Nancy Shores, July 14, 1808.
Betty, John to Betsy Sights, July 11, 1808.
Marable, John H. to Nancy J. Watson, July 13, 1808.
Hunter, Manuel to Judith Lie, May 20, 1808.
Denny, James to Hannah Bell, March 7, 1808.
Hart, Richard to Areena Coonce, March 7, 1808.

Page 84
McNairy, Nathaniel to Catherine B. Hobson, March 4, 1808.
Curry, Isaac to Anne Lambrell, March 28, 1808.
Tuggle, Harris B. to Peggy Bradshaw, April 4, 1808.
Bland, Arthur to Naomi Alexander, Feb. 16, 1808.
Barrow, Matthew to Patsy Childress, July 2, 1808.
Abraham, DeMoss to Elizabeth Newsom, July 8, 1808.
Osteen, Gabriel to Susannah Donelson, March 19, 1808.
Hooper, Thomas to Jane Lovell, Feb. 25, 1808.
Shaffer, Josiah to Elizabeth Binkley, May 21, 1808.
Eakin, William to Mary Daney, May 30, 1808.

Page 85
Glass, John to Peggy Santee, April 13, 1808.
Probast, Wm. G. to Sally Johnston, June 2, 1808.
Chessin, Hosea to Sally Reeves, June 8, 1808.
Ridley, Moses to Catherine Harwood, July 14, 1808.
Jones, John to Martha East, Nov. 7, 1808.
Wortham, John to Jemima Britton, July 26, 1808.
Bradford, Thomas G. to Chloe B. B. Thomas, Aug. 29, 1808.
Farris, Newsom to Elizabeth Taylor, Oct. 31, 1808.
Crawford, Wm. to Barbara Seent, Jan. 7, 1808.

Pritchett, James to Keziah Kennedy, Jan. 7, 1808.

Page 86
Beik, John E. to Lavinia Robertson, Oct. 8, 1808.
Burnett, Reubin to Nancy Seat, Oct. 31, 1808.
Harkreader, Jacob to Sally Halsey, April 14, 1808.
Ferguson, William to Nancy Woodruff, June 28, 1808.
Butler, Robert to Rachel Hayes, Aug. 29, 1808.
Bibb, William to Sally Garrett, Sep. 9, 1808.
Jackson, Henry to Nancy Stubblefield, July 21, 1808.
Cabler, Francis to Jane Smith, July 23, 1808.
Stephens, Bartholomew to Kizziah Linton, July 18, 1808.
Robertson, Felix to Lydia Waters, Oct. 8, 1808.

Page 87
Phillips, John to Polly McFaddin, July 26, 1808.
Smelser, Michael to Eliza Maray, June 16, 1808.
Hurt, Phillips to Polly Allen, June 24, 1808.
Moore, David to Harriet Haywood, June 29, 1808.
Slaybrooks, Levy to Polly Osmon, Sep. 10, 1808.
Jones, Solomon to Betsy Burnham, Sep. 15, 1808.
Titus, James to Nancy Edmondson, May 17, 1808.
Burnard, John to Laura L. Pryor, May 14, 1808.
Turbeville, James to Rebecca Clinton, May 14, 1808.
Murphy, George to Polly Gentry, May 13, 1808.

Page 88
Fey, Jesse to Delany Whitford, March 18, 1808.
Cowgill, Abner to Nancy Earhart, March 8, 1808.
Miller, Jacob to Jane Sutton, Oct. 4, 1808.
Erwin, William to Elizabeth Norton, Sep. 19, 1808.
Erwin, John to Margaret Rivers, Oct. 3, 1808.
Woodward, Jeremiah to Patsy Loyd, Feb. 15, 1808.
Aydelotte, Jasper to Martha Woodward, Feb. 18, 1808.
Sullivan, Jeremiah to Lucinda Hooper, Nov. 30, 1808.
Turbeville, Samuel to Sally Buchanan, Feb. 6, 1808.
Beck, John to Mary Harris, Sep. 19, 1808.

Page 89
Brown, Martin to Sally Huggins, Feb. 11, 1808.
Camp, John to Martha Jones, Sep. 19, 1808.
Brown, John B. to Sarah Huston, Oct. 6, 1808.
Lowe, Richard to Charlotte Jones, Feb. 11, 1808.
Sawyers, William to Honor Sanford, Feb. 3, 1808.
Hart, R. W. to Martha Thompson, Sep. 22, 1808.
George, McClelland to Catherine Williamson, Feb. 1, 1808.
William, Gleaves to Anne Nelson, Sep. 17, 1808.
Goodwin, Michael to Sally Bland, Sep. 20, 1808.
Anderson, Matthew to Phoebe Moody, Sep. 21, 1808.

Page 90
Dew, Jonathan to Nancy Hampton, Jan. 5, 1808.
Kelly, William to Mary Reaves, Jan. 7, 1808.
Stubblefield, Cleming to Penny Shivers, Jan. 10, 1808.

Benningfield, James to Patsy Hooper, Jan. 13, 1808.
Hall, Elisha S. to Sophia W. Talbot, Jan. 11, 1808.
Ritchey, William to Sally Price, Jan. 20, 1808.
Wells, Haney to Lottie Montgomery, Jan. 19, 1808.
James, Joshua to Mary Liles, Nov. 19, 1808.
Brynes, Joseph to Lavinia Stephens, Dec. 23, 1808.
White, Caleb to Susannah Williams, Nov. 2, 1808.

Page 91
Robinson, William P. to Jane Hudson, Dec. 24, 1808.
Greer, Isaac to Tabitha Goodwin, March 18, 1808.
Ralston, James to Easther Shannon, May 7, 1808.
Gossage, Charles to Sarah Pack, May 12, 1808.
Webb, John D. to Sally Childress, April 23, 1808.
Robertson, Reddick to Peggy Dale, April 16, 1808.
Holmes, Wm. to Sally Donelson, May 21, 1808.
Lee, Braxton to Polly Hunter, May 20, 1808.
Edmondson, W. to Martha Buchanan, June 7, 1808.
Tilford, Hugh to Janey Harney, June 5, 1808.

Page 92
Camp, John H. to Dorothy Jones, June 13, 1808.
Madney, Buckner to Elizabeth Sanford, Feb. 3, 1808.
Moore, Ezekiel to Polly Bush, Jan. 19, 1809.
Carney, Vincent to Polly Goldsberry, March 7, 1808.
Seat, Wm. P. to Rebecca Clinton, Dec. 27, 1808.
Drake, Jonathan to Eliza Abernathy, Dec. 25, 1808.
Baugh, Bartly to Nancy Kearny, Dec. 20, 1808.
Corbitt, John to Rachel Cabler, Dec. 6, 1808.
Short, Thomas to Sally Reeder, Nov. 29, 1808.
Moore, Samuel to Jane Dickson, Nov. 23, 1808.

Page 93
Stephens, Jeptha to Sarah Shain, Nov. 11, 1808.
Wilkerson, Wm. to Nancy Baldwin, Nov. 11, 1808.
Byrns, Wm. to Lytha Haboy, Nov. 26, 1808.
McLaughlin, Saml. B. to Rebecca Oliver, Nov. 11, 1808.
Davis, Elijah to Sally Hunter, Nov. 21, 1808.
Thackor, Isaac to Nancy Wells, Nov. 9, 1808.
Wilson, John G. to Mason Winstead, Sep. 15, 1808.
McWhirter, George to Judith Moore, July 26, 1808.
Casey, George to Martha Holland, Aug. 15, 1808.
Pace, Alcey to Sally Stump, Aug. 17, 1808.

Page 94
Adams, Wiles to Nancy Bleakley, Aug. 13, 1808.
Chaffin, Moses to Jane Jones, Aug. 9, 1808.
Pierce, Isaac to Ella Shaw, Aug. 8, 1808.
Ingram, Henry to Susannah Nichols, Aug. 4, 1808.
Lovell, John M. to Susannah Pack, July 27, 1808.
Vorhies, William to Polly Landerson, Sep. 8, 1809.
Mascell, Wm. to Jane Egnes, Sep. 8, 1808.
Cleaves, Wm. to Ruth Price, Feb. 9, 1809.
Porter, James B. to Polly Hudson, May 29, 1809.

Hutton, Charles P. to Mary Hutton, July 11, 1809.

Page 95
Buford, Edward to Rebecca Buford, Oct. 15, 1809.
Nelson, Humphrey to Sally Jackson, July 31, 1809.
Bailey, Henry to Nancy Ogilvie, July 18, 1809.
Thompson, James to Sarah Goodwin, April 24, 1809.
Read, Henry to Elizabeth Peck, May 27, 1809.
McCormack, Richard to Nancy Ragin, March 10, 1809.
Evans, Deal to Sarah Baker, April 6, 1809.
Hopkins, Jason to Alsee Williams, April 19, 1809.
Boyd, Wm. to Sarah Ford, May 4, 1809.
Jones, Jarvis to Jenny Richardson, July 20, 1809.

Page 96
Cobler, John to Phenia Dunn, July 17, 1809.
Dowry, John to Nancy Adams, Dec. 9, 1809.
Harris, Alcey to Sallie West, Sep. 15, 1809.
Coffee, John to Mary Donelson, Oct. 2, 1809.
Barker, Laban to Patsy Parker, Aug. 9, 1809.
Farmer, Samuel to Sally Childress, Feb. 1, 1809
Lytle, William to Jane Hobson, March 21, 1809.
Hutchings, Lemuel to Susannah Owen, April 8, 1809.
Grimes, Philip to Polly Boyd, June 13, 1809.
Harding, John to Hannah Greer, March 16, 1809.

Page 97
Nevins, John to Docas Helburn, April 4, 1809.
Craighead, John B. to June Dickinson, March 21, 1809.
Kelly, John to Nancy Slabaugh, April 5, 1809.
Lovell, Wm. to Elizabeth Smith, March 4, 1809.
Hooper, John to Polly Foster, July 5, 1809.
Rape, Henry to Nancy Pack, May 5, 1809.
Hardin, Howard D. to Nancy Robertson, May 27, 1809.
Hickenbottom, Wm. to Susannah Graham, Aug. 11, 1809.
Smith, Sam to Olley Jones, Nov. 28, 1809.
Joslin, Wm. to Sally Douglas, Nov. 14, 1809.

Page 98
Eastin, Wm. to Rachel Donelson, Oct. 2, 1809.
Hooper, Thomas to Nancy Lovell, April 17, 1809.
Robertson, Christopher to Elizabeth Joslin, April 28, 1809
Allen, Samuel to Susannah Graves, June 24, 1809.
Graves, Henry to Sallie Allen, Oct. 2, 1809.
Calhoun, Thomas to Polly Johnston, Feb. 10, 1809.
Patten, Samuel to Sallie Stevenson, Jan. 31, 1809.
Love, Joseph to Elizabeth Gibson, Feb. 4, 1809.
Chambers, Jacob to Elizabeth Hope, Jan. 7, 1809.
Reeves, Elijah to Patsy Thompson, Nov. 13, 1809.

Page 99
Johnston, Stephen to Kessiah Page, Feb. 14, 1809.
Hunt, Theodoric to Susannah Hooper, July 11, 1809.
Scales, Robert to Sally Perkins, Nov. 17, 1809.

Hail, Mesha to Dorcas Garland, Nov. 22, 1809.
Stogner, Thomas to Sally Gentry, Feb. 13, 1809.
Phelps, Josiah to Patsy Foster, July 19, 1809.
Russell, James to Elizabeth Duren, Dec. 25, 1809.
Martin, Thomas to Patsy Phillips, Sep. 24, 1809.
Williams, John to Mildred B. Morris, Sep. 16, 1809.
Smith, Drury to Lucinda Smith, Dec. 27, 1809.

Page 100
Young, James to Nancy Perry, May 8, 1809.
Parker, William to Susannah Lanier, Feb. 4, 1809.
Adams, Robert to Nancy Willis, May 13, 1809.
Watkins, Joseph P. to Jacintha Seat, May 10, 1809.
Clayton, Henry to Elizabeth Ward, March 1, 1809.
Laird, James to Betsy Shons, Jan. 14, 1809.
Francis, Bell to Elizabeth Allen, Jan. 6, 1809.
Rasberry, William to Sina Hooper, June 1, 1809.
Turbeville, James to Polly Fitzhugh, March 2, 1809.
Hall, Chas. M. to Elizabeth Green, Nov. 20, 1809.

Page 101
Wells, Josiah to Frances Littlepage, March 2, 1809.
McFarlin, Joseph to Cathy Roach, July 15, 1809.
Mixon, John to Nancy Buchanan, March 4, 1809.
Joslin, Daniel to Nancy Harper, July 31, 1809.
Hollandsworth, Joseph to Nancy Hughes, Aug. 18, 1809.
Okelleywood, James to Polly Jones, July 24, 1809.
Hamilton, Wm. H. to Polly Waggoner, July 17, 1809.
Latham, Wm. to Elizabeth Smith, July 21, 1809.
Raney, James to Elizabeth Charlton, Oct. 2, 1809.
Francis, William to Sarah Baldwin, Sep. 28, 1809.

Page 102
Gleaves, Matthew to Betsy Smith, Aug. 19, 1809.
Gilliam, James to Elizabeth Wilkes, Sep. 28, 1809.
Robertson, James to Patsy Finch, Dec. 6, 1809.
Hyde, Benjamin to Milly Cherry, Sep. 26, 1809.
Hooper, Nimrod to Nancy Lucas, Sep. 5, 1809.
Cockrill, James to Sally A. Jones, Aug. 25, 1809.
Lenox, Samuel to Merit Pierce, Dec. 14, 1809.
Tate, Wm. to Lidia Bryant, Dec. 16, 1809.
Peebles, Cordy to Elizabeth Campbell, Nov. 28, 1809.
Feelin, William to Mary Famborough, June 8, 1809.

Page 103
Cole, Thomas to Biron H. Bashan, Feb. 9, 1809.
Hoffman, William to Parmenia Harris, May 27, 1809.
Goodwin, John to Nancy Greer, April 24, 1809.
Lewis, John to Sally Dodd, July 4, 1809.
Morris, Samuel to Winny Richardson, Feb. 9, 1807.
Harrison, William to Polly Goodrich, Aug. 7, 1807.
Mayers, Peter to Betsy Connell, Sep. 8, 1807.
Herring, Wm. to Artimesia Stinnett, -----, 1807.
Shaw, William to Susannah Wray, Feb. 28, 1807.
Nelson, Moses to Betsy McFarland, March 31, 1807.

Page 104
Griffin, George to Elizabeth Swift, April 5, 1807.
Connelly, Peter to Polly Innman, Sep. 29, 1807.
Jones, Isaac to Dorcas Edney, July 11, 1807.
DeMoss, John to Betsy Wade, Aug. 25, 1807.
McArter, James to Hannah Glass, Sep. 5, 1807.
Barron, Willis to Ann E. Beck, June 6, 1807.
Noel, Zacharriah to Polly Grizzard, Dec. 3, 1807.
Hart, Charles to Sally Meek, Nov. 27, 1807.
Watts, Thomas to Betsy Jones, Nov. 27, 1807.
Sample, James to Margaret Dickey, Nov. 4, 1807.

Page 105
Reddin, Maximillian to Polly Love, Nov. 24, 1807.
Hargrave, John to Polly Robertson, Dec. 19, 1807.
Borin, James to Jane Blair, Oct. 19, 1807.
Hill, John to Elizabeth Filts, Nov. 20, 1807.
Scales, Henry to Patsy Edwards, Dec. 5, 1807.
Philan, Richard to Elizabeth Homes, Dec. 3, 1807.
House, Joseph to Alice Birdwell, Jan. 5, 1807.
Bell, Frances to Peggy Bails, July 21, 1807.
Evans, William to Polly Sadler, Sep. 21, 1807.
Dimoner, John to Maria Grimes, Sep. 15, 1807.

Page 106
Williamson, John Jr. to Sally Tate, May 13, 1807.
Newcomb, Thomas to Mary Tennison, Aug. 29, 1807.
Morris, Lemuel to Priscilla Holt, Aug. 28, 1807.
Drmumbrien, Timothy to Christianna Rains, Jan. 10, 1807.
Earthman, James to Elizabeth Drake, July 6, 1807.
Paxon, Reubin to Nancy Mitchell, March 21, 1807.
Kile, William to Patsy Holt, Aug. 7, 1807.
McDaniel, Alexander to Catherine Williams, Sep. 12, 1807.
McQuerry, Micajah to Maria Shelton, Aug. 7, 1807.
Williams, William to Sally Phillips, Feb. 5, 1807.

Page 107
McBride, Joseph to Priscilla Hodge, Jan. 12, 1807.
Marr, John to Sally Blake, April 8, 1807.
Simmons, John to Betsy Thompson, Jan. 20, 1807.
Norris, James to Nancy Blackmore, Oct. 15, 1807.
Swift, John to Betsy Hicklance, Jan. 12, 1807.
Canady, Isaac to Sally Pritchett, Nov. 4, 1807.
Barnes, Samuel to Polly Edmondson, July 22, 1807.
Johnston, Robert to Sally Hillburn, Nov. 7, 1807.
Revis, Elishu to Keziah Berry, Nov. 7, 1807.
Sailors, Dane to Nancy Earhart, Aug. 5, 1807.

Page 108
Dickson, William to Susannah N. Hickman, May 8, 1807.
Reavis, James to Jennie Coon, June 6, 1807.
Brailey, John to Polly Barnes, Aug. 22, 1807.
Newman, Nathan to Polly Gulley, Feb. 25, 1807.
Waggoner, Jacob to Sally Morris, March 12, 1807.
Rucker, Jonathan to Polly Reece, Aug. 3, 1807.

Pirtle, George to Nancy Moore, July 10, 1807.
Northern, William to Martha Kirkpatrick, June 4, 1807.
Blakemon, James to Patsy Taylor, Dec. 17, 1807.
Cantrell, Stephen to Juliet A. D. Windel, Jan. 15, 1807.

Page 109
Newsom, William to Elizabeth Taylor, Oct. 8, 1807.
Oliver, Robert to Nancy Goodwin, Oct. 24, 1807.
Oliver, Enoch to Annie Phelps, Oct. 4, 1807.
Tyree, Richardson to Rosannah Martin, Jan. 8, 1807.
Duncan, William to Polly Wells, Jan. 3, 1807.
Avin, Herbert to Jennie Moss, Feb. 19, 1807.
McKay, Frances to Polly Dean, May 16, 1807.
Clampett, -------- to Susannah Jackson, April 28, 1807.
Binkley, George to Nelly Earthman, May 16, 1807.
Abney, William to Amelia Bate, March 12, 1807.

Page 110
Harley, Jacob to Mary Pyles, Feb. 23, 1807.
Hall, James to Annie Moore, March 23, 1807.
Higgins, William to Nancy Buchanan, March 18, 1807.
Porch, Isaac to Sally Smith, Jan. 12, 1807.
Bently, Richard to Sarah Hayes, Dec. 29, 1806.
Carroll, Samuel to Hulda Davy, Dec. 20, 1806.
Morton, James to Nancy Newsom, Nov. 22, 1806.
Bracken, James to Jane Clark, Nov. 18, 1806.
Watson, John to Martha Edmonds, Dec. 20, 1806.
Harrison, John to Polly Gibson, No date.

Page 111
Old, Michael to Sally Swift, Jan. 12, 1807.
Trim, Elijah to Margery Nicholson, --- 14, 1806.
Williams, John to Nancy Dawson, Nov. 12, 1806.
McKay, David to Sally Harris, Dec. 12, 1806.
Whiteside, Samuel to Cynthia Farris, Oct. 23, 1806.
Swanggs, John to Peggy Bishop, Dec. 13, 1806.
Mann, Robert to Mary Bryant, Nov. 7, 1806.
Webb, James to Michael Harris, Aug. 5, 1806.
Bainbridge, Peter to Lidia Goodman, May 14, 1806.
McConnell, Jno. P. to Patsy Kennedy, June 7, 1806.

Page 112
White, Thomas to Polly McCarmack, Dec. 27, 1806.
Murray, William to Rebecca McKay, May 8, 1806.
Donge, Peter to Tizzy Hooper, May 2, 1806.
Carney, Elijah to Elizabeth C. Goldsberry, May 22, 1806.
McAllister, John to Sally Seagar, March 24, 1807.
Sexton, Jesse to Polly Long, April 11, 1807.
Moss, Benjamin to Nancy Gower, Aug. 6, 1807.
Walker, Wesley to Fanny Lovitt, July 4, 1807.
Gower, Samuel to Celia Koen, Jan. 30, 1807.
Reeves, Edward to Sally Harding, June 11, 1807.

Page 113
Myers, Adam to Elinor Gabriel, June 15, 1807.
Cassellman, Henry to Elizabeth Gillespie, Jan. 31, 1807.
Hopper, Thomas to Mickey Cabler, May 22, 1807.
Hackney, William to Christian Booth, March 10, 1807.
Robertson, Christopher to Nancy Demoss, Oct. 6, 1807.
Robertson, Wm. B. to Leadicia Erwin, April 2, 1807.
Miles, Bird A. to Nancy Cartwright, Feb. 11, 1807.
Stewart, James to Sally Heaton, Jan. 24, 1807.
Barr, Hugh to Sally Cooper, Jan. 28, 1807.
Beatty, Wm. to Penny Bird, Jan. 21, 1807.

Page 114
Walker, Matthew P. to Agnes Hope, March 16, 1807.
Clark, Solomon to Sally Watkins, March 2, 1807.
Rudd, James to Kidey Richardson, Dec. 21, 1807.
Jackson, William to Nancy Eubank, Oct. 6, 1807.
Taylor, Abraham to Sally Sawyer, Dec. 26, 1807.
Reaves, Jonathan to Elizabeth Ridge, Jan. 30, 1807.
Tate, John to Hannah Bryant, Dec. 31, 1807.
Eakin, Robt. W. to Rosanna Johnston, Dec. 29, 1807.
Coon, James to Betsy Pinkly, Dec. 21, 1807.
Reese, Henry to Amelia Clark, Nov. 21, 1807.

Page 115
McAdams, James to Rachel McFarland, Dec. 19, 1807.
Nelson, James B. to Nancy Tucker, Dec. 16, 1807.
Wray, John to Jinnie Ray, Dec. 7, 1807.
Porter, Thomas to Jane McCann, May 30, 1807.
Demumbren, Timothy to Christiana Rains, Jan. 10, 1807.
Morris, Lemuel to Priscilla Holt, Aug. 28, 1807.
Newcom, Thomas to Mary Tenneson, Aug. 29, 1807.
Williamson, John Jr. to Sally Tate, May 13, 1807.
Diamond, John to Maria Grimes, Sep. 15, 1807.
Evans, Wm. to Polly Sadler, Sep. 21, 1807.

Page 116
Bell, Francis to Peggy Bails, July 21, 1807.
House, Joseph to Alsia Bidwell, Jan. 5, 1807.
Phelan, Richard to Elizabeth Homes, Dec. 3, 1807.
Scales, Henry to Patsy Edwards, Dec. 5, 1807.
Hill, John to Elizabeth Felts, Nov. 20, 1807.
Boren, James to Jane Blair, Oct. 19, 1807.
Hargrove, John to Polly Robertson, Dec. 19, 1807.
Beddin, Maximillan to --------(see p. 105), Nov. 24, 1807.
Sample, James to Margaret Dickey, Nov. 4, 1807.
Watts, Thomas to Betsy Jones, Nov. 17, 1807.

Page 117
Hart, Charles to Sally Meek, Nov. 17, 1807.
Noell, Zachriah to Polly Grizzard, Dec. 3, 1807.
Barrow, Walter to Ann Eliza Beck, June 6, 1807.
McCarter, James to Hannah Glass, Sep. 5, 1807.
Demoss, John to Betsy Wade, Aug. 25, 1807.
Jones, Isaac to Dorcas Edney, July 11, 1807.

Connelly, Peter to Polly Inman, Sep. 29, 1807.
Griffin, George to Elizabeth Swift, April 3, 1807.
Nelson, Moses to Betsy McFarland, March 31, 1807.
Shaw, Wm. to Savannah Wray, Feb. 28, 1807.

Page 118
Herring, William to Artemissi Stewart, -----, 1807.
Myers, Peter to Betsy Connell, Sep. 1, 1807.
Harrison, William to Polly Goodrich, Aug. 8, 1807.
Morris, Samuel to Winnie Richardson, Feb. 9, 1807.
Andrews, Gray to Rebecca Walker, March 16, 1807.
Kile, William to Patsy Holt, Aug. 7, 1807.
Fowlkes, Thomas to Mary Parham, Sep. 5, 1811.
Hurt, Floyd to Lucy Owen, Sep. 24, 1811.
Clay, Jonathan to Patsy Taylor, Aug. 23, 1811.
Edgar, Samuel to Agnes Dodson, Aug. 29, 1811.

Page 119
Tatum, Peter to Fanny Jones, Sep. 24, 1811.
Titus, George to Rebecca Wright, Sug. 12, 1811.
Alley, Willis to Patsy Cato, March 14, 1811.
Currin, Robt. P. to Margery M. Nicholson, March 13, 1811.
Speck, Michael to Polly Hooper, Sep. 27, 1811.
Turpin, Aaron to Elizabeth Bostic, April 17, 1811.
Dunn, Jesse to Nancy Cox, May 11, 1811.
Hays, Stockley D. to Lydia Butler, May 15, 1811.
Sutton, Jasper to Susannah Pryor, May 6, 1811.
Butler, Wm. E. to Patsy T. Hays, May 15, 1811.

Page 120
McBride, James to Patsy Vest, May 20, 1811.
McMillin, William to Chloe Pritchett, May 20, 1811.
Wright, Charles to Mary Mosley, May 28, 1811.
Curry, Robt. B. to Jane Owen, June 2, 1811.
McCormack, Wm. to Kizziah Bennett, May 27, 1811.
Talbot, Eli to Delia Waters, May 30, 1811.
McKiernan, Bernard to Marianna C. Waters, June 15, 1811.
McGaughey, Abner to Lavinia Goodwin, Sep. 7, 1811.
Allen, Carter to Wilmoth Branch, Dec. 11, 1807.
Brown, David to Elizabeth Robertson, Dec. 23, 1811.

Page 121
Anderson, Wm. to Elizabeth Taylor, Nov. 27, 1811.
Wright, George to Phoebe Bland, Dec. 24, 1811.
Fox, James to Melitea Lowry, Sep. 24, 1811.
Fitzpatrick, Andrew to Celia Smith, Nov. 30, 1811.
Brown, Robert to Elizabeth Wright, Dec. 13, 1811.
Hainey, Samuel to Fanny Vaughn, Oct. 3, 1811.
Holt, Peter to Jane Adair, Dec. 23, 1811.
Trebble, Shadrack to Anne Hickerson, April 5, 1811.
Sanders, John to Mary Allen, Feb. 4, 1811.
Richardson, John to Cadie Smith, May 4, 1811.

Page 122
Johnston, John to Elizabeth Scales, Feb. 14, 1811.
Barnes, Joel to Minerva Oliver, Feb. 4, 1811.
Compton, John to Patsy Betts, June 8, 1811.
Harris, William to Emily Gibson, April 29, 1811.
Wilson, Joel to Christina Binkley, Oct. 25, 1811.
Pinkerton, David to Celia Barnes, April 6, 1811.
Lucas, John to Rhoda Robertson, June 22, 1811.
Shute, William to Elizabeth Gurley, April 6, 1811.
McGavock, Randall to Sally Rogers, Feb. 28, 1811.
Nixon, William to Catherine Roach, March 20, 1811.

Page 123
Boyd, John to Lavinia Coots, June 22, 1811.
Bailey, John to Margaret Thomas, Jan. 9, 1811.
Moses, James to Delilah Morris, Jan. 2, 1811.
Hailes, Linton to Jennie Wright, April 1, 1811.
Johnston, Charles to Nancy Whitley, Jan. 12, 1811.
Joslin, Burgess to Lovey Kellum, Nov. 29, 1811.
Smith, Benjamin to Peggy Goldsberry, Dec. 17, 1811.
Smith, Guy to Sally Goodwin, Nov. 2, 1811.
Smiley, Robert to Araminta Gibson, Dec. 2, 1811.
Guthrie, Wm. F. to Mary H. Slaughter, Oct. 14, 1811.

Page 124
Evans, William to Sally Lee, Dec. 30, 1811.
Condon, James to Barbara Rains, Nov. 8, 1811.
Simpson, Robert to Sally Wren, Nov. 19, 1811.
Dunnevant, Daniel to Mary Curtis, Aug. 7, 1811.
Lovell, Robert to Sarah Garland, March 23, 1811.
Craig, David to Pelly Buchanan, Sep. 2, 1811.
Pierce, Phillip to Hardy Richardson, Feb. 22, 1811.
Perkins, William to Elizabeth Scott, Sep. 12, 1811.
Winston, William to Polly Cooper, Aug. 21, 1811.
Simonton, Jno. D. to Bitsy Tilley, Aug. 10, 1811.

Page 125
White, Asa to Mary Abston, Sep. 24, 1811.
Kearney, Gustan to Mary M. Smith, Sep. 24, 1811.
Craig, Alexander to Cynthia Kirkpatrick, Sep. 5, 1811.
Morgan, Wm. C. to Nancy B. Sewell, July 21, 1811.
Williams, Littleberry to Margaret Vaulx, Nov. 23, 1811.
Pettus, Stephen to Mary M. Watson, Aug. 2, 1811.
Clemons, James S. to Caroline Deadrick, Feb. 26, 1811.
Pride, Shelton to Barbara Hays, Feb. 10, 1811.
Norman, Nathan to Tabitha Breeding, Feb. 16, 1811.
Shouse, Joseph to Nancy Newcomb, Feb. 25, 1811.

Page 126
Morris, Thomas to Lucrecia Jenkins, Jan. 19, 1811.
Strong, Thos. to Milly Blackmore, Feb. 19, 1811.
Johnson, John to Arsenia Short, Nov. 11, 1811.
Simpkins, Thomas to Sibby Coon, Dec. 28, 1811.
Ross, John to Sarah Blair, Oct. 22, 1811.

Garrett, Richard to Polly Smith, Oct. 8, 1811.
Frazer, John to Mahala Reed, Dec. 2, 1811.
Willis, Amos to Sally Robertson, Dec. 17, 1811.
Stump, Christopher to Rachel Shute, Aug. 3, 1811.
Turner, Lemuel T. to Ann W. Butler, Dec. 27, 1811.

Page 127
Beasley, John to Sarah Cartwright, Aug. 12, 1811.
Vaughn, Wm. to Patsy Paterson, Dec. 2, 1811.
Levey, Thomas to Nancy Pack, March 8, 1811.
Brandon, Thomas to Eliza Sample, March 9, 1811.
Holt, Robert to Polly Shivers, Feb. 11, 1812.
Cody, Chas. H. to Elizabeth Shelton, Dec. 21, 1812.
Cole, John to Chloe Morris, Dec. 30, 1812.
Compton, Wm. to Sally Ozburn, Dec. 5, 1812.
King, Thomas S. to Eliza H. Sewell, April 28, 1812.
Beckton, Asa to Judith Johns, Sep. 26, 1812.

Page 128
Perry, Simpson to Elizabeth Thompson, July 30, 1812.
Taylor, Thomas to Martha Branch, May 25, 1812.
Ragan, Thomas to Kiziah Shaw, March 18, 1812.
Nichol, John to Rachel Bosley, July 8, 1812.
Huie, William to Patsy Garland, March 4, 1812.
Melvin, William to Nancy Shane, Aug. 12, 1812.
Bolton, Claiborne to Nancy Bond, Dec. 24, 1812.
Herring, Solomon to Nancy Rains, July 4, 1812.
Spence, Bretaine to Jenny Forehand, May 9, 1812.
Gates, H.F.D. to Sarah Hall, June 30, 1812.

Page 129
Martin, Alexander to Polly Vest, Sep. 22, 1812.
Abbott, James to Sarah Grimes, April 9, 1812.
Barnes, Jordan to Eunice Oliver, July 28, 1812.
Page, Giles to Henrietta Wilkes, Sep. 15, 1812.
Robertson, Robt. A. to Catherine Fry, Nov. 19, 1812.
Kellum, Edward to Carey Taber, Nov. 9, 1812.
Allen, Walker, to Mary E. Seawell, Oct. 12, 1812.
Page, Jasper to Esther Vick, Oct. 2, 1812
Cason, Stephen to Courtney Chambers, Oct. 2, 1812.
Day, Aaron to Patsy Garrett, Sep. 2, 1812.

Page 130
Winfrey, Valintine to Lucy Patterson, April 17, 1812.
Jabe, James to Peggy Stone, Oct. 14, 1812.
Carter, Christopher to Elizabeth Grizzard, Dec. 17, 1812.
Betts, Jonathan to Betsy Demoss, March 18, 1812.
Davis, John to Sally Williamson, Dec. 16, 1812.
Charlton, Geo. W. to Jane Hamilton, March 23, 1812.
Linton, Alson to Fanny Forkham, July 29, 1812.
Harper, Bretain to Patsy Cook, Jan. 16, 1812.
Everett, Simon to Sally Abernathy, Feb. 13, 1812.
Hillburn, Ambrose to Keziah Waglin, July 1, 1812.

Page 131
Booth, Henry to Polly Peyton, --- 17, 1812.
Miller, Sebrin to Giney McGaugh, June 4, 1812.
Fitzhugh, James to Patsy Bibb, Jan. 1, 1812.
Joslin, James to Anna McElwain, Feb. 4, 1812.
Lovitt, John to Sally Burns, July 20, 1812.
Gleaves, John to Polly Robinson, June 25, 1812.
Wilkinson, Kinchin T. to Martha W. Putney, May 20, 1812.
Hagar, Jonathan to Milly Hedspeth, Aug. 18, 1812.
Shumate, Willis L. to Sally Felts, Sep. 2, 1812.
Blake, John to Betsy A. Morgan, Dec. 23, 1812.

Page 132
White, Lewis to Sally Ray, July 21, 1812.
Moore, William to Patsy Pirtle, Sep. 14, 1813.
Dearing, Anthony to Elizabeth Curtis, Dec. 27, 1813.
Huston, John to Jane Powers, Sep. 13, 1813.
Baker, John to Sally McKain, Sep. 15, 1813.
Edds, William to Holly Vaughn, Sep. 30, 1813.
Cartwright, John to Susannah Ragan, Sep. 22, 1813.
Singleton, Edward to Elizabeth Shaw, Feb. 4, 1813.
Bradford, John to Elizabeth K. Evans, Oct. 25, 1813.
Tottey, Harrison to Patsy Johnston, Sep. 28, 1813.

Page 133
Eaton, John H. to Myra E. Lewis, Dec. 23, 1813.
Bridges, John to Katie Inman, Aug. 23, 1813.
Owen, Henry to Huldy Gardner, Sep. 15, 1813.
Pierce, Jeremiah to Sally Parker, Nov. 19, 1813.
Cannon, Newton to Leah P. Perkins, Aug. 21, 1813.
Brown, Ephriam to Patsy Cooper, Feb. 8, 1813.
Willett, Simon P. to Julia Gillam, Nov. 24, 1813.
Caulfield, James to Fanny Johnston, May 25, 1813.
Thomas, Robert to Sally Wicks, April 17, 1813.
Dodd, Robert to Criolea Conley, May 5, 1813.

Page 134
Harrison, Zachriah to Sally Childriss, April 25, 1813.
Hewlett, George to Nancy Hobson, May 20, 1813.
Jones, John to Milly Greer, Sep. 30, 1813.
Jackson, Alexander to Mary E. Bryan, May 4, 1813.
Gibbons, Jno. C. to Jane B. Graves, Feb. 15, 1813.
McNeese, Hopewell to Nancy Covington, July 13, 1813.
Cooke, Thomas to Juliet G. Fraley, June 10, 1813.
Harris, Alfred M. to Eliza H. Flourney, Sep. 2, 1813.
Landers, Clark to Nancy H. Shields, Oct. 27, 1813.
Settler, Isaac to Matilda Talbot, Oct. 14, 1813.

Page 135
Bedford, Benj. W. to Ferebe White, Sep. 25, 1813.
Demoss, James to Eliza Demoss, Dec. 18, 1813.
Hodges, Robert to Polly Page, Feb. 1, 1813.
Roane, James to Annie C. Irley, Dec. 15, 1813.
Bass, Kinchen C. to Ann Davis, Sep. 7, 1813.

McCoy, Daniel to Nancy Cartwright, Sep. 10, 1813.
Bainhart, Andrew to Nancy Ballentine, Nov. 9, 1813.
Mumford, Marshall B. to Sarah Clark, Nov. 27, 1813.
Mosley, Japtha to Ruthy Turbeville, Dec. 29, 1813.
Benningfield, John to Nancy Russell, July 19, 1813.

Page 136
Brown, Wm. to Mary Green, Aug. 5, 1835.
Williams, Solomon to Elizabeth Stanley, June 1, 1813.
Greer, Benjamin to Peggy Donnelly, May 5, 1813.
Wright, Joseph to Susannah Joiner, June 24, 1813.
Birdwell, Hugh to Lydia McKay, March 12, 1813.
Vick, William to Clarissa Page, July 10, 1813.
Smith, Jesse to Polly Pierce, Feb. 4, 1813.
Kimbro, William G. to Lucinda Basye, Nov. 13, 1813.
Weir, William to Katy McNees, Nov. 2, 1813.
Morgan, George to Fanny Irby, Nov. 16, 1813.

Page 137
Little, Neal to Elizabeth Casey, Aug. 7, 1813.
Creel, Wm. to Elizabeth Bradshaw, Oct. 5, 1813.
Eason, John G. to Julia Ann Deadrick, Aug. 26, 1813.
Tate, Joseph D. to Rachel Brown, April 22, 1813.
Brown, Richard B. to Nancy B. Watkins, Oct. 8, 1813.
Watkins, Wm. E. to Nancy G. Horton, Oct. 8, 1813.
Hicks, John C. to Maria Waters, Oct. 10, 1813.
Stout, S.V.D. to Catherine Tannerhill, Oct. 12, 1813.
Costillow, James to Nancy Douglas, Feb. 1, 1813.
Young, John to Elspa Woods, May 13, 1813.

Page 138
Davy, Richard to Elizabeth Hill, Aug. 18, 1813.
Gilbert, James to Polly Holt, Aug. 20, 1813.
Jones, Dempsey to Susannah Roach, Aug. 5, 1813.
Hardy, Thomas to Lavinia Connelly, Aug. 12, 1813.
Lewis, Samuel to Obedience Felin, Aug. 5, 1813.
Talley, Barnester to Abagail Cravens, Dec. 20, 1813.
Seat, Littleton to Elizabeth Montgomery, June 16, 1813.
Lewis, Wm. B. to Margaret Lewis, Aug. 4, 1813.
Walton, Josiah to Sally Walker, Aug. 6, 1813.
Hill, Thomas to Sally Thomas, Sep. 22, 1813.

Page 139
Vails, Robert to Kezziah Alexander, Dec. 16, 1813.
Simmons, Edward to Sophia D. Carter, June 21, 1813.
Demoss, Henry to Rebecca Wade, Oct. 18, 1813.
Francis, John to Mary Jobe, July 20, 1813.
Howlett, Isaac to Elizabeth M. Ramsey, Aug. 31, 1813.
Bosley, James R. to Elizabeth Scales, Oct. 18, 1813.
Hill, Wm. to Nancy Peebles, Nov. 25, 1812.
McAllister, George to Jane Daniel, Nov. 12, 1812.
Martin, Daniel to Polly McElwain, Dec. 30, 1812.
Sample, Wm. to Margaret Bell, Dec. 29, 1812.

Page 140
Bibb, Benjamin to Susan Ramsey, Jan. 16, 1812.
Burnett, Wm. to Chloe Gwin, Dec. 26, 1812.
Denton, James to Patsy Woodruff, May 11, 1812.
Gower, Wm. G. to Patsy Gower, Feb. 10, 1812.
Gleaves, Michael to Sally Dean, Nov. 2, 1812.
Callithorp, Clayton to Lydia Daniel, Jan. 1, 1812.
Balch, Alfred to Mary W. Lewis, Jan. 12, 1812.
Ogilvie, William to Matilda Blanton, Jan. 28, 1812.
Munroe, William to Patsy Cooper, April 26, 1812.
Rumoner, John to Patsy Glass, Nov. 24, 1812.

Page 141
Brown, Charles to Catherine Faulkner, March 29, 1812.
McCombs, West to Nancy Burnett, Aug. 10, 1812.
Pinkston, Mishek to Sarah Miller, Feb. 24, 1812.
Dillahunty, Wm. to Luzany Greer, Feb. 8, 1812.
Dillard, John B. to Nancy Morris, Nov. 3, 1812.
Perry, Francis S. to Rhoda Thompson, Dec. 30, 1812.
Barns, James to Nelly Sanders, Aug. 5, 1812.
Stratton, Solomon to Polly Equals, Dec. 21, 1812.
Allen, James to Margaret Hamilson, Dec. 2, 1812.
Willis, Wm. to Catherine H. N. Sneed, Dec. 9, 1812.

Page 142
Perkinson, Jackman to Martha Tate, Nov. 19, 1812.
Gower, Wilson to Charlotte Baird, --- 22, 1812.
Stroud, Thomas to Sally Thompson, Feb. 1, 1812.
Reeves, Timothy to Marilla Moody, April 29, 1812.
Davis, Turner to Nancy Edney, May 20, 1812.
Thornton, John to Nancy Miller, Nov. 24, 1812.
McCrory, Thomas to Polly West, May 13, 1812.
Nicholson, Wm. to Phoebe Castleman, Jan. 8, 1812.
Cason, Seth to Elenora Buchanan, Jan. 23, 1812.
Stafford, John to Nancy Thompson, Dec. 21, 1812.

Page 143
Brandon, Wm. to Mary Sample, March 4, 1812.
Hanks, Richard to Sally Dennis, April 5, 1812.
Lewis, George to Libby Grimes, May 14, 1812.
Payne, George W. to Mary Ann Iredell, Aug. 4, 1812.
Herbison, John to Esther Mothershed, March 3, 1812.
Brewer, Wm. to Rachel Phelps, May 14, 1812.
Logue, Josiah to Polly Hood, Aug. 13, 1812.
Robertson, Elijah to Nancy Richardson, Aug. 3, 1812.
White, John to Abigail Dickinson, Nov. 20, 1812.
Dodd, John to Elizabeth Nay, March 20, 1812.

Page 144
League, Hosea to Jennette Horton, Aug. 21, 1812.
Waters, William to Elizabeth Heaton, Jan. 3, 1812.
Thompson, John to Elizabeth Dillahunty, Oct. 17, 1812.
East, Edward H. to Celia Buchanan, Oct. 12, 1812.
McCasland, John to Patsy Shaw, March 19, 1812.
Garland, Elisha to Polly Pack, Jan. 30, 1812.

Covey, John to Martha Watkins, Jan. 17, 1812.
Robertson, Robert A. to Catherine Fry, Nov. 19, 1812.
Parham, William to Nancy Turner, Sep. 28, 1812.
Thompson, Allen to Susanah Kellum, March 23, 1812.

Page 145
Pinkston, James to Lydia Yates, Dec. 21, 1812.
Newton, Robert to Rebecca Barnes, May 11, 1812.
Hardgrove, Skelton to Susannah Loftin, June 6, 1812.
Bennett, Nathan to Elizabeth Martin, Sep. 12, 1812.
Hagan, Henry to Catherine Talbot, March 10, 1812.
Wolf, George W. to Betsy Wright, July 28, 1812.
Bradford, Hugh to Peggy Harrison, Dec. 24, 1812.
Hooper, Absalom to Kitty Lucas, Feb. 1, 1812.
Ferguson, Wm. B. to Rachel Cogburn, Oct. 15, 1812.
Harding, Giles to Charlotte Davis, Sep. 30, 1812.

Page 146
Ferguson, Abby to Peggy Glass, Oct. 23, 1812.
Wilson, Nicholas to Elizabeth Erwin, Oct. 22, 1812.
Cabler, Harris to Sally Edney, Nov. 15, 1812.
Love, David B. to Amelia Castleman, Jan. 6, 1813.
Rape, Peter to Peggy Pack, Jan. 11, 1813.
Darrow, John B. to Elizabeth McGuire, Aug. 26, 1814.
Seat, John B. to Polly H. Drake, Sep. 16, 1814.
Grubbs, Wm. to Kitty Horton, July 20, 1814.
Dunn, Lewis to Judy Mays, Sep. 21, 1814.
Reynolds, Thos. to Elizabeth Cato, Aug. 30, 1814.

Page 147
Wood, Samuel L. to Susannah Gibson, July 28, 1814. Sol. July 31, 1814, Benajah Gray, J.P.
Traylor, James to Polly Patton, Oct. 26, 1814.
Alford, Wm. to Sallie Waller, June 1, 1814.
Folwell, John to Catherine March, April 5, 1814.
Westbrook, Samuel to Lidia West, April 22, 1814.
Dunnagen, John to Susan M. Woodfin, Jan. 1, 1814.
Perry, Noah to Sarah Rogers, Jan. 8, 1814.
Wrenn, George to Aggie McGaugh, Jan. 3, 1814.
Henson, Wm. to Ferebe Vick, Jan. 17, 1814.
Terrill, Micajah to Martha E. Sampson, Jan. 7, 1814.

Page 148
Knight, Wm. to Mary Turbeville, Jan. 1, 1814.
Rush, John to Eliza Morris, Dec. 22, 1814.
Cherry, Wm. to Rebecca Bell, July 9, 1814.
Joyce, Thomas to Charlotte Blackman, May 24, 1814.
Jones, William to Susannah Crawford, Dec. 15, 1814.
Harris, Howell G. to Polly Lyles, Aug. 15, 1814.
Williams, Isaiah F. to Margaret T. Phillips, Dec. 15, 1814.
Allen, John to Peggy Watkins, Sep. 6, 1814.
Lucas, John to Hannah Turbeville, April 5, 1814.
Criddle, Edward to Nancy L. E. Williams, Dec. 6, 1814.

Page 149
Exum, John to Patsy Hannah, March 26, 1814.
Powell, Thomas to Polly Bowers, May 30, 1814.
Greer, Joseph to Polly Mitchell, June 14, 1814.
Henry, Alexander to Peggy Allison, May 23, 1814.
Carter, James to Elizabeth Vest, May 25, 1814.
Logue, Carnes to Peggy Rundell, Oct. 3, 1814.
Veyden, Peterson to Frances Dunivant, Dec. 12, 1814.
Page, John to Tellepe Williams, Feb. 10, 1814.
Bowers, Samuel to Avelena Betts, Nov. 7, 1814.
Mosley, John to Polly Carpenter, Nov. 12, 1814.

Page 150
Bell, Samuel to Betsy Holder, Nov. 23, 1814.
Fletcher, Thos. H. to Sallie Talbot, Jan. 12, 1814.
Smith, Jacob C. to Sally Critz, Aug. 9, 1814.
Cole, Palmon to Lydia Shivers, Aug. 27, 1814.
Griffin, Ira to Elizabeth Ezell, Aug. 27, 1814.
Badger, John to Hannah Roach, July 30, 1814.
Wallace, Reubin to Patsy Page, Jan. 26, 1814.
Brown, Samuel to Polly Dodson, Feb. 4, 1814.
Wheatley, Francis to Rachel Tannerhill, April 2, 1814.
Williams, Jos. N. to Peggy Wright, Aug. 18, 1814.

Page 151
Williams, Elisha to Polly Phillips, May 30, 1814.
Benge, Wm. to Nancy Edmondson, Feb. 10, 1814.
Reeves, George to Mary McCallum, Feb. 21, 1814.
Douglas, Alexander to Anne Costello, Sep. 12, 1814.
Armstrong, Robert to Margaret Nichol, June 9, 1814.
Kirkpatrick, Joseph to Jane Motherhill, June 11, 1814.
Teppy, John to Louise Lee, March 25, 1814.
Patton, Wm. to Patsy Mark, March 31, 1814.
Watkins, Samuel to Martha Peebles, March 31, 1814.
Arant, Wm. to Nennette Nicholas, July 16, 1814.

Page 152
House, Jesse to Nancy Roberts, Oct. 24, 1814.
Legg, Edward to Annie White, Oct. 17, 1814.
Kellam, John to Martha Wade, July 4, 1814.
Lefever, Wm. to Sallie McCaslin, Aug. 12, 1814.
Andrews, Chas. W. to Sally Martin, June 27, 1814.
McDaniel, William to Sophronia W. Campbell, July 26, 1814.
Morris, Martin to Octavia --------, March 29, 1814.
Newton, Wm. to Peggy Bell, Feb. 19, 1814.
Nichol, Alfred to Rebecca Ford, Dec. 14, 1814.
Gower, Wm. to Mary Crutchfield, March 30, 1814.

Page 153
Carter, John to Dolly Burton, Aug. 10, 1814.
Lake, Elijah to Deborah Miller, Sep. 7, 1814.
Worley, Isaiah to Susannah Hutchison, June 22, 1814.
Fitzhugh, Richard to Polly Watson, Nov. 2, 1814.
Menefee, Jarrett to Sally Simpson, May 12, 1814.
Calhoun, Gray to Hannah Anderson, May 21, 1814.

Jackson, Matthew to Elizabeth Eubanks, Dec. 29, 1814.
Morris, Isiah to Hannah Allison, Aug. 6, 1814.
Hobbs, Thomas to Sallie Hobbs, Aug. 6, 1814.
Denton, John to Margaret Williams, Aug. 5, 1814.

Page 154
Wren, Wm. to Elizabeth Harwood, Oct. 3, 1814.
Hutton, Samuel to Polly Levy, Dec. 23, 1814.
Rogers, Feliz to Polly Somerlin, Aug. 19, 1814.
Witherald, James to Margaret Turley, Aug. 24, 1814.
Owen, Jabez to Sally D. Hall, Sep. 8, 1814.
Moses, James to Elizabeth Morris, Nov. 30, 1814.
Howell, Samuel to Anne Barry, Dec. 31, 1814.
Harral, Cadar to Susannah Davenport, Aug. 18, 1814.
Stewart, James to Catherine Payne, Sep. 2, 1814.
Norvell, Moses to Harriet R. West, Feb. 28, 1814.

Page 155
Nimmo, Wesley G. to Elizabeth White, April 27, 1814.
Noles, Butler to Elizabeth Rappe, June 14, 1814.
Barker, John to Patsy Stevenson, June 18, 1814.
Walker, George to Catherine Caffrey, May 13, 1814.
Porter, George to Lydia Porter, Jan. 27, 1814.
Shelton, John to Anne Allen, Jan. 27, 1814.
Hope, Adam to Mary Brown, March 12, 1814.
Wharton, Jessee to Elizabeth Wharton, May 31, 1814.
Burkett, Ephriam to Angeline Nicholas, June 20, 1814.
Valux, Wm. to Mary Hays, July 5, 1814.

Page 156
Dunn, David to Polly Deadrick, June 16, 1814.
Skelly, John to Mary Hartman, July 15, 1814.
Hooper, Churchwell to Nancy Russell, Aug. 23, 1814.
Betts, John to Rutha Glasgow, Sep. 22, 1814.
Williamson, Wm. W. to Elizabeth Phipps, Sep. 10, 1814.
Gains, Horace to Frances Bell, Dec. 23, 1815.
Hyde, Richard to Elizabeth Hooper, March 11, 1815.
Norton, Thomas to Martha Vincent, March 22, 1815.
Lee, Benjamin to Parthenia Stuart, March 20, 1815.
Weaver, John to Polly McMillon, Aug. 8, 1815.

Page 157
Reynolds, Jesse to Peggy Anderson, Aug. 3, 1815.
Watkins, Jacob to Hannah Pugh, Aug. 7, 1815.
Lynch, John to Elizabeth Weaver, Aug. 8, 1815.
Humphries, Daniel to Peggy Seat, Aug. 15, 1815.
Witt, George C. to Charlotte Bosley, Feb. 13, 1815.
Campbell, Wm. to Peggy Bryant, Feb. 4, 1815.
Hyde, Edmond to Rhoda Williams, Feb. 7, 1815.
Temple, Liston to Harriet M. Robertson, March 21, 1815.
Stobaugh, John to Betsy Stobaugh, Jan. 31, 1815.
Rape, Jacob to Patsy Thornton, July 14, 1815.

Page 158
Carroll, Nathaniel to Ann Robertson, Jan. 24, 1815.
Venable, John to Nancy Davis, Oct. 20, 1815.
Morton, Silas to Polly Wright, Oct. 23, 1815.
Williams, Jeremiah to Anne Green, Oct. 9, 1815.
Stanley, John to Matilda Harlin, Oct. 4, 1815.
Dismukes, Geo. R. to Jane Porter, Oct. 7, 1815.
Harris, Asa to Sally Abbott, Oct. 7, 1815.
Cowgill, Elisha to Agnes Wilson, Oct. 2, 1815. Sol. Oct. 5, 1815, Wm. Hall, J.P.
Smith, John H. to Maria Combes, Dec. 20, 1815.
Williams, Robert to Elsie Singletary, Dec. 19, 1815. Sol. Dec. 19, 1815 (?), Thos. Dillahunty, J.P.

Page 159
Wilkes, Benjamin to Anna Patton, Dec. 19, 1815. Sol. Dec. 28, 1815, Zed Allen, J.P.
Hardy, Wm. to Peggy Singletary, Dec. 17, 1815. Sol. Dec. 17, 1815, Thos. Dillahunty, J.P.
Shaw, Ralph to Sally Eakin, Dec. 16, 1815.
Hickman, John P. to Narcissa Weakley, Dec. 16, 1815. Sol. Dec. 19, 1815, T. D. Craighead.
Compton, Henry to Sally Cox, Dec. 16, 1815.
Wright, Thomas to Martha Tutt, Dec. 12, 1815. Sol. Dec. 12, 1815, Wm. Hall, J.P.
Barnes, Dempsy to Polly Sullivan, May 11, 1815.
Phelps, John to Polly Biter, May 26, 1815.
Eastes, Moses to Lucy Hall, June 1, 1815.
Allen, John to Sally Bell, June 6, 1815.

Page 160
McMahon, Richard to Mary Campbell, May 22, 1813.
Vaughn, Johnson to Elizabeth Lowe, June 8, 1815.
Darrah, Christopher to Nancy Binkley, July 17, 1815.
Eckols, Abraham to Nancy Dorris, July 5, 1815.
Young, Daniel to Elenor Cahall, Jan. 23, 1815.
Wright, Elijah to Nancy Wright, July 8, 1815.
Higginbotham, Reubin to Lucretia Vaughn, Jan. 24, 1815.
Melvin, Edmond to Nancy Wright, Nov. 20, 1815.
Tyler, Walter T.G. to Kitty L. Turley, July 17, 1815.
Hobson, John to Susannah Harris, Jan. 3, 1815.

Page 161
Horton, Jas. W. to Sophia W. Davis, Jan. 17, 1815.
Williams, John to Willie Harvey, March 27, 1815.
Holland, Frederick to Sally Craig, April 3, 1815.
Lanier, John to Dicy Parker, March 28, 1815.
McLemon, John C. to Elizabeth Donelson, April 5, 1815.
Anderson, Robt. B. to Elizabeth Mothershed, April 10, 1815
Rogers, George to Fanny Seaborn, April 1, 1815.
Sawyers, Thomas to Patsy Burnett, May 1, 1815.
Elmore, Christopher to Polly Merryman, April 27, 1815.
Francis, Macey to Delia Sheers, May 2, 1815.

Page 162
Fitzgerald, Wm. to Rebecca Patton, May 6, 1815.
Simpkins, Orman Allen to Nancy Reaves, Dec. 27, 1815. Sol. Dec. 29, 1815, Thos. Hickman.
Whitworth, Thos. K. to Icy Pheny Bernard, Dec. 23, 1815.
Dillahunty, Lewis to Lucinda Johnston, Dec. 23, 1815.
Estes, Asa Allen to Naomi T. Marks, Dec. 23, 1815. Sol. Dec. 24, 1815, R. C. Foster.
Tune, James to Darky Dodson, Oct. 23, 1815.
Bell, Thomas to Martha Edmiston, Nov. 10, 1815. Sol. Nov. 14, 1815, Wm. Hume, V.D.M.
Newland, Jesse to Parmelia Lyle, Nov. 21, 1815.
Ridge, William to Telpha Shivers, March 21, 1815.
Fuqua, Joshua to Jane Tait, Oct. 31, 1815.

Page 163
Fitzgerald, James to Elizabeth Smith, Oct. 23, 1815.
Hopkins, Neal to Nancy Johns, Sep. 2, 1815.
Tradwell, Daniel C. to Chloe McDaniel, Sep. 25, 1815.
Fitzhugh, Earl to Peggy Lawrence, Sep. 26, 1815.
Streck, Thomas M. to Barbara Hay, Sep. 4, 1815.
Watkins, Micajah to Nancy Smith, Sep. 26, 1815.
Gilbert, Thomas to Elizabeth Drake, Sep. 9, 1815.
Holly, Edward to Sophia Reynolds, Sep. 28, 1815.
Turner, Wm. to Nancy Price, Sep. 28, 1815.
Martin, James G. to Catherine Donelson, Sep. 27, 1815.

Page 164
Vanduser, John to Sally Ballard, March 2, 1815. Sol. May 4, 1815, Benajah Gray, J.P.
Williams, Thomas to Nancy Dill, March 4, 1815.
Bernard, John to Martha White, Feb. 15, 1815.
Bernard, Wm. to Rosa Cunningham, March 8, 1815.
Pinkerton, James to Rachel Martin, Jan. 31, 1815.
Williamson, Adams to Rebecca Marly, Feb. 13, 1815.
People, Yeaho to Nelly Coffman, Nov. 11, 1815.
Cato, Green to Sally Drake, Aug. 25, 1815.
Brown, John to Rebecca Wills, Nov. 28, 1815.
Dougherty, John to Jane Tucker, Nov. 27, 1815.

Page 165
Hyde, Tazewell to Susan Drake, Nov. 29, 1815. Sol. Nov. 30, 1815, Thomas Hickman.
Harris, Wallace to Peggy Guhrum, Dec. 9, 1815.
Champ, Wiseman to Keziah Cox, Nov. 29, 1815.
Cotton, Allen to Polly Barham, Dec. 9, 1815.
Boyd, George W. to Elizabeth Vaughn, Dec. 9, 1815. Sol. Dec. 10, 1815, David Cloyd.
Abernathy, Freeman to Rachel Drake, Jan. 18, 1816.
McAlister, John to Elizabeth Bosley, Dec. 11, 1816. Sol. Dec. 12, 1816, Wm. Hume V.D.M.
Earhart, Jacob to Sally Strong, April 9, 1816. Sol. April 10, 1816, Peter Fuqua, M.G.

Harding, David M. to Fanny G. Davis, July 15, 1816. Sol. July 17, 1816, R. Hewitt, J.P.
Harris, Matthew to Polly Eubanks, March 16, 1816. Sol. March 17, 1816, E. Gamble, J.P.

Page 166
Nicholas, Elemilech to Peggy Eakins, April 25, 1816.
Nicholas, Jordan to Jenny Shares, March 28, 1816.
Barnes, James to Annice Patterson, Feb. 27, 1816. Sol. Feb. 27, 1816, David Cloyd
Jones, Alexander to Patsy Cockrill, Dec. 18, 1816. Sol. Dec. 19, 1816, Wm. Hume V.D.M.
Hope, Samuel W. to Fanny B. Butt, Jan. 25, 1816.
Clanton, Henry to Polly B. Hailey, Ja. 26, 1816.
McComb, Charles to Susannah Smith, Jan. 29, 1816. Sol. Feb. 8, 1816, Cary Felts.
Hannah, Jas. H. to Elizabeth Crawford, May 20, 1816. Sol. May 20, 1816, W. Tannerhill, J.P.
Hannah, Wm. to Jane Crawford, May 20, 1816. Sol. May 20, 1816.
Settler, Jas. W. to Judith L. Bradford, Feb. 8, 1816. Sol. Feb. 8, 1816, Wm. Hume V.D.M.

Page 167
Cowden, James to Annie B. Bradford, May 19, 1816. Sol. May 19, 1816, Wm. Hume, V.D.M.
Rape, Augustus to Barbara Johnston, Aug. 13, 1816. Sol. Aug. 13, 1816, L. Dawson, M.G.
Jackson, Wm. to Sally Mitchell, April 24, 1816. Sol. May 30, 1816, Wm. Hall, J.P.
Farrar, Landon C. to Ann Walker, June 22, 1816. Sol. July 4, 1816, Edmund Lanier, M.G.
Dougherty, John to Polly Russell, June 24, 1816. Sol. June 30, 1816, G. S. Allen, J.P.
Abernathy, Laban to Lavinia Jordan, June 24, 1816. Sol. June 26, 1816, Jonahan Drake, J.P.
Garland, Jesse to Jane Newson, June 27, 1816. Sol. July 4, 1816, Eldridge Newsom.
Minton, Wm. H. to Rhoda James, June 26, 1816. Sol. July 4, 1816, S. Shannon.
Quinn, Matthew H. to Harriet Elliston, April 2, 1816.
Hall, John B. to Nancy T. Cook, March 30, 1816. Sol. April 30, 1816, Wm. Hall, J.P.

Page 168
Drake, Joshua to Ruthie McCaslin, Jan. 8, 1816. Sol. Jan. 11, 1816, S. Shannon.
Pritchett, Robert to Cena McGaugh, Jan. 11, 1816. Sol. Jan. 18, 1816, Thos. Allen, J.P.
Waggoner, Cornelius to Elizabeth Huffman, Jan. 4, 1816.
Edmondson, Robt. to Ann Meek, Jan. 6, 1816.
Shields, John to Elizabeth Curtis, Feb. 17, 1816. Sol. Feb. 18, 1816, Jas. Whitney.
Cooper, Houston to Tabitha Greer, Feb. 22, 1816.

Joslin, Richard to Polly Becton, March 4, 1816. Sol. March 7, 1816, R. Hewitt, J.P.
Gill, Thomas to Elizabeth Jones, Feb. 27, 1816. Sol. Feb. --, 1816, Joseph Caldwell, J.P.
Christian, Jas. W. to Lavinia Joslin, Feb. 24, 1816.
Vann, Jacob to Sally Woodward, Feb. 24, 1816. Sol. March 7, 1816, S. Shannon.

Page 169
Gwinner, James to Nancy Mays, Feb. 23, 1816. Sol. Feb. 25, 1816, Thos. Kirkman.
Durat, John C. to Jane Taylor, Jan. 2, 1816.
Fuqua, Wm. to Polly Equals, July 29, 1816.
Pennington, Robt. to Betsy Gleaves, July 22, 1816.
Menees, Opal to Polly Barnes, July 4, 1816.
Birdwell, Isaiaih to Susan Pate, Aug. 12, 1816. Sol. Aug. 13, 1816, S. Shannon.
Durrett, Lewis to Sally Tippy, July 29, 1816.
Jordon, Benjamin to Louise Brown, Aug. 9, 1816. Sol. Aug. 13, 1816, Thos. Kirkman.
Nicholson, John to Lucrece Hooper, Aug. 7, 1816. Sol. Aug. 13, 1816, G. S. Allen, J.P.
McCain, Robert to Casey Johnston, Aug. 6, 1816. Sol. (no date given), David W. McLin.

Page 170
Dungey, Thomas to Sally Jones, Aug. 5, 1816.
Hollingsworth, Joseph to Polly Nelson, Aug. 5, 1816. Sol. Aug. 8, 1816, R. Hewitt, J.P.
Sawyers, Dempsy to Courtney Kennedy, May 1, 1816. Sol. May 16, 1816, Levin Edney, M.G.
Peck, Nathaniel to Elizabeth Fairfax, Dec. 5, 1816. Sol. Dec. 5, 1816, R. Hewitt, J.P.
McIntire, Benj. to Fannie Molloy, Aug. 21, 1816.
Hobbs, Littleberry to Anne Adams, Aug. 24, 1816.
Harrison, John to Elizabeth Randall, Dec. 5, 1816.
Claridge, John to Sally Ashley, Aug. 1, 1816. Sol. James Whitney, no date.
Wright, Abraham to Ellen Davis, March 6, 1816. Sol. (Wm. Hume, probably) V.D.M. March 7, 1816.
Drerritt, Joseph to Patsy Vick, March 7, 1816.

Page 171
Hall, Chas. M. to Nancy Steele, March 12, 1816.
Marpant, Brien to Catherine Casper, Jan. 3, 1816.
Brashier, Jacob to Matilda Spicer, Sec. 4, 1816. Sol. Dec. 4, 1816, Jas. Whitney.
Lomax, Alfred to Polly Spicer, Dec. 5, 1816. Sol. Dec. 5, 1816, James Whitney.
Sumner, Exum P. to Temperance Drake, Jan. 9, 1816. Sol. Jan. 11, 1816, R. Weakley.
Greer, Moses to Elizabeth Greer, March 5, 1816.
Scott, Sinclair to Matilda Smith, June 29, 1816. Sol. July 9, 1816, Wm. Anderson, J.P.

Woodward, Edmund to Nancy Baxter, Feb. 14, 1816. Sol. Feb. 22, 1816, Wm. Anderson, J.P.
Hudgins, Pharvale to Parthena Adcock, April 27, 1816. Sol. April 30, 1816, George Wharton, J.P.
Sturdevant, Lewis to Polly Smith, Dec. 12, 1816. Sol. Dec. 12, 1816, Th. Edmiston, J.P.

Page 172
Herring, Beverly to Elenor Logue, May 30, 1816. Sol. S. Shannon, J.P.
Goodwin, Wm. W. to Anne Blackman, May 30, 1816.
Rape, Peter to Sally Funderburk, June 29, 1816. Sol. July 9, 1816, Wm. Anderson, J.P.
Nicholson, Jonathan to Eddy Cox, Feb. 7, 1816. Sol. Feb. 7, 1816, E. Talbot, J.P.
Eakin, Absolom to Sallie Leverton, Aug. 17, 1816.
Williams, Jno. S. to Ann Phillips, Aug. 21, 1816. Sol. (no date), R. Weakley, J.P.
Greer, Moses to Polly Greer, Aug. 1, 1816.
Stephens, Bartholomew to Elizabeth Barnes, Sep. 16, 1816. Sol. Sep. 16, 1816, Levin Edney, M.G.
Gibbs, Austin to Lidia Grooms, Sep. 7, 1816.
Thompson, Jno. P. to Nancy Pierce, Dec. 27, 1816. Sol. Jan. 3, 1817, Jonathan Drake, J.P.

Page 173
Watson, David to Sally Williams, Oct. 29, 1816.
Simpkins, Jos. to Mahala Moore, Dec. 24, 1816. Sol. Dec. 26, 1816, Jonathan Drake, J.P.
Ward, Fleming to Susannah Farmer, (no date).
Brewer, Joseph to Tabitha Tate, Dec. 23, 1816. Sol. Dec. 26, 1816, Jonathan Drake, J.P.
Hobbs, Thomas to Polly Sturtivant, Dec. 23, 1816. Sol. Dec. 27, 1816, Zech Allen, J.P.
Anderson, David to Harriet Haines, May 21, 1816. Sol. May 21, 1816, Wm. Hume V.D.M.
Tennison, John to Polly Strong, May 21, 1816. Sol. May 21, 1816, Peter Fuqua.
Koonce, George to Polly Enlow, June 29, 1816. Sol. June 29, 1816, Levin Edney, M.G.
Hannah, John to Somerville Anderson, June 29, 1816. Sol. July 11, 1816, Wm. Anderson, J.P.
Alford, Lee to Elizabeth Kee, May 20, 1816.

Page 174
White, Willis to Winnie Allen, Feb. 6, 1816.
Hurt, William to Catherine E. Jones, Aug. 27, 1816.
Smith, Edwin to Sally Lowe, Aug. 28, 1816. Sol. Aug. 1816, Joseph Caldwell, J.P.
James, William to Patsy Cloyd, Aug. 17, 1816. Sol. Aug. 18, 1816, Joshua White.
Carter, John to Elizabeth Carter, April 17, 1816. Sol. April 18, 1816, Joel Anderson.

Saunders, Isaac to Elizabeth Miles, April 18, 1816. Sol. April 18, 1816, C. Stump, J.P.
Lynch, William to Elizabeth Kirkpatrick, June 18, 1816. Sol. June 18, 1816, Wm. Hume, V.D.M.
Job, Robert to Polly Long, June 8, 1816. Sol. June ---, 1816, Joel Anderson.
White, Jobey to Fanny Bashaw, June 22, 1816.
Johnson, Andrew M. to Polly Guthrie, July 19, 1816.

Page 175
Hart, John to Susan Kennedy, June 11, 1816.
Wright, James to Susannah Wilson, June 18, 1816.
Adams, James to Mary D. Rogers, July 3, 1816. Sol. July 3, 1816.
John, Diamond to Rebecca Hail, Nov. 14, 1816. Sol. Nov. 21, 1816, G. S. Allen, J.P.
Blair, Ralph A. to Aseneth McFaddin, Nov. 22, 1816. Sol. Dec. 3, 1816, Guy McFadden, M.G.
Mason, Ramsey to Eliza Grundy, Nov. 18, 1816.
Evans, Robert to Lucy Mooring, May 28, 1816. Sol. May 30, 1816, E. Newsom.
Wooten, Daniel to Celia Barnester, Oct. 19, 1816. Sol. Oct. 24, 1816, R. Hewitt, J.P.
Owen, Peter to Charity Hurt, Oct. 14, 1816.
Taylor, Williams to Eliza Cox, Oct. 4, 1816. Sol. Oct. 10, 1816, E. Newsom, J.P.

Page 176
Craig, Alexander to Sally Watkins, Sep. 23, 1816.
Roach, William to Polly Gentry, Sep. 28, 1816. Sol. Oct. 12, 1816, David Cloyd.
Grant, John to Eliza Jones, July 18, 1816. Sol. July 18, 1816, E. Stump, J.P.
Kirkpatrick, Henry to Polly Watkins, Sep. 23, 1816.
Thomas, William to Nancy Rape, June 15, 1816. Sol. June 17, 1816, Eldridge Newsom, J.P.
Dodd, William to Elizabeth Pritchett, Jan. 27, 1816. N. B. Craighead.
Morton, Elisha to Tabitha Mays, Feb. 2, 1816. Sol. Feb. 8, 1816, James Whitehall.
Reeves, George to Rhoda Newsome, Jan. 10, 1816. Sol. Jan. 15, 1816, Wm. Anderson, J.P.
Demoss, Thomas to Betsy Shelton, Jan. 16, 1816. Sol. Jan. 18, 1816, Lewis Edney, M.G.
Hays, Henry to Aggie Briant, Jan. 18, 1816. Sol. Jan. 23, 1816, Wm. Saunders, J.P.

Page 177
Lanier, John to Elizabeth Downey, Nov. 6, 1816. (no date) Jas. Whitsite.
Avantt, Wm. to Elizabeth Simmons, Nov. 2, 1816. Sol. Nov. 7, 1816, Wm. Anderson, J.P.
McNelly -------- to Patsy H. White, Nov. 2, 1816.
Sands, John to Rebecca Lock, Oct. 8, 1816. Sol. Oct. 13, 1816.

Miller, Jas. D. to Nancy Runner, Oct. 19, 1816. Jas. Whitsite.
Stump, Frederick to Catherine Gingery, May 6, 1816. S. Shannon, J.P.
Terhume, Peter to Lucinda Heaton, May 7, 1816. Sol. May 7, 1816, Moses Speer.
Scott, Charles to Anne Miller, May 8, 1816. Sol. May 15, 1816, E. Newsom, J.P.
Haynes, Stephen to Elizabeth Vaughn, May 15, 1816.
Long, James to Ester Work, May 18, 1816.

Page 178
Daniel, Freeman R. to Mary Nicholson, Oct. 30, 1816.
Cason, John to Elizabeth Kibble, Oct. 29, 1816. James Whitsite.
O'Donnelly, Henry to Cynthia Moody, Oct. 29, 1816. Sol. Oct. 30, 1816, Jonathan Drake, J.P.
Miller, Wm. S. to Elizabeth Thornton, Nov. 23, 1816.
Owen, Edmund to Anne Oliver, Nov. 25, 1816.
Pillow, Vincint to Polly Williams, Nov. 30, 1816.
Perry, Norfleet to Rachel Perry, Dec. 3, 1816.
Baker, Samuel to Nancy Eakin, May 11, 1816.
Sutton, Stephen to Nancy Moss, Jan. 30, 1817.
Horn, Wm. H. to Nancy Carpenter, Feb. 1, 1817. Sol. Feb. 2, 1817, Wm. Hall, J.P.

Page 179
Little, Joseph H. to Eliza Allen, Jan. 6, 1817. Sol. Jan. 9, 1817, Joshua White.
Hawkins, James to Nancy Chism, Jan. 8, 1817. Sol. Jan. 14, 1817, R. C. Foster.
Seaborn, Christopher to Amy Felker, Jan. 14, 1817. Sol. Jan. 14, 1817, Wm. Hall, J.P.
Downs, Jas. P. to Polly Moreman, Jan. 20, 1817.
Weaver, Orrin D. to Polly Towsend, Jan. 20, 1817.
Woods, Alexander H. to Polly Evans, Jan. 23, 1817. Sol. Jan. 23, 1817, E. Talbot, J.P.
Stovey, John to Kitty Garland, Jan. 24, 1817. Sol. May 13, 1817, Wm. Anderson.
Gilman, Timothy W. to Mary A. Dennis, Jan. 28, 1817.
Thornton, Nelson to Nancy Hall, Jan. 30, 1817. Sol. Jan. 30, 1817, George Blackburn, Minister.
Abernathy, Charles to Jane Drake, Feb. 10, 1817. Sol. Feb. 12, 1817, Jonathan Drake, J.P.

Page 180
Deets, Frederick to Levinia Hardy, Feb. 11, 1817. Sol. Feb. 11, 1817, James Whitsite.
Shannon, Thos. S. to Catherine Waters, Feb. 19, 1817. Sol. Feb. 19, 1817, Wm. Hume, Minister.
Dobson, Thos. to Sarah McRee, Feb. 27, 1817. Sol. Feb. 27, 1817, Wm. Hall, Acting J.P.
Hynes, Andrew to Nancy Erwin, March 1, 1817. Sol. March 3, 1817, Gideon Blackburn, Minister.

Talbott, Benjamin to Maria Ann Williams, March 4, 1817. Sol. March 4, 1817, Wm. Hume, Minister.
Cook, James to Jane Hope, March 15, 1817. Sol. March 16, 1817, Wm. Hall, J.P.
Standley, Wright to Sally Crockett, March 17, 1817. Sol. March 20, 1817, James Whitsitt.
Smith, Guy to Charlotte Dawson, March 24, 1817. Sol. March 27, 1817, Zech Allen.
Perkins, Nicholas P. to Harriett W. Craddock, March 25, 1817.
McDonald, James to Mary L. Furneville, March 8, 1817.

Page 181
Campbell, John D. to Nancy Hays, March 26, 1817. Sol. March 26, 1817, Wm. Sanders, J.P.
Connell, Wm. to Sally Harris, March 29, 1817. Sol. March 31, 1817, E. Gamble.
Lowrey, Turner to Elilah Robertson, March 31, 1817. Sol. April 29, 1817, S. Shannon.
Wilcox, Thos. to Sally Chism, April 2, 1817. Sol. April 3, 1817, Joel Anderson.
Felker, Jacob to Sally Jackson, April 25, 1817. Sol. April 26, 1817, Peter Fuqua, Min.
Page, John to Polly Harris, May 3, 1817. Sol. May 4, 1817, E. Gamble.
Pulliam, Washington to Tabetha Vest, May 8, 1817. Sol. May 8, 1817, Wm. Hume, Min.
Robertson, John McNairy to Lucy Scales, May 9, 1817. Sol. June 12, 1817, Wm. Hume, Min.
Lewis, John to Ferrebee Feling, May 10, 1817. Sol. May 29, 1817, G. S. Allen, J.P.
Strongfellow, Wm. to Susannah Johnston, May 13, 1817. Sol. May 14, 1817, C. Stump, J.P.

Page 182
Cartwright, David to Elizabeth Cooper, May 13, 1817.
Francis, Macey to Patsy Harper, May 17, 1817. Sol. May 22, 1817, Frederick Reding, J.P.
Williams, Turner to Anna Curren, May 19, 1817.
Byrn, Laura to Nancy Stafford, May 21, 1817. Sol. May 25, 1817, Daniel White.
Patton, Mathew to Polly Work, May 26, 1817.
Trout, George to Catherine Nall, May 29, 1817. Sol. June 21, 1817.
McCasland, Isaac to Nancy Hudgins, May 30, 1817. Sol. May 31, 1817, David Cloyd.
Anthony, Zephiniah H.B. to Mary C. McNees, June 16, 1817. Sol. June 19, 1817, James Whitsitt.
Hardgrove, Lewis to Elizabeth Loftin, June 19, 1817. Sol. June 25, 1817, Zech. Allen.
Wade, Henry to Miranda Thompson, June 3, 1817.

Page 183
Gibson, Jas. M. to Lucy C. Wilkinson, June 23, 1817. Sol. June 23, 1817, T. B. Craighead.

Foster, Ephraim H. to Jane Dickinson, June 23, 1817. Sol. June 24, 1817, Wm. Hume.
White, Lewis to Mildred Ham, June 30, 1817. Sol. July 3, 1817, James Whitsitt.
Cain, John to Aquilla Farmbrough, July 1, 1817.
Eastland, Thomas to Polly Swan, July 3, 1817. Sol. July 3, 1817, G. B. Craighead.
Griffin, George to Tabitha Thomas, July 8, 1817. Sol. July 17, 1817, E. S. Hall.
Maxey, John to Henrietta A. Parker, July 9, 1817. Sol. July 10, 1817, G. B. Craighead.
Boon, James to Elizabeth Douglass, July 14, 1817. Sol. July 20, 1817, Jones, Read, J.P.
Cummins, Wm. to Polly Marlin, July 15, 1817. Sol. July 17, 1817, Zech Allen.
Job, Andrew to Polly Champ, July 23, 1817. Sol. July 27, 1817, W. Russell, J.P.

Page 184
Venable, Hugh B. to Margery Allison, July 25, 1817. Sol. July 31, 1817, Levin Edney, D. of M.L.C.
Crabtree, James to Sarah Lesley, July 31, 1817. Sol. July 31, 1817, B. Gray, J.P.
Roach, Sasnet to Tabitha Johnston, July 31, 1817.
Pierce, John to Augusta Davis, Aug. 4, 1817. Sol. Aug. 7, 1817, Jonathan Drake, J.P.
Herbert, Vincent to Kitty B. Swann, Aug. 5, 1817. Sol. 1817, G. B. Craighead.
Irwin, David to Elizabeth M. Rodgers, Aug. 5, 1817.
Redding, Augustus to Elizabeth Hinkle, Aug. 7, 1817. Sol. Aug. 19, 1817, S. Shannon.
Rowland, Balam to Susannah Murrell, Aug. 8, 1817.
Levy, James to Sally M. Work, Aug. 7, 1817.
Campbell, John to Nancy Helbourne, Aug. 8, 1817.

Page 185
Nelson, John to Rebecca Williams, Aug. 9, 1817. Sol. Aug. 10, 1817, Joel Anderson.
Gardner, John S. to Eliza M. Hans, Aug. 16, 1817. Sol. Aug. 27, 1817, Jas. Whitsitt.
Hays, William to Mary Cowgill, Aug 18, 1817. Sol. (Aug.? 21, 1817, Wm. Saunders, J.P.
Griffin, John to Mary Chism, Aug. 19, 1817. Sol. Aug. 20 1817, Wm. Hall, J.P.
Kurson, Thomas to Nancy Vennable, Aug. 19, 1817.
Osborn, Alfred M. to Patsy Crutcher, Aug. 20, 1817.
Levy, William to Hannah Reaves, Aug. 20, 1817.
Balch, Alfred to Anne Newman, Aug. 26, 1817. Sol. Aug. 27, 1817, Wm. Hume, Min.
Carter, William to Mary Adcock, Aug. 26, 1817. Sol. Aug. 28, 1817, S. Shannon.
Loyons, Jno. B. to Jane McDowell, Aug. 28, 1817.

Page 186
Crabb, Henry to Jane Barrow, Aug. 28, 1817. Sol. Aug. 28, 1817, Wm. Hume, Min.
Slaughter, Francis to Gertrude Lowe, Sep. 1, 1817. Sol. Sep. 11, 1817, Jno. _.Thomonden, V.D.M.
Yeatman, Thos. to Jane Erwin, Sep. 7, 1817. Sol. Sep. 11, 1817, Wm. Hume, V.D.M.
Ludlow, Noah M. to Mary Squires, Sep. 1, 1817. Sol. Sep. 1, 1817, Wm. Hume, V.D.M.
Linton, Samuel to Nancy Butram, Sep. 2, 1817. Sol. Sep. 4, 1817, Levin Edney, Min.
Barham, William to Polly McCollum, Sep. 4, 1817. Sol. Sep. 11, 1817, Levin Edney, Min.
Smith, Thos. to Patsy Gower, Sep. 4, 1817.
Cartmell, Nathan to Isabella Gleaves, Sep. 8, 1817. Sol. Sep. 18, 1817, Wm. Saunders.
Cheatham, Leonard P. to Elizabeth Robertson, Sep. 9, 1817. Sol. Sep. 11, 1817, Wm. Hume, V.D.M.
Anderson, James to Sally Hughes, Sep. 9, 1817. Sol. Sep. 26, 1817, Wm. Anderson.

Page 187
Bradford, Henry C. to Martha Turner, Sep. 18, 1817. Sol. Sep. 18, 1817, Wm. Hume, V.D.M.
Treppard, Wm. to Nancy Ashley, Sep. 25, 1817. Sol. Sep. 25, 1817, James Whitsitt
Armstrong, James to Elizabeth Hodge, Sep. 30, 1817. Sol. Oct. 2, 1817, Zech. Allen.
Perodean, Paul to Sally Carpenter, Oct. 3, 1817. Sol. Oct. 4, 1817, E. Talbot, J.P.
Gleaves, Thos., Jr. to Mary Dean, Oct. 6, 1817. Sol. Oct. 9, 1817, Joshua White.
Boyd, John to Elizabeth McEwen, Oct. 9, 1817. Sol. Oct. 9, 1817, Joseph Love, J.P.
Bevens, Charles to Dolly Woodruff, Oct. 10, 1817. Sol. Oct. 16, 1817, E. Gamble.
Cobler, Christopher to Rebecca Garrison, Oct. 11, 1817. Sol. Oct. 12, 1817, R. C. Foster, J.P.
Haywood, Thos. to Susan Glasgow, Oct. 14, 1817. Sol. G. B. Craighead.
Goodwin, George to Jane T. Buchanan, Oct. 2, 1817. Sol. Oct. 2, 1817, Wm. Hume, V.D.M.

Page 188
Young, John to Caroline Somerville, Oct. 16, 1817.
Drake, Jesse to Rhoda Eddington, Oct. 18, 1817.
McFadden, Ralph S. to Ruth Cox, Oct. 20, 1817. Sol. October, Jos. Caldwell, J.P.
Eakins, Absolom to Susannah Jones, Oct. 21, 1817.
McMannis, Samuel to Julian Condon, Oct. 22, 1817. Sol. by G. B. Craighead.
Garna, William to Lucinda Hill, Oct. 23, 1817. Sol. Oct. 23, 1817, James Whitsitt.
Postly, Samuel to Martha Cowgill, Oct. 29, 1817.

Drake, Wm. J. to Polly Bosley, Oct. 29, 1817. Sol. Oct. 30, 1817, Jonathan Drake.
Childress, Edwin H. to Emily D. Hewitt, Nov. 3, 1817. Sol. Nov. 4, 1817, Wm. Hume, V.D.M.
McElroy, John to Jane Cagle, Nov. 3, 1817.

Page 189
White, Wm. to Eliza Caroline Wharton, Nov. 5, 1817. Sol. by G. B. Craighead (no date).
Jackson, Abraham to Jeney Melvin, Nov. 12, 1817.
Turner, Willie to Maria Thompson, Nov. 13, 1817. Sol. Nov. --, 1817, Joseph Caldwell, J.P.
Jones, Redding B. to Elizabeth Ewell, Nov. 15, 1817. Sol. Nov. 18, 1817, Wm. Saunders, J.P.
Lucas, Abel to Sally Page, Nov. 18, 1817. Sol. Nov. 20, 1817, Th. Edmiston, J.P.
Walker, James to Sally Page, Nov. 18, 1817. Sol. Nov. 20, 1817, Th. Edmiston, J.P.
Brown, Armstead to Tabitha Moody, Nov. 22, 1817. Sol. Nov. 26, 1817, Jonathon Drake, J.P.
Rice, Thomas to Polly Bradshaw, Nov. 25, 1817. Sol. Nov. 26, 1817, Wm. Hall, acting J.P.
Weatherly, Wm. to Serena Gray, Nov. 26, 1817. Sol. Nov. 27, 1817, Guy McFadden.
Stuart, James R. to Janey Lee, Nov. 27, 1817. Sol. Dec. 4, 1817, G. S. Allen, J.P.

Page 190
Betts, Samuel to Elizabeth Hodge, Dec. 2, 1817. Sol. Dec. 1817, Joseph Caldwell, J.P.
Cannon, Willis to Leticia Thompson, Dec. 6, 1817. Sol. Dec. 7, 1817, Wm. Hume, V.D.M.
Humphries, Willie J. to Levica Link, Dec. 9, 1817.
Richardson, Kennedy to Elizabeth Wrenn, Dec. 13, 1817. Sol. Dec. 18, 1817, Levin Edney, Min.
Durdon, Anthony to Helen Hooper, Dec. 17, 1817. Sol. Dec. 18, 1817, Wm. Hume, V.D.M.
Baxter, James to Rebecca Harris, Dec. 18, 1817.
McLaughlin, Wm. H. to Catherine Peebles, Dec. 20, 1817.
Lefloar, Greenwood to Rosa Donnelly, Dec. 2,1817.
Williamson, Wm. to Elizabeth Taylor, Dec. 20, 1817. Sol. Dec. 20, 1817, E. Talbot, J.P.
Porter, Mathew to Sally Wright, Dec. 22, 1817. Sol. Dec. 23, ----, Jas. Whitsitt.

Page 191
Yarbrough, Wm. L. to Elizabeth Furney, Dec. 23, 1817. Sol. Dec. 23, 1817, S. Shannon, J.P.
Hughes, Wm. to Elizabeth Alford, Dec. 23, 1817. Sol. Dec. 25, 1817, J. Whitsitt.
Driver, Abner to Sally Demoss, Dec. 25, 1817. Sol. Dec. 26, 1817, Levin Edney, Min.
Sutton, Wm. to Rachel Dellahunty, Dec. 27, 1817. Sol. Dec. --, 1817, Joseph Caldwell, J.P.

Taylor, James to Rule McCormack, Dec. 29, 1817. Sol. Jan. 2, 1818, Braxton Lee, J.P.
Stull, Samuel to Rachael Mathias, Jan. 1, 1818. Sol. Jan. 1, 1818, Joshua White.
Winstead, Wm. C. to Meddy Davis, Jan. 3, 1818. Sol. Jan. 5, 1818, Levin Edney, Min.
Anderson, Hiram to Susan Newsom, Jan. 5, 1818.
Baird, Willie to Sally Greer, Jan. 6, 1818. Sol. Jan. 15, 1818, E. Newsom.
Dacus, Wm. to Cynthia Dodson, Jan. 6, 1818. Sol. Jan. --, 1818, Joseph Caldwell, J.P.

Page 192
Gower, Elisha to Sally Fowler, Jan. 12, 1818. Sol. Jan. 12, 1818, Braxton Lugis (Lee?).
Whitsitt, Wm. D. to Sarah C. Slaughter, Jan. 14, 1818. Sol. Jan. 15, 1818, Wm. Hume, V.D.M.
Howell, James to Peggy Hartmen, Jan. 17, 1818.
Walters, George to Susannah Taylor, Jan. 22, 1818. Sol. Jan. 22, 1818, W. N. Allen.
Curtis, Constant to Peggy Garter, Jan. 24, 1818. Sol. Feb. 1, 1818, S. Cantrell, J.P.
Atwood, Wm. to Caroline Plummer, Jan. 27, 1818. Sol. Jan. 27, 1818, Wm. Hume, V.D.M.
Clay, Woodie to Orpha Kennedy, Feb. 4, 1818. Sol. Feb. 6, 1818, E. S. Hall, J.P.
Rhea, Wm. to Sarah Bishop, Feb. 5, 1818. Sol. Feb. 5, 1818, Wm. Hume, V.D.M.
White, Jeremiah to Nancy Hill, Feb. 7, 1818. Sol. Feb. 11, 1818, Edmund Lanier.
Wright, John to Judy Hurt, Feb. 12, 1818. Sol. Feb. 12, 1818, Wm. Hall, J.P.

Page 193
Wair, Geo. T. to Julia Ann Branch, Feb. 14, 1818. Sol. Feb. 19, 1818, E. Gamble, J.P.
Owen, Edmond, Jr. to Polly Hope, Feb. 16, 1818. Sol. Feb. 16, 1818, James Whitsitt.
Guess, James to Celia Stewart, Feb. 16, 1818. Sol. Feb. 16, 1818, E. S. Hall, J.P.
Boon, Bryant to Martha Phipps, Feb. 17, 1818. Sol. Feb. 17, 1818, Levin Edney, Min.
Mason, Thomas to Elinor Guthrie, Feb. 21, 1818. Sol. Feb. 25, 1818, Guy McFadden.
Oldham, Chas. to Judith Johnson, Feb. 23, 1818. Sol. March 1, 1818, Joel Anderson.
Roach, Elsy to Caty Stell, Feb. 24, 1818. Sol. Feb. 25, 1818, Guy McFadden.
Hamblem, Jno. M. A. to Mary O. Donelson, Feb. 24, 1818. Sol. Feb. 26, 1818, Wm. Hume, V.D.M.
Sullivant, Bennet M. to Nancy Slavens, March 2, 1818. Sol. March 3, 1818, B. Gray, J.P.
Lock, Jno. W. to Eliza Clark, March 4, 1818. Sol. March 4, 1818, Edward Jones, Min.

Page 194

Crabb, Ralph to Miriam Lewis, March 14, 1818. Sol. (no date), James Whitsitt.

Goodnough, Isiah to Sarah Smith, March 18, 1818. Sol. March 19, 1818, John Cox, L.D., M.E.C.

McGavock, Randall, Jr. to Almira Haines, March 24, 1818. Sol. March 24, 1818, Wm. Hume, V.D.M.

Thornton, Thos. J. to Polly Mays, March 28, 1818. Sol. April 7, 1818, Levin Edney, Min.

Childress, R. O. to Sally Frazier, March 30, 1818. Sol. March 31, 1818, T. B. Craighead.

Gaines, Wm. W. to Sarah Bell, April 1, 1818. Sol. April 2, 1818, Wm. Hume, V.D.M.

Crockett, Andrew to Catherine Bell, April 1, 1818. Sol. April 2, 1818, Wm. Hume, V.D.M.

Fuqua, Jesse to Narcessa Carter, April 2, 1818. Sol. April 2, 1818, Wm. Fuqua.

Equals, Silas to Polly Vick, April 4, 1818.

Williams, William to Mary Dodson, April 2, 1818.

Page 195

Brewer, Wm. to Elizabeth Tait, April 25, 1818. Sol. April 30, 1818, B. Gray, J.P.

Bosworth, Wm. to Marry Ann Penn, May 4, 1818. Sol. May 4, 1818, T. B. Craighead.

Clopton, Sam H. to Maria Harlow, May 7, 1818.

Keen, Joseph to Sarah B. Iredale, May 8, 1818. Sol. May 9, 1818, T. B. Craighead.

Rooker, Caleb to Dinah Joslin, May 15, 1818.

Sullivan, Elisha to Sarah M. Phipps, May 16, 1818. Sol. May 21, 1818, Levin Edney, Min.

Mays, John to Arvena Tucker, June 16, 1818. Sol. June 18, 1818, John Cox, L.D., M.E.C.

Wood, Robert to Sarah B. West, May 19, 1818. Sol. May 19, 1818, Wm. Hume, V.D.M.

Earl, Ralph E. W. to Jane Caffrey, May 21, 1818. Sol. May 21, 1818, Wm. Hume, V.D.M.

Pickle, Robert to Catherine McCanless, May 22, 1818.

Page 196

Mann, David B. to Mary Alexander, June 10, 1818. Sol. June 10, 1818, Wm. Hume, V.D.M.

Cobbs, Jas. H. to Elizabeth Hill, June 15, 1818. Sol. June 18, 1818, Edmund Lanier.

Tait, Waddy to Julia Matilda Coleman, June 17, 1818. Sol. June 17, 1818, Wm. Hume, V.D.M.

Wilson, Robt. to Lucinda Kee, July 1, 1818. Sol. July 10, 1818, Joseph Love.

Martin, Peter H. to Jane Bell, July 2, 1818. Sol. July 2, 1818, Wm. Hume, V.D.M.

Loyd, James to Matilda Morris, July 4, 1818.

Downs, Wm. to Peggy Wilcox, July 7, 1818. Sol. July 9, 1818, Joel Anderson.

Sadler, Jeremiah to Mahaly Earhart, July 8, 1818. Sol. July 17, 1818, R. Weakley, J.P.
Fly, Micajah to Nancy Hardy, July 9, 1818. Sol. July 9, 1818, James Whitsitt.
Harris, Wm. to Lucreasy Barnes, July 14, 1818.

Page 197
Westbrook, Wesley to Susan Dunn, July 15, 1818.
Hubbs, Barri to Sally Harper, July 17, 1818. Sol. July 19, 1818, Wm. Anderson.
Sanders, Gabriel to Jane Hail, July 20, 1818. Sol. July 26, 1818, Benjamin Barrow, Min.
Reynolds, George to Sarah Reeves, July 21, 1818. Sol. July 23, 1818, Wm. Anderson.
McIntire, Robert to Polly Morton, July 21, 1818.
Roads, Newton to Sophia Johnston, July 21, 1818. Sol. July 22, 1818, Levin Edney, Min.
Wright, George to Patsy Sawyers, Aug. 1, 1818.
Phipps, Eldridge N. to Senai Cassellman, Aug. 4, 1818. Sol. Aug. 5, 1818, Levin Edney, Min.
Vick, Joab to Deley Vick, Aug. 5, 1818.
Richardson, Booker to Susannah Robertson, Aug. 10, 1818. Sol. Aug. 27, 1818, Eldridge Newsom.

Page 198
Robertson, Jas. R. to Susan Oldham, Aug. 11, 1818. Sol. Aug. 13, 1818, Wm. Hume, V.D.M.
Lovell, Wm. to Nancy Garland, Aug. 12, 1818. Sol. Aug. 20, 1818, W. Russell, J.P.
Hurt, Henry to Elizabeth Wright, Aug. 17, 1818. Sol. Aug. 18, 1818, Peter Fuqua, Min.
Chandler, George to Nancy Perkins, Aug. 18, 1818. Sol. Aug. 19, 1818, Wm. Hume, V.D.M.
Donaldson, James to Clarnida Richmond, Aug. 18, 1818. Sol. Aug. 19, 1818, Wm. Hume, V.D.M.
Small, Samuel to Cinthia Binkley, Aug. 22, 1818. Sol. Sep. 7, 1818, Iredell Reding, J.P.
Butterworth, Wm. to Nancy Cartwright, Aug. 24, 1818. Sol. Aug. 26, 1818, Edmund Lanier.
Garrett, Rich'd to Rebecca Cannon, Aug. 27, 1818. Sol. Aug. 27, 1818, Wm. Hume, V.D.M.
Dillon, James to Elizabeth Moore, Aug. 29, 1818. Sol. Sep. 1, 1818, James Whitsitt.
Drake, Jno., Jr. to Charlotte R. Witt, Sep. 1, 1818. Sol. Sep. 3, 1818, Wm. Hume, V.D.M.

Page 199
Lewis, Ambrose G. to Jane Watkins, Sep. 1, 1818. Sol. Sep. 1, 1818, Wm. Hume, V.D.M.
Harwell, Frederick to Nancy Black, Sep. 2, 1818. Sol. Sep. 3, 1818, Wm. Hume, V.D.M.
Boyt, James to Patsy Simmons, Sep. 4, 1818. Sol. Sep. 17, 1818, G. S. Allen, J.P.

Hanks, Joshua to Amelia Rape, Sep. 12, 1818. Sol. Sep. 17, 1818, Wm. Anderson.
Stringfellow, Richd. to Hannah Reaves, Sep. 16, 1818. Sol. Sep. 18, 1818, Wm. Anderson.
Palmer, Anthony to Nancy Paul, Sep. 16, 1818. Sol. Sep. 16, 1818, Wm. Hume, V.D.M.
Murry, John M. to Polly Jackson, Sep. 17, 1818. Sol. Sep. 1818, E. Gamble, J.P.
Usery, Masten to Elizabeth Fowler, Sep. 19, 1818. Sol. Oct. 1, 1818, Eldridge Newsom.
Barefield, Daniel to Nancy Grimes, Sep. 21, 1818. Sol. Sep. 29, 1818, Russell, J.P.
Dean, James to Charlotte Horn, Sep. 23, 1818. Sol. Sep. 24, 1818, Will Williams, J.P.

Page 200
Dilworth, Thos. to Susannah Williams, Sep. 24, 1818. Sol. Sep. 24, 1818, Th. Edmiston, J.P.
Foy, James to Mary Daniel, Sep. 25, 1818. Sol. Sep. 27, 1818, Wm. Hume, V.D.M.
Johns, Wm. to Sally Pugh, Sep. 26, 1818. Sol. Sep. 29, 1818, Joel Anderson.
Little, John to Patsy Johns, Sep. 28, 1818. Sol. Sep. 30, 1818, Joel Anderson.
Davis, Joshua to Polly Koen, Sep. 30, 1818. Sol. Sep. 30, 1818, Levin Edney, Min.
Dotson, Limech to Sophia Williams, Oct. 1, 1818. Sol. Oct. 7, 1818, Wm. Hall, J.P.
Brown, Alexander Y. to Rebecca N. Harris, Oct. 9, 1818. Sol. Oct. 15, 1818, Eldridge Newsom.
Rasberry, Geo. to Ferribee Hooper, Oct. 10, 1818. Sol. Oct. 12, 1818, W. Russell, J.P.
Gammill, James to Sally Whites, Oct. 15, 1818. Sol. Oct. 22, 1818, B. Gray, J.P.
Miles, Samuel, Jr. to Bede Lewis, Oct. 19, 1818. Sol. Oct. 29, 1818, G. S. Allen, J.P.

Page 201
Peay, Geo. to Nancy Johnston, Nov. 3, 1818. Sol. Nov. 6, 1818, B. Gray, J.P.
Key, Tandy L. to Delilah Beasley, Nov. 4, 1818.
Harris, James to Elizabeth Maddox, Nov. 5, 1818. Sol. Nov. 5, 1818, Levin Edney.
Scott, Larkin to Peggy Russell, Nov. 7, 1818. Sol. Nov. 10, 1818, W. Russell, J.P.
Scott, Jno. T. to Rebecca Exum, Nov. 9, 1818. Sol. Nov. 10, 1818, Levin Edney, Min.
Downsey, Wm. to Sarah Harwood, Nov. 10, 1818. Sol. Nov. 12, 1818, Levin Edney.
Richardson, Henry to Elizabeth Cox, Nov. 13, 1818. Sol. Nov. 19, 1818, Eldridge Newsom.
Scruggs, Theophelus to Charlotte Perry, Nov. 15, 1818.
Fowlkes, Sam'l to Elizabeth W. Moore, Nov. 18, 1818. Sol. Nov. 21, 1818, Edmund Lanier.

Strong, Thomas to Jene Tibbs, Nov. 18, 1818.

Page 202
Clemons, Isaac to Elizabeth Matthes, Nov. 24, 1818. Sol. Nov. 25, 1818, Edmund Lanier.
Thomas, William to Precilla Cotton, Nov. 24, 1818. Sol. Nov. 24, 1818, Wm. H. White.
Montgomery, Hamilton to Elizabeth Morris, Nov. 24, 1818. Sol. Nov. 25, 1818, Wm. H. Shelton, J.P.
Parkman, David to Margaret Chism, Nov. 25, 1818. Sol. Nov. 26, 1818, Joel Anderson.
Cooper, August to Sally Armstrong, Nov. 25, 1818.
Goodlott, Adam G. to Charlotte P. Campbell, Nov. 26, 1818. Sol. Nov. 26, 1818, Wm. Hume, V.D.M.
Parradise, Parker to Rachel Bayles, Nov. 28, 1818.
Rolston, Geo. to Elizabeth Marshall, Dec. 1, 1818. Sol. Dec. 8, 1818, Joseph Love.
Houton, Daniel to Exit Randall, Dec. 1, 1818.
Miles, Elisha to Sally Lovell, Dec. 5, 1818. Sol. Dec. 10, 1818, Moses Speed.

Page 203
Davis, John to Susan Newton, Dec. 5, 1818.
Hobbs, Collin S. to Theodosia Holmes, Dec. 8, 1818.
Gilbert, Wilson to Nancy Kennedy, Dec. 10, 1818. Sol. Dec. 13, 1818, Joel Anderson.
Daniel, Edward to Thermy Cartwright, Dec. 12, 1818. Sol. Dec. 12, 1818, Levin Edney, Min.
McLaughlin, James to Mary C. Law, Dec. 15, 1818. Sol. Dec. 17, 1818, Wm. Hume, V.D.M.
Mays, Wm. W. to Pennia Fowler, Dec. 15, 1818. Sol. Dec. 17, 1818, Eldridge Newsom.
Crutchfield, Oliver to Polly Burnett, Dec. 18, 1818.
Patterson, Benjamin to Fanny Weakley, Dec. 21, 1818. Sol. Dec. --, 1818, T. B. Craighead.
Bosley, Charles to Eliza Childress, Dec. 23, 1818. Sol. Dec. 24, 1818, Wm. Hume, V.D.M.
Pierson, Isham to Delilah Cross, Dec. 29, 1818.

Page 204
Vaughn, Edward to Elizabeth Cagle, Dec. 30, 1818. Sol. Jan. --, 1819, Jonathan Drake, J.P.
Blurton, John to Elizabeth Tackett, Dec. 30, 1818. Sol. Dec. 31, 1818, Wm. Hall, J.P.
Jones, Benj. B. to Martha M. Haywood, Dec. 31, 1818.
Webber, John to Mancy G. Moore, Dec. 31, 1818. Sol. Jan. 1, 1819, Edmund Lanier.
Marshall, Sam B. to Jane Childress, Dec. 31, 1818. Sol. Dec. 31, 1818, Wm. Hume, V.D.M.
Bournos, Jos. Tansea to Adele Gardette, Jan. 1, 1819. Sol. Jan. 4, 1819, Wm. Hume, V.D.M.
Williamson, Geo. to Lucy Baxter, Jan. 4, 1819. Sol. Jan. 7, 1819, Eldridge Newsom.
Thomas, U. M. to Nancy Marland, Jan. 9, 1819. Sol. Feb. 5, 1819, B. Gray, J.P.

Williams, Wm. to Martha Hall, Jan. 12, 1819. Sol. Jan. 15, 1819, Wm. Hall, J.P.
Freeman, Jas. B. to Elizabeth Denby, Jan. 14, 1819. Sol. Jan. 14, 1819.

Page 205
Sadler, Thomas to Partheny Smith, Jan. 16, 1819. Sol. Jan. 16, 1819, W. Barrow.
James, Smith to Catherine Farmer, Jan. 19, 1819. Sol. Jan. --, 1819, James Whitsitt.
Caldwell, Robt. to Jincy Brown, Jan. 19, 1819. Sol. Jan. 21, 1819, W. Barrow.
Scudder, Phillip J. to Elizabeth Sims, Jan. 20, 1819. Sol. Jan. 21, 1819, Wm. Hume, V.D.M.
Wilcox, James to Polly Kernel, Feb. 10, 1819. Sol. Feb. 11, 1819, Peter Fuqua.
Arthur, Wm. to Mary Ann Godsey, Feb. 11, 1819. Sol. Feb. 11, 1819, Wm. Hume, V.D.M.
Marefield, Thomas to Polly Clay, Feb. 16, 1819. Sol. Feb. 16, 1819, James Whitsitt.
Faulkner, James W. to Francis Tachet, Feb. 22, 1819. Sol. Feb. 28, 1819, W. Barrow.
Baker, Gilbert to Elizabeth Baker, Feb. 23, 1819. Sol. Feb. 24, 1819, Peter Fuqua, Min.
Howsley, Alexander to Wilmouth Bishop, Feb. 24, 1819. Sol. Feb. 24, 1819, Wm. H. White.

Page 206
Abernathy, Laban to Elizabeth Drake, Feb. 27, 1819. Sol. March 23, 1819, Jonathan Drake, J.P.
Neal, Turner to Jane Blair, March 1, 1819. Sol. March 7, 1819, Carey Felts.
Graham, Reuben P. to Nancy S. Thomas, March 3, 1819. Sol. March 4, 1819, Wm. Hume, V.D.M.
Dickson, John M. to Emeline M. Frazor, March 6, 1819. Sol. March --, 1819, T. B. Craighead.
Rutherford, Robt. H. to Evelina Mathis, March 9, 1819.
Smith, Joel to Polly Booten, March 9, 1819. Sol. March 25, 1819, Iredell Reding, J.P.
Carmach, Isaac to Sally Banes, March 11, 1819. Sol. March 11, 1819, S. Shannon.
Pickett, Wm. to Matilda Holder, March 11, 1819. Sol. March 11, 1819, W. Barrow.
Troop, Wm. to Christina Youngblood, March 17, 1819.
McIntosh, Daniel to Mary Charlton, March 24, 1819. Sol. March 24, 1819, Wm. Hume, V.D.M.

Page 207
Buchanan, Alexander to Mary T. Ridley, March 24, 1819. Sol. March 25, 1819, Wm. Hume, V.D.M.
Champ, Richard to Polly Livingston, March 24, 1819. Sol. March 31, 1819, W. Russell, J.P.
Woods, Edward to Sally Trimble, March 27, 1819.

Thompson, Wm. W. to Avelina Jordan, March 31, 1819. Sol. April 8, 1819, Jonathan Drake, J.P.
Duratt, Timothy to Sally Hunter, April 1, 1819.
Cain, Joseph to Parthenia Connell, April 1, 1819.
Bayless, John to Nancy Buel, April 1, 1819. Sol. April 1, 1819, Joseph Love, J.P.
Twigg, Timothy to Elizabeth Roberts, April 1, 1819. Sol. April 6, 1819, B. Gray, J.P.
Sherley, David to Nancy Tachett, April 8, 1819.
Whitaker, Wm. H. to Maria L. Whyte, April 8, 1819. Sol. April 8, 1819, Wm. Hume, V.D.M.

Page 208
Roach, Needham to Fanny B. McNeilly, April 9, 1819. Sol. April 9, 1819, R. C. Foster, J.P.
Allen, Rich'd to Sophia Molloy (col), April 14, 1819. Sol. April 15, 1819, Wm. Hume, V.D.M.
Clinard, John to Polly Cammeron, April 17, 1819. Sol. April 25, 1819, Iredell Reding, J.P.
Drewry, Rich'd to Jemimiah Adams, April 21, 1819. Sol. April 21, 1819, J. Whitsitt.
Wilson, James to Jane Tate, April 24, 1819. Sol. April 29, 1819, Wm. Lounder(?).
Dotson, Harvey to Sally Wilson, April 28, 1819. Sol. April 29, 1819, Wm. Hall, J.P.
Harrod, Thos. to Celia Campbell, May 1, 1819.
Earthman, Isaac to Martha Lanier, May 11, 1819. Sol. May 16, 1819, S. Shannon.
McGavock, Jacob to Louisa C. Grundy, May 11, 1819. Sol. May 11, 1819, Geo. Blackburn, V.D.M.
Clinard, John to Polly Higgins, May 11, 1819. Sol. May 13, 1819, Joseph Love, J.P.

Page 209
Wright, Wm. to Jane H. Wright, May 12, 1819.
Floyd, Jones to Esther Hayes, May 13, 1819.
Harmon, Hardiman to Edith Sadler, May 17, 1819. Sol. May 18, 1819, E. Gamble.
Cruse, Samuel to Harriet Maria Coleman, May 26, 1819. Sol. May 27, 1819, Wm. Hume, V.D.M.
Lane, Owen to Polly Fly, May 31, 1819. Sol. June 3, 1819, Guy McFadden.
Manchester, Willard to Mary S. Taylor, May 31, 1819. Sol. May 31, 1819, Wm. Hume, V.D.M.
Miles, Hardy to Polly Lovell, June 2, 1819. Sol. July 6, 1819, B. Lee, J.P.
O'Donnely, James to Polly Lee, June 7, 1819. Sol. June 8, 1819, Jonathan Drake, J.P.
Barnes, Benjamin to Mary Cato, June 12, 1819.
Jefferson, Thos. to Nancy Dawson, June 12, 1819. Sol. June 17, 1819.

Page 210
Jewell, Joseph to Mary E. Wills, June 14, 1819. Sol. June 15, 1819, John Johnson.
Cloyd, Joshua D. to Frances Newsom, June 15, 1819. Sol. June 24, 1819, Eldridge Newsom.
Lecoq, Frances H. to Rebecca Chapman, June 15, 1819. Sol. June 15, 1819, Wm. Hume, V.D.M.
Page, Absalom to Patsy Woodfork, June 24, 1819. Sol. June 24, 1819, Wm. Wallace, J.P.
Hamilton, Thos. to Sally Owen, July 1, 1819. Sol. July 1, 1819, J. Whitsitt.
Platts, John to Elizabeth Barefoot, July 1, 1819.
Laswell, Henry to Sally Smith, July 5, 1819. Sol. July 15, 1819, Carey Felts.
Donelson, Lemuel to Eliza Whyte, July 13, 1819. Sol. July 15, 1819, Wm. Hume, V.D.M.
Barnes, Benjamin to Polly Whittendon, July 19, 1819. Sol. July 22, 1819, Levin Edney, Min.
Shelton, Wm. to Jane Gower, July 20, 1819. Sol. July 29, 1819.

Page 211
Lemley, Phillip to Eliza Hall, July 21, 1819. Sol. July 22, 1819, Peter Fuqua, Min.
Owen, James to Elizabeth Wray, July 21, 1819.
Lane, Thomas to Rebecca McFaddin, June 24, 1819. Sol. July 1, 1819, B. Gray, J.P.
Fossett, Alexander to Martha Edmonds, July 27, 1819. Sol. July 29, 1819, Wm. Hall, J.P.
Carothers, Wm. to Priscilla McBride, July 28, 1819.
Taylor, Wm. to Priscilla King, July 31, 1819. Sol. Aug. 5, 1819, R. Hewitt.
Raymer, Henry to Elizabeth Smith, Aug. 2, 1819. Sol. Aug. 5, 1819, Iredell Reding, J.P.
Kent, Wm. to Polly Sidebottom, Aug. 4, 1819. Sol. Aug. 4, 1819, Edmund Lanier.
Wills, David to Polly Morris, Aug. 5, 1819. Sol. Aug. 8, 1819, S. Shannon.
Barton, Burges to Jane Scoggins, Aug. 5, 1819.

Page 212
Boner, Henry to Margaret Higgins, Aug. 11, 1819.
Smith, Andrew to Patsy Smith, Aug. 14, 1819. Sol. Aug. 19, 1819, R. Weakley, J.P.
Owens, Marshall to Mary Lewallen, Aug. 17, 1819. Sol. Aug. 19, 1819, Wm. H. Nance, J.P.
Anderson, Solomon to Elizabeth Newsom, Aug. 26, 1819. Sol. Aug. 31, 1819, Wm. H. Shelton, J.P.
Phillips, Mark to Elizabeth Huggins, Aug. 26, 1819.
Gibbs, Thomas to Susan Lester, Aug. 30, 1819.
Moore, Nathan W. to Mary H. Crenshaw, Aug. 31, 1819.
Orr, Wm. to Sally Hedgepath, Sep. 4, 1819. Sol. Sep. 5, 1819, Wm. Hall, J.P.

Wray, Wm. to Levina Harris, Sep. 6, 1819. Sol. Sep. 6, 1819, Wm. Hall, J.P.
Soto, Anthony to Ellen Claxton, Sep. 11, 1819. Sol. Sep. 12, 1819, W. Wallace, J.P.

Page 213
Gibson, John S. to Patsy A. Vaughn, Sep. 14, 1819.
Hughes, Champness to Elizabeth Patton, Sep. 16, 1819.
Phillips, David to Sally Phillips, Sep. 17, 1819.
Johnston, John to Mary Anderson, Sep. 20, 1819.
Smith, Thos. C. to Patsy Vick, Sep. 20, 1819.
Whites, Joshua to Sally Cunningham, Sep. 21, 1819.
Squires, Robt. to Fanny White, Sep. 21, 1819.
Miller, Thomas, Jr. to Clarissa Craddock, Sep. 22, 1819. Sol. Sep. 22, 1819, Wm. Hume, V.D.M.
Wright, Thornton to Juliet Tennison, Sep. 29, 1819. Sol. Sep. 29, 1819, Wm. Hall, J.P.
Sharp, Ambrose to Sarah Cain, Oct. 2, 1819.

Page 214
Brown, Bazzell to Elizabeth Phillips, Oct. 4, 1819.
Redding, Iredale to Patsy Hellums, Oct. 7, 1819. Sol. Oct. 7, 1819, S. Shannon.
Winters, Wm. to Elizabeth Bishop, Oct. 9, 1819.
Shane, Andrew to Martha Green, Oct. 10, 1819. Sol. Oct. 10, 1819, Wm. Hall, J.P.
Vaughn, Samuel to Polly Greer, Oct. 13, 1819. Sol. Oct. 13, 1819, Levin Edney, Min.
Green, Robt. W. to Matilda Porter, Oct. 14, 1819. Sol. Oct. 14, 1819, Geo. Blackburn, V.D.M.
Watkins, Wm. E. to Matilda R. Hewitt, Oct. 18, 1819. Sol. Oct. 20, 1819, Th. Claiborne, acting J.P.
Green, Isiah D. to Margaret Castleman, Oct. 20, 1819. Sol. Oct. 20, 1819, Wm. Hall, J.P.
Hogan, Robt. to Jane Edge, Oct. 21, 1819. Sol. Nov. 1, 1819, Iredell Reding, J.P.
Guy, George to Rebecca Yarbrough, Oct. 23, 1819.

Page 215
McIlwain, John to Abba Greer, Oct. 25, 1819. Sol. Oct. 25, 1819, Wm. Anderson, J.P.
Baker, William to Tabby Cravens, Oct. 25, 1819. Sol. Oct. 28, 1819, Wm. Sanders.
Murrell, Jas. D. to Mary Searcy, Oct. 29, 1819. Sol. Oct. 29, 1819, Wm. Hume, V.D.M.
Mathews, Elisha to Nancy Reaves, Nov. 3, 1819. Sol. Nov. 7, 1819, Wm. Anderson, J.P.
Parker, John C. to Fanny Crutcher, Nov. 4, 1819.
Ramsey, Wm. Jr. to Elizabeth L. Lapsley, Nov. 5, 1819. Sol. Nov. 9, 1819, Th. Edmiston, J.P.
Grant, Geo. to Sophia Bradford, Nov. 1, 1819. Sol. Nov. --, 1819, T. B. Craighead.
Seratt, Joseph to Finey Harvey, Nov. 11, 1819.
Bailey, Wm. to Jane Sutton, Nov. 13, 1819.
Yarbrough, Wm. to Jane Coffman, Nov. 16, 1819.

Page 216

Hood, James to Mary A. Chalmers, Nov. 17, 1819. Sol. Nov. 18, 1819, Wm. Hume, V.D.M.

Adams, Thos. P. to Ann Tennant, Nov. 17, 1819. Sol. Nov. 18, 1819, Wm. Hume, V.D.M.

Fitzhugh, Jno. to Nancy Blackman, Nov. 20, 1819. Sol. Nov. 20, 1819, James Whitsitt.

Strambler, George to Rebecca Jones, Nov. 24, 1819. Sol. Nov. 29, 1819, Levin Edney, Min.

Stump, Jacob to Cassia Hooper, -----------.

Johnston, Rich'd, to Sarah W. Oldham, Nov. 20, 1819. Sol. Nov. 25, 1819, R. Hewitt.

Wood, Fleming P. to Tabitha W. Moore, Dec. 2, 1819.

Criddle, John Jr. to Sally Drake, Dec. 8, 1819.

Bland, Arthur to Polly A. Feltz, Dec. 14, 1819. Sol. Dec. 16, 1819, Benajah Gray, J.P.

Perkins, James W. to Eliza T. Edmiston, Dec. 14, 1819. Sol. Dec. 14, 1819, James Whitsitt.

Page 217

George, Wm. to Martha Ann Cox, Dec. 14, 1819.

Wills, Benjamin to Margaret O. Harnley, Dec. 15, 1819. Sol. Dec. 16, 1819, Wm. Hume, V.D.M.

Williams, Thos. to Patsy Strong, Dec. 18, 1819.

Page, Robt. to Julia Wilks, Dec. 20, 1819. Sol. Dec. 22, 1819, R. Hewitt.

Strong, Thomas to Rhody Shane, Dec. 22, 1819. Sol. Dec. 22, 1819, Peter Fuqua, Min.

Chadwell, John to Polly Thompson, Dec. 23, 1819.

Gainer, Jesse to Merina Cherry, Dec. 23, 1819. Sol. Dec. 24, 1819, Wm. Saunders.

Davis, Daniel to Nancy Lester, Dec. 28, 1819.

Estes, John to Elizabeth Osmore, Dec. 28, 1819. Sol. Dec. 30, 1819, R. C. Foster.

Nix, James to Nancy Caton, Dec. 30, 1819. Sol. -----, ----, T. B. Craighead.

Page 218

Thomas, John to Sally Bradberry, Dec. 30, 1819. Sol. Dec. 30, 1819, Wm. Hume, V.D.M.

Hicks, Marvell to Nancy Green, Jan. 5, 1820.

Talbot, Wm. H. to Caroline Talbot, Jan. 6, 1820. Sol. Jan. 6, 1820, Wm. Hume, V.D.M.

Hughes, John to Nancy Thompson, Jan. 8, 1820. Sol. Jan. 25, 1820, Eldridge Newsom.

McCoy, Dan'l to Sally Hardy, Jan. 11, 1820.

Harding, Thos. to Elizabeth Bosley, Jan. 17, 1820. Sol. Jan. 20, 1820, Wm. Hume, V.D.M.

Linton, Silas to Peggy Pritchett, Jan. 20, 1820. Sol. Jan. 25, 1820, Wm. H. Shelton, J.P.

Brown, Robt. to Sally Conley, Jan. 20, 1820.

Dismukes, Jno. T. to Sarah M. Royster, Jan. 20, 1820. Sol. Jan. --, ----, T. B. Craighead.

McGavock, Jno. to Sally Shall, Jan. 20, 1820. Sol. Jan. 20, 1820, John Johnson.

Page 219
Seat, Robt. M. to Nancy M. Blair, Jan. 24, 1820. Sol. Jan. 24, 1820, John Johnson.
Mitchell, Robt. J. to Martha M. Oldham, Jan. 25, 1820. Sol. Jan. 27, 1820, D. A. Dunham.
Carpenter, Frederick to Taby Holt, Jan. 31, 1820. Sol. Feb. 1, 1820, Joseph Love, J.P.
Jones, Lewis to Milly Spence, Feb. 21, 1820.
Huggins, Jonathan to Elizabeth W. Smith, Feb. 1, 1820. Sol. Feb. 3, 1820, Wm. Hume, V.D.M.
Braughton, John to Nancy White, Feb. 9, 1820. Sol. Feb. 9, 1820, R. C. Foster.
Robertson, Peyton to Ellen Davis, Feb. 11, 1820. Sol. Feb. 14, 1820, Wm. Hume, V.D.M.
Newson, Herbert to Sally Harding, Feb. 12, 1820. Sol. Feb. 17, 1820, R. Hewitt.
Derby, Chas. to Nancy Ann Pulling, Feb. 14, 1820. Sol. Feb. 14, 1820, John Johnson.
Williamson, Benj. S. to Sarah E. Harris, Feb. 14, 1820.

Page 220
Marrs, Hugh to Martha Norton, Feb. 15, 1820.
Martin, Wm. to Sally Pierce, Feb. 21, 1820.
Neely, Wm. to Polly Birdwell, Feb. 22, 1820. Sol. Feb. --, 1820, T. B. Craighead.
Saunders, James to Sarah Cagle, Feb. 23, 1820. Sol. March 2, 1820, Geo. A. Irion.
Butt, Christopher to Nancy Jones, March 4, 1820.
Wright, Benjamin to Elizabeth Lester, March 4, 1820.
Williams, Christopher to Lucinda Lile, March 6, 1820. Sol. March 8, R. Hewitt.
Ridley, George to Polly Vaughn, March 9, 1820.
Robertson, M. C. C. to Peggy Wrenn, March 10, 1820.
Newland, John to Eliza House, March 11, 1820. Sol. March 14, 1820, S. Shannon, J.P.

Page 221
Skiles, Jas. R. to Eliza A. Bell, March 15, 1820. Sol. March 16, 1820, Jas. B. Lapsley.
Spraggins, Asa to Lucreasa Lock, March 15, 1820. Sol. March 19, 1820, Peter Fuqua, Min.
Chadwell, Valentine to Elizabeth Johnston, March 18, 1820.
McFarland, Robert P. to Winney Lloyd, March 20, 1820. Sol. March 20, 1820, Wm. Hume, V.D.M.
Cox, Lorton to Polly Lile, April 13, 1820.
Hopper, John to Jane Eakins, April 5, 1820. Sol. April 9, 1820, Th. Edmiston, J.P.
Rainey, Silas to Polly Reddish, April 8, 1820. Sol. April 8, 1820, Wm. Hume, V.D.M.
Cox, Wm. B. to Priscilla Walker, April 13, 1820. Sol. April 16, 1820, S. Shannon, J.P.
Watson, James to Mary Making Payzer, April 15, 1820. Sol. April 15, 1820, J. P. Erwin, J.P.

Hathaway, Wm. to Ann Hathaway, May 1, 1820. Sol. May 1, 1820.

Page 222

Baker, Isaac L. to Charlotte Lewis, May 3, 1820. Sol. May ----------, T. B. Craighead.

Thomas, Phillip to Aggy (a Mulatto), May 9, 1820. Sol. May 9, 1820, Wm. Hume, V.D.M.

White, Jas. C. to Martha Alexander, May 11, 1820. Sol. July 3, 1820, Wm. H. Nance, J.P.

Bean, Edmund to Peggy Tapper, May 11, 1820. Sol. May 11, 1820, J. P. Erwin, J.P.

Emmons, Cyrenus to Elizabeth Edgar, May 11, 1820.

Buchanan, Jno. K. to Maria L. Saunders, May 18, 1820. Sol. May 18, 1820, James Whitsitt.

Goldsby, Joseph to Patsy Humphreys, May 19, 1820.

Turbeville, Willie to Mary Christenberry, May 20, 1820.

Meed, John to Jane Foster, May 27, 1820.

Pennington, Graves to Martha M. Bondurant, June 3, 1820. Sol. June 7, 1820, T. B. Craighead.

Page 223

Read, Theodorick to Rebecca Sanders, June 6, 1820. Sol. Dec. 28, 1820, W. Wallace, J.P.

Boyd, Joseph to Martha J. Dismukes, June 7, 1820. Sol. June 8, 1820, T. B. Craighead.

Stevens, John to Elizabeth Payzer, June 7, 1820. Sol. June 8, 1820, Wm. Hume, V.D.M.

Webb, Kendal to Mary Dougal, June 8, 1820. Sol. June 8, 1820, John Johnson.

Northern, Samuel to Polly Hodge, June 12, 1820.

Russell, Thomas to Anne Hooper, June 13, 1820. Sol. July 19, 1820, W. Russell, J.P.

Mills, John to Nancy Mills, June 15, 1820.

Winston, John J. to Susan Johnston, June 20, 1820. Sol. June 20, 1820, Thomas Boaz.

Huffman, George to Pheley Mungle, June 22, 1820. Sol. June 22, 1820, Jonathan Drake, J.P.

Adcock, Edward to Sally Davis, June 22, 1820. Sol. June 22, 1820.

Page 224

Bryan, Sherwood to Nancy Johnston, June 29, 1820. Sol. June 30, 1820, S. Shannon, J.P.

Adkinson, Jesse to Ann J. Bridgeforth, July 3, 1820.

Hinton, Wm. M. to Adline Criddle, July 4, 1820.

Trabue, Chas. C. to Agnes G. Wood, July 5, 1820. Sol. July 5, 1820, T. B. Craighead.

Stroud, Willis to Margaret Allen, July 11, 1820. Sol. July 26, 1820, Eldridge Nawsom.

Frazier, Moses B. to Tempy Douglas, July 12, 1820. Sol. July 13, 1820, T. B. Craighead.

Baxter, Jas. to Pheby Burnett, July 15, 1820. Sol. July 23, 1820, E. Newsom.

Warren, Noble to Catherine Robertson, July 19, 1820. Sol. July 23, 1820, Joseph Love, J.P.
Scott, Wm. D. to Nancy Thomas, July 24, 1820. Sol. Nov. 5, 1820, Wm. Hume, V.D.M.
Gillespie, Robt. to Catherine W. Rutherford, July 26, 1820. Sol. July 26, 1820, James Whitsitt.

Page 225
Menefee, Jonas, Jr. to Mary Heaton, Aug. 3, 1820. Sol. Aug. 3, 1820, B. Lee, J.P.
Rape, John to Polly Dunn, Aug. 5, 1820. Sol. Aug. 12, 1820, Eldridge Newsom.
Cook, Reuben to Polly Neely, Aug. 7, 1820. Sol. Aug. 1820, T. B. Craighead.
Lyon, Richard to Elizabeth Hopper, Aug. 10, 1820.
Gulledge, Wm. to Martha Daniel, Aug. 24, 1820. Sol. Aug. 24, 1820, B. H. Lanier, J.P.
Gill, George to Martha R. Marshall, Aug. 25, 1820. Sol. Sep. 24, 1820, S. Shannon.
Bond, John to Sally Cassellman, Aug. 30, 1820. Sol. Aug. 31, 1820, D. A. Dunham.
Smith, Joseph to Eliza Eakins, Aug. 31, 1820. Sol. Aug. 31, 1820, John Johnson.
Hays, David to Hannah Buchus, Aug. 31, 1820. Sol. Aug. 31, 1820, Peter Fuqua.
Cartwright, Thos. M. to Mary Booth, Sep. 12, 1820.

Page 226
Lewis, Wm. C. to Hulda Redding, Sep. 14, 1820. Sol. Sep. 14, 1820, B. H. Lanier, J.P.
Turner, Wm. to Lucinda D. London, Sep. 14, 1820. Sol. Sep. 15, 1820, Wm. Hall, J.P.
Malone, Benjamin to Nancy Gotton, Sep. 20, 1820. Sol. Sep. 21, 1820, Th. Edmiston, J.P.
Crowder, James to Hannah Lowe, Sep. 27, 1820.
Mosely, John to Kitty Osbourne, Oct. 2, 1820. Sol. Oct. 4, 1820, D. A. Dunham, J.P.
Kennedy, James to Nancy Owen, Oct. 3, 1820. Sol. Oct. 4, 1820, Wm. Hall, J.P.
Lock, Joseph to Gilley Wright, Oct. 8, 1820.
Stennett, Benj. M. to Elizabeth Mathews, Oct. 9, 1820. Sol. Oct. 12, 1820, Wm. Herrin, Min.
Wilson, Mathew to Elizabeth Wright, Oct. 9, 1820. Sol. Oct. 9, 1820, James Whitsitt.
Neely, Samuel to Jane Davis, Oct. 11, 1820. Sol. Oct. 12, 1820, T. B. Craighead.

Page 227
Greenhalgh, Jacob to Ann Charlton, Oct. 11, 1820. Sol. Oct. 11, 1820, J. Vardeman, V.D.M.
Erwin, Andrew, Jr. to Elvira Julius Searcy, Oct. 12, 1820. Sol. Oct. 12, 1820, Wm. Hume, V.D.M.
OBryant, Wm. to Lucy Wright, Oct. 14, 1820. Sol. Oct. 18, 1820, Wm. Saunders.

Garrett, Jonathan to Sally Waggoner, Oct. 20, 1820. Sol. Oct. 22, 1820, S. Shannon, J.P.
Spence, Wm. to Pheby Forehand, Oct. 24, 1820.
Smith, Joel R. to Nancy J. Grizzard, Oct. 25, 1820. Sol. Oct. 26, 1820, Wm. Hall, J.P.
Curtis, John to Sally Fowler, Oct. 25, 1820. Sol. Oct. 25, 1820, R. Hewitt, J.P.
Elam, Robt. to Nancy M. Drury, Oct. 25, 1820. Sol. by Jas. Whitsitt.
Glennarrey, Edward to Sarah Sweetman, Oct. 26, 1820. Sol. Oct. 28, 1820, Wm. Hume, V.D.M.
Williams, Wm. to Jane France, Oct. 30, 1820.

Page 228
Jackson, Dyer to Rebecca OBryant, Oct. 31, 1820. Sol. Oct. 31, 1820, Wm. Hall, J.P.
Gardner, Simon to Tobetha Richardson, Nov. 1, 1820. Sol. Nov. 5, 1820, Willie Barrow.
Brierly, Robt. to Sarah Smith, Nov. 4, 1820. Sol. Nov. 23, 1820, Wm. Hume, V.D.M.
Gibson, Wm. to Rebecca Adams, Nov. 14, 1820. Sol. Nov. 14, 1820,A. D. Campbell, Min.
Gardner, Stephen to Darcus Hill, Nov. 14, 1820. Sol. Nov. 15, 1820, Thos. Boaz.
Cooper, Chas. to Maria P. Eastland, Nov. 18, 1820. Sol. Nov. 19, 1820, John Johnson.
Hails, Sharod to Nancy Sullivan, Nov. 22, 1820.
Gower, Wilson to Lucinda Page, Nov. 25, 1820. Sol. Nov. 30, 1820, W. Wallace, J.P.
Anderson, Thos. to Ellender Reaves, Nov. 29, 1820. Sol. Nov. 30, 1820, W. Wallace, J.P.
Hiney, Jacob to Sally Willeford, Dec. 4, 1820. Sol. Dec. 5, 1820, A. D. Campbell, Min.

Page 229
Legrand, Peter, to Anne Coleman, Dec. 5, 1820.
Bailey, Jeremiah to Catherine Waggoner, Dec. 6, 1820
Day, John to Jency Fowler, Dec. 7, 1820. Sol. Dec. 7, 1820, R. Hewitt, J.P.
Abernathy, David to Mary Everett, Dec. 12, 1820. Sol. Dec. 14, 1820, W. Wallace, J.P.
Kennedy, Wm. to Elizabeth Elliston, Dec. 13, 1820. Sol. Dec. 21, 1820, Wm. Herrin.
Cloud, James to Sarah Goodwin, Dec. 20, 1820. Sol. 1820, Levin Edney, M.G.
Hewitt, Hazael to Caroline Newsom, Dec. 20, 1820. Sol. Dec. 21, 1820, Wm. Hume, V.D.M.
Askins, James to Salary Parkman, Dec. 21, 1820.
Brown, Nathanial to Patsy Bell, Dec. 22, 1820.
Yokeley, Henry to Nancy Eddington, Dec. 22, 1820. Sol. Dec. 22, 1820, Wm. Hume, V.D.M.

Page 230
Matlock, John to Polly Fuqua, Dec. 29, 1820. Sol. Dec. 30, 1820, Peter Fuqua, Min.
Germain, Wm. to Sally Berry, July 18, 1798.
Cartwright, James to Mary Kitterlin, Aug. 21, 1798.
Moore, Summerset to Charlotte Blueford, March 15, 1799.
Haile, Wm. to Sally Brown, March 18, 1799.
Lile, Henry to Dinah Evans, March 19, 1799.
Fillitt, Samuel to Sarah Tarkington, March 22, 1799.
Moody, Moses to Jenny Anderson, March 23, 1799.
Nesbitt, Jeremiah to Elizabeth Newbitt, March 29, 1799.
Adams, Frances to Isabella Young, March 29, 1799.

Page 231
Wright, Adam to Peggy Pruett, April 1, 1799.
Summers, Abraham to Nancy Gardner, April 2, 1799.
Martin, Wm. to Polly Smith, April 2, 1799.
Beavers, Joel to Luraney Morris, April 22, 1799.
Thomas, Mark to Rachel Thomas, May 15, 1799.
Mann, John to Susannah Dupree, May 25, 1799.
Reeves, Geo. to Mary Land, May 31, 1799.
Branch, Robt. to Hannah Taylor, June 6, 1799.
Childress, Jno. to Elizabeth Robertson, June 15, 1799.
Mackey, Thos. to Mary Lamasters, June 20, 1799.

Page 232
Barnes, John to Lydia Fowler, June 27, 1799.
Evans, Wm. to Mary Stinnett, June 29, 1799.
McCueston, Robt. to Charity Dunn, July 1, 1799.
McGaugh, Wm. to Polly Patton, July 3, 1799.
Stuart, Wm. to Sarah Bumpass, July 9, 1799.
Hart, Mark to Betsy Kimbro, July 20, 1799.
Titus, George to Joannah Edmondson, July 27, 1799.
Claiborne, Wm. C. C. to Eliza W. Lewis, Aug. 2, 1799.
Holland, Gustavius to Betsy Simpson, Aug. 10, 1799.
Herndon, Joseph to Patsy Coleman, Aug. 26, 1799.

Page 233
McGraw, Jacob to Mary Jane Messeck, Aug. 29, 1799.
McCutchem, James to Martha Patterson, Sep. 10, 1799.
Branch, Robt. to Polly Smith, Sep. 10, 1799.
Young, Peter to Sarah Ross, Sep. 14, 1799.
Thompson, Jas. to Sereana Gearman, Sep. 22, 1799.
Gower, Robt. to Agnes Burnley, Sep. 25, 1799.
Blackburn, Jno. to Lucy Carney, Sep. 29, 1799.
Stump, Jonathon to Martha Johnston, Sep. 30, 1799.
Lovel, James to Catherine Chambers, Oct. 5, 1799.
Compton, Wm. to Susannah Mullin, Oct. 7, 1799.

Page 234
Roach, Brian to Nancy Hanks, Oct. 12, 1799.
Orton, Wm. to Rebecca Williams, Oct. 19, 1799.
McLendon, Dennis to Winifred Greer, Oct. 19, 1799.
Beavers, James to Rhody Gambrel, Oct. 25, 1799.

Sludor, John to Polly McLendon, Oct. 26, 1799.
Fletcher, John to Esther Whitfield, Nov. 5, 1799.
Reaves, Jordon to Mary Magness, Nov. 7, 1799.
Hyde, John to Elizabeth Emmerson, Nov. 11, 1799.
McDaniel, John to Lucy Dawson, Nov. 16, 1799.
Latner, John C. to Elsie Germain, Nov. 17, 1799.

Page 235
Key, Henry to Jane Stuart, Nov. 19, 1799.
Hyde, Henry to Polly Drake, Nov. 12, 1799.
Brown, John to Hannah Standley, Dec. 3, 1799.
Williams, John to Clary Brown, Dec. 7, 1799.
Lewis, Archibald to Eleanora Sappington, Dec. 17, 1799.
Huggins, Chas. to Sarah Little, Dec. 24, 1799.
Evans, Wm. to Nancy Joslin, Dec. 24, 1799.
Morris, Andrew to Elizabeth Earthman, Dec. 24, 1799.
Ridley, Vincent to Lydia Everett, Dec. 28, 1799.
Rains, Jno. to Frances Ogelvie, ---. --, 1800.

Page 236
Tommison, Wm. to Darky Odear, Jan. 1, 1800.
Gowen, Jos. to Polly Fester, Jan. 8, 1800.
Bryant, Hardy S. to Catherine Young, Jan. 17, 1800.
Payton, Jno. W. to Lina Phillips, Jan. 27, 1800.
Green, Thos. to Sally Johns, Jan. 29, 1800.
Germain, James to Anna Hays, Jan. 30, 1800.
Harris, Sam'l B. to Polly Coots, Feb. 1, 1800.
Germain, Tristram to Nicey Bateman, Feb. 2, 1800.
Johnston, James to Juliet Demumby, Feb. 6, 1800.
Orton, Rich'd to Sally Johnston, Feb. 12, 1800.

Page 237
Neely, Samuel to Polly Watkins, Feb. 18, 1800.
Anderson, Wm. P. to Nancy Bell, Feb. 22, 1800.
Huison, Philip to Elizabeth Thompson, March 1, 1800.
Norman, John to Margaret Stockard, March 3, 1800.
Enoch, Davis to Joanna Oliver, March 12, 1800.
Cunningham, John to Polly Patton, March 15, 1800.
Rhoads, John to Elizabeth Hobday, March 19, 1800.
James, Wm. to Elizabeth Walker, March 24, 1800.
Pace, Henning to Martha Bradshaw, March 25, 1800.
Sullivan, Eppes to Sally Sullivan, March 27, 1800.

Page 238
Atherly (or Witherly), Isaac to Polly Robertson, April 16, 1800.
Sludor, Henry to Sally Biggs, April 26, 1800.
Laonard, Isaac to Sophia Neely, May 2, 1800.
Cross, Martin to Polly Hall, May 5, 1800.
Thompson, James to Peggy Buchanan, May 14, 1800.
Hammer, Daniel to Betsy Davis, May 27, 1800.
Perch, Henry to Elizabeth Askins, May 29, 1800.
Hammond, Eli to Polly Owings, May 31, 1800.
Harney, Geo. W. to Jenny McSpaddin, June 3, 1800.

Rice, David to Anna Hayes, June 22, 1800.

Page 239
Hogan, Humphrey to Catherine Fisher, June 24, 1800.
McCollouch, Alexander to Frances Fisher Lenoir, Sep. 11, 1800.
Buchanan, George to Dinah Robertson, Sep. 23, 1800.
Stuart, Andrew to Sarah Drake, Oct. 11, 1800.
Hamilton, John to Polly Tomison, Oct. 29, 1800.
Bell, Hugh to Margaret McKinney, Nov. 15, 1800.
Sullivan, David to Nancy Sullivan, Nov. 23, 1800.
Parvall, John to Peggy Conger, Nov. 29, 1800.
Hamilton, John to Polly Turner, Dec. 1, 1800.
David, James to Elizabeth Reeves, Dec. 1, 1800.

Page 240
Shannon, Samuel to Catherine Motherel, Dec. 10, 1800.
Dyer, Baldy to Polly Taylor, Dec. 13, 1800.
Henry, Hugh to Elizabeth Tamnasson, Dec. 17, 1800.
Cummins, David to Elizabeth Fielder, Dec. 20, 1800.
Turner, Arthur to Elizabeth Glavis, Dec. 29, 1800.
McAfee, Moses to Sally Chamberlain, Dec. 31, 1800.
Boyd, Richard to Nancy Tate, Jan. 3, 1801.
Wright, John to Nancy Eastwood, Jan. 7, 1800.
Collins, John G. to Scerena Donoho, Jan. 3, 1821. Sol. Jan. 11, 1821, A. D. Campbell, Min.
Vaughn, John to Patsy Dunnevant, Feb. 5, 1821.

Page 241
Stuart, Wm. to Elizabeth Lee, Jan. 10, 1821. Sol. Jan. 18, 1821, G. S. Allen, J.P.
Stark, Wm. to Catherine Loving, Jan. 10, 1821. Sol. Jan. 11, 1821, A. D. Campbell, Min.
Standley, Jas. to Nancy Johnston, Jan. 11, 1821.
Hannah, Benj. F. to Mahuldy Greer, Jan. 11, 1821. Sol. Jan. 19, 1821, E. Newsom.
Donelson, Severn to Mary H. Sampson, Jan. 15, 1821. Sol. Jan. 17, 1821, T. B. Craighead.
Green, Stephen to Polly Castleman, Jan. 16, 1821.
Fryer, Alfred to Nancy Puckett, Jan. 18, 1821. Sol. Jan. 21, 1821, B. H. Lanier, J.P.
Brown, John to Elizabeth Lee, Jan. 20, 1821. Sol. Jan. 21, 1821, Peter Fuqua, M.G.
Casselman, Abraham to Eliza Jones, Jan. 20, 1821. Sol. Jan. 20, 1821, Levin Edney, Min.
Hagar, Hollis to Susan Tennison, Jan. 23, 1821. Sol. Jan. 24, 1821, Peter Fuqua, Min.

Page 242
Catron, John to Matilda Childress, Jan. 24, 1821. Sol. Jan. 25, 1821, A. D. Campbell, Min.
Hooper, Alston to Polly Allen, Jan. 24, 1821. Sol. March 25, 1821, W. Russell, J.P.

Knight, John to Polly B. Scott, Jan. 24, 1821. Sol. Jan. 25, 1821, Wm. Hume, V.D.M.
Evans, Samuel to Elizabeth Saluder, Jan. 25, 1821.
Richmond, Bradox to Winney Garrett, Jan. 25, 1821. Sol. Jan. 25, 1821, Jas. Whitsitt.
Earl, Austin to Louisa M. Hail, Jan. 25,1821. Sol. Jan. 25, 1821, C. Stump, J.P.
Drake, Isaac to Louisa Bashaw, Jan. 31, 1821. Sol. Feb. 4, 1821, David Dunn, J.P.
Fluellen, Shaderick to Lydia Page, Feb. 8, 1821. Sol. Feb. 8, 1821, B. H. Lanier, J.P.
Jones, Willie to Margaret Cloyd, Feb. 10, 1821. Sol. Feb. 15, 1821, Jas. Love, J.P.
McCallister, Wilson to Nancy Walker, Feb. 12, 1821.

Page 243
Brittain, James to Mariah Thompson, Feb. 13, 1821. Sol. Feb. 20, 1821, Wm. Hume, V.D.M.
Ostrander, Matthew to Eliza Daniel, Feb. 14, 1821. Sol. Feb. 15, 1821, Wm. Hume, V.D.M.
Ellison, John to Nancy Stewart, Feb. 15, 1821.
Lane, Denne to Susannah McFaddin, Feb. 17, 1821. Sol. March 1, 1821, B. Gray, J.P.
Lanier, Robt. to Eliza A. Criddle, Feb. 22, 1821.
Bedford, Benj. W. to Martha Ann Whyte, March 1, 1821. Sol. March 1, 1821, Wm. Hume, V.D.M.
Simpson, David to Issabella Edgert, March 1, 1821.
Binkley, John to Elizabeth Hurt, March 1, 1821. Sol. March 1, 1821, Wm. Hall, J.P.
Stringfellow, Rich'd to Nancy Seals, March 7, 1821. Sol. March 8, 1821, G. S. Allen, J.P.
Anderson, Isaac to Sally Duratt, March 13, 1821.

Page 244
Keating, Wm. to Anne Chism, March 17, 1821. Sol. March 17, 1821, Carey Feltz.
Forehand, John to Peggy Martin, March 26, 1821.
Pitzer, Wm. to Sarah Miller, March 29, 1821. Sol. March 29, 1821, John Johnson.
Everett, Jesse J. to Milley Wilkinson, March 30, 1821. Sol. April 1, 1821, Jonathan Drake, J.P.
Cartwright, Wm. to Jeney Bell, April 7, 1821.
Knowles, Joseph B. to Mary T. Johnston, April 11, 1821. Sol. April 12, 1821, Wm. Hume, V.D.M.
Hays, Jno. C. to Susan Castleman, April 21, 1821. Sol. April 22, 1821, Peter Fuqua, Min.
Elliston, Wm. to Anne Tenneson, April 27, 1821. Sol. May 1, 1821, Wm. Herrin.
Jones, John N. S. to Eliza Haywood, May 3, 1821. Sol. May 3, 1821, Wm. Hume, V.D.M.
Deaderick, Jno. G. to Eliza E. G. Dunn, May 8, 1821. Sol. May 10, 1821, T. B. Craighead.

Page 245

Joslin, Daniel to Nancy Peal, May 9, 1821. Sol. May 1821, C. Strowitt, Curate of D.C.

Tucker, Woodford to Rebecca Wilder, May 15, 1821. Sol. May 17, 1821, D. A. Dunham, J.P.

Moreland, Edward to Priscilla B. Williams, May 17, 1821.

Crabtree, Benj. to Nancy Bailee, May 17, 1821.

Branch, Wallice to Mary Chapman, May 18, 1821. Sol. Aug. 11, 1821, S. Shannon, J.P.

Edington, Nicholas, Jr. to Eliza Simmons, May 18, 1821. Sol. May 21, 1821, Wm. Hume, V.D.M.

Carroll, McWilliam to Maria F. Meaney, May 19, 1821. Sol. May 20, 1821, B. J. Flag (Flaget, B.P. of Bardstown.

Marlin, Samuel to Charlotte Leah, May 22, 1821. Sol. May 24, 1821, Wm. Barrow.

Harwood, John to Mary Jordan, May 26, 1821. Sol. June 5, 1821, Eldridge Newsom.

Smith, Abraham H. to Charlotte Phelps, May 29, 1821.

Page 246

Stuart, Robt. L. to Sally Carpenter, June 4, 1821. Sol. June 17, 1821, G. S. Allen, J.P.

Pinkerton, Joseph to Elizabeth Bryan, June 5, 1821. Sol. by Wm. Hume.

Rice, Elijah to Mary Ann Cox, June 8, 1821.

Hudgins, John to Polly Kennedy, June 16, 1821. Sol. June 19, 1821, Carey Feltz.

Demoss, Wm. to Byes P. Charter, June 21, 1821. Sol. June 21, 1821, Levin Edney, Min.

Page, Robert to Cassander Phelps, June 25, 1821.

Clinard, Henry to Anne McNeill, June 26, 1821. Sol. Sep. 27, 1821, Iredell Reding, J.P.

Stultz, Jno. H. to Nancy J. Dorris, July 3, 1821. Sol. July 3, 1821, Jas. Whitsitt.

Inman, Lazarus to Elizabeth Malone, July 14, 1821. Sol. July 16, 1821, D. A. Dunham, J.P.

Gordon, James to Ann E. Hewsom, July 17, 1821. Sol. July 17, 1821, Wm. Hume, V.D.M.

Page 247

Williams, Lewis to Elizabeth M. Powell, July 18, 1821. Sol. July 19, 1821, Jonathan Drake, J.P.

Blair, Samuel to Elizabeth Sanders, July 24, 1821. Sol. July 26, 1821, Carey Feltz.

Spence, John to Nancy Ayers, July 26, 1821. Sol. July 26, 1821, A. D. Campbell, Min.

Woodward, Benj. to Harriet Burnett, Aug. 3, 1821. Sol. Aug. 12, 1821, C. Strowitt, Curate of D.C.

Smith, Thomas to Susan Raymer, Aug. 7, 1821. Sol. Aug. 9, 1821, Iredell Reding, J.P.

Brannon, John to Margaret Pearce, Aug. 7, 1821.

Maynard, Rich'd to Letitia Watson, Aug. 8, 1821. Sol. Aug. 8, 1821, W. Barrow.

Ashley, Jesse to Lucinda Holder, Aug. 8, 1821. Sol. Aug. 9, 1821, R. Hewitt.
Erwin, Isaac to Mary W. Nichols, Aug. 8, 1821. Sol. Aug. 9, 1821, Wm. Hume, V.D.M.
Bryn, John R. to Charlotte Logue, Aug. 11, 1821.

Page 248
Chatham, Wm. to Maria Davis, Aug. 15, 1821. Sol. Aug. 16, 1821, Wm. Hume, V.D.M.
Pickering, Wm. to Sally Ingram, Aug. 18, 1821. Sol. Aug. 19, 1821, D. A. Dunham.
Wade, Wm. to Mary Peebles, Aug. 29, 1821. Sol. Aug. 29, 1821, James Whitsitt.
Binkley, David to Drusella Shackleford, Aug. 30, 1821. Sol. Aug. 30, 1821, Peter Fuqua, Min.
Seat, Wm. to Elizabeth Burnett, Sep. 5, 1821. Sol. Sep. 6, 1821, Carey Feltz.
Jonas, James to Charlotte Greer, Sep. 8, 1821.
Sullivent, Isaac B. to Elizabeth Ann Kernel, Sep. 3, 1821.
Wilks, Wm. A. to Nancy Hodge, Sep. 11, 1821. Sol. Sep. 13, 1821, D. A. Dunham.
Key, John to Martha Page, Sep. 11, 1821.
McCance, Elenezer W. to Sarah Latter, Sep. 12, 1821. Sol. Sep. 13, 1821, R. B. Craighead.

Page 249
Farquharson, Robt. to Eliza Porter, Sep. 13, 1821. Sol. Sep. 13, 1821, A. D. Campbell, Min.
Crow, Wm. L. to Sally White, Sep. 13, 1821. Sol. Sep. 13, 1821, Carey Feltz.
Greer, Elijah to Elizabeth Cook, Sep. 13, 1821. Sol. Sep. 13, 1821, Peter Fuqua, Min.
Nichol, Jno. W. to Mary Blair, Sep. 21, 1821.
Thomas, Philip to Aggy Thomas, Sep. 27, 1821. Sol. Sep. 27, 1821, Wm. Hume, V.D.M.
Harris, Howell to Prescilla Harris, Sep. 27, 1821. Sol. Sep. 27, 1821, C. Stowell, Curate.
Nelson, Nichols to Polly Atkinson, Oct. 10, 1821. Sol. Oct. 10, 1821, B. H. Lanier, J.P.
Harris, Ethelrel to Nancy Green, Oct. 13, 1821.
Fuqua, Thos. to Susan Steel, Oct. 17, 1821. Sol. Oct. 18, 1821, Peter Fuqua, Min.
Williams, Wm. S. to Esther Stringfellow, Oct. 17, 1821. Sol. Oct. 18, 1821, Wm. Hume, V.D.M.

Page 250
Cobler, Benjamin to Rebecca Moss, Oct. 17, 1821. Sol. Oct. 17, 1821, Jas. Whitsitt.
Thomas, John to Elizabeth Stewart, Oct. 23, 1821. Sol. Oct. 25, 1821, Th. Edmiston, J.P.
Matsel, Henry to Sarah Wooten, Oct. 23, 1821. Sol. Nov. 1, 1821, Jonathan Drake.
Kennedy, David to Elizabeth Littrell, Oct. 24, 1821.
Hope, Wm. to Mary Walker, Oct. 24, 1821. Sol. Oct. 26, 1821, T. B. Craighead.

Verdon, Barnard to Hannah Clark, Oct. 25, 1821.
Cannady, Milburn to Elizabeth Burnham, Nov. 8, 1821.
Lynn, Jno. E. to Nancy Work, Nov. 6, 1821. Sol. Nov. 8, 1821, Absolom Gleaves.
Hurt, Benjamin to Elizabeth Cassellman, Nov. 14, 1821. Sol. Nov. 15, 1821, Absolom Gleaves.
Greer, John to Myra Green, Nov. 17, 1821. Sol. Nov. 18, 1821, Absolom Gleaves.

Page 251
Newsom, James to Sally Evans, Nov. 17, 1821. Sol. Nov. 18, 1821, G. S. Allen, J.P.
Crawford, John to Nancy Daniel, Nov. 19, 1821. Sol. Nov. 20, 1821, Wm. Hume, V.D.M.
Collins, Starcus to Elizabeth Collinsworth, Nov. 27, 1821. Sol. Dec. 15, 1821, Jacob Browning, R.M.G.
Estes, Wm. W. to Sally Lock, Nov. 30, 1821. Sol. Nov. 30, 1821, Peter Fuqua, Min.
Carney, James to Peggy Hunter, Dec. 1, 1821. Sol. Dec. 6, 1821, W. Wallace, J.P.
Pierce, James to Elizabeth Bacheus, Dec. 3, 1821. Sol. Dec. 6, 1821, Eldridge Newsom.
Cuff, David to Elizabeth Bell, Dec. 4, 1821.
Shivers, Jonas to Elizabeth McCasland, Dec. 14, 1821. Sol. Dec. 21, 1821, S. Shannon, J.P.
King, Lewis to Sarah Cook, Dec. 17, 1821. Dol. Dec. 17, 1821, Peter Fuqua, Min.
Saunders, Jacob to Franky Gower, Dec. 17, 1821. Sol. Dec. 19, 1821, W. Wallace, J.P.

Page 252
Thompson, Robt. to Martha S. R. Jones, Dec. 18, 1821. Sol. Dec. 18, 1821, Wm. Hume, V.D.M.
Kirk, Geo. D. to Eliza Sneed, Dec. 18, 1821. Sol. Jan. 1, 1822, Wm. Hume, V.D.M.
Lucas, Andrew, Jr. to Harriett Belts, Dec. 19, 1821. Sol. Dec. 22, 1821, Robt. Hewitt, J.P.
Killough, James to Parmelia Charter, Dec. 19, 1821.
Vanderville, Jno. to Ann Bryant, Dec. 22, 1821. Sol. Dec. 23, 1821, Wm. Faulkner.
Wright, Jno. B. to Evelina Cato, Dec. 26, 1821.
Manive, John to Rebecca Williamison, Dec. 29, 1821. Sol. Jan. 3, 1822, Wm. Hume, V.D.M.
Hayes, Wm. to Anne Williams, Dec. 31, 1821. Sol. Jan. 3, 1822, Carey Feltz.
Parker, Allen to Gensy Hicks (either 1799 or 1800).
Fitzhugh, Samuel to Elizabeth McCutcheon, Jan. 2, 1822.

Page 253
Feltz, Christopher E. to Nancy Kibble, Jan. 3, 1822. Sol. Jan. 10, 1822, B. Gray, J.P.
Adair, Abner to Elizabeth Leak, Jan. 4, 1822. Sol. Jan. 4, 1822, Wm. Hume, V.D.M.

Raison, Jacob to Sarah Boyles, Jan. 5, 1822, Sol. Jan. 6, 1822, B. H. Lanier, J.P.
Patterson, Moses to Patience Exum, Jan. 9, 1822. Sol. Jan. 20, 1822, Eldridge Newsom.
Seaborne, James to Anne Cassellman, Jan. 18, 1822. Sol. Jan. 20, 1822, Absolom Gleaves, J.P.
Watson, David to Catherine Wolf, Jan. 19, 1822.
Tucker, Wm. to Anny Hodge, Jan. 19, 1822. Sol. Jan. 24, 1822, D. A. Dunham.
Duncan, Thos. A. to Margaret Stothart, Jan. 22, 1822. Sol. Jan. 24, 1822, A. D. Campbell, Min.
Bacchus, Josiah to Susan Pierce, Jan. 22, 1822. Sol. Jan. 24, 1822, Eldridge Newsom.
McLure, Wm. to Martha D. Moore, Jan. 23, 1822. Sol. Jan. 31, 1822, B. Gray, J.P.

Page 254
Wiley, Henry to Jane Gordon, Jan. 23, 1822. Sol. Jan. 23, 1822, Wm. Hume, V.D.M.
Gulledge, Frederick to Polly Fuqua, Jan. 24, 1822. Sol. Feb. 25, 1822, B. H. Lanier, J.P.
Barnwell, David to Elizabeth Haddock, Jan. 26, 1822. Sol. Feb. 5, 1822, B. Gray, J.P.
Wells, Hiram to Patsy James, Jan. 28, 1822. Sol. Jan. 31, 1822, Jonathan Drake.
Pritchett, Benjamin to Joannah Linton, Feb. 4, 1822. Sol. Feb. 11, 1822, Levin Edney, Min.
Howington, Willis to Harriett Gardner, Feb. 9, 1822.
Moore, Isham to Rebecca Barnes, Feb. 11, 1822.
Reaves, Timothy to Ferrebee Russell, Feb. 11, 1822. Sol. Feb. 26, 1822, W. Russell, J.P.
McAllister, James to Barbary Shaw, Feb. 12, 1822.
Smart, Bennett W. to Esther Edmondson, Feb. 13, 1822. Sol. Feb. 14, 1822, Th. Edmiston, J.P.

Page 255
Binkley, Absolom to Aggy Page, Feb. 15, 1822. Sol. Feb. 21, 1822, B. H. Lanier, J.P.
Sailor, Wm. to Hannah Bailey, Feb. 26, 1822.
Hinton, Jno. J. to Martha Ann Turner, March 5, 1822. Sol. March 5, 1822, Will Williams.
Bigley, Edward to Amelia White, March 9, 1822. Sol. March 10, 1822, Thos. Maddin.
Hobday, Joses to Elezette Cartwright, March 12, 1822.
Hall, Elisha to Anna A. Gulliford, March 18, 1822. Sol. March 28, 1822, S. Shannon, J.P.
Smith, Daniel to Elizabeth Jones, March 18, 1822.
Temple, Thos. B. to Elizabeth Hobbs, March 25, 1822.
Bird, John to Emmy Buttrey, March 25, 1822. Sol. March 28, 1822, Th. Edmiston.
Morris, John to Jane Hallums, March 26, 1822. Sol. March 30, 1822, S. Shannon, J.P.

Page 256

White, Wm. to Martha Edmiston, April 29, 1822. Sol. Arpil 30, 1822, Th. Edmiston, J.P.

Scott, Samuel to Polly Scott, May 10, 1822. Sol. May 23, 1822, Wm. Saunders.

Porter, John to Susan Heaton, May 14, 1822. Sol. May 16, 1822, Braxton Lee, J.P.

Cockrill, Mark R. to Susan Collinsworth, May 23, 1822. Sol. May 23, 1822, Wm. Hume, V.D.M.

Puckett, Douglas, Jr. to Maryann Buie, May 23, 1822. Sol. May 28, 1822, B. H. Lanier, J.P.

Hodges, Asia to Melessa Paradise, May 23, 1822. Sol. June 16, 1822, B. H. Lanier, J.P.

Crook, Bignal to Polly Moreman, June 4, 1822. Sol. June 6, 1822, Will Lytle, Chief Jus.

Crawford, Wm. to Darcus Sharp, June 14, 1822.

Woodlin, Wm. to Cassey Felin, June 22, 1822. Sol. June 26, 1822, S. Shannon, J.P.

Hayes, David to Emily Harrison, June 22, 1822. Sol. June 25, 1822, Edward Edwards.

Page 257

Alexander, Wm. to Mary Inman, July 1, 1822. Sol. Levin Edney, Min. (no date given).

East, Addison to Elizabeth Decker, July 4, 1822. Sol. July 4, 1822, Wm. Hume, V.D.M.

Newell, Hugh F. to Mary Anthony, July 4, 1822. Sol. July 4, 1822, Wm. Hume, V.D.M.

McFaddin, Barnett to Lucy Osburn, July 12, 1822. Sol. July 18, 1822, D. A. Dunham.

Westbrook, Turner to Temperance Dunn, July 15, 1822. Sol. July 16, 1822, C. Stedwell, Curate.

Pierce,Isaac to Elizabeth Turner, July 16, 1822. Sol. July 18, 1822, Absolom Gleaves, J.P.

Stephens, Levin to Lurani Sullivant, July 22, 1822. Sol. July 24, 1822, Wm. Herrin.

Schooley, James to Sally Barr, July 29, 1822. Sol. Aug. 6, 1822, W. Russell, J.P.

Askins, Wm. to Polly Jones, July 31, 1822.

Stuart, Thos. H. to Ureny Roach, Aug. 5, 1822.

Page 258

Fletcher, Wm. to Elizabeth Able, Aug. 12, 1822. Sol. Aug. 16, 1822, Absolom Gleaves.

Hayes, John to Martha Whitemore, Aug. 14, 1822. Sol. Aug. 14, 1822, James Whitsitt.

Roach, Jas. C. to Elizabeth Little, Aug. 22, 1822. Sol. Aug. 22, 1822, Levin Edney, Min.

Winn, Edmond to Charity Perkins, Aug. 22, 1822. Sol. Aug. 23, 1822, E. S. Hall.

Melvin, Andrew to Mary Adams, Aug. 26, 1822. Sol. Sep. 5, 1822, Peter Fuqua.

Hobbs, Edward to Ann C. Hill, Aug. 30, 1822.

Fitzgerald, Jonathan to Altiseer Dorris, Sep. 3, 1822.

Barnes, Thomas to Morning Stephenson, Sep. 10, 1822. Sol. Sep. 12, 1822, Thos. Boaz.
Woodward, James to Mary Daniel, Sep. 12, 1822. Sol. Sep. 15, 1822, S. Shannon, J.P.
Hooper, Claiborne Y. to Martha Hooper, Sep. 12, 1822. Sol. Sep. 13, 1822, Wm. Faulkner.

Page 259
Clark, Martin to Charity H. Battle, Sep. 14, 1822. Sol. Oct. 1822, Robt. Paine, Min.
Page, Alfred G. to Tildy Williams, Sep. 17, 1822. Sol. Sep. 19, 1822, Wm. Wallace, J.P.
Smith, Thos. S. to Lydia Thomas, Sep. 18, 1822.
Bullard, Theophelus to Lucy Armstrong, Sep. 19, 1822. Sol. Sep. 19, 1822, Robt. Hewitt, J.P.
Moore, Amos to Elizabeth Ann Luck, Sep. 20, 1822. Sol. Sep. 26, 1822, Thos. Boaz.
Donelson, Wm. to Rachel Donelson, Sep. 24, 1822. Sol. Sep. 26, 1822, Wm. Hume, V.D.M.
Bain, John R. to Nancy Donnald, Sep. 24, 1822. Sol. Oct. 1, 1822, A. D. Campbell, Min.
Seawell, Benj. P. to Eliza Thompson, Sep. 27, 1822.
Brannen, Wm. to Elizabeth W. Sturdi, Sep. 27, 1822.
Hollingsworth, Joseph to Peggy Nelson, Sep. 27, 1822. Sol. Sep. 27, 1822, Jas. Whitsitt.

Page 260
Williams, Lemuel to Harriett Osburn, Oct. 2, 1822.
Jourdan, Williamson V. to Sophia Sugg, Oct. 4, 1822.
Fowlks, Jno. to Mary Turner, Oct. 4, 1822.
Simmons, Chas. to Rebeccah Coshen, Oct. 9, 1822.
Robertson, James to Sally Wilder, Oct. 9, 1822. Sol. Oct. 9, 1822, Robt. Hewitt, J.P.
Turner, Wm. to Elizabeth Cherry, Oct. 12, 1822. Sol. Oct. 16, 1822, Absolom Gleaves.
Herd, George to Sarah Wright, Oct. 14, 1822.
Faulkner, James to Rebecca Woodard, Oct. 15, 1822. Sol. Nov. 1, 1822, S. Shannon, J.P.
Neiblet, Henry to Mariah Bosley, Oct. 17, 1822. Sol. Oct. 22, 1822, Wm. Hume, V.D.M.
Ensley, Enoch to Mary Rains, Oct. 19, 1822.

Page 261
Boyle, Jno. A. to Patsy Roberts, Oct. 19, 1822. Sol. Oct. 22, 1822, Guy McFaddin.
Weaver, Reuben to Celia Vick, Oct. 21, 1822.
Putman, James R. to Sophia Ann Perkins, Oct. 21, 1822. Sol. Oct. 24, 1822, A. D. Campbell, Min.
Rawlings, Edward G. to Margaret Grundy, Oct. 24, 1822. Sol. Oct. 24, 1822, A. D. Campbell, Min.
Kirkpatrick, Jno. to Sally Williamson, Oct. 26, 1822.
Tucker, Anderson to Nelly Smith, Nov. 7, 1822. Sol. Nov. 7, 1822, G. Wilson, J.P.

Stanfield, Goodloe to Lavine Matlock, Nov. 11, 1822. Sol. Nov. 14, 1822, Peter Fuqua, Min.
Vick, Joseph to Dianna Kennedy, Nov. 13, 1822.
Richardson, Wm. S. to Sally Jordan, Nov. 14, 18i2. Sol. Nov. 26, 1822, W. Russell, J.P.
Love, James to Eliza Jefferson, Nov. 25, 1822. Sol. Nov. 26, 1822, Geo. McNeilly.

Page 262
Binkley, Wm. to Sarah Cowgill, Nov. 28, 1822.
McCully, James to Mary Knox, Nov. 29, 1822.
Coltart, Jno. to Jennett Maxwell, Dec. 3, 1822. Sol. Dec. 3, 1822, Wm. Hume, V.D.M.
Vaughn, Edmund W. to Sally Key, Sec. 5, 1822. Sol. Dec. 10, 1822, Th. Edmiston, J.P.
Roach, Henry K. to Chloe Burnham, Dec. 7, 1822. Sol. Dec. 7, 1822, Levin Edney, Min.
Osborne, Thompson to Polly B. Wilks, Dec. 9, 1822. Sol. Jan. 11, 1823, D. A. Dunham.
Tully, Jacob A. to Sarah Jefferson, Dec. 9, 1822. Sol. Dec. 9, 1822, Benjamin P. Sewell, S.P.
Cartmell, Henry R. to Sally Thomas, Dec. 10, 1822. Sol. Dec. 10, 1822, A. D. Campbell, Min.
Spence, John to Rebecca Campbell, Dec. 12, 1822. Sol. Dec. 12, 1822, Wm. Hume, V.D.M.
Washington, Gilbert G. to Elizabeth H. Wharton, Dec. 18, 1822. Sol. Dec. 18, 1822, Wm. Hume, V.D.M.

Page 263
Williams, William S. to Nancy Virgin, Dec. 18, 1822. Sol. Dec. 19, 1822, W. Barron.
Halliday, Alex'd to Elizabeth Graham, Dec. 19, 1822. Sol. Dec. 19, 1822, Wm. Hume, V.D.M.
Hooper, John to Tenny Cullon, Dec. 23, 1822.
Price, John to Sophia E. Overall, Dec. 23, 1822.
Fowler, Thos. J. to Elizabeth Mays, Dec. 24, 1822. Sol. Jan. 2, 1823, Wm. H. Shelton, J.P.
Seay, Samuel to Jane Wharton, Dec. 24, 1822. Sol. Dec. 1822, T. B. Craighead.
Shaw, Wm. to Peggy Campbell, Dec. 27, 1822. Sol. Jan. 1, 1823, S. Shannon, J.P.
Duff, Robt. L. to Lydia Brown, Dec. 31, 1822. Sol. Dec. 31, 1822, A. D. Campbell, Min.
Clifford, Patrick to Bridget Hastie, Jan. 1, 1823. Sol. Jan. 2, 1823, Wm. Lytle, J.P.
Yarborough, James to Peggy Coffman, Jan. 6, 1823.

Page 264
Pipkin, Stewart to Harriet S. Caldwell, Jan. 7, 1823. Sol. Jan. 11, 1823, D. A. Dunham, J.P.
Patterson, Wm. S. to Elizabeth B. Carter, Jan. 7, 1823. Sol. Jan. 9, 1823, Peter Fuqua.
Kinney, Patrick to Mary Cregan, Jan. 7, 1823. Sol. Will Lytle, J.P.

Malone, Calvin to Aloha Bumppass, Jan. 7, 1823. Sol. Jan. 9, 1823, Th. Edmiston, J.P.
Mathews, Edward to Mary Link, Jan. 8, 1823.
Gleaves, Jas. R. to Eliza Wood, Jan. 9, 1823. Sol. Jan. 12, 1823, Peter Fuqua, Min.
Matthias, Stephen to Elizabeth Ann Scott, Jan. 9, 1823. Sol. Jan. 9, 1823, Wm. Saunders.
Hill, James J. to Elizabeth L. Rodgers, Jan. 9, 1823.
Brinkley, Alexander to Hixey Holt, Jan. 10, 1823. Sol. Jan. 12, 1823, B. H. Lanier, J.P.
Walker, Abraham S. to Lenia Phips, Jan. 13, 1823. Sol. Jan. 15, 1823, D. A. Dunham.

Page 265
Alford, Nelson to Elizabeth Hill, Jan. 14, 1823.
Boyd, James to Martha Noles, Jan. 15, 1823. Sol. Jan. 15, 1823, Wm. Hume, V.D.M.
Lightfoot, Henry to Sarah Currin, Jan. 16, 1823. Sol. Jan. 23, 1823, Thos. Edmiston, J.P.
Huie, Richard to Ann Stuart, Jan. 17, 1823.
Bell, Nathaniel to Elenor Johnston, Jan. 18, 1823. Sol. Jan. 23, 1823, Wm. Hume, V.D.M.
Roberts, Mack to Hannah Johnston, Jan. 23, 1823. Sol. Feb. 6, 1823, B. Gray, J.P.
Burnett, Jno. O. to Sally Harris, Jan. 28, 1823. Sol. March 1, 1823, Wm. Herrin, B.M.G.
Finney, Michael to Zilpha McCrory, Jan. 29, 1823. Sol. Feb. 6, 1823, Wm. H. Nance, J.P.
Weaver, Seaborn J. to Mary McGlendon, Feb. 1, 1823. Sol. Feb. 26, 1823, Carey Feltz.
Foster, Jno. L. to Edy Barnes, Feb. 3, 1823.

Page 266
Herren, Joseph to Elizabeth Hall, Feb. 4, 1823. A. D. Campbell, Min.
Lally (or Tally), Reuben to Harriet Rayman, Feb. 10, 1823. Sol. Feb. 13, 1823, S. Shannon, J.P.
Randall, Presly M. to Elizabeth McCarmack, Feb. 10, 1823.
Childress, James W. to Martha Hopkins, Feb. 11, 1823. Sol. Feb. 13, 1823, Wm. Hume, V.D.M.
Summers, Jno. to Tencey Saunders, Feb. 21, 1823.
Leonard, Martin to Elizabeth Garland, Feb. 21, 1823. Sol. Feb. 23, 1823, W. Russell, J.P.
Walkens, John S. to Margaret Allison, Feb. 24, 1823. Sol. Feb. 27, 1823, Benjamin Sewell, S.P.
Smithwick, Edward to Mary Alms, March 1, 1823. Sol. March 2, 1823, B. H. Lanier, J.P.
Williamson, James D. to Eliza Combs, March 3, 1823. Sol. March 4, 1823, Th. Edmiston, J.P.

Page 267
Whitfield, Jno. W. to Susan Phipps, March 8, 1823.
Long, Wm. to Elizabeth Fryer, March 18, 1823. Sol. March 25, 1823, S. Shannon, J.P.

Norvell, Joseph to Agnes Walker, March 22, 1823. Sol. March 23, 1823, Wm. Hume, V.D.M.
Terhune, Jno. to Prudence Heaton, April 1, 1823. Sol. April 3, 1823, B. Lee, J.P.
Turbeville, Jefferson to Mary Jane Moss, April 4, 1823.
Quinn, Matthew H. to Ann T. Parham, April 5, 1823. Sol. April 6, 1823, W. B. Peck, M.G.
Bonds, Nathaniel to Rhody Cassellman, April 8, 1823. Sol. April 8, 1823, D. A. Dunham.
Landsdown, Jno. to Patsy Humphries, April 10, 1823. Sol. April 10, 1823, Will Lytle, J.P.
McClure, Jno. S. to Agnes Vincent, April 12, 1823.
Murdock, Wm. to Lydia Coltharp, April 15, 1823. Sol. April 15, 1823, E. Talbot, J.P.

Page 268
Johnston, Anthony W. to Elizabeth Hobson, April 15, 1823. Sol. April 16, 1823, T. B. Craighead.
Hunter, Isaac to Mary Marshall, April 15, 1823. Sol. April 17, 1823, S. Shannon, J.P.
Osment, Alfred to Nancy Lane, April 18, 1823. Sol. April 21, 1823, Guy McFaddin.
Thompson, John to Mary E. Washington, April 23, 1823. Sol. April 23, 1823, Wm. Hume, V.D.M.
Strong, William to Anne Prickley, April 27, 1823. Sol. April 27, 1823, Peter Fuqua, Min.
Gulledge, John to Priscilla Huggins, April 28, 1823.
Weaver, Williamson to Martha Sluder, May 3, 1823.
Gowen, John J. to Tabitha Hays, May 5, 1823. Sol. May 5, 1823, Jas. Whitsitt.
Alford, William to Sally Hollinsworth, May 6, 1823. Sol. May 8, 1823, Rich'd Dobbs.
Humphrey, Wilson to Elizabeth Waits, May 6, 1823.

Page 269
Cherry, Caleb to Jane Mullin, May 7, 1823. Sol. Sep. 22, 1823, E. Talbot, J.P.
Lawrence, Jno. (col) to Harriet, a woman of color, May 7, 1823. Sol. May 7, 1823, Wm. Hume, V.D.M.
Knight, Graves to Catherine Molloy, May 14, 1823.
Vaughan, Wm. K. to Frances Carpenter, May 14, 1823. Sol. May 13, 1823, Rich'd Dobbs.
Best, Joseph to Laury Sinclair, May 20, 1823. Sol. May, 1823, D. A. Dunham, J.P.
Hooper, Jas. H. to Lucinda G. Stump, May 20, 1823. Sol. May 22, 1823, Wm. Lytle, J.P.
Hailey, James to Catherine Bailey, May 26, 1823. Sol. May 26, 1823, Wm. Lytle, J.P.
McClenden, Jesse to Sarah Burnett, June 2, 1823. Sol. June 3, 1823, Benj. Gray, J.P.
Smith, Joel M. to Charlotte Bateman, June 2, 1823. Sol. June 5, 1823, Rich'd Dobbs.
Cook, James T. to Catherine Hawthorne, June 7, 1823. Sol. June 8, 1823, Wm. Hume, V.D.M.

Page 270
Lofton, Nathaniel to Polly Harris, June 9, 1823.
Demumbrum, John B. to Elizabeth Hollis, June 10, 1823. Sol. June 20, 1823, B. Lee, J.P.
Dozier, Dennis to Harriett Page, June 11, 1823. Sol. June 11, 1823, Will Lytle, J.P.
Jewell, Wm. C. to Mary Smith, June 12, 1823. Sol. June 12, 1823, Rich'd Dobbs.
Williams, Willoughby to Nancy Nichols, June 19, 1823. Sol. June 19, 1823, Wm. Hume, V.D.M.
Brice, John to Martha P. Hudson, June 25, 1823.
Hunter, Jno. T. to Anna Marshall, June 26, 1823.
Armstrong, Wm. to Nancy Irwin, July 1, 1823. Sol. July 1, 1823, A. D. Campbell, M.G.
Fuqua, Joel to Elizabeth Gillaspie, July 2, 1823. Sol. July 4, 1823, Peter Fuqua, M.G.
Sturdevant, Thomas to Catherine Molloy, July 9, 1823.

Page 271
Alford, Wm. to Elizabeth Jones, July 10, 1823. Sol. July 10, 1823, R. C. Foster.
Greer, Asa to Levina Napier, July 12, 1823. Sol. July 17, 1823, Peter Fuqua, M.G.
McAdams, Jesse to Nancy Funk, July 15, 1823. Sol. July 17, 1823, Will Lytle, J.P.
Blair, Thomas to Betsy Phillips, July 19, 1823.
Wallace, Jas. B. to Caroline C. Craddock, July 24, 1823. Sol. July 24, 1823, Rich'd Dobbs.
Minor, Theophelus P. to Myra F. Eakin, July 29, 1823. Sol. July 29, 1823, Wm. Hume, V.D.M.
Cain, Morris to Locky Cobb, July 30, 1823. Sol. July 31, 1823, Will Lytle, J.P.
Hutson, Robt. to Nancy Turnies, July 31, 1823.
Hardgrave, Johnston to Sally Baxter, July 29, 1823.
Manning, Benjamin to Lucretia C. Anthony, Aug. 4, 1823. Sol. Aug. 5, 1823, W. B. Peck, M. G.

Page 272
Horn, Berry to Nancy Fowler, Aug. 7, 1823. Sol. Aug. 12, 1823, W. Russell, J.P.
Cagle, Adam to Pency Pate, Aug. 7, 1823. Sol. Aug. 14, 1823, G. S. Allen, J.P.
Walker, James to Mary Norvelle, Aug. 7, 1823. Sol. Aug. 7, 1823, Rich'd Dobbs.
Gower, Lorenzo D. to Nancy L. Gatlin, Aug. 8, 1823. Sol. Aug. 14, 1823, G. S. Allen, J.P.
Whitside, David to Margaret Wright, Aug. 19, 1823. Sol. Aug. 19, 1823, W. B. Peck, M.G.
Fowler, John H. to Amy J. Hail, Aug. 23, 1823. Sol. Sep. 4, 1823, W. Russell, J.P.
Davis, Loyd to Parmelia Collinsworth, Aug. 28, 1823. Sol. Aug. 28, 1823, Wm. Ramsey, J.P.
Crockett, James to Martha Bell, Aug. 29, 1823. Sol. Aug. 31, 1823, Wm. Hume, V.D.M.

Earhart, John to Elizabeth Crutcher, Sep. 9, 1823. Sol. Sep. 11, 1823, Edmund Lanier.
Carter, Walter O. to Nancy Blair, Sep. 10, 1823. Sol. Sep. 11, 1823.

Page 273
Ham, Elijah to Mary Owen, Sep. 15, 1823. Sol. Sep. 15, 1823, Guy McFaddin.
Odom, Harris H. to Adeline I. Elliston, Sep. 23, 1823. Sol. Sep. 23, 1823, W. B. Peck, M.G.
Welch, Thomas to Eliza Wharton, Sep. 25, 1823. Sol. Sep. 25, 1823, A. D. Campbell, M.G.
Dougall, Joseph to Nancy Ballentine, Sep. 24, 1823. Sol. Sep. 25, 1823, W. B. Peck, M.G.
Exum, Robt. to Eliza Hannah, Sep. 27, 1823. Sol. Sep. 29, 1823, Wm. Herrin, M.G.
Pierce, Spencer to Elizabeth Pierce, Sep. 29, 1823.
Portloch, Wm. to Jane Brown, Sep. 29, 1823.
Dixon, Wallace to Eliza Brady, Oct. 1, 1823.
Arrington, Miles to Nancy K. Clemmons, Oct. 2, 1823.
Jackson, Samuel to Franky Tennisson, Oct. 2, 1823. Sol. Oct. 2, 1823, Peter Fuqua, M.G.

Page 274
Knight, Samuel to Elizabeth Franklin, Oct. 9, 1823.
Hail, Nicholas J. to Eliza Fossett, Oct. 13, 1823. Sol. Oct. 16, 1823, W. Russell, J.P.
Cartwright, Thos. to Polly Orton, Oct. 14, 1823.
Fogg, Francis B. to Mary Rutledge, Oct. 15, 1823. Sol. Oct. 15, 1823, A. D. Campbell, A.G.
Allison, Rich'd H. to Lucy H. Shelton, Oct. 21, 1823. Sol. Oct. 21, 1823, Levin Edney, Min.
McGavock, Frances to Amanda P. Hardin, Oct. 22, 1823. Sol. Oct. 23, 1823, Wm. Hume, V.D.M.
Whitfield, Henry to Martha Ann Loftin, Oct. 22, 1823.
McClure, John to Nancy Whitus, Oct. 22, 1823. Sol. Oct. 23, 1823, Thos. Boaz.
Hiland, Joseph B. to Elizabeth Baxter, Oct. 27, 1823. Sol. Nov. 6, 1823, W. Russell, J.P.
Linck, Joseph to Elizabeth Peck, Oct. 28, 1823. Sol. Oct. 28, 1823, Rich'd Dobbs.

Page 275
Ring, Levi D. to Eliza E. Parker, Oct. 30, 1823. Sol. Oct. 30, 1823, Rich'd Dobbs.
Wilson, Benj. W. to Elinor V. Eakin, Nov. 6, 1823. Sol. Nov. 6, 1823, Wm. Hume, V.D.M.
Donelson, John to Eliza Butler, Nov. 6, 1823. Sol. Nov. 6, 1823, Wm. Hume, V.D.M.
McGavock, Jno. to Elizabeth A. Hinton, Nov. 6, 1823. Sol. Nov. 6, 1823, Rich'd Dobbs.
Craighead, Jno. B. to Lavinia Beck, Nov. 11, 1823. Sol. Nov. 11, 1823, Enoch George.
Drew, Wm. to Eliza Adams, Nov. 12, 1823. Returned day after issue by Willia Barrow.

Vaughn, Thomas to Mary Allen, Nov. 12, 1823. Sol. Nov. 19, 1823, Wm. Hume, V.D.M.
Davis, Elisha to Sally Frey, Nov. 13, 1823. Sol. Nov. 13, 1823, Wm. Hume, V.D.M.
Holstead, Ezra to Martha Ferebee, Nov. 18, 1823. Sol. Nov. 18, 1823, E. Talbot, J.P.
Gibson, Robt. to Jane Adams, Nov. 18, 1823. Sol. Nov. 18, 1823, A. D. Campbell, M.G.

Page 276
Dillon, George K. to Margaret Donley, Nov. 20, 1823. Sol. Nov. 20, 1823, A. D. Campbell, N.G.
Read, David to Harriett Wallace, Nov. 21, 1823. Sol. Dec. 23, 1823, B. Lee, J.P.
Hiland, Henry I. to Rebecca Allen, Nov. 22, 1823. Sol. Dec. 18, 1823, W. Russell, J.P.
Carrington, John B. to Lucy Evans, Nov. 27, 1823. Sol. Jan. 2, 1824, W. Russell, J.P.
Cullum, Lovell H. to Polly Garland, Nov. 28, 1823. Sol. Dec. 4, 1823, W. Russell, J.P.
Pitman, Henry H. to Sally D. Bondurant, Nov. 29, 1823. Sol. 1823.
Carding, Allen D. to Maria W. Hyde, Dec. 3, 1823. Sol. Dec. 4, 1823, Wm. Hume, V.D.M.
Shall, Jacob to Ann James, Dec. 8, 1823. Sol. Dec. 8, 1823, Wm. Hume, V.D.M.
Greer, Ote to Martha Garland, Dec. 11, 1823. Sol.Dec. 23, 1823, W. Russell, J.P.
Feland, James to Sarah Shaw, Dec. 13, 1823. Sol. Dec. 15, 1823, W. Wallace, J.P.

Page 277
Drugan, James to Mary Ann Sanders, Dec. 15, 1823. Sol. Dec. 15, 1823, W. Wallace, J.P.
Brooks, Wm. T. to Jane Stuart, Dec. 17, 1823. Sol. Dec. 18, 1823, Will Lytle, J.P.
Hollingsworth, Geo. to Susan Harvey (Jas. Whitsite), Dec. 18, 1823.
Brown, Wm. W. to Polly Pugh, Dec. 20, 1823.
Linton, James to Sidney Laurence, Dec. 20, 1823. Sol. Dec. 23, 1823, B. Gray, J.P.
Tennesson, Jacob to Sally Wilson, Dec. 20, 1823. Sol. Dec. 23, 1823, Peter Fuqua, M.G.
Jones, Caleb to Dicey Williams, Dec. 22, 1823. Sol. Dec. 25, 1823, Peter Fuqua, M.G.
Aubry, Micajah to Martha W. Wilkinson, Dec. 23, 1823. Sol. Dec. 25, 1823, Thos. Craighead.
Sutton, Rich'd to Judy Bailey, Dec. 23, 1823. Sol. Dec. 25, 1823, Jesse Wharton, J.P.
Newsom, Wm. E. to Eliza H. Davis, Dec. 23, 1823. Sol. Dec. 23, 1823, Wm. Hume, V.D.M.

Page 278
Barham, John to Ann Jackson, Dec. 24, 1823. Sol. Dec. 24, 1823, Levin Edney, Min.

Merryman, Alexander to Sally Philips, Dec. 25, 1823.
Wallace, Eaton to Luiza Page, Dec. 26, 1823. Sol. Jan. 1, 1824, W. Wallace, J.P.
Harmon, Thos. R. to Matilda Hughes, Jan. 1, 1824.
Eubank, Ambrose to Mary Faulkner, Jan. 7, 1824. Sol. Jan. 8, 1824, Jno. M. Chandorn.
Graham, Reuben P. to Mary Ann Shannon, Jan. 7, 1824. Sol. Jan. 7, 1824, Wm. Hume, V.D.M. (Graham was divorced from former wife by Court.)
Whitley, Britton to Milly Charlton, Jan. 10, 1824. Sol. Jan. 15, 1824, Peter Fuqua, M.G.
Davis, Joshua to Maria Jones, Jan. 12, 1824. Sol. Jan. 12, 1824, Levin Edney, M.G.
Richardson, Clinton C. to Martha Brummit, Jan. 19, 1824. Sol. Jan. 27, 1824, Wm. Herrin, M.G.
Marshall, Gilbert to Judith A. Drake, Jan. 20, 1824. Sol. Jan. 21, 1824, S. Shannon, J.P.

Page 279
Brown, Jno. L. to Jane B. Weakley, Jan. 20, 1824. Sol. Jan. 20, 1824, T. B. Craighead, by D. Cash.
Spears, Andrew E. to -------- Williams, Jan. 22, 1824.
Trotter, Robt. to Parmelia Hoffman, Jan. 22, 1824. Sol. Jan. 23, 1824, Wm. Faulkner.
Greer, Walter to Priscilla Greer, Jan. 22, 1824.
Russell, Hiram to Patsy Dawson, Jan. 26, 1824.
Jefferson, Henry to Jane H. Donly, Jan. 27, 1824. Sol. Jan. 28, 1824, Wm. Hume, V.D.M.
Smith, Joel to Eliza Scott, Jan. 28, 1824. Sol. Feb. 5, 1824, Wm. Herrin, M.G.
Hodge, Alva to Easter Phelps, Feb. 6, 1824. Sol. Feb. 11, 1824, R. Hewitt, J.P.
Ford, Wm. to Rachel Cain, Feb. 10, 1824.
Cammeron, Daniel to Sarah Duncan, Feb. 10, 1824. Sol. Feb. 10, 1824, Wm. Hume, V.D.M.

Page 280
Seat, Bernard to Margaret Blair, Feb. 12, 1824. Sol. Feb. 12, 1824, Peter Fuqua, M.G.
Bryan, James to Sarah Richardson, Feb. 14, 1824.
Allen, Alexander to Mary Douglass, Feb. 16, 1824. Sol. Feb. 18, 1824, B. H. Lanier, J.P.
Upshaw, Arthur, M. M. to Martha Ann Jones, Feb. 17, 1824. Sol. Feb. 18, 1824, Wm. Hume, V.D.M.
Johnston, John to Louisa Dunn, Feb. 23, 1824.
Watson, Jonathan to Sarah Woods, March 5, 1824. Sol. March 9, 1824, Wm. H. Nance, J.P.
Reaves, James to Lottie Reaves, March 5, 1824. Sol. March 7, 1824, W. Russell, J.P.
Hooper, Wilson L. to Patsy Russell, March 8, 1824. Sol. March 8, 1824, W. Russell, J.P.
Moore, Isham M. L. to Fanny Johnston, March 11, 1824. Sol. March 11, 1824, S. Shannon, J.P.

Tierman, Nicholas to Mary Ann Holder, March 20, 1824. Sol. April 20, 1824, R. Hewitt, J.P.

Page 281
Overton, Patrick Henry to Rebecca Philips, April 1, 1824.
Randall, Aquilla to Gilly Ferrell, March 1, 1824.
Lefler, Samuel to Nancy Bryant, April 8, 1824. Sol. April 8, 1824, E. Talbot, J.P.
Caldwell, John to Rachel McCormack, April 10, 1824. Sol. April 15, 1824, Wm. Herrin, M.G.
Hudson, Jno. T. to Francis Patey, April 13, 1824. Sol. April 13, 1824, Wm. H. White.
Pigg, Pierce P. to Anne Wright, April 19, 1824. Sol. April 19, 1824, Jas. Whitsitt.
Johnston, Jas. to Ann Lafferty, April 21, 1824.
Spence, Brent to Elizabeth Shute, April 28, 1824. Sol. April 28, 1824, A. D. Campbell, M.G.
Wright, Geo. P. to Mary Grant, May 1, 1824. Sol. May 9, 1824, Wm. Hume, V.D.M.
Hughes, Champness to Sally Thomas, May 3, 1824.

Page 282
Waters, John to Eunice Flint, May 6, 1824. Sol. May 6, 1824, Wm. Hume, V.D.M.
Wehrley, Daniel to Elizabeth Miller, May 10, 1824. Sol. May 11, 1824, Wm. Hume, V.D.M.
Spence, Samuel to Elizabeth Inman, May 10, 1824.
Blackwood, Hiram to Ruthy Clark, May 10, 1824. Sol. May 18, 1824, R. Hewitt, J.P.
Pearl, Dyer to Clarinda Donelson, May 13, 1824. Sol. May 13, 1824, Wm. Hume, V.D.M.
Carney, James to Sarah Powell, May 18, 1824.
Cheatham, Jno. A. to Ann Bass, May 19, 1824. Sol. May 19, 1824, Rich'd Dobbs.
Merritt, Jno. G. to Mary Glasgow, May 26, 1824. Sol. May 27, 1824, J. Pirtle, J.P.
Hite, Samuel to Mary D. Ballentine, May 27, 1824. Sol. May 27, 1824, Peter Fuqua, M.G.
Woodfin, Silas to Susan White, June 2, 1824. Sol. June 2, 1824, Will Williams, J.P.

Page 283
Horn, Matthew to Rachel Arnold, June 2, 1824. Sol. June 4, 1824, R. Hewitt, J.P.
Lester, Sterling H. to Martha A. Wharton, June 15, 1824. Sol. June 15, 1824, Wm. Hume, V.D.M.
Woodcock, Jno. to Margaret Goodlett, June 18, 1824. Sol. June 18, 1824, Wm. Hume, V.D.M.
Warren, Thomas to Charity Wingo, June 19, 1824.
Spence, Nathan to Polly McGinnis, June 19, 1824.
Anderson, Wm. to Nancy Crutcher, June 30, 1824. Sol. July 2, 1824, Jno. M. Chandow.
Saunders, Wm. J. to Mary Chadwell, July 3, 1824.
Ward, Wm. L. to Catherine C. Taylor, July 7, 1824. Sol. July 7, 1824, Wm. Hume, V.D.M.

Farley, Atkinson to Parmelia Johnston, July 10, 1824. Sol. July 13, 1824, Will Lytle, J.P.
Horton, Wm. D. to Rhody B. Love, July 13, 1824. Sol. July 13, 1824, Rich'd Dobbs.

Page 284
Call, Richard K. to Mary L. Kirkman, July 14, 1824. Sol. July 14, 1824, A. D. Campbell, M.G.
Hill, Jno. M. to Phebe Thompson, July 17, 1824. Sol. July 18, 1824, Rich'd Dobbs.
Coldwell, John to Sarah McCully, July 21, 1824.
Kernell, James to Julia Ann Daniel, July 22, 1824. Sol. July 29, 1824, L. Keeling, J.P.
McCrory, Charles to Martha Caldwell, July 26, 1824.
Baker, Hiram to Nancy Saunders, July 26, 1824. Sol. July 29, 1824, Peter Fuqua, M.G.
Bates, Wm. to Elizabeth Cayson, July 29, 1824. Sol. Aug. 3, 1824, Guy McFaddin, J.P.
Allgaier, Jno. to Parmelia Oliver, July 29, 1824. Sol. July 29, 1824, E. S. Hall.
Sanders, David to Sally Forde, Aug. 2, 1824. Sol. Aug. 2, 1824, Peter Fuqua, M.G.
Cole, Jno. to Elizabeth Michael, Aug. 5, 1824.

Page 285
Lee, Stephen to Elizabeth Mayfield, Aug. 7, 1824. Sol. Aug. 12, 1824, W. Russell, J.P.
Phillips, Wm. H. to Elizabeth Maxwell, Aug. 17, 1824. Sol. Aug. 19, 1824, Wm. Hume, V.D.M.
Smith, James to Jane Moss, Aug. 17, 1824. Sol. Aug. 17, 1824, Will Lytle, J.P.
Love, Henry J. to Jane N. Love, Aug. 17, 1824. Sol. Aug. 17, 1824, Rich'd Dobbs.
Glasgow, Isaac L. to Avelina T. Byrn, Aug. 19, 1824. Sol. Aug. 22, 1824, J. Pirtle, J.P.
Pugh, John to Elizabeth Oldham, Aug. 25, 1824. Sol. Aug. 26, 1824, D. A. Dunham, J.P.
Thompson, James to Catherine Crutcher, Aug. 26, 1824. Sol. Aug. 26, 1824, B. Gray, J.P.
Owen, John to Nancy Singltray, Aug. 28, 1824. Sol. Aug. 29, 1824, Guy McFaddin.
House, Jacob to Sally Newell, Aug. 30, 1824. Sol. Sep. 10, 1824, S. Shannon, J.P.
Wood, Stephen to Mary Wray, Sep. 3, 1824. Sol. Sep. 3, 1824, James Whitsitt.

Page 286
Vaughn, David to Sally Thomas, Sep. 9, 1824. Sol. Sep. 9, 1824, Wm. Hume, V.D.M.
Johnson, Jesse to Leathy Bryant, Sep. 9, 1824. Sol. Sep. 9, 1824, Peter Fuqua, M.G.
Knight, Wm. to Bummette Sapington, Sep. 10, 1824.
Wright, Wm. H. to Polly Steel, Sep. 13, 1824. Sol. Sep. 16, 1824, Peter Fuqua, M.G.

Finney, James to Alice Collins, Sep. 13, 1824. Sol. Sep. 16, 1824, Guy McFaddin, J.P.
Donelson, Andrew J. to Emily T. Donelson, Sep. 15, 1824. Sol. Sep. 16, 1824, Wm. Hume, V.D.M.
Mullen, Jno. to Ann Hodges, Sep. 20, 1824. Sol. Sep. 21, 1824, D. A. Dunham, J.P.
Bryan, Samuel to Charlotte Charlton, Sep. 20, 1824. Sol. Sep. 20, 1824, Levin Edney, M.G.
Omps, Benjamin to Lucy Corbett, Sep. 22, 1824.
Melvin, John to Jimemma Brodaway, Sep. 23, 1824. Sol. Sep. 29, 1824, Peter Fuqua, M.G.

Page 287
Loften, Wm. B. to Louisa S. Johns, Sep. 28. 1824. Sol. Sep. 29, 1824, R. Hewitt, J.P.
Knox, James to Mary O. Hobson, Sep. 30, 1824. Sol. Sep. 30, 1824, A. D. Campbell, M.G.
McCoy, Miles to Pheby Clinard, Oct. 4, 1824. Sol. Oct. 5, 1824, Wm. Faulkner.
Yates, Thomas P. to Elizabeth Bashaw, Oct. 5, 1824. Sol. Oct. 7, 1824, J. Pirtle, J.P.
Sneed, Geo. W. to Mary D. Sneed, Oct. 6, 1824. Sol. Oct. 7, 1824, Wm. Hume, V.D.M.
Martin, Thos. to Nancy H. Topp, Oct. 12, 1824.
Clark, Wm. S. to Maria Cook, Oct. 12, 1824. Sol. Oct. 12, 1824, Peter Fuqua, M.G.
Cartwright, Jno. to Fanny Hailey, Oct. 14, 1824.
Binkley, Jno. to Alenida Binkley, Oct. 16, 1824.
Yates, Wm. to Nancy Williams, Oct. 16, 1824. Sol. Oct. 25, 1824, E. S. Hall, J.P.

Page 288
Williams, Jas. B. to Sarah V. Buchanan, Oct. 20, 1824. Sol. Oct. 21, 1824, Wm. Hume, V.D.M.
Welbourne, Enoch to Jane Baker, Oct. 25, 1824. Sol. Oct. 25, 1824, W. Toscinswell, J.P.
Payne, Robt. to Susannah C. Beck, Nov. 5, 1824.
Ewing, Joseph L. to Sarah McGavock, Nov. 11, 1824. Sol. Nov. 11, 1824, Wm. Hume, V.D.M.
Bell, Samuel to Mary McFaddin, Nov. 9, 1824. Sol. Nov. 9, 1824, James Whitsitt.
Reaves, Thos. to Lincy Cullum, Nov. 9, 1824. Sol. Nov. 11, 1824, Jno. M. Lovell, J.P.
Hamilton, Geo. T. to Sally W. Gleaves, Nov. 10, 1824. Sol. Nov. 11, 1824, Absolom Gleaves, J.P.
James, Wm. to Theny Greene, Nov. 12, 1824. Sol. Nov. 12, 1824, E. S. Hall, J.P.
Dunnovent, Humphrey B. to Nachey Owens, Nov. 12, 1824. Sol. Nov. 13, 1824, Wm. Faulkner.
Davis, Chas. to Elizabeth D. Finney, Nov. 13, 1824. Sol. Nov. 14, 1824, Jonathan Drake, J.P.

Page 289
Elliotte, Wm. to Mary Tate Byrn, Nov. 16, 1824. Sol. Nov. 16, 1824, E. P. Connell, J.P.
Bondurant, Jacob M. to Elizabeth C. Read, Nov. 17, 1824. Sol. Nov. 17, 1824, Wm. Hume, V.D.M.
Campbell, Jas. G. to Eliza Phenix, Nov. 17, 1824. Sol. Nov. 17, 1824, Jas. Whitsitt.
Sowell, Shadrack to Margaret Champ, Nov. 23, 1824. Sol. Nov. 28, 1824, J. M. Lovell, J.P.
Puckett, Douglas, Jr. to Polly Ann Fryer, Nov. 27, 1824. Sol. Nov. 27, 1824, B. H. Lanier, J.P.
Huggins, Jno. to Isabella W. Cherry, Nov. 30, 1824. Sol. Dec. 1, 1824, Will Lytle, J.P.
Owen, Elisha to Nancy Seat, Dec. 4, 1824. Sol. Dec. 9, 1824, Guy McFaddin, J.P.
Osment, Granberry to Sally Johnson, Dec. 6, 1824.
Nunnley, Lawson H. to Mildred White, Dec. 7, 1824. Sol. Dec. 7, 1824, R. C. Foster, J.P.
Byrne, Jno. D. to Elizabeth White, Dec. 8, 1824. Sol. Dec. 9, 1824, Will Lytle, J.P.

Page 290
Dunn, Albert G. to Amanda M. Gowen, Dec. 8, 1824. Sol. Dec. 9, 1824, Wm. Hume, V.D.M.
Roundtree, Thomas to Sally Campbell, Dec. 9, 1824. Sol. Dec. 9, 1824, Th. Edmiston, J.P.
Gibbs, David to Dishia Beaver, Dec. 10, 1824.
Bruce, Ezekiel to Tabitha Thomas, Dec. 11, 1824.
Kennedy, Joseph to Jencey Ivey, Dec. 11, 1824.
Hail, Thos. J. to Franky Hooper, Dec. 18, 1824. Sol. Dec. 26, 1824, J. H. Lovell, J.P.
Foster, Jackson to Patsy Overby, Dec. 20, 1824.
Corbett, James to Nancy Cabler, Dec. 22, 1824. Sol. Dec. 23, 1824, Will Lytle, J.P.
Tilford, Hugh to Sally Bowers, Dec. 22, 1824. Sol. Dec. 22, 1824, E. P. Connell, J.P.
McNeill, Thos. F. to Sally Blair, Dec. 22, 1824. Sol. Dec. 23, 1824, Henry White, J.P.

Page 291
Price, Aquilla to Ann Reaves, Dec. 22, 1824. Sol. Dec. 23, 1824, Jno. M. Chaundoin.
Pritchett, Jno. S. to Nancy Pritchett, Dec. 27, 1824. Sol. Dec. 27, 1824, Levin Edney, M.G.
Plummer, Hillary C. to Elizabeth Philips, Dec. 28, 1824. Sol. Dec. 30, 1824, Thos. Edmiston, J.P.
Bostick, Hardin P. to Margaret R. Litton, Dec. 30, 1824. Sol. Dec. 30, 1824, Robt. Paine, M.M.C.
Forbes, Zadach to Louisa M. Earl, Jan. 1, 1825.
Wallace, Hartwell H. to Uphemie Turbeville, Jan. 3, 1825.
Oneill, Asa to Ann Cowgill, Jan. 7, 1825. Sol. Jan. 9, 1825, Absolom Gleaves, J.P.
Eichbaum, Wm. A. to M. C. Sterns, Jan. 6, 1825. Sol. Jan. 6, 1825, Wm. Hume, V.D.M.

Jamison, David S. to Michey Thomas, Feb. 8, 1825. Sol. Feb. 8, 1825, Robt. Paine, M.G.
Chandler, Wm. to Nancy Jackson, Jan. 8, 1825. Sol. Jan. 20, 1825, Absolom Gleaves, J.P.

Page 292
Wilson, Elisha to Sarah Hurt, Jan. 12, 1825. Sol. Jan. 15, 1825, Absolom Gleaves, J.P.
Pope, John to Elizabeth Dunneway, Jan. 15, 1825. Sol. Jan. 17, 1825, Will Lytle, J.P.
Jackson, Abraham to Nancy Hager, Jan. 15, 1825. Sol. Jan. 23, 1825, Absolom Gleaves, J.P.
Huffman, Wm. to Sarah Beavers, Jan. 15, 1825. Sol. Jan. 20, 1825, John M. Chandron.
Williams, James to Patsey Bell, Jan. 17, 1825.
Fossett, Alexander to Mary Edmonds, Jan. 17, 1825. Sol. Jan. 20, 1825, Henry White, J.P.
Seat, Wm. to Nancy Page, Jan. 18, 1825. Sol. Jan. 19, 1825, Peter Fuqua, M.G.
Robertson, M. C. C. to Rebecca Jourdon, Jan. 18, 1825.
Murdoch, Wm. to Cinthia Sellers, Jan. 19, 1825. Sol. Jan. 20, 1825, W. Barron, J.P.
Degrove, Michael E. to Amelia E. Buck, Jan. 19, 1825. Sol. Jan. 19, 1825, E. Talbot, J.P.

Page 293
Jackson, Matthew to Elizabeth Evans, Jan. 19, 1825. Sol. Jan. 20, 1825, W. Barrow, J.P.
Adams, Jno. to Mary A. Cartwright, Jan. 20, 1825. Sol. Jan. 20, 1825, Will Lytle, J.P.
Hite, Hiram to Elizabeth A. Carter, Jan. 25, 1825. Sol. Jan. 27, 1825, Henry White, J.P.
Lewis, Wm. to Polly Mobly, Feb. 26, 1825.
Simmons, Ephriam to Elizabeth Walker, Jan. 31, 1825. Sol. Feb. 3, 1825, Jno. Chandorn.
Tait, Wm. to Taby Garner, Feb. 4, 1825.
Roach, Wm. S. to Elizabeth Sturdevant, Feb. 3, 1825. Sol. Feb. 3, 1825, Levin Edney, M.G.
Hopkins, Wm. to Rebecca Green, Feb. 5, 1825. Sol. Feb. 6, 1825, Will Lytle, J.P.
Patterson, Matthew to Harriet Price, Feb. 5, 1825. Sol. Feb. 6, 1825, Thos. Plaister.
Kernal, Jno. to Polly Wilcox, Feb. 7, 1825. Sol. Feb. 7, 1825, L. Keeling, J.P.

Page 294
Low, Albert P. to Avelina Creighton, Feb. 10, 1825. Sol. Feb. 14, 1825, Absolom Gleaves, J.P.
McGrigger, Jno. to Milberry McDonelson, Feb. 10, 1825. Sol. Feb. 10, 1825, Wm. Hume, V.D.M.
Davidson, Samuel to Hannah Pugh, Feb. 21, 1825.
Davis, Sterling to Elizabeth Edmondson, Feb. 22, 1825. Sol. Feb. 24, 1825, Th. Edmiston, J.P.

McCall, Alexander to Rachel M. E. King, Feb. 24, 1825. Sol. Feb. 24, 1825, Wm. Hume, V.D.M.
Hood, Jno. to Celia Fuqua, Feb. 26, 1825. Sol. March 3, 1825, Guy McFaddin.
Hyde, Jordon to Susan S. Drake, March 1, 1825. Sol. March 3, 1825, Wm. Lytle, J.P.
Smith, Sidney to Rebecca Holloway, March 2, 1825.
Smith, Sidney to Isabella Overby, March 9, 1825.
Hails, Wm. to Maria G. Shaffer, March 10, 1825. Sol. March 10, 1825, Will Lytle, J.P.

Page 295
Martin, Jefferson B. to Elinor H. Hart, March 10, 1825. Sol. March 10, 1825, E. S. Hall.
Feltz, Hardy D. to Joanna Binkley, March 12, 1825. Sol. March 17, 1825, Jno. M. Chandoin, M.G.
Glisson, Thos. G. to Sally Randall, March 12, 1825.
James, Lyman to Mariah C. Goodrich, March 15, 1825. Sol. March 17, 1825, W. Barrow, J.P.
Jobes, Wm. to Sarah Runkle, March 16, 1825. Sol. March 17, 1825, Wm. Hume, V.D.M.
Lovell, Wm. to Malinda Brewer, March 17, 1825. Sol. March 20, 1825, B. Gray, J.P.
Lundy, Henry to Polly Owens, March 17, 1825.
Smith, Wm. to Rebecca Wren, March 18, 1825. Sol. March 21, 1825, Wm. Hume, V.D.M.
Martin, Benjamin to Anna Farmer, March 22, 1825.
Trenea, Wm. Bishop to Hezekiah Kernal, March 23, 1825.

Page 296
Stith, Ferdinand to Cornelia Ann Dickson, March 30, 1825. Sol. March 31, 1825.
Moseley, James to Sarah Colton (or Cotton), April 1, 1825.
Hartman, Andrew to Sarah Matlock, April 22, 1825.
Wallace, Edwin R. to Mary Louisa Lewis, April 4, 1825. Sol. April 5, 1825, Wm. Hume, V.D.M.
Linton, Wm. to Sally Laurence, March 9, 1825. Sol. March 16, 1825, Wm. H. Nance, J.P.
Bell, Hugh to Sarah Sample, April 14, 1825.
Mahan, David to Sally Thomas, April 14, 1825. Sol. April 14, 1825, W. Barrow.
Brown, Jesse to Mary Elizabeth Jewell, April 15, 1825.
Stafford, Elijah to Olive Wright, April 15, 1825.
Goodrich, Robt. C. to Jane Roach, April 16, 1825.

Page 297
Sharp, Jno. M. to Sarah V. Ridley, April 16, 1825. Sol. April 16, 1825, Jas. Whitsitt.
Morris, Joseph to Cynthia Morris, April 20, 1825. Sol. April 20, 1825, Absolom Gleaves, J.P.
Watson, Jas. R. to Catherine Baldridge, April 26, 1825. Sol. May 15, 1825, Wm. H. Nance, J.P.

Cook, Hubbard to Lydia Porter, April 27, 1825. Sol. April 27, 1825, Wm. Hume, V.D.M.
Sample, Thomas to Lucy T. Dodson, April 27, 1825.
Mathis, Allen to Harriet Cartwright, April 30, 1825. Sol. May 1, 1825, E. P. Connell, J.P.
Starkey, Joshua to Nancy Strong, May 2, 1825. Sol. May 8, 1825, Absolom Gleaves, J.P.
Evans, Jas. W. to Franky Rape, May 2, 1825.
Lear, Jno. F. to Elizabeth S. Walker, May 7, 1825. Sol. May 7, 1825, Joseph Norvell, J.P.
Fonville, Jno. B. to Eviline Rutherford, May 9, 1825. Sol. May 12, 1825.

Page 298
Parish, James to Elizabeth Compton, May 11, 1825.
Waggoner, Abraham to Ellender Perry, May 27, 1825. Sol. May 27, 1825, Henry White, J.P.
Deshields, Daniel to Jane Graham, June 1, 1825. Sol. June 2, 1825, Wm. Hume, V.D.M.
Rolston, David to Nancy Basye, June 13, 1825. Sol. June 13, 1825, Will Lytle, J.P.
Weaver, Jonathan W. to Francis Link, June 13, 1825. Sol. June 17, 1825, Thos. Boaz.
Stewart, Wm. to Polly Crance, June 13, 1825.
Smith, Benjamin to Kellury Lester, June 14, 1825. Sol. June 15, 1825, Wm. Faulkner.
Clinard, Philip to Nancy Brumly, June 15, 1825. Sol. June 15, 1825, Wm. Lytle, J.P.
Alexander, James to Sarah Clenard, June 16, 1825. Sol. June 16, 1825, Wm. Lytle, J.P.
Marcum, Uriah to Jane Clinard, June 17, 1825. Sol. June 18, 1825, Wm. Faulkner.

Page 299
Hays, Blackman to Minerve Gowan, June 20, 1825. Sol. June 20, 1825, Jas. Whitsitt.
Stout, Jacob V. D. to Maria Ann B. Anthony, June 30, 1825. Sol. June 30, 1825, Phillip Lindsley.
Baker, Spencer to Peggy Wright, June 30, 1825. Sol. June 30, 1825, Absolom Gleaves, J.P.
Lane, Addison W. to Elizabeth Jones, July 1, 1825. Sol. July 1, 1825, Absolom Gleaves, J.P.
Hope, Wm. to Narcissa M. Sampson, July 12, 1825. Sol. July 13, 1825, Wm. Hume, V.D.M.
Stevenson, Jas. to Ann Farmer, July 13, 1825. Sol. July 14, 1825, R. Hewitt, J.P.
Phipps, Robt. W. to Nancy Work, July 18, 1825. Sol. July 18, 1825, Levin Edney, M.G.
Isham, Strong to Susannah Dunbar, July 22, 1825. Sol. July 24, 1825, Absolom Gleaves, J.P.
Ewing, Randal M. to Martha V. Drake, July 23, 1825. Sol. July 23, 1825, Jas. Whitsitt.
Bilts, Selden to Pernia Conger, July 26, 1825. Sol. July 26, 1825, E. P. Connell, J.P.

Page 300
Steele, Robert to Eliza Dungey, July 29, 1825. Sol. Aug. 4, 1825, Will Lytle, J.P.
Harmon, John to Holly Tucker, July 30, 1825. Sol. July 30, 1825, D. A. Dunham.
Burton, Geo. H. to Elizabeth P. Greer, Aug. 4, 1825. Sol. Aug. 4, 1825, D. A. Dunham.
Carney, Vincent to Hepsey Brinkley, Aug. 5, 1825. Sol. Aug. 5, 1825, B. H. Lanier, J.P.
Nicholson, Elijah to Hailey Brown, Aug. 5, 1825. Sol. Aug. 7, 1825, W. Russell, J.P.
Jackson, Hardy to Sarah Little, Aug. 8, 1825. Sol. Aug. 8, 1825, Levin Edney, M.G.
Warmach, Henry H. to Elizabeth Fly, Aug. 11, 1825.
Moore, John to Mary Stewart, Aug. 13, 1825. Sol. Aug. 18, 1825, Will Lytle, J.P.
Rowland, Joseph to Margaret Murry, Aug. 16, 1825. Sol. Aug. 17, 1825, Wm. Faulkner.
Brewer, Eli to Rhody Fenney, Aug. 18, 1825. Sol. Aug. 18, 1825, Wm. H. Nance, J.P.

Page 301
Curfman, John to Elizabeth Stringfellow, Aug. 20, 1825. Sol. Aug. 21, 1825, Wm. Hume, V.D.M.
Dobbs, David D. to Sally Lester, Aug. 24, 1825. Sol. Aug. 25, 1825, Wm. Faulkner.
Scruggs, Jno. to Sally Ballentine, Aug. 29, 1825.
Simmons, Jesse to Catherine Pierce, Aug. 30, 1825. Sol. Sep. 11, 1825, J. M. Lovell, J.P.
Titue (Titus?), Frazer to Louise Ann Edmondson, Aug. 31, 1825. Sol. Sep. 1, 1825, Wm. Hume, V.D.M.
Shule, Jas. C. to Nancy A. Smith, Sep. 1, 1825.
Ashly, Granberry to Maria Curtis, Sep. 1, 1825. Sol. Sep. 1, 1825, R. Hewitt, J.P.
Philips, Joseph to Dorothy Sumner, Aug. 1, 1825. Sol. Sep. 6, 1825, Wm. Hume, V.D.M.
Williams, Jas. to Mildred C. Noell, Sep. 12, 1825. Sol. Sep. 13, 1825, Henry White, J.P.
Fly, Micajah to Lauretta Low, Sep. 14, 1825. Sol. Sep. 14, 1825, A. D. Campbell, M.G.

Page 302
Owen, Jas. G. to Catherine Saucster, Sep. 20, 1825. Sol. Sep. 20, 1825, Jas. Whitsitt.
Berry, John to Annie Pritchett, Sep. 22, 1825. Sol. Sep. 22, 1825, Levin Edney.
Rear, Hamblin to Nancy Dodson, Sep. 26, 1825.
Martin, Wm. to Delilah McGuire, Sep. 28, 1825. Sol. Sep. 28, 1825, J. Pirtle, J.P.
Hosford, John to Mary Farrow, Sep. 28, 1825. Sol. Sep. 29, 1825, Guy McFaddin.
Campbell, Jas. to Jane R. McCutchen, Sep. 28, 1825. Sol. Sep. 28, 1825, Levin Edney, M.G.

Gilmore, John to Ann Eliza Greene, Oct. 3, 1825. Sol. Oct. 18, 1825, Robt. Paine, M.G.
Donelson, Jacob D. to Agnes P. Sampson, Oct. 3, 1825. Sol. Oct. 4, 1825, Wm. Hume, V.D.M.
Logan, Thomas to Nancy Clark, Oct. 4, 1825. Sol. Oct. 6, 1825, D. A. Dunham.
McLaughlin, James to Matilda Thompson, Oct. 4, 1825.

Page 303
McIntire, James to Margaret Graham, Oct. 4, 1825. Sol. Oct. 4, 1825, A. D. Campbell, M.G.
Litton, Benjamin to Minerva L. Childress, Oct. 5, 1825. Sol. Oct. 5, 1825, Wm. Hume, V.D.M.
Turner, Medicus R. to Minerva Cooper, Oct. 6, 1825. Sol. Oct. 6, 1825, Philip Lindsley.
Hooper, Claiborne Y. to Mary Ann Keeling, Oct. 10, 1825. Oct. 10, 1825.
Wingo, Roland to Rebecca Adcock, Oct. 14, 1825. Sol. Oct. 16, 1825, D. Ralston, J.P.
Rutledge, Frederick to Henrietta Rutledge, Oct. 15, 1825. Sol. Oct. 15, 1825, A. D. Campbell, M.G.
Darrow, Joseph to Martha Morris, Oct. 21, 1825. Sol. Nov. 3, 1825, Jas. Chandoin, J.P.
Walker, Charles to Tabitha Guffing, Oct. 22. 1825. Sol. Oct. 25, 1825, Elijah Kirkman, M.G.
Woodard, Thomas to Susan Fambrough, Oct. 24, 1825. Sol. Oct. 26, 1825, Wm. Faulkner.
Wilks, James to Mary Grizzard, Oct. 24, 1825. Sol. Oct. 24, 1825, J. Pirtle, J.P.

Page 304
Williams, Nathan A. to Susanna Lee, Oct. 24, 1825.
Ament, Samuel P. to Mary Carper, Nov. 1, 1825.
Oliphant, Samuel to Tabitha Charter, Nov. 3, 1825. Sol. Nov. 3, 1825, Jas. Davis.
Dean, Aaron to Jane Binkley, Nov. 3, 1825. Sol. Nov. 14, 1825, B. Liles, J.P.
Crockett, David to Mary Adams, Nov. 8, 1825. Sol. Nov. 8, 1825, A. D. Campbell, M.G.
Brown, Thomas to Delilah Philips, Nov. 9, 1825. Sol. Nov. 10, 1825, Th. Edmiston, J.P.
Risely, George to Elizabeth Abels, Nov. 9, 1825. Sol. Nov. 10, 1825, R. Hewitt, J.P.
Wormach, Mathew to Elizabeth Hackney, Nov. 9, 1825. Sol. Nov. 9, 1825, J. Pirtle, J.P.
Condon, James to Ann Chowning, Nov. 9, 1825.
Tenneson, Jacob to Nancy Goodwin, Nov. 16, 1825. Sol. Nov. 17, 1825, J. M. Lovell, J.P.

Page 305
Brooks, Christopher M. to Sally Taylor, Nov. 16, 1825. Sol. Nov. 17, 1825, Jno. M. Chandoin.
Thomas, James to Elenor F. Meness, Nov. 24, 1825. Sol. Nov. 24, 1825, Jas. Whitsitt.

Sawyers, Ira to Lovey Gray, Nov. 24, 1825. Sol. Nov. 24, 1825, Levin Edney, M.G.
Carper, Alexander to Elzaline Crutcher, Nov. 24, 1825.
Owen, Jno. W. to Polly Seat, Nov. 30, 1825. Sol. Dec. 1, 1825, Jno. Caridge, M.G.
Pierce, Chas. R. to Malinda Anderson, Dec. 2, 1825.
Williams, Jordan E. to Sarah D. Boaz, Dec. 6, 1825.
Knight, Henry to Lusina Cocks, Dec. 5, 1825.
Boaz, Shadrack to Nancy Guthrie, Dec. 6, 1825.
Lane, Drury H. to Agness Wilson, Dec. 7, 1825. Sol. Dec. 9, 1825, Absolom Gleaves, J.P.

Page 306
Shapard, Wm. B. to Margery Childress, Dec. 8, 1825. Sol. Dec. 8, 1825, Wm. Hume, V.D.M.
Baldwin, Wm. to Sarah Melvin, Dec. 14, 1825.
Latapie, Anthony to Sophia Martin, Dec. 15, 1825. Sol. Dec. 15, 1825, Wm. Hume, V.D.M.
Hill, Robt. S. to Elizabeth Gleaves, Dec. 15, 1825.
Murfit, Samuel to Sally Gardner, Dec. 17, 1825.
Stump, Thos. J. to Malinda T. Marshall, Dec. 17, 1825. Sol. Dec. 21, 1825, Wm. Hume, V.D.M.
Edmonds, Maclin B. to Nancy Colye, Dec. 19, 1825.
Hollis, Henry to Ariminta D. Hooper, Dec. 19, 1825. Sol. Dec. 22, 1825, J. M. Lovell, J.P.
Bigelow, Elijah to Maria O. Childs, Dec. 20, 1825. Sol. Dec. 20, 1825, Wm. Hume, V.D.M.
Melvin, Edmond to Nancy Cowgill, Dec. 21, 1825. Sol. Dec. 22, 1825, Absolom Gleaves, J.P.

Page 307
Waggoner, George to Lucinda M. Powell, Dec. 21, 1825. Sol. Dec. 21, 1825, Jonathan Drake, J.P.
Brent, Albert H. to Polly Sutton, Dec. 27, 1825. Sol. Dec. 28, 1825, Will Lytle, J.P.
Wells, Thomas to Eliza Philips, Dec. 27, 1825. Sol. Dec. 27, 1825, Wm. Hume, V.D.M.
Mosier, David to Elizabeth Bennett, Dec. 31, 1825. Sol. Jan. 3, 1826, Jno. Chandoin.
McCoy, Miles to Nancy Stewart, Dec. 31, 1825. Sol. Jan. 1826, Henry White, J.P.
Hagar, Wm. to Martha Bennett, Dec. 31, 1825.
Bell, Jno. to Esther McDaniel, Jan. 2, 1826.
Chillicut, Jas. R. to Jane Gray, Jan. 3, 1826.
Burton, Robt. M. to Martha H. Donelson, Jan. 4, 1826. Sol. Jan. 11, 1826, Wm. Hume, V.D.M.
Martin, Jno. to Matilda Evans, Jan. 2, 1826.

Page 308
Kyser, Philip to Ann Crossweight, Jan. 6, 1826. Sol. Jan. 29, 1826, J. Pirtle, J.P.
Eves, Solomon to Sally Williams, Jan. 6, 1826.
Read, Guillford to Elizabeth Wallace, Jan. 9, 1826. Sol. Jan. 19, 1826, B. Lee, J.P.

Maury, Abraham P. to Mary E. T. Claiborne, Jan. 11, 1826. Sol. Jan. 12, 1826, Wm. Hume, V.D.M.
Beasley, James to Sally Champ, Jan. 14, 1826. Sol. Jan. 19, 1826, J. M. Lovell, J.P.
Smith, Ezekiel to Elmira Shadoin, Jan. 16, 1826. Sol. Jan. 16, 1826, Jonathan Drake, J.P.
Huggins, Robt. to Mary Ann Catoe, Jan. 16, 1826. Sol. Jan. 31, 1826, Geo. McWharton, J.P.
Hitt, James S. to Nancy Cunningham, Jan. 18, 1826. Sol. Jan. 26, 1826, J. Pirtle, J.P.
Cain, James to Jane Smith, Jan. 19, 1826. Sol. Jan. 19, 1826, Wm. Hume, V.D.M.
Lenox, James to Milley Pritchett, Jan. 23, 1826. Sol. Jan. 23, 1826.

Page 309
Edmonds, Allen T. to Rachel Pillow, Jan. 27, 1826. Sol. Jan. 27, 1826, Will Lytle, J.P.
Miles, Wm. to Easter Boyte, Jan. 28, 1826. Sol. Feb. 1, 1826, B. Lee, J.P.
Morris, Isaac E. to Elestus C. Carney, Jan. 31, 1826. Sol. Feb. 2, 1826, B. Lee, J.P.
Adams, Alfred to Elizabeth G. Noell, Feb. 3, 1826.
Deshaza, Wm. G. to Polly Deshaza, Feb. 3, 1826. Sol. Feb. 9, 1826, Wm. Lytle, J.P.
Matlock, Nicholas to Henrietta Binkley, Feb. 9, 1826. Sol. Feb. 9, 1826, B. H. Lanier, J.P.
Adams, Thomas A. to Elizabeth Austin, Feb. 13, 1826.
Horn, Lewis to Teresy Crowder, Feb. 21, 1826.
Haldeman, Jno. to Elvira McClean, Feb. 21, 1826. Sol. Feb. 21, 1826, Wm. Lytle, J.P.
Rowland, Wm. to Delilah Rowland, Feb. 22, 1826. Sol. Feb. 23, 1826, D. Ralston.

Page 310
Gatlin, John to Peggy Gower, Feb. 22, 1826.
Glasgow, Wm. to Jeremiah J. Cartwright, Feb. 23, 1826. Sol. Feb. 23, 1826, E. P. Connell, J.P.
Spence, Marmiam to Sarah Wasson, Feb. 23, 1826. Sol. Feb. 23, 1826, A. D. Campbell, M.G.
Buchanan, Robt. to Elizabeth N. Turley, Feb. 23, 1826. Sol. Feb. 23, 1826, Wm. Hume, V.D.M.
Peay, Thomas to Sarah Waller, Feb. 25, 1826.
Fowler, Daniel to Jane M. Tibb, Feb. 25, 1826. Sol. Feb. 26, 1826, Absolom Gleaves, J.P.
Hunter, Matthew R. to Martha M. Eaton, March 4, 1826. Sol. March 9, 1826, B. Lee, J.P.
Bean, Armistead to Matilda Sneed, March 8, 1826. Sol. March 8, 1826, A. D. Campbell.
Coats, Wm. L. to Elizabeth L. Runkle, March 9, 1826. Sol. March 9, 1826, Wm. Hume, V.D.M.
Jackson, Kindred to Mary Felts, March 13, 1826. Sol. March 14, 1826, Jno. M. Chandoin.

Page 311
Clark, Geo. P. to Unice Ensley, March 14, 1826. Sol. March 22, 1826, D. A. Dunham.
Cummins, Henry G. to Charlotte G. Hyde, March 14, 1826. Sol. March 16, 1826, Th. Edmiston, J.P.
Taylor, Alexander to Martha Williamson, March 15, 1826.
McIver, Evander to Eliza Williams, March 16, 1826. Sol. March 16, 1826, Wm. Hume, V.D.M.
Wilkinson, Jno. M. to Charlotte R. Drake, March 20, 1826. Sol. March 21, 1826, Robt. Paine, M.G.
Brumlove, Isaac to Sarah Buie, March 21, 1826. Sol. March 21, 1826, B. H. Lanier, J.P.
Berry, Wm. G. to Mary W. Bell, March 23, 1826. Sol. March 23, 1826, Wm. Ramsey.
Gay, Henry to Veny Merritt, March 23, 1826. Sol. March 30, 1826, Wm. H. Nance, J.P.
Caltharp, Samuel to Martha Griffis, March 24, 1826. Sol. March 24, 1826, D. Ralston, J.P.
Cobler, Francis to Weltha Harvey, March 24, 1826. Sol. March 26, 1826, Wm. Lytle, J.P.

Page 312
Bugg, Benjamin to Nancy Towns, March 28, 1826. Sol. March 28, 1826, H. White, J.P.
Hollis, Wm. to Elizabeth L. Hooper, March 28, 1826. Sol. March 29, 1826, W. Russell, J.P.
Work, Samuel to Martha Gower, March 29, 1826. Sol. March 31, 1826, J. M. Lovell, J.P.
Wood, Staneel to Lucinda Bashaw, March 30, 1826. Sol. March 30, 1826, Wm. H. White.
Brindley, Robt. to Polly Strown, April 3, 1826. Sol. April 3, 1826, Jno. Davis.
Moore, Frances to Sarah Maxey, April 4, 1826. Sol. April 4, 1826, Robt. Paine, J.P.
McGihee, Geo. W. to Cynthia Ann Campbell, April 6, 1826. Sol. April 6, 1826, Ph. Lindsley.
Hays, Blackman to Elizabeth Compton, April 20, 1826. Sol. Apr. 20, 1826, Jas. Whitsitt.
Douglass, Jonathan to Elizabeth D. Dorris, April 25, 1826. Sol. April 26, 1826, P. S. Fale.
Walker, Levi D. to Sepressa Moore, April 25, 1826. Sol. April 26, 1826, Wm. Lytle, J.P.

Page 313
Morris, Isaac to Belinda Little, April 25, 1826. Sol. April 27, 1826, D. A. Dunham.
Taft, Moses to Elizabeth J. Murrell, April 25, 1826. Sol. April 25, 1826, Wm. Hume, V.D.M.
Randolph, Greenberry to Mary Felts, April 26, 1826. Sol. April 26, 1826, Jno. M. Chandoin.
Wright, John to Elitha S. Munford, April 27, 1826. Sol. April 27, 1826, Wm. Hume, V.D.M.
Cagel, Jacob to Lucy Derrah, May 1, 1826. Sol. May 1, 1826, B. H. Lanier, J.P.

Age, Wm. to Polly Demumbre, May 5, 1826. Sol. May 6, 1826, B. H. Lanier, J.P.
Harpe, Nathaniel to Mariah Murphy, May 11, 1826.
Bryan, Jno. T. to Elizabeth H. Rains, May 12, 1826. Sol. May 12, 1826, Th. Edmiston, J.P.
Stephens, Simon to Rebecca Bell, May 13, 1826. Sol. May 18, 1826, G. W. Charlton, J.P.
Fraser, Daniel M. to Lucy A. Clay, May 19, 1826. Sol. May 25, 1826, Wm. H. White.

Page 314
Lanier, Garrison to Huldah R. Earthman, May 23, 1826. Sol. May 25, 1826, Jno. M. Chandoin.
Norman, Joshua to Ann Way, May 25, 1826. Sol. May 25, 1826, Wm. Lytle, J.P.
Williams, Leonard to Sally Jones, May 27, 1826. Sol. May 28, 1826, Jno. Claridge, M.G.
Harris, Littleberry to Fanny Shaw, May 29, 1826.
Lawson, George to Milley Porter, June 2, 1826.
Hubbell, Wm. T. to Lucretia C. Moorhouse, June 5, 1826. Sol. June 5, 1826, A. W. Johnson, J.P.
Robertson, Wm. E. to Elizabeth Smith, June 6, 1826.
Thomas, Joseph to Eliza Drew, June 10, 1826. Sol. June 11, 1826, Wm. Lytle, J.P.
McCrory, Jno. to Sarah Herrin, June 13, 1826. Sol. June 20, 1826, Wm. Herrin.
Nicholson, Henry to Mary Younglove, June 15, 1826. Sol. June 22, 1826, Wm. Harrin.

Page 315
Hopper, Thomas to Eliza Ann Wall, June 20, 1826, Sol. June 20, 1826, Th. Edmiston, J.P.
Smith, Butler to Mariah Davis, June 21, 1826.
Cunningham, Jas. to Francis Thomas, June 22, 1826. Sol. June 22, 1826, Wm. Lytle, J.P.
Bond, James to Mariah Puckering, June 23, 1826.
Hutchison, Wm. to Elizabeth Lovell, June 24, 1826. Sol. June 25, 1826, Geo. W. Charlton.
Neely, Samuel B. to Prudence Hurt, June 29, 1826. Sol. July 6, 1826, Wm. H. White.
Waggoner, Michael to Sally Morris, June 29, 1826. Sol. July 5, 1826, Thos. Kirkman, J.P.
Guthrie, Dudley to Delilah Kule, July 5, 1826. Sol. July 6, 1826, Wm. Lytle, J.P.
Buchanan, Robt. to Barbara Eastis, July 4, 1826. Sol. July 6, 1826, L. Keeling, J.P.
Shelton, Washington G. to Lucadia Tayler, July 4, 1826.

Page 316
Powell, Benj. R. to Mary Ann G. Butler, July 11, 1826. Sol. July 13, 1826, Wm. Hume, V.D.M.
Brown, Jno. D. to Sarah Wade, July 13, 1826. Sol. July 14, 1826, P. S. Fale.
Harris, Wm. to Lucy Freeman, July 17, 1826. Sol. Aug. 10, 1826, Wm. Harrin.

Smith, Abner to Sarah Jackson, July 17, 1826. Sol. Aug. 4, 1826, Jonathan Drake.
Read, Cain to Mary Waits, July 18, 1826.
Scruggs, James to Margaret Boyd, July 19, 1826. Sol. July 27, 1826, Henry White, J.P.
Pitts, Jesse B. to Nancy Fudge, July 22, 1826. Sol. Aug. 7, 1826, D. A. Dunham.
Shoat, Jacob to Lucy Fulcher, July 22, 1826. Sol. July 23, 1826, Absolom Gleaves, J.P.
Campbell, Hardee to Grace McCormach, July 24, 1826. Sol. July 25, 1826, E. P. Connell, J.P.
Johnston, Miles to Harriet Arterberry, July 24, 1826. Sol. Aug. 2, 1826, Jonathan Drake, J.P.

Page 317
Insel, Thomas to Temperance Whitely, July 25, 1826. Sol. July 26, 1826, Henry White, J.P.
Gowen, Wilford B. to Ursula Rains, July 26, 1826. Sol. July 27, 1826, Wm. Hume, V.D.M.
Harrington, Whitmell to Elizabeth Simpson, July 29, 1826. Sol. Aug. 2, 1826, Jno. M. Chandoin.
Pegram, George to Sally Burnett, Aug. 1, 1826. Sol. Oct. 3, 1826, P. S. Fale.
Williams, Gardner to Bedee Cullom, Aug. 4, 1826. Sol. Aug. 10, 1826, Jno. Jones, J.P.
Dozier, Willoughby to Elizabeth Page, Aug. 5, 1826.
Vick, Josiah to Rebecca Fuqua, Aug. 7, 1826. Sol. Aug. 7, 1826, E. S. Hall, J.P.
Carrington, Wm. to Malvira Russell, Aug. 7, 1826.
Massey, Thos. to Polly Rains, Aug. 10, 1826. Sol. Aug. 10, 1826, Wm. Hume, V.D.M.
Park, Joseph to Eliza St. Clair, Aug. 1, 1826. Sol. Aug. 1, 1826, P. S. Fale.

Page 318
Humphries, Wm. to Elizabeth Hammon, Aug. 18, 1826. Sol. Aug. 20, 1826, Absolom Gleaves, J.P.
Harris, Jno. L. to Eliza S. Goodrich, Aug. 22, 1826. Sol. Aug. 28, 1826, Wm. H. White.
Scruggs, John to Agnes Boyd, Aug. 30, 1826. Sol. Aug. 31, 1826, Wm. Lytle, J.P.
Corn, Simon to Delilah Binkley, Sep. 4, 1826. Sol. Sep. 9, 1826, B. Lee, J.P.
Anderson, Bailes to Jane Jones, Sep. 5, 1826. Sol. Sep. 5, 1826, Levin Edney, M.G.
Wilson, Joseph to Polly Johnson, Sep. 7, 1826.
Cole, Champ T. to Harriett Walker, Sep. 7, 1826. Sol. Sep. 7, 1826, Th. Edmiston, J.P.
Housely, Stephen T. to Nancy Stringfellow, Sep. 12, 1826. Sol. Sep. 14, 1826, Wm. Hume, V.D.M.
Ward, Benjamin to Martha Nice, Sep. 14, 1826. Sol. Sep. 15, 1826, Robt. Hewitt, J.P.
Hooper, Isaac M. to Matilda Dozier, Sep. 19, 1826. Sol. Sep. 24, 1826, J. M. Lovell, J.P.

Page 319
Mullin, Henry to Nancy A. Watson, Sep. 21, 1826. Sol. Sep. 21, 1826, L. Keeling, J.P.
Nash, Wm. to Louisa Temple, Sep. 21, 1826.
Jennett, Harvey to Mahala Young, Sep. 26, 1826. Sol. Sep. 28, 1826, D. A. Dunham.
Morgan, Thos. R. to Ann Swan, Oct. 2, 1826. Sol. Oct. 5, 1826, Wm. Hume, V.D.M.
Deely, Littleton J. to Mary E. Bell, Oct. 2, 1826. Sol. Oct. 3, 1826, Wm. Hume, V.D.M.
Briggs, Jno. to Grace (servant), Oct. 5, 1826. Sol. Oct. 6, 1826, Wm. Lytle, J.P.
Edmiston, Alfred to Nancy Davis, Oct. 7, 1826. Sol. Oct. 7, 1826, Levin Edney, M.G.
England, Titus to Martha Taylor, Oct. 13, 1826. Sol. Oct. 17, 1826, J. Pirtle, J.P.
Pitts, Barnabas to Kitty Haws, Oct. 18, 1826. Sol. Oct. 19, 1826, J. M. Lovell, J.P.
Rainey, Jesse G. to Christianna Rains, Oct. 19, 1826.

Page 320
Hall, Elishu S. to Rhody Boyd, Oct. 19, 1826. Sol. Oct. 19, 1826, P. S. Fale.
Sommerville, Jno. H. to Ann E. Hewitt, Oct. 20, 1826. Sol. Oct. 20, 1826, Wm. Hume, V.D.M.
Lamb, Clinton to Lucinda Hoffman, Oct. 28, 1826. Sol. Nov. 3, 1826, N. B. Pryor.
Knight, Winfield to Nicy Cartwright, Oct. 30, 1826. Sol. Oct. 30, 1826, Jno. Davis.
Bell, Thomas to Sally Johnston, Oct. 31, 1826. Sol. Oct. 31, 1826, A. D. Campbell.
Weeks, Robt. to Clarissa Phelps, Oct. 31, 1826.
Hinkle, Peter to Udoxey Tait, Nov. 1, 1826. Sol. Nov. 7- 1826, Jno. M. Chandoin.
Warmach, Wm. to Patsy Wright, Nov. 1, 1826.
Arnold, Wm. to Martha E. Robertson, Nov. 4, 1826. Sol. Nov. 5, 1826, Robt. Paine, M.G.
Miles, Wm. H. to Coraen H. Lee, Nov. 4, 1826.

Page 321
McAfee, Thomas to Nancy Blair, Nov. 4, 1826.
Brown, Morgan W. to Ann Maria Childress, Nov. 4, 1826. Sol. Nov. 7, 1826, Wm. Hume, V.D.M.
Harris, Howell to Polly Berry, Nov. 6, 1826. Sol. Nov. 8, 1826, Thos. Kirkman, J.P.
Scruggs, Edward to Jane Boyd, Nov. 6, 1826.
McKinney, Wm. C. to Harriet A. Wray, Nov. 8, 1826. Sol. Nov. 8, 1826, Jas. Whitsitt.
McDowell, Samuel to Sarah Piland, Nov. 10, 1826. Sol. Sep. 23, 1827, Thos. Scott, J.P.
Byrns, Thos. D. to Lydia Crawford, Nov. 17, 1826. Sol. Nov. 23, 1826, B. H. Lanier.
Moore, James B. to Mary Goodrich, Nov. 22, 1826. Sol. Nov. 29, 1826, Geo. W. Charlton, J.P.

Greer, Gardner to Polly Brady, Nov. 25, 1826. Sol. Nov. 27, 1826, B. H. Lanier.
Chandler, Jas. L. to Susan P. Mitchell, Nov. 27, 1826. Sol. Nov. 28, 1826, Absolom Gleaves, J.P.

Page 322
Waggle, Elbert to Eliza Baker, Nov. 28, 1826. Sol. Nov. 1826, J. Pirtle, J.P.
Stone, Levi B. to Franky Ashley, Nov. 29, 1826. Sol. Nov. 30, 1826, John Claridge, M.G.
Perry, Littleton to Eletha Page, Nov. 29, 1826.
Wyatt, Isaac to Elenor McCutcheon, Nov. 30, 1826. Sol. Dec. 5, 1826, Wm. Hume, V.D.M.
Duncan, Alexander to Susan Cabler, Nov. 30, 1826. Sol. Nov. 30, 1826, Jas. Whitsitt.
Horn, Henry to Elizabeth Thomas, Dec. 9, 1826.
Greer, Brison to Lucinda Napier, Dec. 13, 1826. Sol. Dec. 14, 1826, Jno. Jones, J.P.
Cutchen, Lemuel R. to Ann W. Matthews, Dec. 16, 1826.
Gower, Russell to Nancy Boyte, Dec. 16, 1826. Sol. Dec. 21, 1826, B. Lee, J.P.
McCain, John to Elizabeth Nance, Dec. 16, 1826. Sol. Dec. 21, 1826, Banajah Gray, J.P.

Page 323
Pinkerton, John to Sophia Lile, Dec. 18, 1826. Sol. Dec. 18, 1826, Simpson Shephard.
Binkley, Jas. to Lucindy Smith, Dec. 18, 1826. Sol. Dec. 21, 1826, Jno. M. Chandoin.
Dill, John to Polly Goodwin, Dec. 19, 1826.
Weeks, Henry to Lydia Francis, Dec. 19, 1826.
Aust, John to Elizabeth Cassellman, Dec. 19, 1826.
O Brient, John to Mahala Wilson, Dec. 19, 1826. Sol. Dec. 21, 1826, Absolom Gleaves, J.P.
Burton, Samuel C. to Sarah Jane Wade, Dec. 21, 1826.
Vaulx, Joseph to Susan E. Hobson, Dec. 21, 1826. Sol. Dec. 21, 1826, A. D. Campbell, M.G.
Cox, Wm. to Polly Graham, Dec. 23, 1826. Sol. Dec. 24, 1826, Thos. Scott, J. P.
Eddington, Nicholas to Ester Cantrell, Dec. 23, 1826. Sol. Jan. 2, 1827, Wm. Lytle, J.P.

Page 324
Drake, Logan to Susan Cheek, Dec. 26, 1826.
Wallace, Wm. P. to Edy Corbitt, Dec. 28, 1826. Sol. Dec. 31, 1826, Wm. Lytle, J.P.
Russell, Stephen to Rebecca Work, Dec. 30, 1826. Sol. Dec. 31, 1826, J. M. Lovell, J.P.
Talley, Wm. to Nancy Underwood, Jan. 4, 1827. Sol. Jan. 5, 1827, Wm. H. White.
Thomas, Joseph to Frances Fleming, Jan. 6, 1827. Sol. Jan. 8, 1827, Wm. Lytle, J.P.
Whiteside, Thomas to Sarah Bell, Jan. 6, 1827. Sol. Jan. 6, 1827, Jas. Whitsitt.

Greer, Wm. to Ann Jones, Jan. 8, 1827. Sol. Jan. 11, 1827, Jno. Jones, J.P.
Smith, Calvin M. to Jane E. Love, Jan. 9, 1827. Sol. Jan. 9, 1827, Wm. Hume, V.D.M.
Jackson, Woodson to Mary W. Jackson, Jan. 11, 1827. Sol. Jan. 11, 1827, Wm. Lytle, J.P.
Adams, Sterling H. to Nancy Manley, Jan. 12, 1827. Sol. Jan. 18, 1827.

Page 325
Allen, Ramey to Lucinda Caruthers, Jan. 13, 1827.
Thompson, David G. to Polly Anderson, Jan. 15, 1827. Sol. Jan. 18, 1827, Wm. Herrin.
Bell, Zachriah to Rebecca Lee, Jan. 18, 1827.
Steel, Jas. to Judidah H. Wood, Jan. 19, 1827
Tobourn, Henry to Bethiel Carter, Jan. 23, 1827. Sol. Jan. 23, 1827, Absolom Gleaves, J.P.
McClendon, Clark to Milley Burnett, Jan. 26, 1827. Sol. Jan. 27, 1827, Jno. Claridge, M.G.
Holt, Henry to Mary Wills, Jan. 29, 1827. Sol. Jan. 31, 1827, Wm. Lytle, J.P.
Dorris, Wm. D. to Rebeccah Shivers, Feb. 1, 1827.
Arnold, Jno. H. to Mary Ann Bryant, Feb. 3, 1827. Sol. Feb. 4, 1827, H. White, J.P.
Myers, Jacob to Cynthia Myers, Feb. 3, 1827. Sol. Feb. 3, 1827, Wm. Lytle, J.P.

Page 326
Evans, Lorenzo D. to Susannah Rape, Feb. 3, 1827. Sol. Feb. 22, 1827, J. M. Lovell, J.P.
Washington, Jas. G. to Susan Thomas, Feb. 5, 1827. Sol. Feb. 5, 1827, P. S. Fall.
Lyon, Alpheus to Eliza Dunn, Feb. 7, 1827. Sol. Feb. 7, 1827, Wm. Hume, V.D.M.
Sadler, John G. to Martha Barnwell, Feb. 9, 1827. Sol. Feb. 21, 1827, Banajah Gray, J.P.
Jackson, Abner to Judith Jackson, Feb. 9, 1827. Sol. Feb. 9, 1827, Absolom Gleaves, J.P.
Davidson, Wm. to Mary Jackson, Feb. 13, 1827. Sol. Feb. 14, 1827, Jesse Shelton, J.P.
Branch, Chas. to Elizabeth Scruggs, Feb. 13, 1827. Sol. Feb. 15, 1827, Henry White, J.P.
Rutland, Wm. B. to Nancy Little, Feb. 17, 1827.
Cobb, Jno. P. to Ann Head, Feb. 17, 1827. Sol. Feb. 18, 1827, E. P. Connell, J.P.
Oliphant, Thos. J. to Avelina Eakins, Feb. 17, 1827. Sol. Feb. 22, 1827, Banajah Gray, J.P.

Page 327
White, Peter M. to Jean Neely, Feb. 28, 1827. Sol. March 1, 1827, Wm. H. White.
Fall, Jas. to Frances Love, March 1, 1827. Sol. March 1, 1827, P. H. Lindsley.

Brown, Aris to Emily Cartwright, March 1, 1827. Sol. March 1, 1827, Wm. Hume, V.D.M.
Hamilton, Jas. to Sarah Warmoth, March 3, 1827.
Hill, Wm. W. to Polly Robinson, March 5, 1827. Sol. March 5, 1827, B. H. Lanier, J.P.
Ruleman, Jacob to Mary Fay, March 8, 1827. Sol. March 8, 1827, Wm. Hume, V.D.M.
Wilkinson, Benj. to Amandy McDaniel, March 13, 1827.
Coon, Shadrach to Susan Davis, March 15, 1827. Sol. March 20, 1827, Wm. Lytle, J.P.
New, Martin to Sarah Probart, March 16, 1827. Sol. March 20, 1827, Wm. Hume, V.D.M.
Alford, Jno. to Jane Logan, March 16, 1827. Sol. March 17, 1827, R. Hewitt, J.P.

Page 328
Peelar, Hazlewood W. to Sarah Copely, March 19, 1827. Sol. March 19, 1827, Absolom Gleaves, J.P.
Lenox, James to Judy Fuqua, March 19, 1827. Sol. April 19, 1827, B. Lee, J.P.
Henry, John to Nancy Costilo, March 19, 1827. Sol. March 19, 1827, Isaac Hunter.
Winchester, Jabez to Louisa Demunbrum, March 26, 182_.
Huntsinger, Jacob to Cynthia Miller, March 31, 1827. Sol. March 31, 1827, G. M. Cox, J.P.
Holmes, Vivian B. to Susan B. Wigginton, April 2, 1827. Sol. April 5, 1827, P. S. Fall.
Moses, Henley to Avelina Carney, April 2, 1827. Sol. April 3, 1827, Wm. Lytle, J.P.
Lewis, Nathan to Catherine Smith, April 3, 1827. Sol. May 3, 1827, Edmund Lanier.
Taylor, Bailey W. to Delilah Austin, April 3, 1827. Sol. April 3, 1827, Jas. W. Allen.
Campbell, Wm. P. to Lucy Ann Wiggington, April 5, 1827- Sol. April 5, 1827, P. S. Fall.

Page 329
Richardson, David M. to Paulina Seargant, April 5, 1827. Sol. April 5, 1827, Wm. Hume, V.D.M.
Ezell, James to Jane Work, April 12, 1827. Sol. April 1827, Jno. C. Hicks, M.G.
Mussellman, Abraham to Sally Thompson, April 16, 1827. Sol. April 16, 1827, Wm. Lytle, J.P.
Jackson, Jacob D. to Frances Adkison, April 19, 1827. Sol. April 20, 1827, Isaac Hunter.
Casey, Shadrack to Sarah Jones, April 21, 1827. Sol. April 21, 1827, Levin Edney, M.G.
Patton, Thomas to Susan Morris, April 21, 1827. Sol. April 21, 1827, Jno. Jones, J.P.
Jefferson, Thos. B. to Martha Graves, April 23, 1827.
Williams, Christopher C. to Jane E. Nichols, April 24, 1827. Sol. April 24, 1827, Wm. Hume, V.D.M.
Clay, Joseph W. to Elizabeth V. Harding, April 24, 1827. Sol. April 26, 1827, Wm. Hume, V.D.M.

Sanderson, Geo. E. to Merilla T. Eaton, April 27, 1827. Sol. May 3, 1827, Wm. Lytle, J.P.

Page 330

Alexander, John to Luticia Phelps, May 4, 1827. Sol. May 5, 1827, Wm. Lytle, J.P.
Scoggins, Geo. W. to Sarah Underwood, May 5, 1827.
Stephenson, John to Nancy Grooms, May 7, 1827. Sol. May 7, 1827, Wm. Lytle, J.P.
Rucks, James to Luiza V. Brown, May 16, 1827. Sol. May 16, 1827, Philip Lindsley.
Wilkins, Winchester to Rebecca Lano, May 18, 1827.
Smith, Major L. to Rebecca Vincent, May 19, 1827. Sol. May 19, 1827, E. S. Hall, J.P.
Reason, Peter to Lucinda McDaniel, May 22, 1827.
Perkins, Samuel to Nancy Richardson, May 24, 1827. Sol. May 24, 1827, Wm. Hume, V.D.M.
Spear, Nathan A. to Sally Hardgrave, May 28, 1827.
Jackson, Lucas to Winney Dickinson, June 2, 1827.

Page 331

Jones, Thomas to Anne Moss, June 9, 1827.
Foster, Shelton to Malinda Adams, June 9, 1827. Sol. June 14, 1827, Wm. Lytle, J.P.
Campbell, Jno. W. to Jane Eliza Porter, June 12, 1827. Sol. June 13, 1827, Wm. Hume, V.D.M.
Veal, Dempsey to Nancy Read, June 13, 1827. Sol. June 14, 1827, John Jones, J.P.
Donelson, William to Elizabeth Anderson, June 14, 1827. Sol. June 14, 1827, Wm. Hume, V.D.M.
Jackson, Wm. to Elizabeth Robertson, June 23, 1827. Sol. July 12, 1827, Wm. Lytle, J.P.
Brumley, Jno. to Rebeccah Mullins, June 25, 1827.
Glasgow, Jno. C. to Elizabeth Smith, June 28, 1827. Sol. June 28, 1827, Thos. Scott, J.P.
Bowers, Stephen C. to Margaret Hackney, June 29, 1827. Sol. July 12, 1827, E. P. Connell, J.P.
Smith, Edmund B. to Sally Hardgrave, June 30, 1827. Sol. July 1, 1827, Thos. Scott, J.P.

Page 332

McGraw, George to Lucy Stearman, July 9, 1827. Sol. July 11, 1827, Wm. Lytle, J.P.
Shaw, George to Jane Terry, July 11, 1829.
Fly, Enoch to Mary Harwood, July 12, 1827. Sol. July 12, 1827, P. S. Fall.
Buchanan, Moses R. to Sarah V. Ridley, July 12, 1827. Sol. July 12, 1827, J. Whitsitt.
Baird, Zebulon to Elizabeth Fuqua, July 14, 1827. Sol. July 19, 1827, Jas. T. Tompkins.
Foster, Wm. S. to Nancy Lynn, July 14, 1827. Sol. July 14, 1827, J. Pirtle, J.P.
Bower, Wm. P. to Jane Byrn, July 16, 1827. Sol. July 19, 1827, E. P. Connell, J.P.

Bland, Isaac to Lucy Wright, July 17, 1827. Sol. July 20, 1827, Wm. Lytle, J.P.
Waggoner, Mathias to Martha Gee, July 17, 1827.
Lester, German to Elizabeth B. Lewis, July 19, 1827. Sol. July 19, 1827, Wm. Hume, V.D.M.

Page 333
Barnes, Randal M. to Elizabeth Crowder, July 22, 1827. Sol. Aug. 27, 1827, Jno. Davis.
Stark, Joal to Cordelia Randal, July 23, 1827. Sol. July 23, 1827, E. P. Connell, J.P.
Baldwin, Wm. to Margaret Champ, July 25, 1827. Sol. July 25, 1827, Absolom Gleaves, J.P.
Carey, Pleasant to Mariah Trudel, July 25, 1827.
Bridgeford, Wm. to Susan Sneed, July 28, 1827.
Drake, James F. to Hannah Marshall, Aug. 7, 1827. Sol. Aug. 15, 1827, Jno. M. Chandoin.
Morgan, Thos. to Martha Barnes, Aug. 8, 1827.
Turner, Robt. B. to Sophronia L. Boyd, Aug. 9, 1827. Sol. Aug. 9, 1827, Wm. Hume, V.D.M.
Quinton, Allen to Margaret Cowerdon, Aug. 9, 1827. Sol. Aug. 9, 1827, P. S. Fall.
Harper, Wm. to Mildred L. McQuary, Aug. 13, 1827. Sol. Aug. 16, 1827, Thos. Scott, J.P.

Page 334
Farmer, Erles to Barbary Wells, Aug. 15, 1827. Sol. Aug. 16, 1827, Wm. Lytle, J.P.
Farmer, Samuel to Martha Parkman, Aug. 22, 1827. Sol. Aug. 23, 1827, Wm. Lytle, J.P.
McWhirter, Geo. F. to Nancy Seat, Aug. 22, 1827. Sol. Aug. 22, 1827, German Baker.
Bryant, Wm. to Anna O. Bryant, Aug. 30, 1827. Sol. Aug. 30, 1827, Absolom Gleaves, J.P.
Tait, David to Artemessa Perkins, Aug. 31, 1827. Sol. Sep. 1, 1827.
Work, Robt. to Hetis Hooper, Sep. 4, 1827. Sol. Sep. 6, 1827, J. M. Lovell, J.P.
Clark, Pleasant to Narcissa Scott, Sep. 4, 1827.
Mullin, Jno. B. to Sarah V. Garrett, Sep. 4, 1827. Sol. Sep. 5, 1827, James W. Allen.
Horn, Stephen H. to Mary Kimbro, Sep. 8, 1827. Sol. Sep. 8, 1827, J. Whitsitt.
Gray, Jackson to Margaret Carpenter, Sep. 5, 1827. Sol. Sep. 5, 1827, Edmund Lanier.

Page 335
Bashaw, Benjamin to Sarah Williamson, Sep. 8, 1827. Sol. Sep. 9, 1827, Wm. H. White.
Gravis, Thos. F. to Sarah Roberts, Sep. 11, 1827. This marriage forbidden and never performed.
Barry, Richard H. to Mary L. May, Sep. 13, 1827. Sol. Sep. 13, 1827, Wm. Hume, V.D.M.
Johnson, James to Nancy Kirkpatrick, Sep. 17, 1827.
Dozier, Willoughby to Elizabeth Page, Sep. 22, 1827.

Grawosz, Thos. F. to Sarah Roberts, Sep. 22, 1827.
Murry, Mark W. to Temperance Murry, Sep. 24, 1827. Sol. Sep. 24, 1827, Wm. Lytle, J.P.
Jones, Jno. H. to Harriet E. Whitehead, Sep. 27, 1827. Sol. Sep. 28, 1827, R. C. Foster, J.P.
Barrow, Washington to Ann M. Shelby, Sep. 27, 1827. Sol. Sep. 27, 1827, Wm. Hume, V.D.M.
Thornton, Jno. G. to Margaret E. Moxey, Sep. 29, 1827. Sol. Oct. 4, 1827, Jas. W. Allen.

Page 336
Burress, Wm. to Emelia Parkman, Oct. 1, 1827. Sol. Oct. 4, 1827, Henry White, J.P.
Spurlock, Grandison to Ann Scott, Oct. 2, 1827. Sol. Oct. 2, 1827, Wm. Hume, V.D.M.
Morton, Samuel to Emeline Woods, Oct. 2, 1827.
Bradley, Stephen W. to Jane Howlett, Oct. 3, 1827. Sol. Oct. 3, 1827, P. S. Fall.
Hoover, Philip to Sarah Ann E. Priestly, Oct. 4, 1827. Sol. Oct. 4, 1827, Wm. Hume, V.D.M.
Harney, Perry to Lucinda Owen, Oct. 4, 1827. Sol. Oct. 4, 1827, Banajah Gray, J.P.
Ball, Israel to Olly Walton, Oct. 5, 1827. Sol. Oct. 5, 1827, Absolom Gleaves, J.P.
McFarlin, Thomas to Hetty Reaves, Oct. 11, 1827.
Chickering, John to Sarah Waits, Oct. 15, 1827.
Dean, Moses to Mary Binkley, Oct. 15, 1827.

Page 337
Carper, John to Nancy Williams, Oct. 16, 1827.
Beaty, Jno. to Nancy Buie, Oct. 22, 1827. Sol. Oct. 23, 1827, Wm. Hume, V.D.M.
Jackson, Burrel to Elizabeth Harris, Oct. 22, 1827. Sol. Oct. 25, 1827, Thos. Scott, J.P.
Crutcher, Larkin to Amelia Clark, Oct. 24, 1827. Sol. Oct. 25, 1827, Jno. M. Chandoin.
Beach, Jno. B. to Elizabeth Marshall, Oct. 30, 1827. Sol. Oct. 31, 1827, Jno. Atkinson.
Reaves, John to Polly Johnson, Oct. 30, 1827. Sol. Jan. 15, 1828, Thos. Kirkman, J.P.
Greer, Vincent to Susannah Stevens, Oct. 31, 1827. Sol. Nov. 2, 1827, Absolom Gleaves, J.P.
Curtis, Jas. to Sarah Griffin, Oct. 31, 1827. Sol. Oct. 31, 1827, E. S. Hall.
Porter, Jas. A. to Amanda I. McNairy, Nov. 1, 1827. Sol. Nov. 1, 1827, Wm. Hume, V.D.M.
Cassellman, John to Martha Hurt, Nov. 3, 1827. Sol. Nov. 6, 1827, Absolom Gleaves, J.P.

Page 338
Rollings, Henry to Martha A. Dunn, Nov. 7, 1827. Sol. Nov. 7, 1827, Wm. Hume, V.D.M.
Alderson, Rich'd S. to Louisa Cobler, Nov. 9, 1827. Sol. Nov. 9, 1827, Wm. Lytle, J.P.

Barnes, Wm. to Mary Whitley, Nov. 10, 1827.
Hays, Robt. to Methursy Wilson, Nov. 10, 1827. Sol. Dec. 27, 1827, Wm. Saunders.
Rountree, Nathaniel to Catherine Lee, Nov. 10, 1827.
Hamilton, Absolom to Olly Cutchen. Nov. 10, 1827.
Lewis, Washington to Cynthia Small, Nov. 12, 1827. Sol. Nov. 14, 1827, Levin Edney, J.P.
Cunningham, Samuel to Sarah Brother, Nov. 14, 1827. Sol. Nov. 14, 1827, Wm. Lytle, J.P.
Dickey, James to Rosanna B. Wood, Dec. 14, 1827.

Page 339
Sims, Walter to Mary Eliza Egbert, Nov. 14, 1827. Sol. Nov. 15, 1827, Wm. Hume, V.D.M.
Knight, John to Cynthia DeMoss, Nov. 14, 1827.
Melvin, John to Nancy Wilson, Nov. 14, 1827. Sol. Nov. 16, 1827, Absolom Gleaves, J.P.
Athey, Thomas J. to Lucy W. Brooks, Nov. 15, 1827. Sol. Nov. 15, 1827, P. S. Fall.
Hooper, Isaac N. to Mary Hoven, Nov. 17, 1827.
Todd, Jno. N. to Mary Ann Morgan, Nov. 22, 1827. Sol. Nov. 22, 1827, P. S. Fall.
Humphries, Reuben to Elizabeth Cook, Nov. 22, 1827. Sol. Nov. 22, 1827, Absolom Gleaves, J.P.
Garrison, Geo. W. to Martha Kellum, Nov. 24, 1827. Sol. Nov. 26, 1827, W. Russell, J.P.
Blair, Samuel to Rebecca Sparkman, Oct. 26, 1827. Sol. Nov. 29, 1827, Henry White, J.P.
Biggs, Jas. to Elizabeth Wray, Nov. 26, 1827. Sol. Nov. 29, 1827, Wm. Lytle, J.P.

Page 340
McCutcheon, Patrick to Mary Reed, Nov. 26, 1827. Sol. Nov. 27, 1827, Wm. Hume, V.D.M.
Beasley, James to Hannah Cowgill, Dec. 1, 1827.
Boaz, David to Lucinda White, Dec. 3, 1827.
Felts, Jno. to Dicey C. Pigg, Dec. 4, 1827. Sol. Dec. 5, 1827, Henry White, J.P.
Shivers, Asa to Tennessee Page, Dec. 6, 1827. Sol. Dec. 6, 1827, Henry White, J.P.
Baker, Jno. W. to Levina Bowers, Dec. 8, 1827. Sol. Dec. 9, 1827, E. P. Connell, J.P.
Farish, Edmond to Lucy Jane Martin, Dec. 12, 1827. Sol. Dec. 18, 1827, Wm. Hume, V.D.M.
Walton, David H. to Mary Pritchard, Dec. 13, 1827. Sol. Dec. 20, 1827, Levin Edney, M.G.
Dickey, James to Rosanna B. Wood, Dec. 14, 1827. Sol. Dec. 19, 1827, L. Redding, J.P.
Cullum, Gains F. to Cynthia A. Hooper, Dec. 14, 1827. Sol. Dec. 16, 1827, J. M. Lovell, J.P.

Page 341
Garland, Felix to Lucinda Hooper, Dec. 17, 1827. Sol. Dec. 20, 1827, W. Russell, J.P.

Phea, Jno. S. to Sarah P. Scales, Dec. 17, 1827. Sol. Dec. 18, 1827, Jno. Haynie, M.G.
Mooreman, Chas. W. to Sarah Keeling, Dec. 18, 1827. Simpson Shepherd.
Booth, Wm. to Polly Rule, Dec. 18, 1827.
Cook, Moses to Lucinda S. Wright, Dec. 18, 1827. Sol. Dec. 21, 1827, Geo. W. Charlton, J.P.
Murrey, Robt. to Hodessa Thompson, Dec. 19, 1827. Sol. Dec. 19, 1827, Wm. Hume, V.D.M.
Dunnegan, Jas. J. to Elizabeth M. Weakley, Dec. 20, 1827. Sol. Dec. 20, 1827, Wm. Hume, V.D.M.
Clay, Sidney P. to Isabella Read, Dec. 20, 1827. Sol. Dec. 20, 1827, Philip Lindsley.
Cayce, James to Mary Ann McEwing, Dec. 22, 1827. Sol. Dec. 24, 1827, Wm. Hume, V.D.M.
Underhill, Jno. P. to Rachel Owens, Dec. 22, 1827.

Page 342
Johnson, Anderson to Elizabeth Drummond, Dec. 25, 1827. Sol. Dec. 25, 1827, R. Weakley, J.P.
Rape, Daniel to Emelia Lovell, Dec. 28, 1827. Sol. Jan. 10, 1828, W. Russell, J.P.
Roach, Lewis W. to Sally McDaniel, Dec. 29, 1827.
Dodson, Presley to Leanna Waller, Dec. 31, 1827.
Foxhall, Jas. to Amanda Johnson, Dec. 31, 1827. Sol. Jan. 2, 1828, Wm. Lytle, J.P.
Holloway, John to Polly Manly, Jan. 1, 1828.
Nichol, John to Harriet Marford, Jan. 1, 1828. Sol. Jan. 1, 1828, Philip Lindsley.
Dunneway, Griffin J. to Eliza M. Ewing, Jan. 1, 1828. Sol. Jan. 3, 1828, Wm. Hume, V.D.M.
Melvin, Andrew to Elizabeth Chandler, Jan. 2, 1828. Sol. Jan. 3, 1828, Absolom Gleaves, J.P.
Dortch, Jesse L. to Nancy W. Adams, Jan. 3, 1828. Sol. Jan. 3, 1828, Robert Paine, M.G.

Page 343
Radford, John to Rebecca Williamson, Jan. 4, 1828. Sol. Jan. 10, 1828, Wm. H. White.
Pritchard, Benjamin to Catherine W. Newsom, Jan. 7, 1828. Sol. Jan. 10, 1828, Jno. Davis.
Lee, Stephen to Maria Peebles, Jan. 9, 1828.
Callaghan, Philip to Maria Carroll, Jan. 10, 1828. Sol. Jan. 10, 1828, Wm. Lytle, J.P.
Wilson, Jno. W. to Mary Ann Badger, Jan. 10, 1828. Sol. Jan. 10, 1828, P. S. Fall.
Brown, Berryman to Catherine E. Marshall, Jan. 10, 1828. Sol. Jan. 10, 1828, P. S. Fall.
Hatcher, Elijah to Delilah Greer, Jan. 12, 1828.
Ashley, Martin to Mary Logan, Jan. 12, 1828. Sol. Jan. 24, 1828, Wm. Lytle, J.P.
West, Mathias S. to Martha P. Bruce, Jan. 17, 1828. Sol. Jan. 1828, Simpson Shephard.

Maynor, Pleasant to Nancy Bailey, Jan. 18, 1828. Sol. Jan. 21, 1828, Wm. Hume, V.D.M.

Page 344
Ranier, Jno. to Elizabeth Age, Jan. 19, 1828. Sol. Jan. 21, 1828, Jno. M. Chandoin, M.G.
Quinn, Lott to Elinor Holloway, Jan. 22, 1828. Sol. Jan. 22, 1828, J. Whitsitt.
Burgis, Thomas to Margaret Logan, Jan. 22, 1828. Sol. Jan. 24, 1828, R. Hewitt, J.P.
Alford, Nelson to Elizabeth Hill, Jan. 23, 1828. Sol. Jan. 23, 1828, Moses Speer, M.G.
Hill, Jno. T. to Georgianna Beck, Jan. 23, 1828. Sol. Jan. 23, 1828, Wm. Hume, V.D.M.
Watkins, Thomas to Pembroke Cartwright, Jan. 28, 1828. Sol. Jan. 31, 1828, Wm. Hume, V.D.M.
Stuart, John to Harriet Park, Jan. 29, 1828. Sol. Jan. 29, 1828, Wm. Lytle, J.P.
Green, James to Jane Wiggin, Jan. 30, 1828. Sol. Jan. 31, 1828, Wm. Lytle, J.P.
Mitchell, Jno. T. to Sally Jordon, Feb. 2, 1828. Sol. Feb. 1828, J. Pirtle, J.P.
Robinson, James C. to Susan Litton, Feb. 6, 1828. Sol. Feb. 6, 1828, Wm. Hume, V.D.M.

Page 345
Davis, John to Nancy Barr, Feb. 8, 1828. Sol. Feb. 10, 1828, Reubin Chandoin, D._.
Rupard, John to Louise Boon, Feb. 11, 1828. Sol. Feb. 13, 1828, Jno. C. Hicks, M.G.
Wiley, Enisley to Hannah Leslie, Feb. 12, 1828. Sol. Feb. 12, 1828, Will Lytle, J.P.
Reasoner, Peter to Polly Barker, Feb. 15, 1828. Sol. Feb. 17, 1828, B. H. Lanier, J.P.
Johnson, Isaac to Nancy Furnveel, Feb. 15, 1828.
Dark, Chas. S. to Margaret Winchester, Feb. 20, 1828. Sol. Feb. 21, 1828, E. P. Connell, J.P.
Merritt, Gibson to Sarah Rains, Feb. 20, 1828. Sol. Feb. 20, 1828, J. Whitsitt.
Blair, John to Jane Mann, Feb. 22, 1828. Sol. Feb. 28, 1828, Geo. W. Charlton, J.P.
Higgins, Wm. H. to Janisha Shell, Feb. 23, 1828. Sol. Feb. 24, 1828, Wm. H. Nance, J.P.
Wilson, Elijah to Ann C. Brooks, Feb. 26, 1828. Sol. Feb. 26, 1828, P. S. Fall.

Page 346
Fitzgerald, Bird to Julia Dodson, Feb. 26, 1828. Sol. March 13, 1828, Wm. Saunders.
Dwyer, Joseph to Catherine Dwyer, Feb. 26, 1828. Sol. Feb. 29, 1828, Will Williams, J.P.
Long, Thos. to Mary M. Porter, Feb. 28, 1828. Sol. Feb. 28, 1828, Wm. Lytle, J.P.

Louther, George to Mary Zolar, March 4, 1828. Sol. March 4, 1828, Wm. Lytle, J.P.
Claiborne, Thos. B. to Mary Maxwell, March 5, 1828. Sol. March 6, 1828, Wm. Hume, V.D.M.
Holt, Thos. to Rosanna Herbert, March 8, 1828. Sol. March 13, 1828, Th. Edmiston, J.P.
Valentine, Nicholas to Patience Morris, March 10, 1828. Sol. March 10, 1828, Wm. Lytle, J.P.
Brooks, Christopher to Sally Hutchinson, March 19, 1828. Sol. March 19, 1828, Wm. Lytle, J.P.
Noaks, Chas. H. to Eveline A. Cartwright, March 19, 1828. Sol. March 24, 1828, E. P. Connell, J.P.
March, Jesse D. to Sarah Thompson, Nov. 20, 1828. Sol. Nov. 20, 1828, P. S. Fall.

Page 347
Binkley, Isaac to Patsy Wilson, March 21, 1828. Sol. April 3, 1828, Jno. Hall, J.P.
Burgis, Lorenzo D. to Harriet Curtis, March 26, 1828. Sol. March 27, 1828, Will Lytle, J.P.
Felts, Wm. G. to Celia Ann Moore, March 28, 1828. Sol. March 28, 1828, Geo. W. Charlton, J.P.
Burk, Wm. to Agatha Mullen, March 28, 1828.
Brooks, Richard P. to Mary H. Newsom, March 27, 1828.
Enochs, Alfred to Eliza S. Fambrough, March 31, 1828. Sol. April 3, 1828, Wm. Hume, V.D.M.
Fisher, Frederick E. to Ann W. Buck, April 1, 1828. Sol. April 1, 1828, Wm. Hume, V.D.M.
Collier, Wyatt to Jennett Walker, April 2, 1828. Sol. April 3, 1828, Wm. Hume, V.D.M.
White, Edmund to Mary Mullen, April 10, 1828.
Ament, Thos. W. to Malinda Gholson, April 10, 1828. Sol. April 10, 1828, Jas. Rowe, M.G.

Page 348
McGraw, Elijah to Elizabeth Adcock, April 12, 1828.
Claridge, Henry to Elizabeth Hamilton, April 14, 1828.
Miller, Joseph to Nancy Boyles, April 15, 1828. Sol. April 20, 1828, B. H. Lanier, J.P.
Davis, Thos. to Sally Carlisle, April 16, 1828. Sol. April 16, 1828, Wm. Lytle, J.P.
Dickinson, Chas. H. to Ann Maria Turner, April 17, 1828. Sol. April 17, 1828, Wm. Hume, V.D.M.
Tennison, Matthew to Sarah W. Reaves, April 22, 1828. Sol. April 22, 1828, S. McManus, J.P.
Pigg, Nelson W. G. to Evelinah Felts, April 23, 1828.
Byrn, James T. to Mary Dorris, April 26, 1828. Sol. Sep. 4, 1829, E. P. Connell, J.P.
Davis, Preston W. to Amanda C. Sumner, April 30, 1828. Sol. April 30, 1828, Wm. Hume, V.D.M.
Waters, Thos. J. to Susan Smith, May 6, 1828. Sol. May 7, 1828, Wm. Hume, V.D.M.

Page 349
Simpson, Elias H. to Adeline Fisher, May 8, 1828. Sol. May 8, 1828, Wm. Hume, V.D.M.
Smith, Wm. to Julian Scott, May 14, 1828. Sol. Aug. 29, 1828, Thos. Ferelin.
Cropper, Wm. to Elizabeth Norwood, April 21, 1828.
Menees, Henry C. to Elizabeth Norment, May 22, 1828. Sol. May 22, 1828, J. Whitsitt.
Burnett, Henry to Sally Ballentine, May 24, 1828. Sol. May 24, 1828, Geo. W. Charlton, J.P.
Forbes, Zadok to Nancy Strong, May 26, 1828. Sol. May 26, 1828, S. McManus, J.P.
Nelson, Benjamin to Ann Patterson, May 29, 1828. Sol. May 29, 1828, Henry White, J.P.
Fain, Samuel to Susan S. Wharton, June 3, 1828. Sol. June 3, 1828, Wm. Hume, V.D.M.
Rayburn, Jno. K. to Sarah Jane Lytle, June 5, 1828. Sol. June 5, 1828, Wm. Hume, V.D.M.
Armstrong, Wm. to Lucy Baxter, June 7, 1828. Sol. June 7, 1828, Thos. Scott, J.P.

Page 350
Dean, John to Ann W. Matthews, June 9, 1828.
Childress, Geo. C. to Margaret L. Vance, June 12, 1828. Sol. June 12, 1828, Wm. Hume, V.D.M.
Cherry, Robt. to Mary Ann Davis, June 12, 1828. Sol. June 13, 1828, L. Keeling, J.P.
Walsh, Hency C. to Ann McConnell, June 16, 1828.
Donelson, Stockley to Philian Lawrence, June 19, 1828. Sol. June 19, 1828, Wm. Hume, V.D.M.
Mitchell, Philip H. to Sarah A. Allen, June 19, 1828. Sol. June 19, 1828, Wm. Hume, V.D.M.
Barnes, Andrew J. to Martha Foster, June 26, 1826. Sol. June 26, 1828, Wm. H. Nance, J.P.
Watts, Jesse B. to Margaret S. Scott, June 30, 1828. Sol. June 30, 1828, Wm. Hume, V.D.M.
Binkley, Adam to Julisa Morris, June 30, 1828. Sol. July 6, 1828, B. Lee, J.P.
Woodfin, Ryland H. to Francis M. Allen, June 30, 1828. Sol. July 1, 1828, Wm. Hume, V.D.M.

Page 351
Birdwell, Andrew to Elizabeth H. Page, July 1, 1828. Sol. July 1, 1828, Th. Edmiston, J.P.
Cooper, Chas., Jr. to Ann Pope, July 2, 1828. Sol. July 3, 1828, Henry White, J.P.
Binkley, Henry to Nancy A. Gleaves, July 5, 1828. Sol. July 8, 1828, Peter Fuqua, M. G.
Call, Peter H. to Amanda M. Bondurant, July 7, 1828.
Scott, Abner to Polly Kennedy, July 8, 1828.
Green, Wm. to Elizabeth Jackson, July 15, 1828. Sol. July 15, 1828, Wm. Lytle, J.P.
Reaves, Burwell to Sally Smith, July 21, 1828. Sol. July 27, 1828, Reuben Chandoin, M.G.

Minter, Jno. T. to Maria White, July 22, 1828. Sol. July 22, 1828, Jas. Rowe.
Moore, Gilman to Elizabeth Evans, July 22, 1828. Sol. July 23, 1828, P. S. Fall.
Barr, Jno. to Metilda Smith, July 23, 1828. Sol. July 27, 1828, Reuben Chandoin.

Page 352
Brown, Thomas to Nancy Ellison, July 26, 1828. Sol. July 26, 1828, Levin Edney, M.G.
White, Chas. P. to Sally Pegram, July 29, 1828. Sol. July 31, 1828, Thos. Ferebee.
Radford, Jasper S. to Evelina E. McBride, July 31, 1828. Sol. July 31, 1828, L. Keeling, J.P.
Willis, Walter to Catherine Wilson, Aug. 4, 1828. Sol. Aug. 28, 1828, Wm. Hume, V.D.M.
Nelson, Matthew to Sibella T. Watkins, Aug. 6, 1828. Sol. Aug. 7, 1828, Wm. Hume, V.D.M.
Foulks, Wm. P. to Mary Ann Fowlkes, Aug. 8, 1828. Sol. Aug. 14, 1828, Wm. Lytle, J.P.
Hyde, Tazewell to Eliza Ann Drake, Aug. 12, 1828. Sol. Aug. 14, 1828, P. S. Fall.
Morton, Barzillai G. to Margaret Howell, Aug. 12, 1828. Sol. Aug. 14, 1828, Th. Edmiston, J.P.
Sims, Jno. W. to Margaret Johnson, Aug. 20, 1828.
Goodrich, Sterling W. to Mary A. Goodrich, Aug. 27, 1828. Sol. Aug. 1828, Simpson Shephard.

Page 353
Gower, Lewis G. to Polly Fowler, Aug. 30, 1828.
Spence, Wm. G. to Mary Stogner, Sep. 1, 1828. Sol. Sep. 2, 1828, J. M. Chandoin.
Byrn, Stephen W. to Mary Boker, Sep. 2, 1828. Sol. Sep. 7, 1828, S. P. Connell, J.P.
Blackwood, Hiram to Sally Arterberry, Sep. 2, 1828. Sol. Sep. 3, 1828; R. Hewitt, J.P.
Holt, Lewis P. to Mary Powell, Sep. 4, 1828.
Wade, Geo. W. to Winney R. Hopper, Sep. 6, 1828. Sol. Sep. 22, 1828, Thos. Ferebee.
Parkerson, Jas. to Tennessee Scott, Sep. 10, 1828. Sol. Sep. 11, 1828, Thos. Ferebee.
Warmach, Thos. to Harriet Byrn, Sep. 12, 1828. Sol. Oct. 7, 1828, E. P. Connell, J.P.
Huffman, Solomon to Sarah Smith, Sep. 16, 1828.
Hackney, Daniel to Nancy Moss, Sep. 16, 1828. Sol. Sep. 17, 1828, E. P. Connell, J.P.

Page 354
Speice, James to Ann Leak, Sep. 20, 1828. Sol. Sep. 20, 1828, Wm. Hume, V.D.M.
Williams, Zippo to Rebecca Hail, Sep. 23, 1828. Sol. Sep. 24, 1828, W. Russell, J.P.
Lyles, Hilary to Mary Heaton, Sep. 24, 1828. Sol. Sep. 24, 1828, S. Shephard.

Foster, Devid to Virie Williams, Sep. 25, 1828. Sol. 25, 1828, Wm. H. Nance, J.P.
Franklin, James to Mary Ann Smith, Sep. 30, 1828. Sol. Sep. 30, 1828, Wm. Lytle, J.P.
Brown, Wm. L. to Louisa A. Gibbs, Sep. 30, 1828. Sol. Oct. 30, 1828, P. S. Fall.
Huff, John to Ann Cockrill, Oct. 1, 1828. Sol. Oct. 3, 1828, Wm. Warker.
Cole, Abel to Martha W. Lee, Oct. 1, 1828.
Wetherill, John to Virginia W. Foster, Oct. 4, 1828. Sol. Oct. 4, 1828, Wm. Hume, V.D.M.
Handoin, Jno. W. to Sally Coltharp, Oct. 7, 1828. Sol. Oct. 16, 1828, Jno. M. Chandoin, M.G.

Page 355
Mitchell, Zachriah to Minerva Davis, Oct. 8, 1828. Sol. Oct. 8, 1828, Levin Edney, M.G.
Brown, Joseph P. to Mary L. Brown, Oct. 11, 1828.
Jackson, Wiley to Mary McCrory, Oct. 18, 1828. Sol. Oct. 18, 1828, Levin Edney, M.G.
Green, Oliver to Elizabeth Womble, Oct. 18, 1828. Sol. Oct. 18, 1828, Wm. Lytle, J.P.
Smith, Abraham to Catherine Powell, Oct. 18, 1828. Sol. Oct. 20, 1828, Wm. Lytle, J.P.
Wheeler, Wm. to Parrilee Lester, Oct. 20, 1828.
Brummell, Wm. to Jane Johnson, Oct. 21, 1828. Sol. Oct. 29, 1828, Jas. Tarrant, M.G.
Martin, Jas., Jr. to Elizabeth Brinkley, Oct. 21, 1828.
Russell, Mills to Margaret Harding, Oct. 21, 1828. Sol. Oct. 22, 1828, Jno. Davis, J.P.
Wise, Henry A. to Ann E. Jennings, Oct. 23, 1828.

Page 356
Jackson, Daniel B. to Mary Moorefield, Oct. 23, 1828. Sol. Oct. 23, 1828, Wm. Lytle, J.P.
Speice, Thos. to Mary Shelton, Oct. 25, 1828. Sol. Oct. 27, 1828, Wm. Lytle, J.P.
Donelson, Stephen to Matilda S. Moore, Oct. 28, 1828. Sol. Oct. 28, 1828, James Rowes.
Hall, Allen A. to Mary Newman, Oct. 28. 1828. Sol. Oct. 28, 1828, Wm. Hume, V.D.M.
Ware, Wm. K. to Amelia Taylor, Nov. 5, 1828. Sol. Nov. 6, 1828, Wm. Lytle, J.P.
Rains, Wilford H., to Maria Gowen, Nov. 5, 1828. Sol. Nov. 5, 1828, J. Whitsitt.
Jordan, Norfleet to Emeline Shandoin, Nov. 6, 1828. Sol. Nov. 12, 1828, W. Russell, J.P.
David, Wm. D. to Louisa Meader, Nov. 10, 1828. Sol. Nov. 12, 1828, Wm. Lytle, J.P.
Washington, Wm. L. to Susan P. Trimble, Nov. 13, 1828. Sol. Nov. 13, 1828, Wm. Hume, V.D.M.
Page, Wm. to Lucy Harris, Nov. 18, 1828.

Page 357
Felts, Thos. to Courtenay Miles, Nov. 19, 1828.

Homar, Daniel to Polly Allen, Nov. 24, 1828. Sol. Nov. 26, 1828, Wm. Lytle, J.P.
Morgan, Benjamin to Frances Basye, Nov. 26, 1828. Sol. Dec. 7, 1828, J. Pirtle, J.P.
Sullivan, Drewry to Martha Barnes, Nov. 26, 1828. Sol. Dec. 28, 1828, G. W. Charlton, J.P.
Kibby, Alexander to Martha Morris, Nov. 27, 1828.
Thompson, Jas. P. to Rachel Shelby, Nov. 27, 1828. Sol. Nov. 27, 1828, Wm. Hume, V.D.M.
Edney, Newton to Sally Pritchett, Nov. 27, 1828.
Bell, Jno. to Jane Gooch, Nov. 29, 1828.
Garland, Samuel to Nancy Benningfield, Dec. 1, 1828. Sol. Dec. 4, 1828, J. M. Lovell, J.P.
Sharp, Jas. G. to Tabitha Baker, Dec. 1, 1828. Sol. Dec. 4, 1828, Will Sanders.

Page 358
White, Joseph to Arney Owen, Dec. 1, 1828. Sol. Dec. 4, 1828, Th. Edmiston, J.P.
McKnight, Thos. W. to Martha B. Woodard, Dec. 1, 1828.
Jackson, Warren to Minerva Garrett, Dec. 4, 1828. Sol. Dec. 4, 1828, Simpson Shephard.
Kellum, Henry to Lucinda Williams, Dec. 4, 1828. Sol. Dec. 5, 1828, Jno. C. Hicks, M.G.
Thompson, Samuel W. to Margery Ann Bryan, Dec. 8, 1828. Sol. Dec. 8, 1828, Levin Edney, M.G.
Martin, Frederick to Patsy Lee, Dec. 9, 1828.
Ray, Henry D. to Lenora K. Glasgow, Dec. 10, 1828. Sol. Dec. 11, 1828, E. P. Connell, J.P.
Wolf, James to Nancy Linton, Dec. 10, 1828.
Paul, Isaac to Susan Nance, Dec. 11, 1828.
Fawcet, James to Elizabeth G. Russell, Dec. 11, 1828 Sol. Dec. 23, 1828, J. M. Lovell, J.P.

Page 359
Mayfield, Sutherlin S. to Sarah Waller, Dec. 15, 1828. Sol. Dec. 17, 1828, Th. Edmiston, J.P.
Vest, Samuel to Ann Chadwell, Dec. 17, 1828. Sol. Dec. 24, 1828, Jas. Whitsitt.
Jones, Joseph W. to Charlotte G. Ellis, Dec. 17, 1828.
Gregory, Jno. to Letitia White, Dec. 18, 1828. Sol. Dec. 18, 1828, Wm. Lytle, J.P.
Casey, Samuel to Jemima Cheek, Dec. 18, 1828.
Haynes, Robert S. to Catherine Moulton, Dec. 22, 1828. Sol. Dec. 22, 1828, Wm. Lytle, J.P.
Chavons, Wm. to Celia Corke, Dec. 22, 1828. Sol. Dec. 23, 1828, S. McManus, J.P.
Mitchell, Benj. to Elizabeth Shivers, Dec. 23, 1828. Sol. Dec. 23, 1828, Simpson Shephard.
Guinn, Wm. M. to Caroline M. Sampson, Dec. 23, 1828.
Elmore, Wm. A. to Panther Estes, Dec. 26, 1828. Sol. Dec. 26, 1828, Simpson Shephard.

Page 360
Luton, Jesse to Mary Sims, Dec. 26, 1828. Sol. Dec. 26, 1828, Simpson Shephard.
Pasquel, Henry to Jane Sanders, Dec. 29, 1828.
Williams, Benjamin W. to Susan Battle, Dec. 30, 1828. Sol. Dec. 30, 1828, Wm. Hume, V.D.M.
Smith, Ralph P. to Ann Nicholson, Dec. 31, 1828. Sol. Jan. 1, 1829, Ph. Lindsley.
Carper, Sampson P. to Levina Austin, Jan. 1, 1829.
Musgrove, Edward F. to Angelina M. Lanier, Jan. 2, 1829. Sol. Jan. 2, 1829, Wm. Hume, V.D.M.
Hyde, Edmund to Christiana Rains, Jan. 7, 1829. Sol. Jan. 8, 1829, Wm. Hume, V.D.M.
Bass, Jno. M. to Malonia C. Grundy, Jan. 7, 1829. Sol. Jan. 7, 1829, Wm. Hume, V.D.M.
Hawkins, Robt. to Rosetta Inyard, Jan. 7, 1829. Sol. Jan. 8, 1829, Wm. Lytle, J.P.
Boyd, Whitmell H. to Sally S. Biddle, Jan. 7, 1829. Sol. Jan. 7, 1829, Wm. Hume, V.D.M.

Page 361
Johnson, Joseph H. to Harriet Richmond, Jan. 8, 1829. Sol. Jan. 8, 1829, P. S. Fall.
Paul, Samuel W. to Mary Jane Baird, Jan. 13, 1829. Sol. Jan. 15, 1829, Wm. Hume, V.D.M.
Erwin, Jas. to Margaret Caldwell, Jan. 13, 1829. Sol. Jan. 15, 1829, Wm. Hume, V.D.M.
Gross, Geo. S. to Evelina Clinard, Jan. 14, 1829. Sol. Jan. 15, 1829, Wm. Lytle, J.P.
Davis, Jackson C. to Elizabeth Patterson, Jan. 15, 1829. Sol. Jan. 15, 1829, Wm. Lytle, J.P.
Williams, Robt. J. to Jane Turner, Jan. 20, 1829. Sol. Jan. 20, 1829, Wm. Lytle, J.P.
Thomason, Spencer to Sarah Shivers, Jan. 20, 1829. Sol. Jan. 21, 1829, Wm. Lytle, J.P.
Adams, Samuel H. to Sarah P. Hill, Jan. 26, 1829.
Goodrich, Jas. M. to Susan P. Wills, Jan. 27, 1829. Sol. Jan. 27, 1829, Wm. Lytle, J.P.
Gupton, James to Sally Hail, Jan. 29, 1829.

Page 362
Gower, Abel B. to Alpha David, Jan. 30, 1829. Sol. Feb. 3, 1829, Wm. Lytle, J.P.
Hooper, Churchill to Elizabeth Jordan, Jan. 30, 1829. Sol. Feb. 1, 1829, J. M. Lovell, J.P.
Scruggs, Oglesby to Ann M. Howlett, Feb. 2, 1829.
Summers, Thomas to Nancy Cheatham, Feb. 7, 1829. Sol. Feb. 8, 1829, P. S. Fall.
Campbell, Wm. to Francis Gill, Feb. 7, 1829. Sol. Feb. 7, 1829, Ph. Lindsley.
Hurt, Wm. to Elizabeth H. Bowers, Feb. 9, 1829. Sol. Feb. 10, 1829, Wm. H. White.
Merriman, Jesse T. to Mary Holmes, Feb. 10, 1829.
Norwood, Thos. to Mildred Bell, Feb. 10, 1829.

Bradfute, Robert to Sarah S. Sneed, Feb. 10, 1829. Sol. Feb. 10, 1829, James Guinn, M.G.
Searles, John to Elizabeth Goodrich, Feb. 11, 1829. Sol. Feb. 19, 1829, Hays Blackman, J.P.

Page 363
Page, Solomon C. to Harriett A. Moore, Feb. 14, 1829. Sol. Feb. 14, 1829, Jas. Givin, M.G.
Thompson, Wm. P. to Ann J. Whiteside, Feb. 14, 1829. Sol. Feb. 14, 1829, J. Whiteside.
Corbit, Dempsy to Catherine Turbeville, Feb. 16, 1829. Sol. Feb. 16, 1829, Wm. H. Nance, J.P.
Sanders, Stephen to Elizabeth Johnston, Feb. 19, 1829. Sol. Feb. 26, 1829, Guy McFaddin.
Mathes, Alexander R. to Caroline Connell, Feb. 19, 1829. Sol. Feb. 24, 1829, Will Lytle, J.P.
Newland, Wm. to Mary Puckett, Feb. 23, 1829.
Parrish, Woodson to Margaret Harman, Feb. 23, 1829. Sol. Feb. 24, 1829, Jas. Givin, M.G.
McCombs, Baptist to Emile W. Wooton, Feb. 24, 1829. Sol. Feb. 24, 1829, Jas. Givin, M.G.
Graves, David to Mary Hudson, Feb. 24, 1829. Sol. Feb. 26, 1829, Wm. H. White.
Fussell, John to Judida White, Feb. 24, 1829. Sol. Feb. 24, 1829, J. Whitsitt.

Page 364
Evans, Wm. T. to Mary Ann Hobbs, March 2, 1829. Sol. March 2, 1829, Levin Edney, M.G.
Hollis, James S. to Judy Fuqua, March 2, 1829. Sol. March 2, 1829, Will Lytle, J.P.
Adams, Abner to Lucy Manley, March 5, 1829.
Bellsnyder, Thomas to Polly M. Hopkins, March 5, 1829. Sol. March 5, 1829, Will Lytle, J.P.
Frazier, Ephriam to Lucinda Frazier, March 6, 1829. Sol. March 6, 1829, Robt. Hewitt, J.P.
Cravens, John to Winnefred Tally, March 7, 1829. Sol. March 8, 1829, Wm. Saunders.
Finn, Thos. to Sarah Cobbs, March 9, 1829. Sol. March 10, 1829, Wm. Hume, V.D.M.
Smith, Robert to Nancy Estes, March 11, 1829. Sol. March 11, 1829, U. H. Quinn.
Raimer, George to Hester Booten, March 11, 1829. Sol. March 12, 1829, Jno. M. Chandoin.
Leah, Jno. C. to Mary W. Baldridge, March 14, 1829. Sol. March 15, 1829, Wm. H. Nance, J.P.

Page 365
Gee, Wm. to Mary Burton, March 17, 1829. Sol. March 17, 1829, Simpson Shephard.
Carney, Asa to Cressy Martin, March 17, 1829.
McCombs, Gabriel to Nancy C. Smith, March 21, 1829.
Noell, Reuben to Sally Noell, March 23, 1829. Sol. March 24, 1829, E. P. Connell, J.P.

Johnson, Joseph to Catherine Garrett, March 25, 1829.
Pinkard, Edward W. to Mary B. Caldwell, March 26, 1829. Sol. March 26, 1829, J. Whitsitt.
Langston, Obediah to Ann Vandike, March 26, 1829.
Tucker, Wesley J. to Nancy Greer, March 28, 1829. Sol. Sol. April 2, 1829, Will Lytle, J.P.
Seat, David to Sarah Burnett, April 3, 1829.
Neal, Samuel to Mary L. Fitzhugh, April 6, 1829. Sol. April 16, 1829, Hays Blackman, J.P.

Page 366
Winburn, Wm. M. to Ann B. Walker, April 7, 1829. Sol. April 7, 1829, U. H. Quinn.
Greer, James to Hannah Dellahunt, April 13, 1829. Sol. April 16, 1829, Wm. Herrin.
Dickinson, Wm. to Mary Jane McGuire, April 21, 1829.
Dean, Aaron to Narcissa Binkley, May 2, 1829.
Corder, Thos. L. to Susannah Park, May 11, 1829. Sol. May 12, 1829, E. P. Connell, J.P.
Varden, Edmund to Ann Patrick, May 12, 1829.
Bennett, Wm. to Mary Sneed, May 16, 1829. Sol. May 20, 1829, Wm. Hume, V.D.M.
Maddeaux, Wm. D. to Jane Check, May 16, 1829.
Redout, Wm. L. to Louise Scales, May 28, 1829.
Butler, Augustine W. to Mary D. Hyde, June 3, 1829. Sol. June 4, 1829, Wm. Hume, V.D.M.

Page 367
Leher, Jno. P. T. to Margaretta White, June 5, 1829. Sol. June 7, 1829, Jas. Givin, M.G.
Rosenbaum, Jno. to Lucy Wilkenson, June 6, 1829.
Chandler, Wm. to Ruthy Nichols, June 10, 1829.
Boyd, Jno. to Lamira S. Ewing, June 11, 1829. Sol. June 11, 1829, P. S. Fall.
Stanley, Wright to Mary C. McBride, June 20, 1829.
Odom, Wm. to Mary Lee, June 23, 1829.
Booth, Wm. to Mary Ann Cunningham, June 24, 1829. Sol. June 25, 1829, E. P. Connell, J.P.
Sweeny, Hugh to Sarah W. Downey, June 24, 1829. Sol. June 24, 1829, Levin Edney, M.G.
Newell, McNairy to Levinie Bosley, June 24, 1829. Sol. June 25, 1829, Wm. Hume, V.D.M.
McMahon, Wm. to Sarah R. Rogers, July 2, 1829. Sol. July 8, 1829, B. H. Lanier, J.P.

Page 368
Scruggs, Edward to Jane Boyd, July 4, 1829. Sol. July 9, 1829, Will Lytle, J.P.
Bell, Wm. H. to Maria Wilkinson, July 6, 1829. Sol. July 9, 1829, Wm. Hume, V.D.M.
Cullum, Jeremiah W. to Elizabeth T. Hooper, July 10, 1829. Sol. Aug. 20, 1829, J. M. Lovell, J.P.
Talbot, Thos. J. to Sarah Ann Hinton, July 15, 1829. Sol. July 16, 1829, P. S. Fall.

Garrett, Wm. W. to Susan Faulkner, July 19, 1829. Sol. July 30, 1829, Will Lytle, J.P.
Bland, Joseph A. to Serena T. Walker, July 18, 1829.
Gresham, Austin to Eliza O. Burge, July 23, 1829. Sol. July 23, 1829, J. Whitsitt.
Tucker, Jas. H. to Mary Lazenberry, July 25, 1829.
Buckner, James M. to Minerva B. Cook, July 27, 1829.
Dunnevant, Joseph to Martha Curtis, Aug. 4, 1829.

Page 369
Sanders, Wm. to Emeline Williams, Aug. 13, 1829. Sol. Aug. 13, 1829, Will Lytle, J.P.
Harrison, Jno. E. to Martha Cobler, Aug. 15, 1829. Sol. Aug. 16, 1829, Hays Blackman, J.P.
Brumfield, David to Margaret Chesser, Aug. 17, 1829.
Jessup, Wm. to Leatha Knight, Aug. 19, 1829.
Edgin, Jno. A. to Leatha Coleman, Aug. 17, 1829.
Jones, Jas. C. to Sarah W. Mumford, Aug. 24, 1829. Sol. Aug. 27, 1829, Wm. Hume, V.D.M.
Harris, Gideon to Elsey McGuinnis, Aug. 31, 1829.
Howlett, Stockley H. to Susan Ramsey, Sep. 2, 1829. Sol. Sep. 10, 1829, Th. Edmiston, J.P.
Harman, Jefferson to Eliza Capps, Sep. 10, 1829. Sol. Sep. 10, 1829, Will Lytle, J.P.
Butts, Wilson to Eliza Jane Kingston, Sep. 11, 1829. Sol. Sep. 16, 1829, Jno. C. Hicks, M.G.

Page 370
McEwin, Felix G. to Elizabeth C. Howard, Sep. 14, 1829. Sol. Sep. 17, 1829, Wm. Hume, V.D.M.
Harwell, Frederick to Susannah Clark, Sep. 16, 1829. Sol. Sep. 17, 1829, Will O. Williams, J.P.
Andrews, Wm. to Olivia F. Read, Sep. 24, 1829. Sol. April 24, 1829, P. S. Fall.
Wilcocks, Benj. A. to Sarah Fudge, Sep. 29, 1829. Sol. Oct. 1, 1829, L. Keeling, J.P.
Stump, Albert G. to Ann Dozier, Sep. 29, 1829. Sol. Oct. 1, 1829, Will Lytle, J.P.
Alford, Jno. T. to Nancy Reaves, Nov. 2, 1829. Sol. Nov. 5, 1829, Th. Edmiston, J.P.
Lusk, Robert to Matilda F. Fairfax, Oct. 7, 1829. Sol. Oct. 7, 1829, Wm. Hume, V.D.M.
Kernell, Wm. D. to Ursula Tankersley, Aug. 8, 1829. Sol. Aug. 8, 1829, Will Lytle, J.P.
Chapoinel, Peter to Emeline Jennings, Oct. 8, 1829.
Harris, Robt. B. to Nancy Eubanks, Oct. 8, 1829. Sol. Oct. 8, 1829, B. Lee, J.P.

Page 371
Smith, Jason to Nancy Cox, Oct. 10, 1829. Sol. Oct. 12, 1829, Reuben Chandoin.
Lucas, Washington R. to Martha M. Crutcher, Oct. 14, 1829. Sol. Oct. 14, 1829, Wm. Hume, V.D.M.

Brady, Robt. to Nancy Wright, Oct. 15, 1829. Sol. Oct. 15, 1829, Wm. Hume, V.D.M.
Turner, Jas. H. to Lucinda Pilcher, Oct. 15, 1829. Sol. Oct. 15, 1829, Jas. Gwin, M.G.
Hume, Fountain to Alcina A. Austin, Oct. 21, 1829. Sol. Oct. 21, 1829, F. E. Pitts, M.G.
Parker, Samuel to Susan Snow, Oct. 24, 1829. Sol. Oct. 24, 1829, F. E. Pitts, M.G.
Johns, Joel to Sophia Dickinson, Dec. 24, 1829. Sol. Dec. 24, 1829, Will Lytle, J.P.
Stringfellow, Hiram P. to Lucy Brummet, Oct. 24, 1829. Sol. Oct. 27, 1829, Wm. Herrin.
Roach, Lewis W. to Jane Orten, Nov. 2, 1829. Sol. Nov. 8, 1829, Jno. Davis.
Alford, Jno. T. to Nancy Reaves, Nov. 2, 1829. Sol. Nov. 5, 1829, Thos. Edmiston, J.P.

Page 372
Cook, Lewis to Matilda Hughs, Nov. 3, 1829.
Bain, Jno. R. to Sarah E. Crockett, Nov. 5, 1829.
Clay, Joshua to Harriet Patterson, Nov. 5, 1829. Sol. Nov. 9, 1829, H. White, J.P.
Shelton, Franklin to Nancy Shelton, Nov. 5, 1829. Sol. Nov. 30, 1829, Thos. Ferebee.
Bolten, Joel to Polly Bush, Nov. 5, 1829. Sol. Nov. 12, 1829, Jno. Hall, J.P.
Carter, Jno. C. to Levinia Miers, Nov. 9, 1829. Sol. Nov. 12, 1829, H. White, J.P.
Baker, Wm. to Elmira Questinberry, Nov. 10, 1829. Sol. Nov. 10, 1829, P. S. Fall.
O'Rielly, James C. to Matilda Adams, Nov. 17, 1829.
Strother, Geo. T. to Mary Ann Roberts, Nov. 19, 1829. Sol. Nov. 19, 1829, Wm. Lytle, J.P.
Harding, Wm. G. to Mary S. McNairy, Nov. 19, 1829. Sol. Nov. 19, 1829, Wm. Hume, V.D.M.

Page 373
McNiell, Edward H. to Mary McCutcheon, Nov. 23, 1829. Sol. Dec. 3, 1829, Wm. Hume, V.D.M.
Tanner, Thos. W. to Levica Irby, Nov. 24, 1829. Sol. Nov. 24, 1829, Will Lytle, J.P.
Parish, Francis to Fanny Dismukes, Nov. 26, 1829. Sol. Nov. 26, 1829, Will Lytle, J.P.
Mays, Wright to Patsy Pegram, Nov. 26, 1829. Sol. Dec. 3, 1829, Jno. C. Hicks, M.G.
Pilcher, Mason to Lucretia Hubble, Nov. 26, 1829. Sol. Nov. 26, 1829, P. S. Fall.
Williams, Jno. T. to Sarah Gullidge, Dec. 10, 1829. Sol. Dec. 10, 1829, Will Lytle, J.P.
Wright, Jas. W. to Martha Tate, Dec. 10, 1829.
Lee, Vinson to Polly Richardson, Dec. 10, 1829. Sol. Dec. 19, 1829, Reuben Chandoin.
Cassellman, Wm. to Mariah H. Bush, Dec. 10, 1829. Sol. Dec. 16, 1829, Jno. Hall, J.P.

Hurt, Wm. to Mariah Brown, Dec. 12, 1829. Sol. Dec. 17, 1829, Jno. Hall, J.P.

Page 374
Douglass, Harry L. to Jane A. Crabb, Dec. 15, 1829. Sol. Dec. 15, 1829, Phillip Lindsley.
O'Briant, James to Sarah Cassellman, Dec. 15, 1829. Sol. Dec. 15, 1829, Absolom Gleaves, J.P.
Exum, Arthur to Catherine Taylor, Dec. 15, 1829. Sol. Dec. 23, 1829, Jno. C. Hicks, M.G.
Snowden, Samuel B. to Jane W. Hume, Dec. 17, 1829. Sol. Dec. 17, 1829, Wm. Hume, V.D.M.
Harris, Wm. to Elizabeth M. Thompson, Dec. 18, 1829. Sol. Dec. 18, 1829, Wm. Hume, V.D.M.
Pitts, Burrell to Elizabeth Hous, Dec. 19, 1829. Sol. Dec. 20, 1829, W. Russell, J.P.
Shadoin, Lewis to Mary Coltharp, Dec. 21, 1829. Sol. Dec. 23, 1829, Jno. M. Chandoin.
Coltharp, Wm. to Eliza Betts, Dec. 23, 1829. Sol. Dec. 27, 1829, E. P. Connell, J.P.
Johnston, Burrell P. to Louisa Cato, Dec. 22, 1829. Sol. Dec. 24, 1829, Jno. Hall, J.P.
McKnight, Wm. W. to Elizabeth Woodard, Dec. 23, 1829.

Page 375
Luter, Banj. W. to Rachel Smiley, Dec. 24, 1829. Sol. Dec. 24, 1829, Will Lytle, J.P.
Fisher, Benj. F. to Elizabeth B. Lee, Dec. 24, 1829. Sol. Dec. 24, 1829, H. White, J.P.
Wilds, Wm. to Franky Reaves, Dec. 26, 1829. Sol. Dec. 29, 1829, Moses Speed, M.G.
McGuines, James to Jane Jackson, Dec. 28, 1829. Sol. Dec. 29, 1829, Jno. M. Chandoin.
Scales, Jas. to Jane D. Loving, Dec. 29, 1829. Sol. Dec. 29, 1829, P. S. Fall.
Marshall, Frederick to Lucy Ann Marshall, Dec. 31, 1829. Sol. Dec. 31, 1829, S. McManus, J.P.
Matthews, Alexander to Eliza M. Love, Jan. 6, 1830. Sol. Jan. 6, 1830, Will Lytle, J.P.
Elliston, Joseph T., Jr. to Martha A. Mitchell, Jan. 6, 1830. Sol. Jan. 6, 1830, A. L. P. Green, M.G.
Hite, Samuel t- Jane Stuart, Jan. 7, 1830. Sol. Jan. 7, 1830, H. White, J.P.
Green, Thos. J. to Sarah A. Wharton, Jan. 8, 1830. Sol. Jan. 8, 1830, Wm. Hume, V.D.M.

Page 376
Coen, James to Maria Wingfield, Jan. 11, 1830. Sol. Jan. 12, 1830, Will Lytle, J.P.
Johnson, Lewis to Nancy Lee, Jan. 13, 1830. Sol. Jan. 13, 1830, Peter Fuqua, M.G.
Harris, James H. to Nancy Cooper, Jan. 13, 1830. Sol. Jan. 13, 1830, Wm. Hume, V.D.M.
Wright, Wm. to Priscilla Reaves, Jan. 13, 1830.

Ellis, Littleton to Polly Wright, Jan. 13, 1830. Sol. Jan. 14, 1830, Jno. Hall, J.P.
Towns, Leonard to Martha Cassellman, Jan. 18, 1830. Sol. Jan. 24, 1830, Geo. W. Charlton, J.P.
Gorman, James O. to Martha A. T. Hewlett, Jan. 20, 1830. Sol. Jan. 20, 1830, W. Landswell, J.P.
Boyte, John to Elizabeth Gower, Jan. 20, 1830.
Bland, Samuel L. to Mahala Binkley, Jan. 22, 1830. Sol. Jan. 29, 1830, Jno. Hall, J.P.
Logue, David to Susan Winchester (or Randal), Jan. 23, 1830. Sol. Feb. 7, 1830, J. Pirtle, J.P.

Page 377
Farrow, Thos. to Mahala Bowlin, Jan. 25, 1830.
Ballow, Thos. W. to Martha A. Ballow, Jan. 25, 1830. Sol. Jan. 27, 1830, Ambrose F. Driskill, M.G.
Reese, Thos. to Ann Hall, Jan. 25, 1830. Sol. Jan. 26, 1830, Reuben Payne, J.P.
Parrish, James G. to Mary Ashley, Jan. 26, 1830. Sol. Jan. 26, 1830, Simpson Shephard.
Fletcher, Peyton to Sarah W. Graves, Jan. 26, 1830. Sol. Jan. 26, 1830, Will Lytle, J.P.
Minor, Richard to Martha Norvell, Jan. 27, 1830. Sol. Jan. 28, 1830, Jno. M. Chandoin.
Harris, Wm. to Martha Dennis, Jan. 30, 1830. Sol. Feb. 11, 1830, Reuben Chandoin.
Frazer, Jno. to Louisa Perch, Jan. 30, 1830. Sol. Jan. 30, 1830, Levin Edney, M.G.
Carter, Garret to Sally Nichelson, Feb. 1, 1830. Sol. Feb. 15, 1830, Will Lytle, J.P.
Hurt, Jno. to Jane Wright, Feb. 6, 1830.

Page 378
Grubbs, Thos. W. to Mary Castleman, Feb. 9, 1830. Sol. Feb. 17, 1830, Geo. W. Charlton, J.P.
Sanders, Noell to Mary McCord, Feb. 9, 1830.
Harris, Fleming to Elizabeth Leah, Feb. 9, 1830. Sol. Feb. 10, 1830, Wm. Hume, V.D.M.
Stewart, Wm. to Sarah Greer, Feb. 12, 1830. Sol. Feb. 18, 1830, Wm. Hume, V.D.M.
Felts, Thomas to Elizabeth Harris, Feb. 12, 1830. Sol. Feb. 14, 1830, B. Lee, J.P.
Barnes, Martin to Elizabeth Wright, Feb. 13, 1830. Sol. Feb. 16, 1830, Geo. W. Charlton, J.P.
Hiett, Granthom to Priscilla Harper, Feb. 13, 1830. Sol. Feb. 14, 1830, R. Weakley, J.P.
Roberts, Wm. to Sarah J. Chowning, Feb. 15, 1830. Sol. Feb. 15, 1830, J. Whitsitt.
Stewart, Wm. to Elizabeth Ann Lay, Feb. 15, 1830. Sol. Feb. 18, 1830, W. White, J.P.
Hill, Wm. to Nancy Weaver, Feb. 18, 1830. Sol. Feb. 18, 1830, Will Lytle, J.P.

Page 379
Hiland, Geo. W. to Martha Morris, Feb. 18, 1830. Sol. March 2, 1830, Reubin Chandoin.
Edmonds, Sterling to Eliza Brown, Feb. 18, 1830.
Green, Jno. B. to Josephine Peach, Feb. 18, 1830. Sol. Feb. 18, 1830, Jas. Givin, M.G.
Harper, Sterling J. S. to Levithia Reaves, Feb. 20, 1830.
Blakey, Geo. D. to Lucy L. Thomas, Feb. 23, 1830. Sol. Feb. 23, 1830, Jas. Givin, M.G.
Drake, Eli to Martha Ann Gleaves, Feb. 24, 1830, Sol. Feb. 24, 1830, P. S. Fall.
Mayfield, Jno. W. to Catherine Dick, Feb. 25, 1830. Sol. Feb. 25, 1830, Thos. Hickman.
Sanders, Isaac to Patsy Gower, March 2, 1830.
Gunter, Green B. to Sinai Lucas, March 3, 1830. Sol. March 3, 1830, J. Whitsitt.
Richardson, Alex. to Nancy Richardson, March 8, 1830.

Page 380
Hardy, Wm. to Icypheny Watkins, March 15, 1830.
Marshall, Jno. J. to Mary Whiffle, March 16, 1830. Sol. March 16, 1830, Will Lytle, J.P.
Barnes, Reddeck to Sarah H. Brierly, March 18, 1830.
Brinkley, Eli to Catherine Swigart, March 22, 1830.
Hill, James S. to Mary Earnest, March 23, 1830. Sol. March 23, 1830, H. White J.P.
Fowlkes, Jno. B. to Martha Turner, March 24, 1830. Sol. Mar. 24, 1830, Will Lytle, J.P.
Cross, Nathaniel to Ann Caroline Bonney, April 3, 1830. Sol. April 3, 1830, Th. Lindsley.
Read, Matthew to Harriet Walding, April 6, 1830. Sol. April 7, 1830, B. H. Lanier, J. P.
Byrns, Wm. A. to Elizabeth Williams, April 7, 1830. Sol. April 22, 1830, E. P. Connell, J.P.
Deal, Wm. to Nancy Mayfield, April 7, 1830. Sol. April 8, 1830, W. Russell, J.P.

Page 381
Neal, Richard P. to Caroline R. Buck, April 8, 1830.
Thompson, David G. to Elizabeth McElwain, April 12, 1830. Sol. April 15, 1830, Thos. Ferebee.
Waggoner, Christopher to Sarah Patrick, April 10, 1830. Sol. April 21, 1830, Absolom Gleaves, J.P.
Gates, Jas. to Catherine Dinwidie, April 19, 1830.
Johnson, Jas. to Alianna Hill, April 22, 1830. Sol. April 28, 1830, Wm. Lytle, J.P.
Curfman, Wm. to Mary Ann Atkinson, April 26, 1830.
Taylor, Jas. to Polly Dyer, April 29, 1830. Sol. April 29, 1830, Jno. P. Erwin, J.P.
Harrison, Wm. H. to Mary Ann Morment, May 3, 1830. Sol. May 3, 1830, J. Whitsitt.
Glasgow, Wm. to Martha Logan, May 5, 1830. Sol. May 7, 1830, Thos. Scott, J.P.

Page 382
Harding, Wm. to Elizabeth H. Clopton, May 6, 1830. Sol. May 12, 1830, Wm. Hume, V.D.M.
Shaw, James L. to Marinda Harder, May 6, 1830. Sol. May 6, 1830, Reuben Payne, J.P.
Johnson, Wm. J. to Mary Russell, May 8, 1830. Sol. May 8, 1830, J. Whitsitt.
Anderson, Isaac to Nancy Simmons, May 8, 1830. Sol. May 30, 1830, Jno. C. Hicks, M.G.
Bobs, Thos. to Nancy Armstrong, May 12, 1830. Sol. May 13, 1830, N. B. Pryor, J.P.
Holmes, Phineas to Eliza J. Read, May 13, 1830. Sol. May 13, 1830, Wm. Hume, V.D.M.
Rine, Geo. J. to Mary M. Ridley, May 17, 1830. Sol. May 19, 1830, P. S. Fall.
Bray, Wm. R. to Parmelia Eakin, May 17, 1830. Sol. May 17, 1830, Levin Edney, M.G.
Perry, Allen M. to Talitha Cartwright, May 28, 1930.
Johnson, Nimrod to Susan Burnett, May 29, 1830.

Page 383
Williamson, Henry G. to Nancy R. Hogan, June 2, 1830. Sol. June 3, 1830, Robt. Davis, M.G.
Ellidge, Ambrose to Mary Cherry, June 3, 1830. Sol. June 3, 1830, Will Lytle, J.P.
Sims, Wm. P. to Minerva W. Harn, June 3, 1830. Sol. June 3, 1830, J. Whitsitt.
Young, Daniel to Mary J. Drake, June 9, 1830. Sol. June 9, 1830, Will Lytle, J.P.
Ridley, Hause H. to Sarah Everitt, June 9, 1830.
Wills, Andrew L. to Susan Ann Brown, June 16, 1830. Sol. June 16, 1830, Wm. Hume, V.D.M.
Nanney, Wm. to Elizabeth Farmer, June 19, 1830. Sol. June 23, 1830, Will Lytle, J.P.
Hughes, Lynch to Nancy Little, June 22, 1830. Sol. June 24, 1830, Jas. Givin, M.G.
Foster, Shelton to Sarah Hopper, June 22, 1830.
Phillips, Joel to Jane Gee, June 23, 1830.

Page 384
Milom, Andrew to Talitha Cartwright, June 24, 1830. Sol. June 24, 1830, N. B. Pryor, J.P.
Wright, Jonathon to Elvira Hewgley, June 25, 1830. Sol. July 6, 1830, H. White, J.P.
Horn, Joseph to Nancy McDaniel, June 26, 1830. Sol. June 29, 1830, Jno. C. Hicks, M.G.
Currell, Jas. S. to Nancy Ann Roberts, July 2, 1830. Sol. July 3, 1830, Hays Blackman, J.P.
Beatty, Edward to Eliza Jane Holmes, July 6, 1830. Sol. July 8, 1830, Wm. Hume, V.D.M.
Raybourn, Samuel S. to Susan P. Davis, July 10, 1830. Sol. July 11, 1830, Wm. Hume, V.D.M.
Anderson, Wm. to Elizabeth Childs, July 12, 1830. Sol. July 19, 1830, Absolom Gleaves, J.P.

Hicks, Edward D. to Nancy W. Davis, July 14, 1830. Sol. July 14, 1830, Wm. Hume, V.D.M.
Love, Wm. to Sarah Walker, July 20, 1830. Sol. July 29, 1830, J. Pirtle, J.P.

Page 385
Thompson, John to Elizabeth N. Buchanan, July 24, 1830. Sol. July 25, 1830, G. Baker, M.G.
Stewart, Jno. Gurnett S. to Elizabeth Dungey, July 24, 1830. Sol. July 24, 1830.
Kinney, Oria A. to Mary A. Fall, July 28, 1830, Sol. July 28, 1830, Wm. Hume, V.D.M.
Willis, Jno. to Julia Hawkins, July 28, 1830. Sol. July 28, 1830, J. Whitside.
Brown, Rich'd K. to Sarah Ann Hurt, Aug. 5, 1830. Sol. Aug. 5, 1830, Will Lytle, J.P.
Williams, Wm. A. to Catherine P. Turner, Aug. 7, 1830. Sol. Aug. 10, 1830, S. Shannon, J.P.
Porter, Solomon to Hannah Finley, Aug. 19, 1830. Sol. Aug. 19, 1830, Jas. Givin, M.G.
Graham, Jno. to Elizabeth Brown, Aug. 23, 1830. Sol. Aug. 24, 1830, Will Lytle, J.P.
Dashields, Jno. to Barbara Graham, Aug. 25, 1830. Sol. Aug. 25, 1830, Will Lytle, J.P.
McCormack, Berry to Lucy H. Wanen, Aug. 25, 1830. Sol. Aug. 25, 1830, A. L. Green, M.G.

Page 386
Lea, Wm. to Lucinda How, Aug. 26, 1830.
Hutton, Wm. B. to Martha Dillahunt, Aug. 30, 1830. Sol. Aug. 31, 1830, Jno. C. Hicks, M.G.
Gee, Jno. P. to Ann C. Baker, Aug. 31, 1830. Sol. Aug. 31, 1830, S. Shephard.
Mitchell, Benjamin to Lucretia Craig, Sep. 4, 1830. Sol. Sept. 5, 1830, N. B. Pryor, J.P.
Pike, Josiah to Paralee Venable, Sep. 7, 1830. Sol. Sep. 8, 1830, E. P. Connell, J.P.
Smith, Elijah to Lurena Mullen, Sep. 8, 1830. Sol. Sep. 8, 1830, E. S. Hall, J.P.
Vandervoort, Peter, Jr. to Mary Biddle, Sep. 10, 1830. Sol. Sept. 14, 1830, Geo. Weller, M.G.
Chesser, James to Catherine Best, Sep. 15, 1830.
Malloch, Benjamin to Hilley Bell, Sep. 14, 1830. Sol. Sep. 16, 1830, H. White, J.P.
Allen, Jones W. to Almyra McKay, Sep. 20, 1830. Sol. Sep. 23, 1830, Will Lytle, J.P.

Page 387
Wharton, Joseph P. to Caroline C. Hewitt, Sep. 21, 1830. Sol. Sep. 21, 1830, Wm. Hume, V.D.M.
Posey, Thos. to Sarah Gulliford, Sep. 28, 1830. Sol. Oct. 19, 1830, Reubin Payne, J.P.
Jones, Jno. to Fanny Cullum, Sep. 29, 1830. Sol. Oct. 6, 1830, J. M. Lovell, J.P.

Martin, Geo. W. to Lucinda O. R. Donelson, Sep. 29, 1830. Sol. Sep. 30, 1830, Jas. Givin, M.G.
Gross, Michael S. to Adie Connell, Sep. 29, 1830. Sol. Sep. 30, 1830, Will Lytle, J.P.
Hall, Theodorich to Bridgett Cliford, Sep. 30, 1830. Sol. Sep. 30, 1830, Will Lytle, J.P.
Wilson, Joseph to Martha Johnson, Oct. 2, 1830. Sol. Oct. 10, 1830, S. Shannon, J.P.
Homes, Jno. to Lucy Ann Philips, Oct. 4, 1830.
Stewart, Wm. to Drusilla Johnson, Oct. 11, 1830. Sol. Oct. 19, 1830, Absolom Gleaves.
Logan, Jno. to Minerva Clark, Oct. 13, 1830. Sol. Oct. 14, 1830, Will Lytle, J.P.

Page 388
Oliver, Jno. C. to Cynthia Lawrence, Oct. 14, 1830.
Williams, Wm. H. to Minerva Wilborn, Oct. 20, 1830. Sol. Oct. 21, 1830, Wm. H. White, J.P.
Holcoum, Wm. to Lucinda Singleton, Oct. 23, 1830. Sol. Oct. 24, 1830, James Givin, M.G.
Evans, Jno. to Zane E. Demoss, Oct. 25, 1830. Sol. Oct. 25, 1830, Levin Edney, M.G.
Deshazo, Rich'd to Jane Lakin, Oct. 25, 1830. Sol. Oct. 25, 1830, Wm. L. Willis, J.P.
Neal, Ralph to Sarah Hartman, Oct. 25, 1830.
Lee, Jesse A. to Jarmett Edmonds, Oct. 26, 1830.
McIlwain, Wm. to Charlotte Greer, Oct. 28, 1830. Sol. Nov. 4, 1830, Thos. Ferebee.
Binkley, Henry to Mary Bernet, Nov. 1, 1830.
Baldwin, Henry, Jr. to Mary F. Dickson, Nov. 1, 1830. Sol. Nov. 2, 1830, Geo. Weller, M.G.

Page 389
Diffee, Wm. to Lucy White, Nov. 1, 1830. Sol. Nov. 3, 1830, Will Lytle, J.P.
Tucker, Jno. E. to Sarah Hughes, Nov. 4, 1830.
Shewell, Thos. to Augusta Anderson, Nov. 6, 1830. Sol. Nov. 6, 1830, Philip Lindsley.
Merryman, Jno. A. to Mary Ann Galliher, Nov. 8, 1830. Sol. Nov. 8, 1830, Wm. L. Willis, J.P.
Cunningham, Enoch to Isabella Tinnin, Nov. 8, 1830. Sol. Nov. 11, 1830, E. P. Connell, J.P.
Simpson, Jno. S. to Eugenia C. Saunders, Nov. 9, 1830. Sol. Nov. 10, 1830, Geo. Waller, M.G.
Marshall, Josiah to Minerva E. Ezell, Nov. 11, 1830. Sol. Nov. 12, 1830, Will Lytle, J.P.
Hill, Marcus R. to Ann Elizabeth Tucker, Nov. 18, 1830.
Maxwell, Jno. to Mary Leek, Nov. 19, 1830. Sol. Nov. 25, 1830, Wm. H. Nance, J.P.
Felts, Milos Cary to Amelia Burnett, Nov. 19, 1830.

Page 390
Vardin, Andrew to Sally Spence, Nov. 23, 1830. Sol. Dec. 7, 1830, Jno. Davis.

Stratton, Henry M. to Hannah A. Snow, Nov. 24, 1830. Sol. Nov. 24, 1830, F. E. Pitts.
Christie, Itia to Elizabeth Lee, Nov. 27, 1830. Sol. Dec. 2, 1830, Thos. Scott, J.P.
Lee, Joel to Catherine Parrish, Dec. 1, 1830.
Vaught, Elias to Susan Williams, Dec. 2, 1830.
Campbell, Josiah E. to Dorinda T. Howlett, Dec. 2, 1830. Sol. Dec. 2, 1830, Th. Edmiston, J.P.
Woods, Eli L. to Rachel Myers, Dec. 3, 1830. Sol. Dec. 5, 1830, Wm. Hume, V.D.M.
Dorris, Anderson to Elizabeth Homes, Dec. 6, 1830. Sol. Dec. 7, 1830, Will Lytle, J.P.
Matthews, James G. to Mary Ann Chilnell, Dec. 6, 1830.
White, Henry to Rebecca Ford, Dec. 8, 1830. Sol. Dec. 8, 1830, N.B. Pryor, J.P.

Page 391
Taylor, Isaac to Izzy Creighton, Dec. 8, 1830. Sol. Dec. 8, 1830, Jas. Whitsitt.
Marshall, Jno. C. to Eliza Jane Cloyd, Dec. 8, 1830. Sol. Dec. 8, 1830, Jno. Board, M.G.
Watts, Hance H. to Frances Norman, Dec. 9, 1830.
Mallory, Philip to Martha F. Nance, Dec. 9, 1830. Sol. Dec. 9, 1830, A.L.P. Green, M.G.
Edney, Jesse Lee to Cynthia Stewart, Dec. 11, 1830. Sol. Dec. 12, 1830, Thos. Scott, J.P.
Williams, Willie to Louisa Johnson, Dec. 13, 1830. Sol. Dec. 16, 1830, B. Gray, J.P.
Davis, John to Emily Gower, Dec. 13, 1830.
Goss, Jno. D. to Elizabeth Buie, Dec. 13, 1830. Sol. Dec. 14, 1830, Abner McDowell.
Goodrich, Edmund W. to Lucy Ann Goodrich, Dec. 14, 1830. Sol. Dec. 15, 1830, J. Keeling, J.P.
Manley, Jno. to Sarah Satterfield, Dec. 15, 1830. Sol. Dec. 16, 1830, J. Wharton.

Page 392
Mathis, James D. to Sarah Jane Allen, Dec. 15, 1830. Sol. Dec. 16, 1830, L. Keeling, J.P.
Leath, Wm. to Mary Laughlin, Dec. 15, 1830. Sol. Dec. 23, 1830, Hays Blackman, J.P.
Wheeler, Stephen to Martha E. Allen, Dec. 15, 1830.
Masefield, Henry to Mary Oliver, Dec. 17, 1830.
Wheeler, James to Emily Morris, Dec. 18, 1830. Sol. Dec. 24, 1830, S. Shannon, J.P.
Pickard, Geo. W. to Nancy Bryant, Dec. 18, 1830. Sol. Dec. 18, 1830, Levin Edney, M.G.
Bryant, Jno. M. to Jane Moss, Dec. 18, 1830. Sol. Dec. 18, 1830, Levin Edney, M.G.
Howard, James to Martha Cheatham, Dec. 20, 1830. Sol. Dec. 21, 1830, Wm. Hume, V.D.M.
Jackson, Jno. T. to Hannah Stubblefield, Dec. 21, 1830.
Allen, Jno. to Parthene Estis, Dec. 21, 1830. Sol. Dec. 21, 1830, Wm. L. Willis, J.P.

Page 393
Jenkins, Robt. to Susan Graves, Dec. 23, 1830. Sol. Dec. 23, 1830, Wm. H. White.
Wilson, Oliver H. to Sarah Green, Dec. 23, 1830. Sol. Dec. 23, 1830, P. S. Hall.
Brown, Alfred S. to Jennett Tarpley, Dec. 26, 1830. Sol. Dec. 26, 1830, A.L.P. Green, M.G.
Tucket, Jno. W. to Jane Mitchell, Dec. 27, 1830. Sol. Dec. 27, 1830, Wm. L. Willis, J.P.
Compton, Jno. to Sarah Butterworth, Dec. 27, 1830. Sol. Jan. 11, 1831, Reuben Payne, J.P.
Biggs, Alex'd to Sarah Dean, Dec. 30, 1830.
Dowdy, Wm. W. to Bannistine E. Herron, Jan. 1, 1831.
Gorman, Wm. E. to Emily Allen, Jan. 2, 1831. Sol. Jan. 2, 1831, N. B. Pryor.
Haynes, Aaron to Sarah G. M. Barry, Jan. 5, 1831. Sol. Jan. 6, 1831, Wm. Lytle, J.P.
Gilman, Jas. S. to Elizabeth Earhart, Jan. 6, 1831. Sol. Jan. 6, 1831, Jas. Givin, M.G.

Page 394
Washington, Thomas to Mary Osborn, Jan. 11, 1831. Sol. Jan. 11, 1831, Geo. Weller, M.G.
Shute, Lee to Margaret Dunn, Jan. 12, 1831. Sol. Jan. 12, 1831, Wm. Hume, V.D.M.
Morris, Josiah H. to Sarah Mitchell, Jan. 12, 1831. Sol. Jan. 13, 1831, J. Pirtle, J.P.
Bass, Jno. to Temperance Ann Sumner, Jan. 13, 1831. Sol. Jan. 13, 1831, Wm. Hume, V.D.M.
Ellis, Wm. F. to Adeline Moore, Jan. 17, 1831
Cartwright, David to Jane Cunningham, Jan. 18, 1831.
Williams, Lemuel to Sarah Holmes, Jan. 18, 1831.
Luter, Elisha to Cynthia Woodward, Jan. 19, 1831. Sol. Feb. 20, 1831, S. Shannon.
Pegram, Wm. to Agnis Mays, Jan. 19, 1831. Jno. C. Hicks.
Hunt, Tilman S. to Nancy Bailey, Jan. 19, 1831

Page 395
James, Thos. H. to Anne Bowen, Jan. 20, 1831. Sol. Jan. 20, 1831, Jas. Givin, M.G.
Updegraff, Joseph to Fanny Haney, Jan. 26, 1831.
Shields, Wm. to Maria Clay, Jan. 27, 1831. Sol. Jan. 27, 1831, P. S. Fall.
Fairfax, Jas. B. to Ann Tennessee Noles, Jan. 28, 1831. Sol. Jan. 28, 1831, N. B. Pryor, J.P.
Tarkington, Burrell W. to Maria W. Charter, Feb. 1, 1831. Sol. Feb. 1, 1831, Levin Edney, M.G.
Morgan, John to Martha Smith, Feb. 2, 1831.
Thompson, Samuel M. to Cynthia McCrory, Feb. 8, 1831. Sol. Feb. 17, 1831, Wm. Herrin.
Smith, Richard to Hannah Brim, Feb. 16, 1831. Sol. Feb. 16, 1831, Jas. Givin, M.G.
Still, Wm. H. to Elizabeth Mars, Feb. 22, 1831. Sol. Feb. 23, 1831, Jno. M. Holland.

Curd, Price to Martha Gleaves, Feb. 23, 1831. Sol. March 17, 1831, Peter Fuqua, M.G.

Page 396
Callender, Thomas to Mary Sangster, Feb. 23, 1831. Sol. Feb. 24, 1831, Wm. Hume, V.D.M.
Menees, Jno. E. to Mary Ham, March 1, 1831. Sol. March 1, 1831, Jas. Whitsitt.
Mays, Joseph to Eliza Barum,March 1, 1831. Sol. March 1, 1831, Levin Edney, M.G.
Carper, McCoy to Susan Foster, March 2, 1831.
Simmons, James to Phoebe Grimes, March 2, 1831.
Sneed, Wm. T. to Elizabeth G. Critchlow, March 7, 1831.
Griffin, Dawson to Elizabeth Logan, March 8, 1831. Sol. March 10, 1831, Will Lytle, J.P.
Patton, James to Sally Tenneson, March 11, 1831.
Ayers, Baker to Margaret Sumners, March 12, 1831. Sol. March 13, 1831, H. White.
Neely, Jacob to Penelope Sandy, March 16, 1831. Sol. March 17, 1831, Wm. H. White.

Page 397
Saffarans, David to Elizabeth Wills, March 16, 1831. Sol. March 17, 1831, F. E. Pitts, M.G.
Collins, Thomas to Louise Harris, March 19, 1831.
Butler, Levi D. to Nancy Ellis, March 19, 1831. Sol. April 1, 1831, Jno. Hall, J.P.
Pilkington, Wm. B. to Martha Mitchell, March 23, 1831. Sol. March 24, 1831, Wm. H. White.
Shivers, Noah to Emeline Shafer, March 23, 1831. Sol. March 24, 1831, Abner McDowell.
Abbey, Rich'd to Mary Ann Compton, March 24, 1831. Sol. March 24, 1831, Wm. Hume, V.D.M.
Cartwright, Jefferson to Margaret Payne, March 24, 1831. Sol. March 24, 1831, Jas. Givin, M.G.
Dobbs, Jno. R. to Eliza Menees, March 29, 1831.
Bell, Robt. J. to Zyranna Brown, April 4, 1831. Sol. April 7, 1831, Hays Blackman, J.P.
Binkley, Peter to Tabitha Morris, April 2, 1831.

Page 398
Moore, Thomas to Frances Marlin, April 5, 1831. Sol. April 7,1831, Wm. L. Willis, J.P.
Green, Thos. C. to Mary Ann Peel, April 9, 1831.
Wise, James to Frances Fisher, April 11, 1831. Sol. April 12, 1831, A.L.P. Green, M.G.
Everett, Thomas to Elizabeth Bennett, April 22, 1831. Sol. April 24, 1831, R. Hewitt, J.P.
Baker, Ebijah to Rebecca Holloway, April 23, 1831.
Winfrey, Thos. A. to Panthea Elmore, April 22, 1831. Sol. April 22, 1831, Wm. Hume, V.D.M.
Sutton, Thos. to Saludia Burns, May 4, 1831.
Stephens, Lovey to Elizabeth Jackson, May 4, 1831.

Williams, David to Priscilla Shelby, May 5, 1831. Sol. May 5, 1831, Geo. Weller, M.G.
Elam, Edward to Catherine Binkley, May 4, 1831. Sol. May 5, 1831, G. W. Charlton, J.P.

Page 399
Denton, James to Rhoda Spence, May 7, 1831. Sol. May 10, 1831, Jno. Berry, J.P.
Wallace, Benj. R. B. to Tabitha W. Bradshaw, May 9, 1831.
Flinn, Jno. to Mary Witcher, May 13, 1831. Sol. May 13, 1831, Wm. L. Wills, J.P.
Rogers, Wm. to Elizabeth Bouton, May 17, 1831. Sol. May 19, 1831, Pinckney C. Posey, M.G.
Thomas, Jefferson to Jane Roden, May 17, 1831. Sol. May 17, 1831, Will Lytle, J.P.
Shelton, Robt. W. to Matilda M. Mann, May 23, 1831.
Reese,David to Sarah Burnett, May 22, 1831. Sol. May 23, 1831, Wm. Herrin.
Sutton, Thos. to Candois Alexander, May 26, 1831. Sol. Nov. 9, 1831, Jno. C. Hicks, M.G.
Key, Martin J. H. to Elizabeth Shumate, May 26, 1831.
Grayson, Henry to Sally Harrison, May 30, 1831.

Page 400
Stewart, Wm. to Mary Allen, May 31, 1831.
Puckett, Jones to Nancy Frensley, June 1, 1831. Sol. June 1, 1831, Jno. Stump, J.P.
Bledsoe, Moses to Isabella McCauley, June 9, 1831. Sol. June 9, 1831, S. Shannon, J.P.
Blake, Daniel to Emma P. Rutledge, June 9, 1831. Sol. June 9, 1831, Geo. Weller, M.G.
Owen, Rich'd C. to Harriet F. Reeves, July 9, 1831.
Estes, Robt. P. to Eliza Cartwright, June 16, 1831. Sol. June 16, 1831, Wm. Hume, V.D.M.
Dunneway, Sam. P. to Sarah Pope, June 18, 1831. Sol. June 19, 1831, G. G. Washington, J.P.
Boaz, Joshua to Mary Whites, June 18, 1831. Sol. June 27, 1831, Benejah Gray, J.P.
Warmach, Wm. to Racel Baker, June 20, 1831. Sol. June 21, 1831, J. Pirtle, J.P.
Horton, Robinson to America Ridley, June 25, 1831. Sol. July 3, 1831, James Whitsitt.

Page 401
Corbitt, Wm. A. to Lucinda Elverby, June 25, 1831. Sol. June 26, 1831, G. G. Washington, J.P.
Smith, Willie to Mary Stringfellow, July 4, 1831. Sol. July 10, 1831, Reuben Chandoin, D.D.
Murrey, Joshua to Nancy M. Vick, July 6, 1831.
Quimby, Caswell K. to Classie Hopper, July 7, 1831. Sol. July 7, 1831, G. G. Washington, J.P.
Wood, Johnson to Mary Questenberry, July 7, 1831. Sol. July 14, 1831, G. G. Washington, J.P.

Hinton, Harrison B. to Rachel T. Turner, July 14, 1831. Sol. July 15, 1831, Will Lytle, J.P.
Jackson, Washington to Emily Gilliam, July 16, 1831. Sol. July 16, 1831, Levin Edney, M.G.
Miles, Hardy D. to Caroline Lovell, July 18, 1831. Sol. July 27, 1831, B. Lee, J.P.
Owen, Wm. to Elizabeth Owen, July 19, 1831. Sol. July 21, 1831, Th. Edmiston, J.P.
Scott, Robt. to Margaret Spiece, July 22, 1831.

Page 402
Greer, Isaac to Peggy Richardson, July 23, 1831. Sol. July 23, 1831, Wm. Herrin.
Cox, Bray G. to Elizabeth Marshall, July 29, 1831. Sol. July 29, 1831, Abner McDowell.
Hail, Thos. J. to Eveline Ambrose, Aug. 1, 1831. Sol. Aug. 2, 1831, James Givin, M.G.
Cassedy, Alexander A. to Emeline Cantrell, __________.
Austin, Geo. W. to Nancy R. Boaz, Aug. 5, 1831.
Stubblefield, Wm. to Melissa Martin, Aug. 6, 1831. Sol. Aug. 7, 1831, Will Lytle, J.P.
Barclay, Shadrack to Lucinda Allen, Aug. 6, 1831. Sol. Aug. 6, 1831, Will Lytle, J.P.
Dermote, Joseph W. to Parthena Ellis, Aug. 9, 1831. Sol. Aug. 14, 1831, G.W. Charlton, J.P.
Hite, Henry to Ann Brannon, Aug. 10, 1831. Sol. Aug. 11, 1831, Thos. Ferebee.
Colquitt, Wm. L. to Lucy E. Thompson, Aug. 11, 1831. Sol. Aug. 11, 1831, Jno. M. Holland, M.G.

Page 403
Hart, Micajah to Mary Ann Reynolds, Aug. 11, 1831. Sol. Aug. 11, 1831, Jas. Givin, M.G.
Reynolds, Wm. to Jane Clemmons, Aug. 11, 1831. Sol. Aug. 11, 1831, Jas. Givin, M.G.
Galloway, Samuel to Catherine Haynes, Aug. 12, 1831.
White, Wm. F. to Catherine L. White, Aug. 13, 1831. Sol. Aug. 19, 1831, Geo. Weller, M.G.
Beazley, Laban to Sidney Campbell, Aug. 13, 1831. Sol. Aug. 13, 1831, S. Shannon, J.P.
Armstrong, Jno. to Matilda Brown, Aug. 19, 1831.
Cox, Melvin G. to Elizabeth Ann Bumpass, Aug. 29, 1831.
Mayfield, Isaac to Elizabeth Patterson, Aug. 20, 1831. Sol. Aug. 21, 1831, W. Russell, J.P.
Allison, Alexander to Mary Pritchett, Aug. 22, 1831. Sol. Aug. 22, 1831, Levin Edney, M.G.
Hester, David to Mary Bowen, Aug. 25, 1831. Sol. Aug. 26, 1831, Jas. Givin, M.G.

Page 404
Green, James H. to Mary D. Menefee, Aug. 26, 1831. Sol. Sep. 1, 1831, Abner McDowell.
Dunlap, James to Mary Loftin, Aug. 26, 1831. Sol. Aug. 28, 1831, Wm. Herrin.

Burton, Thos. to Mary Ann Midlin, Aug.27, 1831. Sol. Aug. 28, 1831, Abner McDowell.
Everitt, Kincheon to Elizabeth Work, Aug. 29, 1831.
Page, Jefferson to Louisa Quisenberry, Aug. 30, 1831. Sol. Aug. 30, 1831, Abner McDowell.
Perry, Thomas to Malinda Binkley, Aug. 31, 1831. Sol. Aug. 31, 1831, Peter Fuqua, M.G.
Hall, Robt. B. to Mary M. Musgrove, Sep. 1, 1831.
Deckard, Wm. to Eliza Carlisle, Sep. 2, 1831. Sol. Sep. 2, 1831, Will Lytle, J.P.
Gambill, Wm. H. B. to Mary H. Gray, Sep. 2, 1831.
Duncan, Robt. P. to Lucy Aydelette, Sep. 2, 1831. Sol. Sep. 6, 1831, Thos. Scott, J.P.

Page 405
Carper, Thos. to Polly Wolf, Sep. 8, 1831.
Williamson, Jno. L. to Jane Williamson, Sep. 6, 1831. Sol. Sep. 8, 1831, Ezekial Cloyd.
Martin, Wm. to Nancy Brown, Sep. 7, 1831. Sol. Sep. 7, 1831, Will Lytle, J.P.
Williamson, Robt. T. to Harriet Williamson, Sep. 10, 1831. Sol. Sep. 11, 1831, E. P. Connell, J.P.
Shall, Ephriam P. to Ann B. Spence, Sep. 15, 1831. Sol. Sep. 15, 1831, Wm. Hume, V.D.M.
Porch, Henry to Delilah Dillahunt, Sep. 20, 1831. Sol. Sep. 20, 1831, Levin Edney, M.G.
Armour, Wm. to Elizabeth Carter, Sep. 23, 1831. Sol. Oct. 12, 1831, Reubin Chandoin, D.D.
Richardson, Alfred to Phoebe Bryant, Sep. 24, 1831.
Glasgow, Geo. W. to Elizabeth Shelhorn, Sep. 26, 1831. Sol. Sep. 29, 1831, J. Pirtle, J.P.

Page 406
Claird, Wm. to Martha Dodson, Sep. 28, 1831.
Cain, Robt. B. to Mary L. Lawrence, Sep. 29, 1831. Sol. Sep. 29, 1831, Wm. Hume, V.D.M.
Pugh, Henry H. to Sarah Lyle, Sep. 29, 1831. Sol. Sep. 29, 1831, Jno. M. Holland, M.G.
Thompson, Jas. M. to Polly A. Clark, Oct. 1, 1831. Sol. Oct. 27, 1831, Wm. Harrin.
Dean, Jas. to Jane Moore, Oct. 4, 1831. Sol. Oct. 4, 1831, Will Lytle, J.P.
Mullin, Thos. to Dovey Connelley, Oct. 9, 1831. Sol. Oct. 20, 1831, Th. Edmiston, J.P.
Green, Alex'd L. P. to Mary A. E. Elliston, Oct. 19, 1831. Sol. Oct. 19, 1831, Jno. M. Holland, M.G.
Alley, Joseph to Fanny Jones, Oct. 20, 1831. Sol. Oct. 20, 1831, Will Lytle, J.P.
Baker, Wm. D. to Mary Fuqua, Oct. 22, 1831. Sol. Nov. 3, 1831, Jno. Hall, J.P.
Alston, James to Jane Johnston, Oct. 25, 1831. Sol. Oct. 25, 1831, Wm. Hume, V.D.M.

Page 407
Wilson, Jno. H. to Lucy Ann Smith, Oct. 26, 1831. Sol. Oct. 27, 1831, Thos. Scott, J.P.
Rayworth, Egbert A. to Leodocia J. Boyd, Oct. 26, 1831. Sol. Nov. 2, 1831, Wm. Hume, V.D.M.
Ivey, Isaac to Nancy Spence, Oct. 28, 1831. Sol. Oct. 28, 1831, Levin Edney, M.G.
Cook, Chas. to Mary Owen, Oct. 31, 1831.
Campbell, Jas. G. to Jane A. Phenix, Oct. 31, 1831.
Ramer, Geo., Sr. to Mary Moses, Nov. 1, 1831. Sol. Nov. 2, 1831, J. Sims, J.P.
Wilson, Wm. T. to Elizabeth Underwood, Nov. 1, 1831.
Hall, Henry to Martha Belsher, Nov. 2, 1831.
Duke, Nimrod W. to Susan Waggoner, Nov. 3, 1831. Sol. Nov. 3, 1831, S. Shannon.
Neely, Samuel to Martha Sander, Nov. 3, 1831. Sol. Nov. 11, 1831, Wm. H. White

Page 408
Spencer, Henry to Zerilla Ballentine, Nov. 5, 1831. Sol. Nov. 24, 1831, Geo. W. Martin.
Blain, Lindsey to Elizabeth Petty, Nov. 7, 1831. Sol. Nov. 8, 1831, Thos. Scott, J.P.
Prim, Lorenzo D. to Mary E. Currin, Nov. 9, 1831.
Donelson, John to Prudence Gower, Nov. 10, 1831.
Williams, Elisha to Sarah H. Ridley, Nov. 10, 1831. Sol. Nov. 10, 1831, R. C. Foster.
Brown, John to Polly Dillingham, Nov. 14, 1831. Sol. Nov. 17, 1831, Thos. Scott, J.P.
Mandley, David to Sally Collins, Nov. 14, 1831. Sol. Nov. 18, 1831, Will Lytle, J.P.
Green, Thos. to Sarah Cobler, Nov. 16, 1831. Sol. Nov. 17, 1831, James Whitsitt.
Pennington, Jno. W. to Elizabeth P. Dodson, Nov. 16, 1831. Sol. Nov. 18, 1831, Wm. H. White.
Shearon, Thos. W. to Lettetia H. Bewer, Nov. 17, 1831. Sol. Nov. 17, 1831, James Givin, M.G.

Page 409
Whittemore, Fountain to Lucretia Stephenson, Nov. 19, 1831.
Rutledge, Henry A. to Caroline Nicholson, Nov. 23, 1831. Sol. Nov. 24, 1831, Geo. Weller, M.G.
Smith, Jno. B. to Louisa J. Scruggs, Nov. 23, 1831. Sol. Nov. 23, 1831, Jno. M. Holland, M.G.
Page, Jesse W. to Arabella Folwell, Nov. 23, 1831. Sol. Nov. 23, 1831, Wm. Hume, V.D.M.
Greer, Green B. to Lucinda Robertson, Nov. 29, 1831. Sol. Dec. 19, 1831, W. E. Watkins.
Woodson, Wm. to Tennessee Lowe, Dec. 3, 1831. Sol. Dec. 8, 1831, Wm. Hume, V.D.M.
Coggins, Robt. C. to Nancy S. Jones, Dec. 3, 1831. Sol. Dec. 8, 1831, J. Browning, J.P.
Moore, Alfred to Mary C. S. Cox, Dec. 6, 1831.

Pegram, Roger to Caroline Williams, Dec. 7, 1831. Sol. Dec. 7, 1831, Jno. C. Hicks, M.G.
McLean, Chas. D. to Jane E. Smith, Dec. 8, 1831.

Page 410
Fields, Fielding to Mary P. Allen, Dec. 10, 1831. Sol. Dec. 10, 1831, Jas. Givins, M.G.
Anderson, Wm. to Elizabeth Barton, Dec. 13, 1831. Sol. Dec. 20, 1831, Thos. Scott, J.P.
Cook, Bennett to Sarah M. W. Daniel, Dec. 14, 1831. Sol. Dec. 18, 1831, Thos. Ferebee.
Cabler, Edwin S. to Rebecca M. Leach, Dec. 15, 1831. Sol. Dec. 15, 1831, A. L. P. Green.
Wright, James W. to Marianne Clement, Dec. 15, 1831. Sol. Dec. 15, 1831, Jas. Whitsitt.
Neely, Geo. W. to Harriet White, Dec. 20, 1831. Sol. Dec. 21, 1831, James Givin, M.G.
Thrift, Branch O. to Margaret Hagey, Dec. 21, 1831. Sol. Dec. 22, 1831, James Givin, M.G.
Thomas, Henry S. to Eveline Reeves, Dec. 24, 1831.
Pilcher, Merritt S. to Nancy Barron, Dec. 26, 1831. Sol. Dec. 26, 1831, Wm. Hume, V.D.M.
Gee, Joshua I. to Elizabeth A.C. Williamson, Jan. 2, 1832. Sol. Jan. 3, 1832, Wm. H. White.

Page 411
Wright, Jno. A. to Julia A. Bibb, Jan. 7, 1832. Sol. Jan. 7, 1832, Will Lytle, J.P.
Johnson, Esquire to Patsy Earhart, Jan. 13, 1832. Sol. Jan. 17, 1832, Levin Edney, M.G.
Gower, Wm. T. to Lucy Knight, Jan. 18, 1832. Sol. Jan. 19, 1832, Thoas. Ferebee.
Shute, Philip C. to Hannah P. DeMoss, Jan. 18, 1832. Sol. Jan. 19, 1832, Wm. Hume, V.D.M.
Whiteside, Henry to Zippora Skillem, Jan. 19, 1832. Sol. Jan. 19, 1832, James Whitsitt.
Connell, Giles to Kitty Tennin, Jan. 21, 1832. Sol. Jan. 26, 1832, J. Pirtle, J.P.
Matterson, Joel to Polly Hollingsworth, Jan. 23, 1832. Sol. Jan. 26, 1832, H. White.
Erwin, Jas. to Frances A. Jefferson, Jan. 24, 1832. Sol. Jan. 24, 1832, Martin Clark, M.G.

Page 412
Hainson, Thos. T. to Rebecca Allen, Jan. 25, 1832. Sol. Jan. 25, 1832, Wm. Saunders, J.P.
Ward, Wm. B. to Sarah P. Wells, Jan. 25, 1832. Sol. Jan. 25, 1832, Geo. Weller.
Capps, Caleb to Tabitha Fowler, Jan. 25, 1832.
Buchanan, Wm. M. to Susan Everett, Jan. 26, 1832. Sol. Jan. 26, 1832, Jas. Whitsitt.
Ewing, Orville to Milbrey H. Williams, Jan. 26, 1832. Sol. Jan. 26, 1832, Wm. Hume, V.D.M.
Watkins, Geo. P. to Melinda Walker, Jan. 30, 1832.

Thomas, Wm. H. to Jane Bailey, Jan. 31, 1832. Sol. Jan. 31, 1832, J. B. McFerrin, M.G.
Keys, Rich'd to Katy Kendall, Feb. 1, 1832.
Owen, Frederick, Sr. to Susannah Moore, Feb. 4, 1832.
McCollum, Jno. D. to Zillah W. Smith, Feb. 6, 1832. Sol. Feb. 7, 1832, Hays Blackman, J.P.

Page 413
Cox, Benjamin to Irean Watkins, Feb. 6, 1832. Sol. Feb. 9, 1832, W. E. Watkins.
Kimbro, Samuel to Elizabeth V. Nance, Feb. 11, 1832. Sol. Feb. 22, 1832, Jas. Whitsitt.
Tucker, Joel C. to Winnefred Owen, Feb. 13, 1832. Sol. Feb. 13, 1832, L. D. Overall.
Spear, Jesse L. to Jane R. Williams, Feb. 15, 1832. Sol. Feb. 15, 1832, Jno. C. Hicks, M.G.
Hazelings, Wm. to Eliza Rankins, Feb. 15, 1832.
Neely, Joshua to Priscy Ann Estis, Feb. 15, 1832. Sol. Feb. 16, 1832, H. White.
Ewing, Wm. L. to Nancy R. Thompson, Feb. 15, 1832. Sol. Feb. 16, 1832, J.G.H. Speer, M.G.
Ellis, Jesse to Sally Hager, Feb. 16, 1832. Sol. Feb. 22, 1832, Jno. Hall, J.P.
Harness, Jno. to Fanny Waller, Feb. 18, 1832. Sol. Feb. 23, 1832, Wm. H. White.
Walker, Wm. to Milley Bess, Feb. 22, 1832.

Page 414
Smith, Geo. W. to Susan Sneed, Feb. 23, 1832. Sol. Feb. 23, 1832, Wm. Hume, V.D.M.
Hill, Daniel B. to Margaret J. Stout, Feb. 23, 1832. Sol. Feb. 23, 1832, Wm. Hume, V.D.M.
Laseter, Timothy to Sarah Powell, Feb. 25, 1832.
Harris, James to Elizabeth McNeill, Feb. 25, 1832. Sol. March 4, 1832, J. Browning, J.P.
Etherage, John to Mary Ann Jane Dennis, Feb. 29, 1832. Sol. March 4, 1832, J.M. Lovell, J.P.
McCall, Wm. to Eliza Ann Haile, Feb. 29, 1832. Sol. Feb. 29, 1832, J.B. McFerrin, M.G.
Gravis, Thos. F. to Martha Roberts, Feb. 29, 1832. Sol. Feb. 29, 1832, Will Lytle, J.P.
Smith, Rich'd to Martha Bell, March 1, 1832.
Harlow, Levi to Martha Hazlerig, March 1, 1832. Sol. March 5, 1832, E.S. Hall, J.P.
Hall, Allen A. to Sophia Chester, March 1, 1832. Sol. March 1, 1832, Wm. Hume, V.D.M.

Page 415
Ford, Jno. P. to Anne S. Jefferson, March 5, 1832. Sol. March 5, 1832, L.D. Overall.
Chaponel, Anthony to Mary Humerithhouse, March 6, 1832. Sol. March 7, 1832, Simpson Shephard.
Crooks, Jno. to Polly Armstrong, March 7, 1832. Sol. March 7, 1832, Will Lytle, J.P.

Tucker, Wm. to Ann C. Zachery, March 10, 1832. Sol. March 11, 1832, Will Lytle, J.P.
Age, Cader to Eliza Ann Bell, March 12, 1832. Sol. March 13, 1832, Jas. Sims, J.P.
Lytle, Jno. S. to Sarah S. Boyd, Feb. 13, 1832. Sol. March 14, 1832, Geo. Weller, M.G.
Young, Jas. to Rebecca R. Hogg, March 14, 1832. Sol. March 15, 1832, Wm. Hume, V.D.M.
Waldron, Wm. to Sarah Patton, March 15, 1832. Sol. March 15, 1832, Wm. H. Nance, J.P.
Cartwright, Jno. H. to Kitty Connell, March 17, 1832. Sol. March 17, 1832, J. Pirtle, J.P.
Jamison, Rich'd to Sarah Melvin, March 20, 1832. Sol. March 22, 1832, Absolom Gleaves, J.P.

Page 416
Comfort, Joseph W. to Nancy A. Williams, March 28, 1832. Sol. March 28, 1832, J. B.McFerrin, M.G.
Dotson, Marshall to Emily Brown, March 28, 1832.
Dabbs, Jno. R. to Eliza Menoes, March 29, 1832. Sol. March 31, 1832, Jas. Whitsitt.
Bates, Robt. to Jane Powell, April 14, 1832. Sol. April 16, 1832, E. P. Connell.
Pritchard, Wm. to Mary M. Poyzer, April 25, 1832. Sol. April 25, 1832, Wm. Hume, V.D.M.
Bang, Wm. F. to Jane R. W. Jelton, April 25, 1832. Sol. April 25, 1832, Jas. Givin, M.G.
Moore, James D. to Ann S. Keeling, April 26, 1832. Sol. April 26, 1832, J. B. McFerrin, M.G.
Dodson, Wm. T. to Elizabeth Stewart, April 30, 1832.
Troublefield, Green B. to Eliza R. Clark, May 2, 1832. Sol. May 8, 1832, Wm. Harrin.
Moore, Robert L. to Martha Clay, May 3, 1832. Sol. May 3, 1832, J. B. McFerrin, M.G.

Page 417
Smith, Benjamin D. to Harriet S. Criddle, May 3, 1832. Sol. May 3, 1832, Wm. Hume, V.D.M.
Sears, Green to Lucy Ann Woodward, May 5, 1832. Sol. May 6, 1832, Thos. Scott, J.P.
Peck, Jno. to Temperance B. Thompson, May 8, 1832. Sol. May 8, 1832, Abner McDowell.
Cooper, Washington to Mary J. H. Menefee, May 9, 1832. Sol. May 9, 1832, Jas. Whitsitt.
Shelter, Phil to Virginia A. Wharton, May 10, 1832. Sol. May 10, 1832, Wm. Hume, V.D.M.
Steele, Joseph to Elizabeth Martin, May 10, 1832. Sol. May 10, 1832, J. W. Horton, J.P.
Brown, John to Melsindy Carney, May 19, 1832.
Bumpass, Washington to Eliza Gilliam, May 19, 1832. Sol. May 20, 1832, Walter Sims, J.P.
Smith, Thos. to Courtney Boyte, May 29, 1832. Sol. June 10, 1832, B. Lee, J.P.

Green, Hiram to Susan Garet, May 30, 1832. Sol. May 31, 1832, Wm. Hume, V.D.M.

Page 418

Wright, Aaron to Margaret J. Thomas, May 31, 1832. Sol. May 31, 1832, Peter S. Gayle.

Peters, Thomas to Uracia Collins, May 31, 1832. Sol. June 2, 1832, James Givin, M.G.

Vanyck, Abraham to Elizabeth Cantrell, June 6, 1832. Sol. June 7, 1832, Wm. Hume, V.D.M.

Burge, Pennington to Julia White, June 14, 1832. Sol. June 14, 1832, Will Lytle, J.P.

Stewart, Wm. to Meranda Ichmon, June 16, 1832. Sol. June 16, 1832, Absolom Gleaves.

Gleaves, Michael H. to Mary Ann D. Gleaves, June 18, 1832. Sol. June 28, 1832, Will Lytle, J.P.

Stanfield, Green to Elizabeth Wolf, June 19, 1832.

Perkins, James M. to Susanna E. Currey, June 21, 1832. Sol. June 21, 1832, Wm. Hume, V.D.M.

Shepherd, Thomas to Ann E. Lawrence, June 21, 1832. Sol. June 21, 1832, James Givin, M.G.

Buchanan, Rich'd to Martha Murphy, June 23, 1832.

Page 419

Standley, Shadrach to Nelly Binkley, June 25, 1832.

McGraw, Jno. C. to Susannah B. Willis, June 28, 1832. Sol. June 28, 1832, Jno. B. McFerrin, M.G.

Mullin, Solomon to Christiana Shule, June 29, 1832. Sol. June 29, 1832, Wm. Hume, V.D.M.

Dotson, Thos. to Martha Jones, June 30, 1832. Sol. June 30, 1832, Levin Edney, M.G.

Thompson, Wm. H. to Jane Clow, July 8, 1832. Sol. July 8, 1832, Robt. Paine, M.G.

Conner, Cornelius to Minerva A. Eakin, July 12, 1832. Sol. July 12, 1832, Wm. Hume, V.D.M.

Burton, Wm. to Cynthia Davis, July 17, 1832.

Will, Mills to Lydia Bartlett, July 18, 1832. Sol. July 18, 1832, Will Lytle, J.P.

Turner, Jno. H. to Mary J. Parker, July 20, 1832.

Johnson, Jno. to Nancy Bainal, July 25, 1832. Sol. July 26, 1832, Abner McDowell.

Page 420

Dotson, Geo. C. to Sarah Jackson, July 25, 1832.

Ament, Henry to Mary Graham, July 25, 1832. Sol. July 26, 1832, J. B. McFerrin, M.G.

Marchant, Jordan M. to Elvira W. Lawrence, July 27, 1832. Sol. July 27, 1832, Jas. Givin, M.G.

Garrett, Geo. H. to Rebecca Duke, Aug. 5, 1832. Sol. Aug. 6, 1832, Wm. James, J.P.

Earthman, Jno. H. to Lucinda H. Earhart, Aug. 6, 1832. Sol. Aug. 9, 1832, Daniel Buie, J.P.

Sullivant, Gilbert to Lucinda Morris, Aug. 11, 1832. Sol. Aug. 15, 1832, Jno. Hall, J.P.

McGoldrick, Edward P. to Harriet D. Merryman, Aug. 14, 1832. Sol. Aug. 14, 1832, D. Long, M.G.
Shule, Andrew W. to Fanny Stewart, Aug. 21, 1832. Sol. Aug. 21, 1832, Will Lytle, J.P.
Crichlow, Branker to Adaline Bibb, Aug. 23, 1832. Sol. Aug. 23, 1832, Hays Blackman, J.P.
Bauldin, John to Elizabeth Smith, Aug. 16, 1832. Sol. Aug. 16, 1832, Will Lytle, J.P.

Page 421
Meness, Benjamin to Eliza Walker, Aug. 23, 1832. Sol. Aug. 23, 1832, Jas. Whitsitt.
Sanders, Chas. to Anne Rawlings, Aug. 28, 1832. Sol. Aug. 29, 1832, Wm. Hume, V.D.M.
Scales, Robt. H. to Elizabeth Ballard, Aug. 29, 1832.
Taylor, Bartlet to Polly Taylor, Aug. 31, 1832. Sol. Sep. 6, 1832, Jno. Davis.
Harris, Matthew to Nancy Underwood, Sep. 3, 1832.
Grainger, Jacob to Catherine Day, Sep. 6, 1832.
Phelps, Silas M., Jr. to Issabella Huggins, Sep. 10, 1832. Sol. Sep. 13, 1832, Jno. Hall, J.P.
Allen, Dixon to Louisa C. Brown, Sep. 13, 1832. Sol. Sep. 13, 1832, Wm. Hume, V.D.M.
Harmon, Rich'd to Sarah Hughes, Sep. 13, 1832. Sol. Sep. 13, 1832, Jas. Givin, M.G.
Merritt,Hansel to Mary Noel, Sep. 13, 1832. Sol. Sep. 13, 1832, Peter S. Gayle.

Page 422
Grooms, Rich'd to Sarah Harmon, Sep. 14, 1832. Sol. Sep. 14, 1832, James Givin, M.G.
Donelson, Thos. J. to Emma Y. Farquhar, Sep. 15, 1832. Sol. Sep. 17, 1832, Geo. Weller, M.G.
Wray, James to Elizabeth M. Frazier, Sep. 17, 1832. Sol. Sep. 18, 1832, Wm. H. White.
Pickard, Allen to Margaret Pinkerton, Sep. 17, 1832. Sol. Sep. 18, 1832, Levin Edney, M.G.
Porter, James to Mary Erwin, Sep. 20, 1832. Sol. Sep. 20, 1832, Ph. Lindsley.
Hickey, Calvin M. to Mary Jane Scott, Sep. 20, 1832. Sol. Sep. 20, 1832, Geo. Weller, M.G.
Green, Hansel to Susan Craddock, Sep. 20, 1832.
Bailey, James to Lucinda Brown, Sep. 21, 1832. Sol. Sep. 21, 1832, A.L.P. Green, M.G.
Baker, Jno. R.M. to Martha S. Warmoth, Sep. 22, 1832.
Lowe, Nevi (Neri?) to Elizabeth Keeling, Sep. 25, 1832. Sol. Sep. 25, 1832, L. D. Overall.

Page 423
Randolph, Jas. to Sarah Adcock, Sep. 26, 1832. Sol. Aug. 4, 1832, Daniel Bond.
Morris, Robt. to Eliza Jones, Sep. 26, 1832. Sol. Sep. 26, 1832, Levin Edney, M.G.
Barrett, Alexander to Ann Patterson, Sep. -7, 1832. Sol. Sep. 27, 1832, Wm. Hume, V.D.M.

Campbell, Geo. W. to Sally Shaw, Sep. 29, 1832. Sol. Oct. 1, 1832, S. Shannon, J.P.
Linch, Arren to Sally Johnson, Oct. 1, 1832.
Hudson, Joseph to Judith Earthman, Oct. 2, 1832.
Brewer, Jas. M. to Ann M. Austin, Oct. 3, 1832. Sol. Oct. 3, 1832, L. D. Overall.
Stennett, Geo. to Elizabeth Graham, Oct. 4, 1832.
Wilson, Geo. to Mary A. Richardson, Oct. 5, 1832. Sol. Oct. 7, 1832, Jno. Chilton, M.G.
Roach, Jesse to Eleanor Whites, Oct. 6, 1832.

Page 424
Harris, Wm. to Mary P. Shelton, Oct. 9, 1832.
Hise, Elijah to Elvira Stewart, Oct. 9, 1832. Sol. Oct. 9, 1832, James Givin, M.G.
Holman, James T. to Clementine H. Boyd, Oct. 11, 1832. Sol. Oct. 11, 1832, Wm. Hume, V.D.M.
Mosby, James C. to Elizabeth P. Gwynne, Oct. 11, 1832. Sol. Oct. 11, 1832, Alex L. P. Green, M.G.
Cissna, Wm. to Mary Bennett, Oct. 11, 1832. Sol. Oct. 11, 1832, Will Lytle, J.P.
Talley, Nelson to Sarah Raymond, Oct. 11, 1832. Sol. Nov. 1, 1832, S. Shannon, J.P.
Sullivant, Lessonby to Rosena Waggoner, Oct. 15, 1832, by G. W. Charlton, J.P.
Patterson, Wm. to Ruhama House, Oct. 16, 1832.
Adkisson, Wm. to Mary Curfman, Oct. 17, 1832.
Cayce, Joseph F. to Isabella R. White, Oct. 17, 1832. Sol. Oct. 17, 1832, Jas. Smith.

Page 425
Maxey, Powhatton W. to Julia Hobbs, Oct. 18, 1832. Sol. Oct. 18, 1832, L. D. Overall.
Casey, Martin R. to Rebecca I. Gilliam, Oct. 23, 1832.
Bingham, Thos. W. to Patsy B. Stewart, Oct. 24, 1832.
Childress, Jno. to Mary Ann Goode, Oct. 24, 1832. Sol. Oct. 24, 1832, Wm. Hume, V.D.M.
Brown, Nathaniel to Catherine Bowen, Oct. 25, 1832. Sol. Oct. 25, 1832, J. B. McFerrin, M.G.
Webster, Daniel to Jane Patrick, Nov. 1, 1832. Sol. Nov. 2, 1832, Walter King, J.P.
Stephens, Lovet to Elizabeth Jackson, Nov. 7, 1832. Sol. Nov. 7, 1832, E. Goodrich, J.P.
McKnight, Erwin to Elizabeth Brighton, Nov. 6, 1832. Sol. Nov. 8, 1832, Jas. Sims, J.P.
Sturdivant, Wm. to Canzada Cowgill, Nov. 9, 1832. Sol. Nov. 12, 1832, A. G. Conell.
Hodges, Anderson to Louisa Cochran, Nov. 9, 1832. Sol. Nov. 15, 1832, Will Lytle, J.P.

Page 426
Kimbro, Isaac N. to Ludecy Kimbro, Nov. 10, 1832.
Howard, Mimmecan H. to Rebecca Porter, Nov. 10, 1832. Sol. Nov. 11, 1832, Wm. Hume, V.D.M.

Wallace, Wm. P. to Lethe Gant, Nov. 13, 1832.
Patterson, Wm. M. to Lovahanna Hows, Nov. 13, 1832.
Ramer, Henry to Azillah McCormack, Nov. 14, 1832. Sol. Nov. 22, 1832, J. Browning, J.P.
Garrett, Greenberry to Mary A. Spear, Nov. 15, 1832. Sol. Nov. 15, 1832, A.L.P. Green, M.G.
Green, Jonathan to Dorothy Grooms, Nov. 15, 1832. Sol. Nov. 15, 1832, Will Lytle, J.P.
Hill, John H. to Mary Casey, Nov. 15, 1832. Sol. Nov. 15, 1832, John Davis.
Joiner, Wm. to Cardine Turner, Nov. 20, 1832. Sol. Nov. 21, 1832, E. P. Connell, J.P.
Steel, Edward G. to Lucy I. Rawlins, Nov. 24, 1832. Sol. Nov. 24, 1832, Wm. Hume, V.D.M.

Page 427
Rucker, Benjamin A. to Elizabeth Waller, Nov. 24, 1832. Sol. Nov. 29, 1832, D. C. McLoed, M.G.
Thompson, Wm. P. to Issabella Whitside, Nov. 24, 1832.
Carter, Samuel J. to Ann C. Vaulx, Nov. 27, 1832. Sol. Nov. 27, 1832, J. Whitsitt.
Thompson, Jno. to Martha M. Rawlings, Nov. 27, 1832. Sol. Nov. 27, 1832, Wm. Hume, V.D.M.
Murphy, Jas. to Susan Fairley, Nov. 28, 1832. Sol. Nov. 28, 1832, Will Lytle, J.P.
Whitfield, Wm. to Elizabeth Newsom, Dec. 4, 1832. Sol. Dec. 4, 1832, Levin Edney, M.G.
Gaibra, Jas. S. to Mary Shepherd, Dec. 5, 1832. Sol. Dec. 6, 1832, A.L.P. Green, M.G.
Wilson, Robt. to Matilda Thornhill, Dec. 6, 1832. Sol. Dec. 6, 1832, Wm. Hume, V.D.M.
Yarborough, Edward to Lucinda Blain, Dec. 10, 1832.
Birdwell, Samuel to Sarah E. Bashaw, Dec. 11, 1832. Sol. Dec. 12, 1832, Wm. H. White.

Page 428
Culpepper, James H. to Elizabeth Swinney, Dec. 12, 1832. Sol. Dec. 13, 1832, Jas. Whitsitt.
Dotson, Isaiah Y. to Catherine Dotson, Dec. 13, 1832.
Waggoner, Thos. J. to Nancy Stubblefield, Dec. 15, 1832.
Meadows, Henderson to Nancy Stearman, Dec. 15, 1832. Sol. Jan. 22, 1833, W. E. Watkins.
Buffington, John to Martha Foster, Dec. 18, 1832. Sol. Dec. 18, 1832, Will Lytle, J.P.
Lay, Thomas to Helena Williams, Dec. 19, 1832. Sol. Dec. 28, 1832, Will Lytle, J.P.
Gray, Mason I. to Mary W. Cox, Dec. 19, 1832.
Gee, Norvell P. to Martha Wilson, Dec. 20, 1832. Sol. Dec. 20, 1832, Wm. H. White.
Bryant, Wm. to Nancy Sturdivant, Dec. 20, 1832.
Parrish, Absolom to Susan Tilford, Dec. 20, 1832. Sol. Dec. 21, 1832, A.L.P. Green, M.G.

Page 429
Ewing, Edwin, H. to Rebecca P. Williams, Dec. 20, 1832. Sol. Dec. 20, 1832, Wm. Hume, V.D.M.
Hughs, Claiborne W. to Sarah Knight, Dec. 21, 1832.
Steerman, Geo. W. to Elizabeth Allen, Dec. 24, 1832.
Newsom, Wm. to Levinia Gower, Dec. 24, 1843.
King, Christopher B. to Sarah Blair, Dec. 25, 1832.
Jarnegan, Carey to Judith Fuller, Dec. 26, 1832.
Sturdivant, Herbert A. to Harriet Baker, Dec. 26, 1832. Sol. Jan. 6, 1833, Absolom Gleaves, J.P.
Stovall, Caleb T. to Lydia Jefferson, Dec. 28, 1832.
Buchanan, Charles to Catherine Philips, Dec. 28, 1832.
Goodlet, Adam G. to Eliza T. Turner, Jan. 1, 1833. Sol. Jan. 1, 1833, Dan Ralston.

Page 430
Levin, Lewis C. to Ann C. Hays, Jan. 2, 1833. Sol. Jan. 2, 1833, Geo. Weller, M.G.
Mosby, Wm. T. to Elizabeth Ann Tilford, Jan. 2, 1833. Sol. Jan. 3, 1833, Wm. Hume, V.D.M.
Rogers, Benjamin to Mary Ann Hite, Jan. 3, 1833. Sol. Jan. 3, 1833, Will Lytle, J.P.
Harris, David P. to Martha Proctor, Jan. 5, 1833.
Johnson, George J. to Martha Spain, Jan. 9, 1833. Sol. Jan. 10, 1833, P. B. Robinson, A.M.
Francis, Joseph to Eliza Speace, Jan. 10, 1833. Sol. Dec. 12, 1833, A.L.P. Green, M.G.
Provine, John to Catherine Ralston, Jan. 11, 18-3.
Smith, Sidney to Eliza Jane Wharton, Jan. 10, 1833. Sol. Jan. 10, 1833, Wm. Hump, V.D.M.
Cunningham, Edward to Susan T. Dismukes, Jan. 15, 1833.
Meado, Richard to Margaret Clark, Jan. 15, 1833.

Page 431
McPherson, Cornelius to Mary Griffin, Jan. 16, 1833.
Cartwright, John to Laney Compton, Jan. 16, 1833. Sol. Jan. 17, 1833, Hays Blackman, J.P.
Pembleton, Wm. to Levinia Dejarnett, Jan. 16, 1833. Sol. Jan. 17, 1833, Absolom Gleaves, J.P.
Hoge, Jno. M. to Sarah Farrar, Jan. 17, 1833. Sol. Jan. 18, 1833, J. Browning, J.P.
Campbell, Patrick W. to Lucy W. Athey, Jan. 18, 1833. Sol. Jan. 20, 1833, Peter S. Gayle.
Ivey, Wilson to Lavinia Graham, Jan. 18, 1833.
Jackson, Wm. O. to Lucy Lazenby, Jan. 24, 1833.
Dennison, John R. to Rebecca Owen, Jan. 28, 1833.
Postlethwaight, Jno., Jr. to Sarah H. Johns, Jan. 31, 1833.
Abby, Anthony S. to Susan L. Compton, Jan. 31, 1833. Sol. Jan. 31, 1833, Wm. Hume, V.D.M.

Page 432
Castleman, Andrew E., Jr. to Nancy Redding, Jan. 31, 1833. Sol. Jan. 31, 1833, Dan Ralston.

Jones, Chas. A. to Nancy Waggoner, Feb. 1, 1833. Sol. Feb. 7, 1833, G. W. Charlton, J.P.
Douglas, Wm. to Peggy Colbs, Feb. 1, 1833. Sol. Feb. 7, 1833, James Sims, J.P.
Binkley, Wm. to Caroline Wilson, Feb. 5, 1833. Sol. Feb. 7, 1833, Peter Fuqua, M.G.
Kingston, Wm. to Sophronia Russell, Feb. 5, 1833. Sol. Feb. 7, 1833, Thos. Ferebee.
Barrett, John to Frances Adkinson, Jan. 6, 1833. Sol. Feb. 7, 1833, Jno. Wright, J.P.
Lovell, Benjamin P. to Dorothy H. Hooper, Feb. 8, 1833. Sol. Feb. 21, 1833, Wm. Russell, J.P.
Cullum, James T. to Elizabeth Hooper, Feb. 8, 1833. Sol. Feb. 10, 1833, J. M. Lovell, J.P.
Shane, James to Zenith Guthrie, Feb. 9, 1833.
Phelps, Miles B. to Mahala Bland, Feb. 11, 1833. Sol. Feb. 15, 1833, John Hall, J.P.

Page 433
Hailey, Harvid to Elizabeth Kingston, Feb. 12, 1833.
Tenneson, Abraham W. to Elizabeth Young, Feb. 12, 1833. Sol. Feb. 14, 1833, Wm. Herrin.
Driver, Burrell to Rebecca McGuffey, Feb. 16, 1833. Sol. Feb. 18, 1833, Jno. Wright, J.P.
Green, Jas. W. to Sarah Ann Hallahar, Feb. 18, 1833.
Mulherrin, Chas. to Elizabeth D. Pope, Feb. 23, 1833. Sol. Feb. 23, 1833, Abner McDowell.
Baldridge, Jno. L. to Susan Gutchen, Feb. 26, 1833.
Brown, John M. to Eliza B. Harrison, March 1, 1833. Sol. March 1, 1833, Robt. Davis, M.G.
Reddick, Jno. to Martha Langford, March 2, 1833. Sol. March 1, 1833, Jno. Wright, J.P.
Leake, Joseph to Jane Wilmoth, March 5, 1833.
Duke, Henry R. to Nancy Peoples, March 9, 1833.

Page 434
Capps, John to America Casbear, March 9, 1833.
Newton, Lytle to Betsy Evans, March 22, 1833. Sol. April 3, 1833, Thos. Ferebee.
Rutledge, Thos. to Mary Boyd, March 29, 1833. Sol. April 1, 1833, Thos. Scott.
Lovell, Wm. H. to Laurahanny House, March 30, 1833. Sol. April 4, 1833, Thos. Ferebee.
Cullum, Jesse P. to Susan A.M.V. Hooper, April 2, 1833. Sol. April 5, 1833, Wm. Russell, J.P.
Johnson, Wm. to Jane Dobson, April 2, 1833. Sol. April 6, 1833, A. Gee.
Smith, Wm. to Elizabeth Rainey, April 4, 1833. Sol. April 4, 1833, Wm. Hume, V.D.M.
King, George to Ann Ransom, April 11, 1833. Sol. April 11, 1833, P. B. Robinson, A.M.
Knight, Wm. to Louisa Pickle, April 12, 1833.
Lanier, Lewis H. to Huldah I. Morris, April 16, 1833. Sol. April 18, 1833, Dan Bond, J.P.

Page 435
Boyt, Felix to Martha Payne, April 16, 1833. Sol. April 18, 1833, B. Lee, J.P.
Drew, Moses to Elizabeth Stell, April 18, 1833.
Irwin, Jas. to Mary McPherson, April 19, 1833. Sol. April 19, 1833, Will Lytle, J.P.
Hall, Jno. to Mary Pillows, April 20, 1833. Sol. April 21, 1833, Jno. Beard, M.G.
Brown, Jno. E. to Mary Williams, April 21, 1833. Sol. April 21, 1833, P. B. Robinson, A.M.
Bigley, John to Betsy Wright, April 29, 1833. Sol. May 7, 1833, Jno. Hall, J.P.
Kinnaird, Joseph K. to Susan Ann Tomlin, May 1, 1833. Sol. May 19, 1833, Hays Blackman, J.P.
Patterson, Andrew J. to Issabella Hays, May 7, 1833.
Avery, Wm. H. to Harriet Anderson, May 7, 1833. Sol. May 7, 1833, Wm. Hume, V.D.M.
Bird, Moses to Martha Hodges, May 27, 1833.

Page 436
Stewart, Wm. to Nancy Hailey, May 22, 1833. Sol. May 23, 1833, A.L.P. Green.
Murrell, James M. to Sicily M. Nance, May 28, 1833. Sol. May 28, 1833, James Whitsitt.
Perry, Burrell, Jr. to Elizabeth T. Gleaves, June 4, 1833. Sol. June 27, 1833, Jno. Hall, J.P.
Skeggs, Thos. L. to Mary Jane Drennon (alias Boyd), June 11, 1833. Sol. June 13, 1833, P.B.Robinson, A.M.
Scales, Jeremiah to Delilah Bosley, June 11, 1833. Sol. June 13, 1833, P.B.Robinson, A.M.
Rainey, Wm. to Elizabeth Rowland, June 11, 1833.
Butcher, Wm. to Joanna Thomas, June 13, 1833. Sol. June 13, 1833, James Givins, A.M.
Gower, Joel to Mary Gower, June 15, 1833. Sol. June 16, 1833, B. Lee, J.P.
Stothart, Alexander H. to Sarah Ann Bosley, June 26, 1833. Sol. June 27, 1833, James Givin, M.G.
Norvell, Caleb C. to Catherine N. Carroll, June 27, 1833. Sol. June 27, 1833, Ph. Lindsley.

Page 437
Reeves, Elisha G. to Elizabeth Crisp, June 28, 1833. Sol. July 5, 1833, Wm. Herrin.
Petway, Jno. S. to Caledonia Gordon, July 1, 1833.
Phelan, Druey to Mary Gilliam, July 3, 1833.
Bridges, Smith to Tempe Loftin, July 4, 1833. Sol. July 6, 1833, Thos. Ferebee, J.P.
Merryman, Robt. B. to Ruth Wingo, July 4, 1833. Sol. July 4, 1833, J. Browning, J.P.
Mayfield, Jas. S. to Sophia Ann Crutchor, July 10, 1833. Sol. July 10, 1833, A. M. Bryan.
Vann, Jacob to Margaret Shaw, July 11, 1833. Sol. July 16, 1833, S. Shannon, J.P.
Binkley, Jos. S. to Martha S. Steele, July 13, 1833.

Work, Robert to Caroline Bradshaw, July 15, 1833. Sol. July 18, 1833, W. E. Watkins.
Gibson, Joseph F. to Sophia W. Hall, July 16, 1833. Sol. July 16, 1833, P. B. Robinson, A.M.

Page 438
Simmon, Dan'l to Sarah Boyle, July 18, 1833.
Jennings, Isaac R. to Maria L. Felts, July 19, 1833.
Pigg, Robert F. to Maria L. Felts, July 22, 1833. Sol. July 22, 1833.
Babbitt, Harrison P. to Susan C. Frensley, July 24, 1833.
Flood, Hardy to Eliza Arnold, July 25, 1833. Sol. July 25, 1833, Thos. T. Read, J.P.
Hart, Wm. D. to Elizabeth E. Owens, Aug. 7, 1833.
Allen, Sam'l M. to Catherine E. Doughty, Aug. 3, 1833. Sol. Aug. 3, 1833, A.L.P. Green, M.G.
Williams, David to Zibi Hailey, Aug. 10, 1833.
Spenco, Joseph to Eliza Pinkerton, Aug. 15, 1833. Sol. Sep. 11, 1833, Thos. Ferebee, J.P.
Penuel, Alanson to Nancy Gibson, Aug. 17, 1833. Aug. 1833, Barnard Phillips, M.G.

Page 439
Jackson, Wm. to Martha Miles, Aug. 19, 1833.
Call, Joseph to Tempe White, Aug. 19, 1833.
Kirkwood, Wm. R. to Mahala S. Farmer, Aug. 22, 1833.
Wade, Thomas to Mary Shephard, Aug. 27, 1833. Sol. Aug. 27, 1833, Jas. Green, M.G.
Earhart, Nimrod to Elizabeth Stewart, Aug. 27, 1833. Sol. Sep. 6, 1833, John Hall, J.P.
Redd, Parm B. to Jane A. Sangster, Aug. 28, 1833.
Frendsley, Wm. D. to Mary Ann Carney, Aug. 29, 1833.
Atkinson, Howell S. to Charlotte White, Aug. 29, 1833. Sol. Aug. 29, 1833, P. B. Robinson, A.M.
Witty, Jno. C. to Frances Wistion, Aug. 29, 1833. Sol. Aug. 30, 1833, Absolom Adams.
Marean, Thos. J. to Lindevent Lenon, Aug. 30, 1833.

Page 440
Stroud, Geo. W. to Elizabeth Johnson, Sep. 2, 1833. Sol. Sep. 6, 1833, Jno. Hall, J.P.
Hayes, George to Priscilla Taylor, Sep. 3, 1833.
House, Ambrose to Margaret Wetherall, Sep. 3, 1833. Sol. Sep. 4, 1833, P. B. Robinson, A.M.
Hoover, Andrew J. to Martha Shute, Sep. 4, 1833. Sol. Sep. 4, 1833, J. T. Edgar.
Carney, Jno. B. G. to Catherine P. Binkley, Sep. 9, 1833.
Warmack, Richard to Elizabeth A. Byrn, Sep. 11, 1833. Sol.----------, Jno. C. Bowers.
Mosley, Thos. D. to Ann C. Goodner, Sep. 13, 1833.
Tilford, Daniel to Mary Parker, Sep. 14, 1833. Sol. Sep. 17, 1833, Jas. Goin, M.G.
McFerrin, John B. to Almyra A. Probast, Sep. 18, 1833. Sol. Sep. 19, 1833, A.L.P. Green, M.G.

Cotton, Hardy to Louisa Saunders, Sep. 18, 1833.

Page 441
Burke, Carter to Eliza E. Perry, Sep. 19, 1833. Sol. Sep. 19, 1833, Wm. H. Hagans, J.P.
Franklin, Milton B. to Vessy Tait, Sep. 21, 1833.
Duke, Wm. S. to Martha A. Simpkins, Sep. 21, 1833.
Reaves, Peter to Emily A. Owen, Sep. 24, 1833. Sol. Sep. 30, 1833, H. Owen, J.P.
Jackson, Jas. to Elizabeth Melvin, Sep. 25, 1833.
Young, Wm. C. to Sophia P. Gleaves, Sep. 25, 1833. Sol. Sep. 25, 1833, Wm. Lytle, J.P.
Rieff, Joseph to Susan Leech, Sep. 26, 1833. Sol. Sep. 26, 1833, Will Lytle, J.P.
Cawley, Jas. to Nancy Madden, Oct. 1, 1833. Sol. Oct. 1, 1833, Jno. Wright, J.P.
Murphy, Geo. W. to Martha Williams, Oct. 4, 1833. Sol. ----------, Levin Edney.
Ezell, Lafayette to L. J. Baker, Oct. 9, 1833.

Page 442
Gower, Joseph to Elizabeth Allen, Oct. 10, 1833.
Johnson, Wm. H. to Lilly Ann Burnett, Oct. 14, 1833. Sol. Oct. 30, 1833, John Hall, J.P.
Carter, Nelson P. to Ann C. Spivey, Oct. 18, 1833. Sol. Oct. -----, Bernard Phillips, M.G.
Claiborne, Algimon S. to Mary E. Topp, Oct. 19, 1833. Sol. Oct. 20, 1833, Abner McDowell.
Tait, Andy to Addell A. Livingston, Oct. 21, 1833. Sol. Oct. 21, 1833, Thos. J. Barker.
Wilkinson, Jno. C. to Emily Ballard, Oct. 21, 1833. Sol. Oct. 21, 1833, John Beard, M.G.
Donelson, John to Laura M. Lawrence, Oct. 22, 1833. Sol. Oct. 24, 1833, J. T. Edgar.
Tant, Filson to Lucinda Thompson, Oct. 23, 1833.
Winchester, V. P. to Samuela Price, Oct. 23, 1833. Sol. Oct. 23, 1833, D. W. Lindsley.
Rasberry, Thomas to Ann Harris, Oct. 24, 1833.

Page 443
Shute, Jno. A. to Nancy H. Watkins, Oct. 24, 1833. Sol. Oct. 24, 1833, Robt. A. Lapsley.
Simpson, Wm. to Hulda Binkley, Oct. 28, 1833.
Morton, Allen to Louisa R. Morton, Oct. 30, 1833. Sol. Oct. 31, 1833, Wm. H. Nance, J.P.
White, Beverly W. to Issabella B. Anderson, Oct. 31, 1833. Sol. Oct. 31, 1833, J. T. Edgar.
Akin, Allen to Sally Boyd, Nov. 2, 1833. Sol. Nov. 4, 1833, A.L.P. Green.
McPherson, Jas. B. to Nancy Rhodes, Nov. 5, 1833. Sol. --------, Wm. Roach.
McIver, Jno. to Jane R. Martin, Nov. 5, 1833. Sol. Nov. 5, 1833, J. T. Edgar.
Miller, James to Elizabeth Miller, Nov. 6, 1833. Sol. Nov. 7, 1833, A. Adams, M.G.

Hutton, Wm. D. to Virginia Ferebee, Nov. 6, 1833. Sol. Nov. 7, 1833, Wm. Roach.
Huff, John to Jane E. Cockrill, Nov. 7, 1833. Sol. Nov. 7, 1833, Absolom Adams, M.G.

Page 444
Hall, Henry to Betsy Belcher, Nov. 7, 1833. Sol. Nov. 20, 1833, Thos. Scott.
Carter, James C. to Nancy Buchanan, Nov. 9, 1833.
Watson, Wm. P. to Mary Logan, Nov. 9, 1833. Sol. Nov. 10, 1833, S. Pirtle, J.P.
Pegram, Glenn to Caroline Phipps, Nov. 9, 1833. Sol. Nov. 14, 1833, Wm. Roach.
Little, Jno. C. to Nancy Jackson, Nov. 12, 1833. Sol. Nov. 14, 1833, Wm. Roach.
Ralston, William to Harriet M. Waller, Nov. 14, 1833.
Rainey, William to Drusilla Durham, Nov. 18, 1833. Sol. Nov. 18, 1833, Wm. Lytle, J.P.
Cross, James B. to Cynthia M. Wright, Nov. 20, 1833.
Edwards, Hugh to Eveline E. Phipps, Nov. 20, 1833. Sol. Nov. 21, 1833, Wm. Roach.
Snell, Rosseau S. to Louisa M. Robertson, Nov. 20, 1833. Sol.Nov. 20, 1833, J. B. McFerrin, M.G.

Page 445
Cagle, Geo., Sr. to Temperance Vester, Nov. 21, 1833. Sol. Nov. 24, 1833, David Abernathy, J.P.
Porter, Henry to Agnes Thomas, Nov. 21, 1833.
Stein, Albert to Caroline Troost, Nov. 21, 1833. Sol. Nov. 21, 1833, P. H. Lindsley.
Curd, Richard D. to Emily E. Hall, Nov. 26, 1833. Sol. Dec. 12, 1833, Jno. Beard, M.G.
Wright, Jno. to Damaris Parham, Nov. 27, 1833. Sol. Dec. 2, 1833, A. Goode.
Gibson, Lorenzo to Louisa C. Thomas, Nov. 28, 1833. Sol. Nov. 29, 1833, A.L.P. Green, M.G.
Rains, Hance H. to Margaret C. Buchanan, Nov. 28, 1833. Sol. Nov. 28, 1833, Abner M. Dowell.
Newberry, James to Nancy Pulleu, Nov. 28, 1833. Sol. Nov. 28, 1833, Jno. P. Erwin, J.P.
Smith, Joel to Lucinda Cagle, Nov. 30, 1833.
Peek, Wm. to Jane Wade, Nov. 30, 1833.

Page 446
Basham, James W. to Charlotte Cherry, Dec. 3, 1833. Sol. Dec. 5, 1833, A. Goode.
Work, Joseph A. to Thersa Allen, Dec. 3, 1833. Sol. Dec. 19, 1833, J. M. Lovell, J.P.
McGavock, David to Caroline Pugsley, Dec. 4, 1833. Sol. Dec. 6, 1833, Geo. Weller.
Gray, Pierce to Mary J. Blackman, Dec. 5, 1833.
Demumbrae, Wm. R. to Eliza Betts, Dec. 6, 1833. Sol. ----------, Jno. C. Bowers.
Bonds, Joshua to Ann Haley, Dec. 7, 1833. Sol. Dec. 8, 1833, Wm. Roach.

Work, Robert to Elizabeth W. Hollis, Dec. 11, 1833.
Heyl, Lewis J. to Charlotte DiJone, Dec. 12, 1833.
Dailey, Robert to Frances Scott, Dec. 14, 1833. Sol. Dec. 25, 1833, Thos. Scott.
Norman, Henry to Jane Merryman, Dec. 16, 1833. Sol. Dec. 17, 1833, Fountain E. Pitts.

Page 447
Williams, Lewis to Charlotte M. Rains, Dec. 17, 1833. Sol. Dec. 17, 1833, J. T. Edgar.
Danks, Jno. W. to Catherine P. Moore, Dec. 17, 1833. Sol. Dec. 17, 1833, Fountain S. Pitts.
McBride, John to Sophia B. Carter, Dec. 17, 1833.
Brown, Walter to Fredonia Johnson, Dec. 18, 1833. Sol. Dec. 18, 1833, Abe. Goode.
Manley, Pleasant to Tennessee Quimby, Dec. 18, 1833. Sol. Dec. 19, 1833, Jas. Whitsitt.
Binns, Wm. A. to Mary G. Garnet, Dec. 19, 1833.
Turner, Richard A. to Ann Drake, Dec. 19, 1833.
Waters, Perry to Louisa D. Butler, Dec. 2, 1833. Sol. Dec. 21, 1833, Dan'l Buie, J.P.
McDonald, Alexander to Mary C. Harper, Dec. 3, 1833. Sol. Dec. 24, 1833, J. T. Edgar.
Frederick, Wm. M. to Caroline L. McCasland, Dec. 24, 1833.

Page 448
Cherry, John to Sarah Finch, Dec. 24, 1833. Sol. Dec. 26, 1833, Wm. H. White.
Taylor, Jonathan to Mary Ann Hall, Dec. 24, 1833. Sol. Dec. 24, 1833, Thos. Scott.
Estes, Josiah to Henrietta White, Dec. 26, 1833.
Jeffries, Henry to Caroline E. Cayce, Dec. 26, 1833. Sol. ----------, Abner McDowell.
Puckett, Jordon to Mary Ann Adcock, Dec. 27, 1833. Sol. Dec. 29, 1833, Dan'l Buie, J.P.
White, John to Lurana Estes, Dec. 27, 1833. Sol. Dec. --, 1833, B. Phillips, M.G.
Hearn, Ebenezer to Ann Dickens, Dec. 30, 1833.
Carney, Ennis B. to Utility W. Lewis, Jan. 31, 1834.
Stevenson, Vernon K. to Elizabeth Childress, Jan. 28, 1834. Sol. Jan. 28, 1834, O. B. Hayes.
Read, Joel to Sarah H. Smith, Dec. 28, 1833. Sol. Dec. 28, 1833, J. Whitsitt.

Page 449
Young, William to Jane Earthman, Jan. 27, 1834. Sol. Jan. 30, 1834, Wm. Lytle.
Powell, Barton P. to Mary Walker, Jan.27, 1834.
Ramer, Geo. to Sarah Cole, Jan. 27, 1834.
Dana, Russell to Mary Martin, Jan. 23, 1834.
Beard, Richard to Cynthia G. Castleman, Jan. 21, 1834. Sol. Jan. 21, 1834, Abner McDowell.
Warmath, Thomas to Ann C. McFaddin, Jan. 20, 1834. Sol. Jan. 23, 1834, Peter A. Gayle.

Mickley, James E. to Sophy Morgan, Jan. 18, 1834. Sol. Jan. 19, 1834, A.L.P. Green.
Marshall, Wm. J. to Lucinda Wright, Jan. 14, 1834. Sol. Jan. 16, 1834, Jno. Beard, M.G.
Bledsoe, Jesse to Martha C. Williams, Jan. 13, 1834. Sol. Jan. 23, 1834, E. Goodrich, J.P.
Thompson, Joseph to Caroline Grubbs, Jan. 9, 1834. Sol. Jan. 9, 1834, R. A. Lapsley, M.G.

Page 450
Dunnaway, William M. to Sarah E. Buchanan, Jan. 7, 1834. Sol. Jan. 9, 1834, Abner McDowell.
Goodrich, Harrison to Mary Sirls, Jan. 7, 1834. Sol. Jan. 8, 1834, E. H. East, J.P.
Johnson, Isham to Nancy Smith, Jan. 2, 1834. Sol. Jan. 16, 1834, Jno. Hall, J.P.
Adkison, Daniel to Nancy Curfman, Feb. 3, 1834.
Chisholm, Rufus K. to Emeline Neugent, Feb. 4, 1834.
Hudson, Richard to Martha Ann Butler, Feb. 5, 1834. Sol. Feb. 6, 1834, Wm. Roach.
Smith, Samuel to Susan Smith, Feb. 6, 1834.
Boyte, Jonathan to Elizabeth Simmons, Feb. 6, 1834.
Branch, Lewis to Martha Scruggs, Feb. 10, 1834. Sol Feb. 19, 1834, Reubin Payne, J.P.
Kozer, Timothy to Ellen T. Laughton, Feb. 10, 1834. Sol. Feb. 11, 1834, J. T. Edgar, M.G.

Page 451
Kirby, Jno. M. to Margaret H. M. White, Feb. 11, 1834. Sol. Feb. 11, 1834, A.L.P. Green, M.G.
Petty, Jas. H. to Mary Jane Bradby, Feb. 11, 1834. Sol. Feb. 12, 1834, Wm. Lytle, J.P.
Coleman, Christian to Elizabeth Adcock, Feb. 12, 1834. Sol. Feb. 27, 1834, Dan'l Buie, J.P.
Smith, Jno. H. to Caroline Morton, Feb. 13, 1834. Sol. Feb. 14, 1834, Thos. J. Reid, J.P.
Walker, Jas. M. to Mary A. McLemore, Feb. 20, 1834. Sol. Feb. 20, 1834, J. T. Edgar, J.P.
Campbell, Albert G. to Sarah Pierce, Feb. 22, 1834.
Burges, Geo. W. to Nancy Alford, Feb. 24, 1834. Sol. Feb. 27, 1834, Wm. Lytle, J.P.
Marshall, Edward to Mary A. Cheatham, Feb. 25, 1834. Sol. Feb. 25, 1834, J. A. Barrett, J.P.
Shelby, Carter to Nancy Harrison, Jan. 1, 1834.
Zachary, Bartlett to Sarah C. Kimbro, Jan. 2, 1834.

Page 452
Finch, Wm. S. to Edith Waller, Jan. 6, 1834. Sol. Jan. 8, 1834, Reubin Paine, J.P.
Burnett, Richard to Polly Ballentine, March 12, 1834. Sol. March 14, 1834, Geo. W. Charlton.
Newell, Thos. H. to Jane Graham, March 13, 1834. Sol. March 13, 1834, A.L.P. Green, M.G.
Chaffer, Richard W. to Catherine Dorris, March 17, 1834. Sol. March 20, 1834, James Green, M.G.

Lee, Henry to Elizabeth Pegram, March 18, 1834. Sol. March 18, 1834, Thos. Ferebee.
Robinson, John to Nancy M. Allen, March 21, 1834.
Baker, Jarman to Mary J. Reace, March 24, 1834. Sol. March 27, 1834, J. T. Edgar, M.G.
Mitchell, Pleasant H. to Ann Ridley, April 5, 1834. Sol. -----, 1834, P. Fuqua.
Spargo, Jno. D. to Elizabeth Green, April 8, 1834. Sol. April 8, 1834, Thos. J. Reid, J.P.
Hooker, Moseley to Mary Noble, April 11, 1834. Sol. April 12, 1834, J. T. Edgar, M.G.

Page 453
Ledyard, Wm. I. to Frances L. Erwin, April 14, 1834. Sol. April 14, 1834, J. T. Edgar, M.G.
Wilburn, Jno. G. to Eliza A. White, March 4, 1834. Sol. March 6, 1834, Reuben Payne, J.P.
Couch, Jno. A. to Margaret Parrish, March 6, 1834. Sol. March 6, 1834.
Smith, Jackson to Nancy Buchanan, March 7, 1834. Sol. ----------, 1834, Jas. Whitsitt.
Green, Gardner to Jemima Gibbs, March 8, 1834.
Tate, Thomas J. to Rebecca Aikin, March 9, 1834. Sol. March 9, 1834, Wm. Lytle, J.P.
Warmack, Edward to Jemima Hackney, March 10, 1834. Sol. ----------, 1834, Jno. V. Bowers.
Hawkins, Willis M. to Elizabeth M. Sanders, March 11, 1834. Sol. March 11, 1834, J. T. Edgar, M.G.
Calloway, Geo. W. to Catherine P. Noel, April 17, 1834. Sol. April 1834, Bernard Philips, M.G.
McKinney, Caleb to Lucretia Green, April 19, 1834.

Page 454
McCrory, Robt. E. to Catherine Lazanby, April 21, 1834.
Castleman, Lewis to Louisa Tucker, April 24, 1834.
Sluder, Aaron B. to Elizabeth W. Garner, April 24, 1834.
Deadrick, Foilding to Ann L. B. Cooper, April 24, 1834. Sol. April 24, 1834, J. T. Edgar, M.G.
Lambert, Hezikiah to Jane Brown, April 28, 1834.
Bashaw, Jos. E. to Ann Sampson, April 29, 1834, by E. Goodrich, J.P.
Gunter, Green B. to Mary Lucas, April 30, 1834. Sol. May 1, 1834, James Whitsitt.
Corbett, Willie B. to Elizabeth Moore, May 1, 1834. Sol. May 1, 1834, Wm. Lytle, J.P.
Martin, R.C.K. to Priscilla Douglas, May 1, 1834. Sol. May 1, 1834, Geo. Weller.
Dozier, Joseph to Jane Cullum, May 7, 1834, by M. Harris, J.P.

Page 455
Parks, Jno. J. to Jane Bashears, May 8, 1834. Sol. May 8, 1834, W. M. Lytle, J.P.
Hows, Rasa to Nancy Lovell, May 12, 1834. Sol. May 15, 1834, Thos. Ferebee.

Hill, Robert to Louisa Harrison, May 15, 1834. Sol. May 15, 1834, A.L.P.Green.
Bryan, Hardy W. to Margaret K. McGavock, May 16, 1834. Sol. May 16, 1834, J. T. Edgar.
Phillips, Jas. to Susan Spain, May 17, 1834.
Rieff, Orren M. to Matilda A. Tambrio, May 19, 1834. Sol. May 19, 1834, Saml S. Moody.
Dean, Jabez to Mary Jane Hill, May 20, 1834. Sol. May 20, 1834, Jas. Whitsett.
May, James F. to Eliza F. Phillips, May 21, 1834.
Stratton, Madison to Mary A. Snow, May 21, 1834. Sol. May 21, 1834, A.L.P. Green, M.G.
Finch, Wm. to Mary Stephens, May 22, 1834.

Page 456
Goodwin, Green B. to Mary Ann Goodwin, May 22, 1834. Sol. May 22, 1834, Jas. Whitsett.
Hail, Jefferson to Frances Nelson, May 23, 1834. Sol. May 23, 1834, Wm. Lytle, J.P.
Coverly, John to Ann Sumner, May 31, 1834.
Bugg, Sam'l H. to Catherine Smiley, June 3, 1834. Sol. June 3, 1834, J. T. Edgar, J.P.
Hill, Isaac to Paulina P. Carter, June 3, 1834. Sol. June 3, 1834, Bernard Phillips, M.G.
Jennings, Isaac to Julia Ann Pearsons, June 4, 1834.
Brown, Wm. B. to Catherine Bearden, June 9, 1834. Sol. June 11, 1834, Thos. Ferebee, J.P.
Irwin, James to Elizabeth Nanny, June 11, 1834. Sol. June 18, 1834, Wm. Lytle, J.P.
Atkinson, Wm. J. to Brunella Stockton, June 12, 1834.
Drenen, Espy C. to Maria Castleman, June 14, 1834. Sol. June 14, 1834, Abe Green, J.P.

Page 457
Bandy, Geo. to Minerva Hellums, June 20, 1834. Sol. June 20, 1834, Abe Green, J.P.
Rimon, Chas. H. to Prudence Reddick, June 21, 1834. Sol. June 22, 1834, Wm. Lytle, J.P.
Scruggs, Allen to Catherine Galloway, June 21, 1834. Sol. June 21, 1834, Thos. J. Reid, J.P.
Knowles, Leander to Frances M. Stout, June 23, 1834. Sol. June 23, 1834, A. Adams, M.G.
Ridley, Geo. T. to Mary Dotson, June 25, 1834.
Oliphant, Henry to Rebecca Driver, June 26, 1834.
Cattharp, John to Elizabeth Haley, June 26, 1834. Sol. June 26, 1834, Thos. J. Reid, J.P.
Newby, James to Susan Howlett, July 1, 1834.
Bailey, Spiler H. to Maria Clark, July 2, 1834. Sol. July 2, 1834, F. E. Pitts, M.G.
Masterson, Thos. G. to Christina I. Roane, July 3, 1834. Sol. July 3, 1834, J. T. Edgar, M.G.

Page 458
Dodson, Wm. T. to Mary Rodgers, July 5, 1834.

Fryer, Stockley D. to Nancy Dickens, July 9, 1834. Sol. July 9, 1834, S. Shannon, J.P.
Frazer, Stephen D. to Elizabeth Foulks, July 12, 1834.
Dismukes, Geo. E. to Harriet N. Williams, July 14, 1834. Sol.. July 15, 1834, A. P. Porter.
Castlemen, Wm. W. to Martha Tennison, July 16, 1834. Sol. July 16, 1834, Wm. Donelson.
Smith, Thos. to Elizabeth A. Robertson, July 17, 1834. Sol. July 17, 1834, T. J. Edgar, M.G.
Wehrley, Dane to Sarah Hall, July 17, 1834. Sol. July 17, 1834, Jas. Green, M.G.
Smith, Burton to Elizabeth Fox, July 18, 1834.
Thomas, Peter to Martha Ballentine, July 23, 1834. Sol. July 23, 1834, Thos. J. Read, J.P.
Hardeman, Franklin to Catherine C. Wilson, July 26, 1834. Sol. July 27, 1834, Geo. Weller, M.G.

Page 459
Grant, Francis to Fereby Nash, July 26, 1834.
Aikin, Wm. to Sarah Couch, July 31, 1834, by Samuel S. Moody.
Brown, Benjamin F. to Ann James, Aug. 5, 1834.
Hows, Brinkley to Ann Allen, Aug. 5, 1834.
Hume, Alfred to Louisa H. Bradford, Aug. 6, 1834. Sol. Aug. 12, 1834, O. W. Hays.
Neely, Thos. B. to Mary Ann Shaw, Aug. 7, 1834. Sol. Aug. 14, 1834, Wm. Ralston.
Nash, John to Lucy F. Jordan, Aug. 8, 1834. Sol. Aug. 14, 1834, Wm. H. White.
Stewart, Andrew to Nancy Johnson, Aug. 14, 1834. Sol. Aug. 14, 1834, Wm. Lytle, J.P.
Bigley, Thos. W. to Nancy Patrick, Aug. 14, 1834. Sol. Aug. 14, 1834, Wm. T. Senter.
Neely, Elisha to Lucinda Lamb, Aug. 16, 1834. Sol. Aug. 17, 1834, Samuel S. Moody, M.G.

Page 460
Cobbs, James H. to Sarah Brunch, Aug. 18, 1834. Sol. Aug. 18, 1834, Jos. B. Knowles, J.P.
Hite, Horatio to Margaret Stewart, Aug. 26, 1834. Sol. Aug. 26, 1834, E. H. East, J.P.
Stewart, John to Mahala Corbitt, Aug. 30, 1834, by Jas. Whitsitt.
Wright, Thos. to Eliza Ann Mayo, Sep. 2, 1834.
Morgan, James to Mary Tindall, Sep. 2, 1834. Sol. Sep. 2, 1834, R.B.C. Howell, M.G.
Allen, Thos. J. to Jane I. Hart, Sep. 3, 1834. Sol. Sep. 4, 1834, R. A. Lapsley, M.G.
Cheeney, Hampton J. to Mary E. Smith, Sep. 4, 1834.
Hooper, Jesse E. to Charlotte C. Fawcett, Sep. 12, 1834. Sol. Sep. 15, 1834, Thos. Scott.
Binkley, Adam to Sally Wren, Sep. 17, 1834.
Hill, Williams to Nancy Williams, Sep. 26, 1834.

Page 461
Wood, David S. to Susan B. Childs, Sep. 26, 1834. Sol. Oct. 7, 1834, Geo. W. Charlton, J.P.
Garland, Samuel to Mary Walltrip, Sep. 26, 1834. Sol. Oct. 5, 1834, L. P. Cheatham, J.P.
Wright, John to Jane Wright, Sep. 29, 1834.
Garner, Thos. to Evaline Law, Sep. 29, 1834. Sol. Sep. 29, 1834, Jas. Garland, J.P.
Bruce, John to Catherine Swift, Sep. 30, 1834. Sol. Sep. 30, 1834, J. Pirtle, J.P.
Buffington, Anderson to Paralle Cabler, Oct. 1, 1834. Sol. Oct. 1, 1834, Elihu Robinson.
Cullom, Wm. to Zaney Boyd, Oct. 2, 1834. Sol. Oct. 15, 1834, Thos. Scott.
Brewer, Rodham to Elizabeth Hooper, Oct. 2, 1834.
Scott, Peyton L. to Mary Ann Hunt, Oct. 4, 1834. Sol. Oct. 5, 1834.
Dean, Francis A. L. to Jane Alley, Oct. 17, 1834. Sol. Oct. 17, 1834, Jno. Wright, J.P.

Page 462
Stainback, J. W. H. to Martha C. Epps, Oct. 15, 1834.
Mayfield, Peter to Martha Proctor, Oct. 18, 1834.
Adcock, John to Jane Adcock, Oct. 18, 1834. Sol. Oct. 30, 1834, Dan Buie, J.P.
Jefferies, Stephen to Affie Moore, Oct. 20, 1834.
Thompson, Young to Julia Ann Scott, Oct. 24, 1834. Sol. Nov. 2, 1834, Thos. Ferebee.
Dozier, Nimrod W. to Susanna Williams, Oct. 25, 1834. Sol. Nov. 15, 1834, Wm. Shelton, J.P.
Fields, Wm., Jr. to Minerva H. Mays, Oct. 30, 1834.
Simmons, Jackson to Sarah Harris, Oct. 31, 1834.
Smith, Wm. to Julia Davis, Nov. 1, 1834.
Wilson, Luke to Eliza Jane Dungee, Oct. 30, 1834.

Page 463
Brown, James to Elizabeth Boyd, Nov. 3, 1834.
Kingston, Wm. to Matilda Roach. Oct. 31, 1834. Sol. Nov. 4, 1834, R. C. Goodgoin, M.G.
Barnard, Joseph to Susan E. Bateman, Nov. 6, 1834. Sol. Nov. 7, 1834, A.L.P. Green, M.G.
Whitworth, Isaac to Mary Skelley, Nov. 7, 1834.
Johnston, James to Cassandra Woodlin, Nov. 8, 1834.
Eaton, Ransom W. to Therisa Crockett, Nov. 13, 1834.
Martin, John to Susan Brinkley, Nov. 11, 1834.
Love, Jno. T. to Hannah A. Stratton, Nov. 13, 1834. Sol. Nov. 19, 1834, J. B. McFerrin, M.G.
Jones, Joel L. to Minerva Turner, Nov. 15, 1834. Sol. Nov. 16, 1834, Jno. Holland, M.G.
Mann, Thos. J. to Edith S. Evans, Nov. 14, 1834.

Page 464
Bryant, Archibald H. to Winnie House, Nov. 17, 1834. Sol. Nov. 17, 1834, Jno. Davis, J.P.

Gray, Henry W. to Mary Boyd, Nov. 20, 1834.
Green, Jas. H. to Margaret Drake, Nov. 22, 1834. Sol. Nov. 22, 1834, Abner McDowell.
Wood, Thos. J. to Rebecca Steele, Nov. 24, 1834. Sol. Nov. 28, 1834, P. Fuqua.
Warner, Edw'd W. to Mary J. Berryhill, Nov. 25, 1834. Sol. Nov. 26, 1834, J. T. Edgar, M.G.
Boyd, Wm. to Bertha Walker, Nov. 28, 1834.
Grizzard, Greenville to Nancy M. Cole, Dec. 3, 1834. Sol. Dec. 4, 1834, J. Pirtle, J.P.
Cone, Guilford to Emeline Murphy, Dec. 3, 1834. Sol. Dec. 5, 1834, Robt. C. Goodgoin, M.G.
Stephenson, George to Frances E. Boaz, Nov. 28, 1834. Sol. Dec. 4, 1834, Wm. H. Nance, J.P.
Stump, Frederick H. to Nannie B. Dozier, Dec. 6, 1834. Sol. Dec. 11, 1834, W. M. Smith, M.G.

Page 465
Green, Henry to Harriet Henry, Dec. 6, 1834. Sol. Dec. 18, 1834, Wm. Heverin.
Sturman, Washington to Malinda Fowler, Dec. 7, 1834. Sol. Dec. 7, 1834, B. Spinner, J.P.
Yeatman, Henry T. to Sarah Ann West, Dec. 8, 1834. Sol. Dec. 8, 1834.
Haddick, David to Malinda C. Baldridge, Dec. 8, 1834. Sol. Dec. 9, 1834, B. Gray, J.P.
Boyte, Felix G. to Elizabeth Simmons, Dec. 11, 1834.
Harding, Job to Zaney Dillahunt, Dec. 16, 1834. Sol. Dec. 17, 1834, Jno. Davis, J.P.
Gordon, James to Issabella McNairy, Dec. 16, 1834. Sol. Dec. 16, 1834, J. T. Edgar, M.G.
Brown, Wm. to Jane Brookman, Dec. 17, 1834.
Collins, Caliborne S. to Elizabeth W. Jones, Dec. 20, 1834, Sol. Dec. 23, 1834, Wm. Roach.
Newsom, Wm. to Sarah Gowers, Dec. 22, 1834. Sol. Dec. 30, 1834, Jno. Davis, J.P.

Page 466
Hoskins, Robt. T. to Tennessee Abernathy, Dec. 22, 1834. Sol. Dec. 23, 1834, David Abernathy, J.P.
Jenkins, George to Elenor Goodwin, Dec. 23, 1834. Sol. Dec. 25, 1834, T. Fanning, M.G.
Lowe, Alexander to Susan A. Boyd, Dec. 24, 1834.
Graves, Sherrod G. to Peggy Neeley, Dec. 24, 1834.
Harris, James to Eliza Underwood, Dec. 24, 1834. Sol. Dec. 25, 1834, David Abernathy, J.P.
Sneed, Alexander E. to Elizabeth Guthrie, Dec. 29, 1834. Sol. Dec. 30, 1834, W. H. Nance, J.P.
Phillips, Thomas to Elizabeth Caldwell, Dec. 30, 1834. Sol. Jan. 7, 1835, J. W. Whitsitt.
Harrison, Thomas to Indiana C. Reeves, Dec. 31, 1834. Sol. Jan. 1, 1835, Wm. Shelton, J.P.
Cutchin, Saml R. to Mary Walden, Jan. 3, 1835. Sol. Jan. 4, 1835, Banajah Gray, J.P.

Warner, Wm. S. to Sarah Wood, Jan. 1, 1835. Sol. Jan. 1, 1835, A.L.P. Green, M.G.

Page 467
Finch, Wm. S. to Edith Waller, Jan. 6, 1835.
Powell, Edmund L. to Julia G. Davis, Jan. 12, 1835. Sol. Jan. 15, 1835, A.L.P. Green.
Polk, Jno. T. to Susan Baldridge, Jan. 12, 1835. Sol. Jan. 15, 1835, Benajah Gray, J.P.
Drake, Blount W. to Mary D. Hyde, Jan. 13, 1835. Sol. Jan. 15, 1835, F. E. Pitts, M.G.
Appleton, Wm. to Lucinda Russell, Jan. 15, 1835. Sol. Jan. 29, 1835, Wm. Shelton, J.P.
Earheart, Adam to Mary Sturtevant, Jan. 15, 1835. Sol. Jan. 18, 1835, Wm. Saunders.
Britt, Arthur to Mary J. McCutchin, Jan. 22, 1835. Sol. Jan. 22, 1835, F. E. Pitts, M.G.
Talbott, Enoch M. to Emiline Shivers, Jan. 22, 1835. Sol. Jan. 22, 1835, Thos. J. Reid, J.P.
Yates, David to Caroline Carter, Jan. 22, 1835. Sol. Jan. 25, 1835, Jno. Davis, J.P.
Robertson, Jesse to Mary A. Vaughn, Jan. 24, 1835. Sol. Feb. 5, 1835, B. Gray, J.P.

Page 468
Whitfield, Thomas J. to Sallie L. Dillahunty, Jan. 26, 1835. Sol. Jan. 27, 1835, Wm. Roach.
Wadkins, James to Sarah Pugh, Jan. 31, 1835.
Purdy, John to Evelina Chapman, Feb. 3, 1835. Sol. Feb. 5, 1835, F. E. Pitts.
Smith, McDaniel to Diana Pugh, Feb. 3, 1835. Sol. Feb. 9, 1835, Jas. Givin, M.G.
Hall, Theodrich to Evelina Cartwright, Feb. 9, 1835. Sol. Feb. 10, 1835, J. Pirtle, J.P.
Carney, Elijah M. H. to Sarag R. Frensley, Feb. 11, 1835.
Alley, Henry to Elizabeth Spicer, Feb. 11, 1835. Sol. Feb. 12, 1835, A.L.P. Green.
Evans, Wm. H. to Margaret A. Charlton, Feb. 17, 1835.
Kennedy, Ashley to Polly Cato, Feb. 17, 1835. Sol. Feb. 19, 1835, David Abernathy, J.P.
Zachery, Robt. to Nannie L. Tucker, Feb. 19, 1835. Sol. Feb. 21, 1835, John Morton.

Page 469
Petty, Isaac H. to Lucinda Singleton, Feb. 23, 1835.
Work, Andrew to Catherine Griffin, Feb. 23, 1835.
Arrington, Larkin to Burnette Binkley, Feb. 23, 1835. Sol. March 4, 1835, Allen Knight, J.P.
Boyd, Jonathon to Jane Maxey, Feb. 24, 1835.
Anderson, John to Mary Marshall, Feb. 24, 1835. Sol. Feb. 24, 1835, Jno. Wright, J.P.
Jones, Holloway to Ruth Rhodes, Feb. 25, 1835. Sol. Feb. 25, 1835, Wm. Roach.
Osborne, Thos. H. to Sarah A. M. Thomas, Feb. 26, 1835.

Petway, Wm. to Martha Hobson, Feb. 26, 1835. Sol. Feb. 26, 1835, F. E. Pitts, M.G.
Carney, Joshua to Sina Binkley, March 3, 1835.
Miller, Jno. C. to M. A. M. Mumford, March 3, 1835. Sol. March 3, 1835, F. E. Pitts, M.G.

Page 470
Johnson, Robert to Nancy Rawling, March 3, 1835. Sol. March 3, 1835, B. Spence, J.P.
Dun, Maclin to Nannie Evans, March 3, 1835. Sol. March 4, 1835, Thos. Ferebee.
Vick, Joel to Elizabeth Dean, March 5, 1835.
Hughes, Oliver to Sarah Morton, March 5, 1835. Sol. March 5, 1835, Thos. J. Redd, J.P.
Regan, Joseph to Cornelia Marshall, March 5, 1835. Sol. March 5, 1835, A.L.P. Green, M.G.
Bell, Munroe to Beulah C. Fursman, March 9, 1835. Sol. March 9, 1835, J. T. Edgar, M.G.
Woodward, Geo. P. to Sarah E. Carter, March 10, 1835.
Ellis, Wm. F. to Nellie Chaser, March 10, 1835.
Bransford, Jacob to Maria Hagey, March 12, 1835.
Herring, Beverly to Sarah Watson, March 12, 1835, by Jno. C. Bowers.

Page 471
Kiser, Horace P. to Emeline Maynard, March 31, 1835. Sol. April 20, 1835, J. T. Edgar, M.G.
Lowe, Lewis to Mary E. Sumner, April 1, 1835. Sol. April 2, 1835, A.L.P. Green, M.G.
Mosby, Wm. T. to Sarah E. Gaines, April 2, 1835.
Johnston, John L. to Caroline J. Hickey, April 6, 1835. Sol. April 9, 1835, Thos. Morton.
Randolph, Lewis to Elizabeth A. Martin, April 7, 1835. Sol. April 9, 1835, R. A. Lapsley, M.G.
Parker, Geo. W. to Elizabeth A. Barry, April 9, 1835. Sol. April 9, 1835, R.B.C. Howell, M.G.
Hope, Samuel R. to Mary E. Brown, April 9, 1835. Sol. April 9, 1835, Jno. W. Hannar, M.G.
Shivers, John C. to Zilpha Dorris, April 9, 1835. Sol. April 9, 1835, Jas. Givin.
Piniham, John to Linsey Piniham (no date given).
McCabe, Wm. to Mary Ann Leak, April 13, 1835. Sol. April 13, 1835, Jas. Givin, M.G.

Page 472
Driver, Henry to Elizabeth Maclin, April 14, 1835. Sol. April 14, 1835, Jas. Givin, M.G.
Tarver, Byrd R. to Jane W. Leak, April 18, 1835. Sol. April 18, 1835, J. T. Edgar, M.G.
Monday, John to Martha Babbitt, April 20, 1835.
Harris, Wm. to Elizabeth Alexander, April 20, 1835. Sol. April 23, 1835, Thos. Ferebee.
Dean, Wm. to Minerva Gower, April 22, 1835. Sol. April 26, 1835, Thos. Hickman, J.P.
Barley, Thos. H. to Susan O. Fortune, April 23, 1835.

Anderson, Wm. W. to Melissa Cato, April 28, 1835. Sol. April 30, 1835, Geo. W. Charlton, J.P.
Griffith, Thomas to Nannie Brown, May 7, 1835. Sol. May 7, 1835, Jas. Givin, M.G.
Vance, Elisha L. to S. Brooks, May 7, 1835. Sol. May 7, 1835, J. T. Edgar, M.G.
Harrison, Rolla to Mary Galbrath, May 9, 1835. Sol. May 13, 1835, E. P. Carnell, J.P.

Page 473
McKain, Elisha to Abby Mason, May 9, 1835.
Frazier, Wm. to Margaret Nicholson, May 12, 1835.
Hooper, Wm. C. to Mary Riggins, May 16, 1835. Sol. May 28, 1835, W. M. Shelton.
Alfred, Patrick to Tabitha Firbus, May 17, 1835.
Butler, Robert to Elizabeth Bean, May 19, 1835. Sol. May 20, 1835, F. G. Ferguson, M.G.
Jones, Caleb to Eliza M. Hume, May 23, 1835. Sol. May 24, 1835, Geo. Weller, M.G.
Wayne, Wm. to Margaret Harris, May 26, 1835. Sol. May 26, 1835, E. H. East, J.P.
Blanchard, Carey H. to Mary G. Overton, May 28, 1835. Sol. May 28, 1835, J. B. Reynolds, M.G.
Hickerson, Warner to Mary Merritt, June 1, 1825.
Hunter, Jacob to Mary Bolton, June 1, 1835. Sol. June 4, 1835, Jno. Wright, J.P.

Page 474
Cotton, Chas. to Frances Pilant, June 2, 1835. Sol. ----------, Thos. Martin.
Young, Daniel to Susannah Drake, June 3, 1835.
Miles, Saml. to Tabitha Appleton, June 4, 1835. Sol. June 27, 1835, Wm. Shelton, J.P.
Horney, Perry to Ruth Waggoner, June 4, 1835.
Camp, James T. to Mary F. Walker, June 5, 1835. Sol. June 5, 1835, A.L.P. Green.
McCulley, Wm. to Jane Biter, June 6, 1835. Sol. June 10, 1835, Wm. Saunders.
Menefee, Jonas H. to Elvina Scales, June 9, 1835. Sol. June 11, 1835, R.B.C. Howell.
Green, L.S.S. to Sarah R. Smith, June 11, 1835. Sol. June 11, 1835, J. W. Hanner, M.G.
Cross, Powhatan to Martha Barlow, June 13, 1835.
Bell, Wm. H. to Martha A. Robertson, June 18, 1835. Sol. June 18, 1835, James Givin, M.G.

Page 475
McNairy, Jno. S. to Elizabeth Alloway, June 18, 1835. Sol. June 18, 1835, Geo. Willis, M.G.
Hewlett, Wm. to Jane G. Gilman, June 25, 1835. Sol. June 25, 1835, J. W. Hanner, M.G.
Barnester, Nathaniel H. to Amelia Stone, June 26, 1835. Sol. June 30, 1835, Jno. Wright, J.P.
Williams, Plummer to Nannie B. Joslin, June 27, 1835.

Miles, Wm. to Eliza W. Lovell, June 29, 1835. Sol. July 1, 1835. Wm. Shelton.
Matthews, John G. to Julia Ann Currin, Oct. 13, 1834.
Cox, Archibald D. to Elizabeth Adams, Oct. 9, 1834.
McCampbell, Isaac N. to Eliza Jane Cole, Oct. 16, 1834. Sol. Oct. 16, 1834, D. L. Alexander.
Farrar, Samuel M. to Sarah E. Whitsitt, Oct. 14, 1834, by Jas. Whitsitt, M.G.
Work, John F. to Nancy E. Jones, Oct. 24, 1834. Sol. Oct. 30, 1834, Thos. Ferebee.

Page 476
Clay, Joshua to Sarah G. Ballou, Nov. 10, 1834.
Miles, William to Eliza W. Lovell, June 1, 1835. Sol. June 29, 1835, Wm. Shelton, J.P.
Williams, Plummer to Nancy B. Joslin, July 27, 1835.
Barnester, Nathaniel H. to Amelia Stone, June 26, 1835. Sol. June 30, 1835, Jno. Wright, J.P.
Hewlett, William to Jane Gilman, June 25, 1835. Sol. June 25, 1835, J. W. Hanner, M.G.
McNairy, John S. to Elizabeth Alloway, June 18, 1835. Sol. June 18, 1835, Geo. Weller, M.G.
Bell, Wm. H. to Martha A. Robertson, June 18, 1835. Sol. June 18, 1835, James Garlin, M.G.
Cross, Powhatton to Martha Barlow, June 14, 1835.
Greene, L.S.S. to Sarah R. Smith, June 11, 1835. Sol. June 11, 1835, J. W. Hanner, M.G.
Jones, Thomas to Frances Connell, July 8, 1835. Sol. July 9, 1835, J. T. Edgar, M.G.

Page 477
Mullen, Reuben W. to Sophronia Bibb, July 10, 1835.
Thompson, Wm. P. to Ann Hearn, July 1, 1835. Sol. July 23, 1835, F. G. Ferguson, M.G.
Hooper, Wm. to Nancy Brown, July 3, 1835.
Nevins, John to Elizabeth Haynes, July 1, 1835. Sol. July 1, 1835, Jas. Givins, M.G.
Saunders, Wm. to Esther Jones, July 1, 1835.
Lovell, Holman R. to Ann Brown, July 1, 1835.
Gilliam, Wm. L. to Margaret H. Ord, July 13, 1835. Sol. July 30, 1835, Eps Connell, J.P.
Barton, John to Tennessee Young, July 15, 1835. Sol. July 15, 1835, Thos. Ferebee.
Exum, Elijah S. to Sarah E. Carter, July 15, 1835. Sol. Aug. 10, 1835, Thos. Scott.
Cabler, Jno. L. to Mary A.T. Zachery, July 15, 1835. Sol. July 15, 1835, E. H. East, J.P.

Page 478
Foster, Benj. F. to Agnes E. Temple, July 21, 1835. Sol. July 21, 1835, Tolbert Fanning, B.C.C.
Adkinson, William to Amaline Scott, July 22, 1835.
Dismukes, John D. to Nancy Williamson, July 22, 1835.

Dabbs, Thos. C. to Isabella Burgess, July 22, 1835. Sol. July 23, 1835, Tolbert Fanning, B.C.C.
Loving, Gabriel to Elizabeth McGuin, July 22, 1835. Sol. July 23, 1835, M. H. Quinn, M.G.
Spence, Joseph to Polly McDaniel, July 24, 1835. Sol. July 29, 1835, Robt. C. Goodgoin, M.G.
Crutcher, William to Emma C. Pike, July 29, 1835. Sol. July 30, 1835, Geo. Weller, M.G.
Sandy, Wm. to Florida Howlett, Aug. 3, 1835.
Cargill, Henry A. to Mary P. Hays, Aug. 5, 1835. Sol. Aug. 5, 1835, Geo. Weller, M.G.
Dunnevant, Abram to Ann McCoold, Aug. 6, 1835.

Page 479
Smith, John to Sally Capps, Aug.15, 1835. Sol. Aug. 17, 1835, E. H. East, J.P.
Monks, Franklin to Maria Coleman, Aug. 18, 1835.
Butler, Nathaniel W. to Ann P. Marshall, Aug. 19, 1835. Sol. Aug. 21, 1835, J. T. Edgar, M.G.
Lyons, Jno. B. to Eliza Merryman, Aug. 20, 1835. Sol. Aug. 21, 1835, J. T. Edgar, M.G.
Brumaker, Frederick to Bell Ann Graham, Aug. 20, 1835. Sol. Aug. 21, 1835, Thos. J. Read, J.P.
Short, Wesley to Alseleh Whitley, Aug. 22, 1835.
Glasgow, Jesse to Hannah Boyd, Aug. 22, 1835. Sol. Sep. 2, 1835, Thos. Ferebee, J.P.
Jones, Daniel to Celia Forhand, Aug. 26, 1835.
Silbird, William to Sarah Morris, Aug. 26, 1835.
Porter, Joseph Y. to Ellen Porter, Aug. 26, 1835. Sol. Aug. 26, 1835, Robt. A. Lapsley.

Page 480
Walker, Allen to Elizabeth Forhand, Aug. 29, 1835.
Ellis, Green to Rebecca Deal, Aug. 29, 1835. Sol. Sep. 11, 1835, Thos. Hickman, J.P.
Woodfin, Ryland H. to Henrietta Bailey, Sep. 1, 1835. Sol. Sep. 2, 1835, A.L.P. Green.
Whitfield, John to Mary G. Hutton, Sep. 1, 1835. Sol. Sep. 2, 1835, Levin Edney, M.G.
Cook, Granville to Elenor P. Long, Sep. 2, 1835. Sol. Sep. 3, 1835, J. W. Hanner, M.G.
Miller, Alexander to Agnes Wates, Sep. 3, 1835. Sol. Sep. 6, 1835, P. S. Gayle, M.G.
Tate, Lorenzo to Jonanna Chavons, Sep. 7, 1835.
Roach, Admiral G. to Mary A. Stringfellow, Sep. 7, 1835. Sol. Sep. 17, 1835, Levin Edney, M.G.
Perry, Robert to Nancy Boyd, Sep. 11, 1835.
Cole, Isaac to Margaret Weaver, Sep. 12, 1835.

Page 481
Odell, Thos. J. to Harret Bryan, Sep. 16, 1835.
Trimble, John to Margaret D. McEwen, Sep. 7, 1835. Sol. Sep. 16, 1835, J. T. Edgar, M.G.
Sevier, John to Milley A. Singleton, Sep. 17, 1835.

Hanks, Jackson to Eliza Harris, Sep. 21, 1835. Sol. Sep. 21, 1835, F. G. Ferguson.
Riggs, Samuel I. to Medora C. Cheatham, Sep. 23, 1835. Sol. Sep. 23, 1835, J. T. Edgar.
Nix, James E. to Frances Johnson, Sep. 26, 1835. Sol. Oct. 7, 1835, R. C. Goodgoin, M.G.
Stamp, Philip S. to Susanna B. Menefee, Sep. 30, 1835. Sol. Oct. 1, 1835, R.B.C. Howell, M.G.
Tardiff, Peter to Mary P. Sanders, Sep. 30, 1835. Sol. Sep. 30, 1835, J. T. Edgar, M.G.
Leach, Samuel to Rhoda M. Barker, Oct. 1, 1835.
Livingston, Wm. to Elenor R. Nichol, Oct. 1, 1835. Sol. Oct. 1, 1835, J. T. Edgar, M.G.

Page 482
Turnage, James to Sophia O'Brien, Oct. 1, 1835. Sol. Oct. 1, 1835, John Wright, J.P.
Sullivan, Willis W. to Martha Ann Porch, Oct. 8, 1835.
Courtney, Micajah to Adine A. Woods, Oct. 12, 1835. Sol. Oct. 13, 1835, R. A. Lapsley, M.G.
Rucker, Benjamin to Eliza Welch, Oct. 13, 1835. Sol. Oct. 14, 1835, Simpson Shepherd.
Perkins, Joseph W. to Mary R. Talbot, Oct. 17, 1835. Sol. Oct. 18, 1835, Robt. A. Lapsley.
Binkley, Asa N. to Martha Drenard, Oct. 21, 1835.
Hartman, James to Elizabeth Sirles, Oct. 22, 1835. Sol. Oct. 27, 1835.
Powell, Seymons to Elizabeth East, Oct. 22, 1835. Sol. Oct. 22, 1835, James Givan, M.G.
Davis, James H. to Eliza Thomas, Oct. 24, 1835.
Smith, Wynne B. to Nancy Allen, Oct. 24, 1835.

Page 483
Bell, John to Jane Yeatman, Oct. 24, 1835. Sol. Oct. 25, 1835, J. T. Edgar, M.G.
Duke, Thos. N. to Bertha Clemmons, Oct. 27, 1835. Sol. Oct. 29, 1835, Thos. J. Read, J.P.
Ezell, McGregor to Rosanna Baker, Oct. 28, 1835.
Hamilton, Hamadither to Evarilla McMurry, Oct. 31, 1835, by James Whitsitt.
Buchanan, Jno. K. to Elizabeth C. McEwen, Nov. 2, 1835.
Burnett, Leonard to Martha Hartman, Nov. 2, 1835. Sol. Nov. 5, 1835, E. H. East, J.P.
Webb, Kendal to Rhoda Dyer, Nov. 5, 1835. Sol. Nov. 5, 1835.
Hight, Doctor C. to Charity Oats, Nov. 7, 1835. Sol. Nov. 8, 1835, Wm. Herrin.
Hugh, Haffy to Emiline Thweatt, Nov. 9, 1835. Sol. Nov. 9, 1835, J. T. Edgar, M.G.
Boyd, Nicholas H. to Emeline M. Campbell, Nov. 9, 1835. Sol. Nov. 12, 1835, R. A. Lapsley, M.G.

Page 484
Jones, Lewis to Nancy A. Wilson. Nov. 12, 1835. Sol. Nov. 12, 1835, E. H. East, J.P.

Davis, James to Sarah Russell, Nov. 14, 1835. Sol. Nov. 17, 1835, R. C. Goodgoin.
Sparkman, Samuel to Sarah Eastes, Nov. 17, 1835. Sol. Nov. 19, 1835, Daniel Judd.
Hart, Jesse to Emeline Gale, Nov. 27, 1835. Sol. Nov. 27, 1835, R. A. Lapsley, M.G.
Smith, Thomas to Lucretia Cagle, Nov. 28, 1835. Sol. Nov. 29, 1835, D. Abernathy, J.P.
Rosser, David to Harriett Chadwell, Nov. 28, 1835. Sol. Nov.29, 1835.
Burnett, Leonard to Elizabeth Woodard, Nov. 30, 1835. Sol. Dec. 15, 1835, A. Thompson
Hill, John to Paulina A. Cattley, Dec. 3, 1835.
Gaulding, Wallthal to Rebecca Word, Dec. 3, 1835.
Hall, Wm. M. to Jane Alcorn, Nov. 11, 1835. Sol. Nov. 11, 1835, J. T. Edgar.

Page 485
Turner, Jas. H. to Cornelia J. Dyer, Dec. 3, 1835. Sol. Dec. 3, 1835, J. B. McFerrin, M.G.
Poindexter, Wm. G. to Elizabeth Marshall, Dec. 4, 1835. Sol. Dec. 5, 1835, W. R. Helms, J.P.
Pyron, Jno. C. to Nancy C. Pratt, Dec. 5, 1835.
Thompson, Jas. H. to Roxina C. Harris, Dec. 7, 1835. Sol. Dec. 10, 1835, Tolbert Fanning, E.C.C.
Williams, Elmon W. to Louisa Bell, Dec. 8, 1835. Sol. Dec. 10, 1835, John Beard, M.G.
Allison, Thos. G. to Sarah Vaughn, Dec. 9, 1835. Sol. Dec. 11, 1835, S. B. Giles.
Wright, William to Rachel Cook, Dec. 12, 1835.
Green, James M. to Elibeth H. Hyde, Dec. 12, 1835.
Williams, Benjamin to Tabitha Johnson, Dec. 12, 1835.
Dickinson, Henry to Elizabeth Horn, Dec. 15, 1835.

Page 486
White, Andrew J. to Margaret McEwing, Dec. 17, 1835. Sol. Dec. 17, 1835, M. M. Marshall.
Cato, William to Jane Peebles, Dec. 17, 1835. Sol. Dec. 22, 1835, David Abernathy, J.P.
Orton, Samuel R. to Ann Pinkerton, Dec. 22, 1835.
Baker, Andrew J. to Eliza Aiken, Dec. 24, 1835.
Marshall, Elihu S. to Elizabeth Fairley, Dec. 24, 1835. Sol. Dec. 24, 1835, Tolbert Fanning, E.C.C.
Sadler, Burrell B. to Rachel Stokes, Dec. 28, 1835.
Potter, James O. to Gilley Ann Sneed, Dec. 29, 1835.
Spain, John A. to Eliza A. Hartley, Dec. 30, 1835.
Hudson, Wm. G. to Mary M. Allen, Dec. 31, 1835. Sol. Dec. 31, 1835, J. B. McFerrin, M.G.
Wilds, John T. to Eliza Campbell, Dec. 31, 1835. Sol. Dec. 31, 1835, Levin Edney, M.G.

Page 487
Tucker, Harvey to Amelia Williams, July 14, 1836. Sol. July 14, 1836, J. W. Hanner, M.G.

Drake, Charles A. to Rhoda L. Neely, July 10, 1836.
Davis, Larned to Mary Marlin, June 21, 1836. Sol. June 21, 1836, Thos. Callender, J.P.
Bradford, Robert to Eliza T. Hart, June 29, 1836. Sol. June 30, 1836, Robt. A. Lapsley, M.G.
Moore, Jas. R. to Issabella L. Smith, June 20, 1836.
Wilson, George to Eugenia G. Kingsley, June 28, 1836. Sol. June 28, 1836, J. T. Edgar, M.G.
Jones, Sion to Sally Edwards, Feb. 29, 1836. Sol. March 7, 1836, Thos. Scott.
Conwell, L. S. to M. S. Combs, June 18, 1836. Sol. June 18, 1836, J. T. Edgar, M.G.
Walker, Leroy P. to Elizabeth Hudnall, June 20, 1836. Sol. June 21, 1836, J. T. Edgar, M.G.
Stansberry, Langley to Tennessee Norman, July 7, 1836. Sol. July 7, 1836, Jno. B. McFerrin, J.P.

Page 488
Grammas, James to Mary Ann Harrison, July 5, 1836. Sol. July 6, 1836, A.L.P. Green, M.G.
Mitchell, J. W. to Elizabeth Burks, April 5, 1836. Sol. April 5, 1836, John Wright, J.P.
Hager, Geo. W. to Minerva J. Clements, April 6, 1836. Sol. April 14, 1836, John Beard, M.G.
Allen, James to Jane Johnson, June 30, 1836. Sol. July 1, 1836, J. T. Edgar, J.P.
Humphrys, Julius to Amy Eliza Lathroop, June 28, 1836. Sol. June 29, 1836, J. T. Edgar.
McDaniel, George to Susanna Diggons, July 14, 1836, by Geo. Wills, Rector.
Howington, James W. to Rachel Rhodes, Aug. 4, 1836, by Wm. Roach.
Leonard, Simeon to Frances Holt, July 28, 1836. Sol. July 28, 1836, R.B.C. Howell, M.G.
Marshall, Wm. to Mary Ann Lawrence, July 27, 1836. Sol. July 27, 1836, Jas. Green, M.G.
Pyron, Chas. S. to Mary Ann Cotton, July 27, 1836.

Page 489
Matthews, Howard to Virginia Lawrence, July 27, 1836. Sol. July 27, 1836, J. T. Edgar, M.G.
McGinnis, Augustus to Almyra Pen, July 25, 1836. Sol. July 25, 1836, James Green.
Cagle, Geo. J. to Elizabeth Smith, July 18, 1836. Sol. July 20, 1836, Wm. Drake, J.P.
Hudnall, Thos. to Rachel Douglas, July 20, 1836.
White, James to Rebecca Williams, July 25, 1836. Sol. July 26, 1836, J. T. Edgar, M.G.
Jarnett, Nathan G. to Maria A. Wair, July 20, 1836.
Mitchell, Sam. V. to Elizabeth A. Garrett, July 16, 1836. Sol. July 16, 1836, J. W. Hanor.
Harrison, Thos. B. to Ann Speece, Aug. 16, 1836, by Jo Norvell, J.P.

Rhodes, H.M.C. to Harriet Jones, Aug. 12, 1836, by Wm. Roach.
Ellis, William to Phebe Shegog, March 21, 1836.

Page 490
Morrow, John to Sarah Ann Gilliam, Aug. 5, 1836. Sol. Aug. 5, 1836, J. W. Hanner, M.G.
Mayo, Benjamin to Caroline Thomas, Aug. 4, 1836. Sol. Aug. 6, 1836, Wm. J. Drake.
Rhodes, Elisha to Julia Jones, Aug. 4, 1836.
Horn, Littleton to Elizabeth McDaniel, March 24, 1836. Sol. March 24, 1836, R. C. Goodgoin, M.G.
Allen, Manion to Eliza E. Scruggs, March 26, 1836. Sol. April 3, 1836, Reuben Payne, J.P.
Pike, John to Susan Ragan, March 26, 1836, by Jno. C. Bowers.
Strange, Palmer to Eliza Long, March 28, 1836.
Baker, Andrew J. to Eliza Jones, March 19, 1836.
Binkley, Jacob to Mary Jane Frensley, March 19, 1836. Sol. April 11, 1836, Thos. J. Reace, J.P.
Brooks, M.D. to F. H. Milissa McGowen, Aug. 17, 1836. Sol. Aug. 18, 1836, Jno. B. McFerrin, M.G.

Page 491
Stalcup, Alfred to Mary Shivers, Aug. 17, 1836. Sol. Sep. 2, 1836, D. Ralston, J.P.
Roscoe, Peyton to Sarah Kirkpatrick, Jan. 22, 1836.
Thomas, Jesse to Elizabeth Litton, Jan. 20, 1836. Sol. Jan. 20, 1836, Jno. B. McFarrin, M.G.
Craig, James T. to Mary E. Robertson, Jan. 19, 1836. Sol. Jan. 20, 1836, A.L.P. Green, M.G.
Scott, Wm. A. to Ann Nicholson, Jan. 19, 1836.
Richardson, David P. to Ellen M. Bosworth, Jan. 15, 1836. Sol. Jan. 18, 1836, Jno. B. McFerrin, M.G.
Clark, Richard to Susan G. ---------, Jan. 14, 1836. Sol. Jan. 14, 1836, R.B.C. Howell, M.G.
Griffin, Pleasant to Parmelia Cowgill, Jan. 14, 1836. Sol. 1836, Peter Fuqua.
Saunders, Richmond to Mary Raspberry, Jan. 5, 1836.
Pierce, Richard J. to Sallie A. E. Campbell, Jan. 12, 1836.

Page 492
Greer, Joseph to Martha Tennison, Jan. 2, 1836. Sol. Jan. 3, 1836, Wm. Herrin.
Edney, Edmund to Elizabeth Kennedy, Nov. 7, 1836.
Puckett, Ethelrid to Nannie E. Garrett, Jan. 5, 1836. Sol. Jan. 6, 1836, A.L.P. Green, M.G.
Morgan, Rufus M. to Jane L. Williams, May 26, 1836. Sol. May 26, 1836, R.B.C. Howell, M.G.
Foster, William to Mary Owen, May 24, 1836. Sol. May 24, 1836, Wm. H. Hagans, J.P.
Harrison, Wm. to Micky Corbitt, May 23, 1836. Sol. May 26, 1836, J. Whitsett.

Smiley, Thos. T. to Emeline R. Norvell, March 30, 1836. Sol. March 31, 1836, Ph. Lindsley.
Cole, Jo G. to Jane Dillehay, May 18, 1836. Sol. May 18, 1836, Caleb Weedin.
Anderson, Nehemiah to Ann C. Duncan, Jan. 30, 1836. Sol. Jan. 31, 1836, Jno. B. McFerrin, M.G.
Russell, James to Miriam Russell, Jan. 27, 1836. Sol. Feb. 7, 1836, Jno. Davis.

Page 493
Smith, Davidson M. to Elinor M. Clow, Jan. 25, 1836. Sol. Jan. 28, 1836, A.L.P. Green, M.G.
Smith, Wyley to Catherine Jones, Jan. 25, 1836. Sol. Jan. 26, 1836, J. M. Cleag, J.P.
Cox, Crosby to Elizabeth Barrett, Jan. 23, 1836. Sol. Feb. 7, 1836, E. H. East, J.P.
Ewing, Andrew to Margaret Hynes, Feb. 4, 1836. Sol. Feb. 4, 1836, Philip Lindsley.
Aldrich, Joseph A. to Susan C. Joyce, Feb. 3, 1836. Sol. Feb. 4, 1836, Jno. B. McFerrin, M.G.
Hambrick, Jerry to Ursula Brown, Feb. 1, 1836. Sol. Feb. 3, 1836, H. Thompson.
Stephens, Needham to Angeline Brooks, Jan. 30, 1836. Sol. Jan. 31, 1836, Robt. A. Lapsley, M.G.
Owen, Campbell W. to Catherine Seay, Feb. 7, 1836.
Burnett, Wm. C. to Elizabeth Lee, Feb. 8, 1836. Sol. Feb. 10, 1836, A. Thompson.
Spain, Jno. N. to Eliza A. Hartley, Dec. 30, 1835. Sol. Jan. 1, 1836, A.L.P. Green, M.G.

Page 494
Hail, Hampton to Harriet Woods, Feb. 18, 1836. Sol. March 3, 1836, Wm. H. Nance, J.P.
Roler, John to Elizabeth Woods, Feb. 18, 1836. Sol. March 3, 1836, Wm. H. Nance, J.P.
Stegar, Charles to Nanny Tucker, Feb. 19, 1836.
Morgan, F. H. to Mary S. Jennings, June 4, 1836.
Hall, Sam'l S. to Haddassar Neely, June 3, 1836. Sol. June 6, 1836, O. B. Hays, J.P.
Dover, Isaac to Prithey P. Howerton, June 8, 1836.
Fagundus, Thesdon to Lavinia Sanders, May 3, 1836. Sol. May 4, 1836, R.B.C. Howell, M.G.
Cowgill, Moses to Martha Binkley, May 14, 1836.
Stewart, Robert to Sarah L. Clemons, May 5, 1836. Sol. May 5, 1836, R.B.C. Howell, M.G.
Scruggs, Theophalis to Winny Allen, May 12, 1836.

Page 495
Steger, Samuel to Sarah Ann Moon, Oct. 19, 1836.
Holmes, Wm. to Frances M. Huggins, Dec. 10, 1836. Sol. Dec. 10, 1836, Thos. Fuqua.
Hill, Wm. W. to Dicy Wilson, April 13, 1836. Sol. April 14, 1836, Allen Knight, J.P.

Childress, Geo. C. to Rebecca Jennings, Dec. 12, 1836. Sol. Dec. 12, 1836, J. T. Edgar, M.G.
Vaugn, Johnson to Eliza Berry, April 6, 1836. Sol. April 8, 1836, S. B. Giles.
Walker, Wm. to Catherine Earhart, April 18, 1836. Sol. April 18, 1836, P. Fuqua.
Power, Jno. F. to Adeline Pew, April 16, 1836. Sol. April 17, 1836, Jno. Wright, J.P.
Anderson, Benj. C. to Sally Burton, April 16, 1836. Sol. April 20, 1836, Allen Thompson, J.P.
Cole, James H. to Elizabeth Walker, April 16, 1836, by Jno. C. Bowers.
Binkley, Hiram to Nancy Morris, April 16, 1836.

Page 496
Humphreys, Samuel to Dorcas Price, April 13, 1836. Sol. April 16, 1836, A.L.P. Green, M.G.
Pyles, Smith to Hannah Parks, April 13, 1836. Sol. April 14, 1836, Daniel Justin.
Connell, Thos. J. to Mary Ann Hamblen, Sep. 19, 1836.
Herman, Duncan N. to Elenor R. Robertson, Sep. 20, 1836. Sol. Sep. 20, 1836, Philip Lindsley.
Spence, James to Elizabeth Cummins, Sep. 22, 1836.
Webb, N. E. to Catherine M. Clinard, Sep. 24, 1836. Sol. Sep. 24, 1836, James Green, M.G.
Clark, Elias to Margaret Biggs, Jan. 1, 1836.
Daniel, David to Helen Lay, Nov. 23, 1836. Sol. Dec. 1, 1836, Wesley Warren.
Swan, Orange to Sarah McFarland, June 15, 1836. Sol. June 15, 1836, R.B.C. Howell, M.G.
Espy, Robert to Eliza W. Johnson, Nov. 24, 1836. Sol. Nov. 25, 1836, A.L.P. Green, M.G.

Page 497
Austin, Jason H. to Lucinda L. Johnston, Nov. 21, 1836. Sol. Nov. 24, 1836, Wm. H. Hagans, J.P.
Sampley, Joseph to Catherine Butrey, Dec. 19, 1836. Sol. Dec. 24, 1836, Thos. Allison.
Roberts, Alescis to N.E.T. Moonfield, Dec. 29, 1836. Sol. Dec. 30, 1836, A.L.P. Green, M.G.
Lenon, Paten H. to Sarah Austin, Dec. 17, 1836. Sol. Dec. 22, 1836, Wm. H. Hagans,J.P.
Stainback, J.W.H. to Mary E. Spain, Nov. 16, 1836. Sol. Nov. 17, 1836, A.L.P. Green, M.G.
Cross, Wm. E. to Henrietta Sirls, Dec. 17, 1836. Sol. Dec. 30, 1836, H. Towns, J.P.
Crunk, Joseph H. to Susan E. Pratt, Nov. 10, 1836. Sol. Nov. 10, 1836, Robt. Davis, M.G.
Wright, Robt. T. to Mary B. Phillips, Nov. 9, 1836, by Jas. Whitsett.
Whitly, Micajah to Mary Parks, Dec. 21, 1836. Sol. Dec. 21, 1836, E.S. Hale, J.P.
Gibson, Robt. to Rosanna Adams, Nov. 11, 1836. Sol. Nov. 11, 1836, J. T. Edgar, M.G.

Page 498
Fulcher, Edward to Rachel Johnson, Nov. 16, 1836. Sol. Nov. 16, 1836, Wm. H. Hagans, J.P.
Briley, John G. to Sarah Ann Gillman, Nov. 7, 1836.
Fox, James to Susan Waggoner, Nov. 7, 1836.
Poarch, Jno. C. to Louisa Cardy, Oct. 31, 1836.
Rhodes, Newton to Alcey Heath, Nov. 1, 1836, by Wm. Roach.
Campbell, James to Jane McCrary, Dec. 15, 1836. Sol. Dec. 15, 1836, Jno. Wright, J.P.
Shelton, Jesse to Sarah Ann Barclift, Oct. 29, 1836.
Brooks, Jno. T. to Theresa Cowgill, Oct. 31, 1836.
Wallace, Wm. W. to Mary A. W. Barry, Dec. 13, 1836. Sol. Dec. 13, 1836, R.B.C. Howell, M.G.
Walker, Wm. to Martha Price, Aug. 17, 1836.

Page 499
Jones, Jefferson to Agnes McCrory, Aug. 19, 1836, by Wm. Roach.
Stewart, Jas. H. to Mary Matlock, Aug. 30, 1836. Sol. Sep. 1, 1836, E. H. East, J.P.
Dascomb, Jno. to Caroline Horn, Aug. 30, 1836. Sol. Aug. 30, 1836, Jno. B. McFerrin, M.G.
Howlett, Addison B. to Elizabeth Clemons, Nov. 26, 1836. Sol. Nov. 30, 1836, S. G. Burney, M.G.
Harris, Jno. P. to Elizabeth Gibbs, Nov. 26, 1836.
Hill, Samuel to Jane Howlett, Nov. 29, 1836.
Brown, James to Sophia Bundy, Dec. 2, 1836.
Burr, Wm. G. to Elizabeth Rundalls, Dec. 7, 1836. Sol. Dec. 7, 1836, D. Ralston, J.P.
Philips, Asa R. to Sarah Ann Wright, Nov. 26, 1836.
Briley, Thos. B. to Rebecca Wolf, Dec. 27, 1836.

Page 500
Haines, Charles to Harriet McDaniel, Dec. 31, 1836. Sol. Jan. 1, 1837, R. C. Goodgoin, M.G.
Ferebee, Thos. H. to Mary Greer, Sep. 2, 1836. Sol. Sep. 4, 1836, Jas. Davis, J.P.
Merchant, Wm. S. to Nancy Lockby, Sep. 5, 1836. Sol. Sep. 6, 1836, Daniel Judd.
Beasley, Bennet H. to Susan Carper, Sep. 6, 1836. Sol. Sep. 6, 1836, R.B.C. Howell.
Castleman, David to Louisianna Cayce, Sep. 7, 1836. Sol. Sep. 8, 1836, Robt. Bradford, J.P.
Wright, H. M. to Amelia Ann Williams, Sep. 7, 1836.
Chadoin, Jesse to Nancy Simmons, Sep. 8, 1836.
Dement, George Thomas to Ann E. Richmond, Sep. 13, 1836. Sol. Sep. 1836, J. W. Davis, M.G.
Austin, Wm. to Hannah Gillman, Sep. 15, 1836.
Read, David to Ann Litton, Sep. 1, 1836.

Page 501
Smith, Jno. P. to Mary Langston, Oct. 15, 1836. Sol. Oct. 16, 1836, Jno. Bransford, M.G.

Rice, Robert R. to Mary Ann Shirly, Oct. 11, 1836. Sol. Oct. 11, 1836, J. T. Edgar, M.G.
Finley, James to Elizabeth W. Bell, Oct. 10, 1836.
Mathis, Henry to Lucinda Ray, Oct. 5, 1836. Sol. Oct. 6, 1836, David Abernathy, J.P.
Hawkins, Nathan to P. Howerton, Oct. 9, 1836. Sol. Oct. 9, 1836, Jno. Corbett, J.P.
Stewart, Arthur to Martha Cabler, Oct. 1, 1836. Sol. Oct. 6, 1836, Jno. Corbett, J.P.
Smith, Wm. to Susan Mayo, Sep. 28, 1836. Sol. Sep. 28, 1836, David Abernathy, J.P.
Sailors, Jno. to Elenor Hogan, Sep. 26, 1836.
Stubblefield, Madison to Amanda Young, Oct. 18, 1836. Sol. Oct. 20, 1836, Wm. J. Drake, J.P.
Cantrell, Stephen, Jr. to Louisa Horn, Oct. 18, 1836. Sol. Oct. 18, 1836, J. Y. Burney, M.G.

Page 502
Holt, Henry to Louisa Harris, Sep. 24, 1836.
Morgan, F. H. to Mary S. Jennings, June 4, 1836. Sol. June 5, 1836, J. T. Edgar, M.G.
McLean, A. Andrews to Louisa E. Quinn, Oct. 25, 1836. Sol. Oct. 25, 1836, A.L.P. Green, M.G.
Lassiter, Frederick to Mary A. Draper, Oct. 20, 1836. Sol. Oct. 22, 1836, E. P. Connell, J.P.
Fanning, Tolbert to Charlotte Fall, Dec. 21, 1836. Sol. Dec. 22, 1836, Phillip Lindsley, M.G.
Cloyd, Preston to Mary F. Castleman, Dec. 22, 1836.
Manlove, Joseph E. to Caroline L. Hyde, Dec. 22, 1836. Sol. Dec. 22, 1836, J.S.G. Strickland, M.G.
Fry, Freeman to Mahala Wiggins, Dec. 24, 1836. Sol. Dec. 25, 1836, Daniel Jude.
Kay, Reubin L. to Elspha M. Walker, Aug. 25, 1836. Sol. Aug. 25, 1836, R. A. Lapsley, M.G.
Wilson, John to Mary Grizzard, May 31, 1836, by Jno. C. Bowers.

Page 503
Carr, Jesse D. to Louisa A. Brewer, Oct. 26, 1836. Sol. Oct. 27, 1836, A.L.P. Green, M.G.
Buchanan, James to Amanda McMurrey, April 26, 1836. Sol. April --, 1836, J. T. Edgar, M.G.
Lovell, Chas. G. to Jinsy A. W. Hooper, Oct. 29, 1836. Sol. Nov. 2, 1836, Wm. Shelton, J.P.
Bandy, Williamson B. to Susan Brown, Jan. 2, 1836. Sol. 1836, P. Fuqua.
Drake, Isaac to Rhoda Neely, July 10, 1836. Sol. July 10, 1836, J. T. Edgar, M.G.
Morehead, Geo. to Millie Ann Surveyor, Feb. 18, 1836. Sol. Feb. 18, 1836, L. P. Cheatham, J.P.
Clay, Joseph W. to Buthenia H. Walker, March 5, 1836. Sol. March 10, 1836, Tolbert Fanning, M.G.
Love, Joseph to Sarah Gleaves, Feb. 20, 1836.
Terry, Nathaniel G. to Ann Hays, March 9, 1836. Sol. March 16, 1836, J. M. Clay, J.P.

Rives, Peter G. to Eliza Arnold, March 17, 1836, by Geo. Weller, M.G.

Page 504

Long, John to Lucinda McDaniel, March 10, 1836. Sol. March 11, 1836, Jno. Davis, J.P.

Sills, Joseph to Mary F. Young, April 28, 1836. Sol. April 28, 1836, R.B.C. Howell, M.G.

Strange, Parham to Milly Long, April 30, 1836. Sol. May 1, 1836, Thos. Ferebee, J.P.

Fox, Amos to Sarah J. Young, April 28, 1836. Sol. April 28, 1836, R.B.C. Howe-l, M.G.

McMahon, Morgan to Sarah Trenton, May 12, 1836. Sol. May 12, 1836, Jno. A. Shute, J.P.

Sayers, Charles to Maria E. Cowan, May 12, 1836. Sol. May 12, 1836, Thos. Callender, J.P.

Madaris, Grady to Mary E. Smith, April 21, 1836. Sol. April 21, 1836, Jas. Whitsett.

Chadwell, Gideon to Lucinda Whittemon, April 18, 1836. Sol. April 19, 1836, Jas. Whitsett.

Erwin, Hugh to Margery Bosley, Feb. 23, 1836. Sol. Feb. 23, 1836.

Dodson, Archibald to Lydia Van Hook, Feb. 24, 1836. Sol. Feb. 24, 1836, Jno. Wright, J.P.

Page 505

Everett, Blake B. to Nancy Balthrop, Feb. 22, 1836. Sol. March 1, 1836, Thos. W. Sheron.

Ginett, Andrew to Martha Earls, Feb. 25, 1836. Sol. Feb. 25, 1836, Jno. W. Hanner, M.G.

Scott, Alexander to Mary J. Hobson, March 1, 1836.

Young, Joseph R. to Nancy Burgiss, March 1, 1836. Sol. March 2, 1836, E. S. Hale, J.P.

Brown, Jesse to Mary Hester, Feb. 5, 1836. Sol. Feb. 5, 1836, J. B. McFerrin, M.G.

Boswell, James to Narcissa Hughes, Feb. 10, 1836.

Ward, Albert G. to Maria G. Baker, Feb. 16, 1836.

Roller, John to Elizabeth Woods, Feb. 18, 1836.

Capps, Robert to Lydia Bess, Dec. 21, 1836.

Baker, James to Mary Jones, Feb. 19, 1836.

Page 506

Thruston, John to Lucretia O. Shrague, March 9, 1837. Sol. March 9, 1837, J. T. Edgar, M.G.

Dennison, Marshall to Mary J. Vanderville, June 20, 1837. Sol. June 20, 1837, Thos. Fuqua.

Brown, J. P. W. to Jane Nichol, Nov. 10, 1837. Sol. Nov. 16, 1837, J. T. Edgar, M.G.

Brown, Wm. to Jane Allen, June 6, 1837.

Miller, Thos. J. to Nancy J. Welburn, April 11, 1837. Sol. April 11, 1837, Jno. Wright, J.P.

Jent, James N. to Sarah Harris, July 19, 1837.

Tucker, Armistead C. to Sarah Ann Tucker, July 15, 1837. Sol. July 15, 1837, C. McDaniel, J.P.

McWhirter, Sam C. to Mary K. Swin, July 18, 1837.
Young, William to Mary Hall, July 24, 1837.
Pegram, Edward to Catherine Burnett, Oct. 10, 1837.

Page 507
Chilton, Thos. W. to Catherine Phillips, Oct. 12, 1837. Sol. Oct. 12, 1837, J. W. Davis, M.G.
Mitchell, Wm. N. to Martha J. Williams, April 19, 1837.
Phillips, Geo. W. to Susan Jane Wright, Oct. 14, 1837. Sol. Oct. 19, 1837, Jas. Whitsitt.
Carney, John to Sally Ford, Aug. 21, ----, by Reubin Payne, J.P.
Dreyfus, Isaac to Lucy Royster, Aug. 17, 1837. Sol. Aug. 17, 1837, R.B.C. Howell,M.G.
Elliott, Collins D. to Elizabeth --------, Aug. 19, 1837. Sol. Aug. 19, 1837, J. B. McFerrin, M.G.
Bankhead, Jas. to Elizabeth Flint, May 16, 1837. Sol. May 16, 1837, J. T. Edgar, M.G.
Topp, Robertson to Elizabeth L. Vance, April 27, 1837. Sol. April 27, 1837, J. T. Edgar, M.G.
Rains, Felix R. to Mary E. H. Rains, Nov. 30, 1837. Sol. Nov. 30, 1837, J. T. Edgar, M.G.
Alderson, Thomas to Rebecca Compton, Feb. 27, 1837. Sol. Feb. 28, 1837, J. T. Edgar, M.G.

Page 508
Woods, James, Jr. to Elizabeth S. Crockett, Aug. 30, 1837. Sol. Aug. 31, 1837, J. T. Edgar, M.G.
Yeargin, William to Malvina H. Rucks, May 23, 1837. Sol. May 23, 1837, J. T. Edgar, M.G.
Smith, Pleasant to Mary Jane Ewing, Feb. 16, 1837. Sol. Feb. 16, 1837.
Trimble, Thos. C. to Fannie E. Williams, May 23, 1837. Sol. May 23, 1837, J. T. Edgar.
Mahoney, Stephen J. to Teresa Callan, Nov. 16, 1837. Sol. Nov. 23, 1837, J. T. Edgar, M.G.
Harris, Wm. H. to Margaret A. Scales, Sep. 6, 1837. Sol. Sep. 12, 1837, Jas. Whitsitt.
Shumate, J.J.D.R. to Mary Warmath, Sep. 6, 1837.
Lapsley, Jas. M. to Elizabeth A. Hall, Sep. 11, 1837.
Camp, Wm. C. to Elizabeth K. Morgan, Aug. 28, 1837. Sol. Aug. 29, 1837, J.L.G. Strickland, M.G.
Swain, Thomas to Harriet Osment, July 24, 1837. Sol. Wm. Hagans, J.P.

Page 509
Lucas, W.H.F. to Catherine Shields, June 3, 1837. Sol. June 4, 1837, R.L. Andrews.
Brilsford, John to Mary Ann Cook, June 7, 1837. Sol. June 7, 1837, R.B.C. Howell, M.G.
Brown, Wm. to Jane Allen, June 6, 1837. Sol. June 6, 1837, Jno. H. Wright, J.P.
Stow, Ebenezer to Elizabeth A. Castleman, April 29, 1837. Sol. April 30, 1837, Jas. Whitsitt.

Matthias, Thomas to Jane Wray, April 27, 1837. Sol. April 27, 1837, Jno. Wright, J.P.
Brittle, Milton P. to Sarah McMurry, April 26, 1837. Sol. April --, 1837, J. W. Davis, M.G.
Burnett, Ira J. to Elizabeth Bland, Oct. 9, 1837. Sol. Oct. 10, 1837, E. H. East, J.P.
Edmondson, Jno. to Matilda J. Wilson, April 27, 1837.
Moake, Jacob to Martha W. Harris, Oct. 9, 1837.
Saunders, Jno. F. to Lucinda J. Austin, Sep. 30, 1837. Sol. Sep. 30, 1837, Wm. H. Hagans, J.P.

Page 510
Burlington, John to Mary A. Hollingsworth, Oct. 7, 1837. Sol. Oct. 8, 1837, Jas. Whitsett.
Mitchell, Wm. N. to Martha J. Williams, April 19, 1837. Sol. April 19, 1837, A.L.P. Green, M.G.
Morris, Isaac (col.) to Harriett Summers, April 13, 1837. Sol. April 13, Reubin Payne, J.P.
Brooks, Christopher to Ann L. Kinsly, April 19, 1837. Sol. April 19, 1837, Robt. L. Andrews.
Crawford, A. C. to Martha A. Lytle, April 18, 1837. Sol. Sep. 18, 1837, Phillip Lindsley.
Burgess, A. B. to Helen M. Stratton, April 18, 1837. Sol. April 18, 1837, Phillip Lindsley.
Elkin, Robert to Peggy Morton, April 13, 1837. Sol. April 27, 1837, John Morton.
Drew, Edward to Hannah Butcher, Sep. 13, 1837. Sol. Sep. 13, 1837, R. Moody, M.G.
Martin, Benjamin F. to Narcissa Allen, Aug. 30, 1837. Sol. Aug. 31, 1837, J.G.L. Strickland, M.G.
Hite, Robt. C. to Rebecca Diamond, June 15, 1837. Sol. June 22, 1837, Wm. Shelton, M.G.

Page 511
Freeman, Clinton L. to Sarah L. McMurray, June 1, 1837. Sol. June 1, 1837, Jas. Whitsitt.
Wallace, Jno. M. to Sarah E. Smith, Aug. 5, 1837. Sol. Aug. 5, 1837, J. Whitsitt.
Ellis, Azariah to Catherine Hagar, Aug. 9, 1837. Sol. Aug. 10, 1837, Thos. Fuqua.
Jackson, Levin E. to John Taylor, Aug. 11, 1837. Sol. Aug. 13, 1837, Jno. Davis, J.P.
Poston, Alex. H. to Adeline T. Bosley, Aug. 15, 1837. Sol. Aug. 15, 1837, R.B.C. Howell, M.G.
Riggs, Jas. to Charlotte Napier, Aug. 16, 1837. Sol. Aug. 16, 1837, R. A. Lapsley, M.G.
Owen, Wm. to Ketturah Waller, Jan. 20, 1837.
Brown, Hughly to Matilda Inman, Jan. 19, 1837.
Elliott, Collins D. to Elizabeth Porterfield, Aug. 19, 1837.
Lapsley, Joseph M. to Elizabeth A. Hall, Sep. 11, 1837. Sol. Sep. 12, 1837, R. Lapsley.

Page 512
Trousdale, Bryson B. to Maria Smith, Jan. 25, 1837. Sol. Jan. 26, 1837, J. T. Edgar, M.G.
Shull, John to Elizabeth Holloway, Jan. 21, 1837.
Brooks, Wm. T. to Janette Baker, Jan. 25, 1837.
Harris, Allen P. to Eliza Jane Drake, Jan. 28, 1837. Sol. Feb. 2, 1837, D. Ralston, J.P.
Newsom, Joseph to Martha Adkisson, Jan. 31, 1837. Sol. Feb. 2, 1837, Ira Davis, J.P.
Grizzard, Granville D. to Martha A. Bumpass, Jan. 31, 1837. Sol. Feb. 2, 1837, Wm. B. Carpenter.
Castleman, Preston to Eliza Castleman, Feb. 6, 1837. Sol. March 15, 1837, Jas. H. Cook, J.P.
Pritchitt, Jno. C. to Angeline Adcock, July 13, 1837.
Cole, Robt. A. to Charlotte C. Marlin, July 13, 1837. Sol. July 13, 1837, Robt. L. Anderson.
Estes, John to Mary Brackett, July 11, 1837.

Page 513
Kimble, Thos. D. to Eliza Boggs, July 5, 1837. Sol. July 5, 1837, J. T. Edgar, M.G.
Dorris, Thomas to Lydia Byrn, July 3, 1837. Sol. July 9, 1837, Jno. Wright, J.P.
Morrison, Andrew to Sarah Lawrence, July 1, 1837. Sol. July 2, 1837, R.B.C. Howell, M.G.
Harris, John B. to Evelin Woodward, June 28, 1837.
Adcock, Beverly to Paralee Paradise, June 27, 1837. Sol. June 30, 1837, D. Ralston, J.P.
Wright, Jesse to Martha Wright, June 20, 1837. Sol. June 27, 1837, Jas. H. Cook, J.P.
Anderson, Dan'l S. to Elizabeth Barkly, July 10, 1837. Sol. July 11, 1837, Danl Judd.
Grizzard, Wm. M. to Mary A. Bumpass, Jan. 3, 1837. Sol. Jan. 4, 1837, Wm. B. Carpenter.
Herrin, Chas. J. to Martha Abernathy, Jan. 5, 1837. Sol. Jan. 5, 1837, David Abernathy, J.P.
Bandy, Williamson B. to Susan Brown, Jan. 2, 1837.

Page 514
Samuel, Addison L. to Mary P. Scott, Jan. 13, 1837. Sol. Jan. 14, 1837, A.L.P. Green, M.G.
Harrison, Caleb G. to Eliza Aikin, Jan. 8, 1837. Sol. Jan. 8, 1837, Jno. Wright, J.P.
Adcock, Henry to Minerva Fryer, Jan. 9, 1837. Sol. Jan. 15, 1837, D. Ralston, J.P.
Phillips, Jesse H. to Margaret J. May, Jan. 16, 1837. Sol. Jan. 19, 1837, J. T. Edgar, M.G.
Higginbotham, Wm. to Amanda M. Sturdivant, June 20, 1837. Sol. June 22, 1837, R.B.C. Howell, M.G.
Lovell, Napoleon B. to Julia Diamond, Jan. 17, 1837. Sol. Jan. 17, 1837, Wm. Shelton, J.P.
Clodfelter, Jacob to Martha Nelms, June 20, 1837. Sol. June 20, 1837, James Green, M.G.
Phillips, Wm. J. to Virginia Robertson, June 17, 1837.

Carter, Danl F. to Mary J. Buntin, Feb. 15, 1837. Sol. Feb. 23, 1837.
Lovell, Jno. H. to Parthena C. Hooper, Jan. 17, 1837. Sol. Jan. 22, 1837, Wm. Shelton, J.P.

Page 515
Fullmer, Jno. S. to Mary Ann Price, May 24, 1837. Sol. May 24, 1837, R.B.C. Howell, M.G.
Boyte, Felix G. to Elizabeth Simmons, May 24, 1837.
Glascock, E. R. to Olivia F. Andrews, May 25, 1837. Sol. May ------, J. W. Davis, M.G.
Bloodworth, Bedford to Polly Sullivan, May 17, 1837. Sol. May 17, 1837, David Abernathy, J.P.
Leak, Josephus C. to Pamila Farley, May 17, 1837. Sol. May 18, 1837, Robert L. Andrews.
Enochs, Alfred to Mary F. Camp, May 18, 1837. Sol. May 18, 1837, J.L.G. Strickland, M.G.
Lassiter, Elisha H. to Elizabeth Vaughn, May 16, 1837.
Woodfolk, Wm. W. to Ellen D. Horton, May 11, 1837. Sol. May 11, 1837, R.B.C. Howell, M.G.
Corbett, Felix M. to Sarah C. Anderson, April 12, 1837. Sol. April 12, 1837, Danl. Judd.
Peak, Simmons to Delitha B. Nugent, May 10, 1837. Sol. May 10, 1837, John Bransford, M.G.

Page 516
Hall, Richard to Ann L. Johnson, April 12, 1837.
Dungey, Wm. to Elizabeth Dungey, May 27, 1837, by P. Fuqua.
Andrews, James to Mary McIntyre, July 26, 1837. Sol. July 26, 1837, J. B. Knowles, J.P.
Ward, John H. to Ann S. Reed, July 26, 1837. Sol. July ------, J. W. Davis, M.G.
Morgan, Lewis to Mary Ann Parker, July 27, 1837.
Hooper, Wm. C. to Mary Ann Cullom, Aug. 2, 1837. Sol. Aug. 6, 1837, Wm. Shelton, J.P.
McLendon, Thos. J. to Haley F. Ellis, July 31, 1837.
Hill, Jas. S. to Celia A. Abernathy, Sep. 4, 1837. Sol. Sep. 5, 1837, B. M. Barnes, J.P.
Rives, Felix R. to Catherine Hopper, June 15, 1837.
Murpo, Wm. B. to Eveline R. Sims, Nov. 1, 1837. Sol. Nov. 1, 1837, P. W. Maxey, J.P.

Page 517
Waggoner, Saml. D. to Margaret Huggins, March 14, 1837. Sol. March 14, 1837, Thomas Fuqua.
Davis, Seth L. to Mary Moss, Dec. 19, 1837. Sol. Nov. 21, 1838.
White, Jacob to Elizabeth Hofman, Feb. 16, 1837.
Wood, Edward G. to Anestine Hall, Oct. 25, 1837.
Hally, John to Elizabeth Norton, Oct. 27, 1837. Sol. Oct. 27, 1837, Jno. M. Robertson.
Wiley, Levi to Mary Wright, Nov. 11, 1837. Sol. Nov. 30, 1837, Jas. H. Cook, J.P.

Robinson, J. B. to Marie A. Hewlett, Nov. 14, 1837. Sol. Nov. 14, 1837, A.L.P. Green.
Abernathy, Jas. to Elizabeth Deal, Sep. 19, 1837. Sol. Sep. 19, 1837, Wm. P. Drake.
Page, Jas. H. to Mary A. Quisenberry, Oct. 18, 1837. Sol. Oct. 19, 1837, J. W. Davis, M.G.
Hoffman, Jas. W. to Mary Jane Gravett, July 25, 1837. Sol. July, J. W. Davis, M.G.

Page 518
Mahoney, Stephen J. to Thersa Callen, Nov. 16, 1837.
Harris, Jno. B. to Eveline Woodard, June 28, 1837. Sol. Aug. 12, 1837, Thos. Scott, J.P.
Boyd, Robert to Rachel Gwin, Nov. 27, 1837. Sol. Nov. 27, 1837, Jno. Wright, J.P.
Ryall, Thos. C. to Elizabeth Scudder, Dec. 21, 1837. Sol. Dec. 21, 1837, J. Thos. Wheat, M.G.
Hinton, Harrison B. to Maria T. Sumner, Nov. 30, 1837. Sol. Nov. 30, 1837, A.L.P. Green.
Johnson, John W. to Martha Johnson, April 8, 1837. Sol. April 8, 1837, Jno. Corbitt, J.P.
Parker, Felix, Jr. to Martha C. Oakford, Nov. 19, 1837. Sol. Nov. 19, 1837, J. M. Wheat, M.G.
Hows, John to Catherine Jones, Dec. 12, 1837. Sol. Dec. 14, 1837, S.B. Davidson, J.P.
Shelton, Wm. H. to Sally Jane Greer, Dec. 13, 1837. Sol. Dec. 19, 1837, Wm. Herrin, M.G.
Dozier, Grundy to Sarah Page, Feb. 13, 1837. Sol. Feb. 18, 1837, Wm. Shelton, J.P.

Page 519
Goodrich, Thomas C. to Eliza Foster, Feb. 12, 1837. Sol. Feb. 12, 1837, Jo. Norvell, J.P.
Pease, Jno. B. to Elizabeth W. Dibrell, Feb. 13, 1837. Sol. Feb. ------, J. W. Davis, M.G.
Franklin, Washington to Mahala S. Petty, Feb. 15, 1837, by Thos. Callender, J.P.
Maynor, Pleasant to Jane M. Iredale, Feb. 21, 1837. Sol. Feb. 21, 1837, F. E. Pitts, M.G.
Wozencraft, Oliver M. to Lamiza A. Pamsey, Feb. 21, 1837. Sol. Feb. 23, 1837, F. E. Pitts, M.G.
Alford, Guthridge to Celia Johnson, Sep. 23, 1837. Sol. Sep. 24, 1837, E. H. East, J.P.
Baxter, Nathaniel to Martha O. Hamilton, Sep. 19, 1837. Sol. Sep. 19, 1837, Robt. Hardin, M.G.
Childress, Lotin to Susan B. Willis, Sep. 21, 1837. Sol. Sep. 21, 1837, Robt. L. Andrews.
Garner, Brice M. to Sarah Shaffer, May 10, 1837. Sol. May 10, 1837, J. W. Davis, M.G.
Hart, Jno. H. to Mary Ann Bosworth, Oct. 19, 1837. Sol. Oct. 19, 1837, J. W. Davis, M.G.

Page 520
Hibdon, Andy to Martha Holder, Oct. 10, 1837. Sol. Oct. 10, 1837, Jno. M. Robertson.

Redd, John P. to Jane Pegram, Oct. 18, 1837. Sol. Dec. 4, 1837, R. C. Goodgoin, M.G.
Bennett, Wm. to Betsy Ann Bess, Dec. 16, 1837. Sol. Dec. 16, 1837, Thos. Callender, J.P.
Ellis, Thos. to Nancy C. Chesser, Dec. 9, 1837. Sol. Dec. 10, 1837, David Abernathy, J.P.
Singleton, Ander J. to Prissy M. Winston, Aug. 24, 1837. Sol. Aug. ------, J. W. Davis, M.G.
Major, Thos. to Elizabeth Gibbs, Nov. 5, 1837. Sol. Nov. 29, 1837, Wm. Shelton, J.P.
Villeplait, A. S. to Sarah A. Roscoe, Dec. 28, 1837. Sol. Dec. 28, 1837, Thos. J. Wheat, J.P.
Suiter, James to Mary Bell, Nov. 4, 1837. Sol. Nov. 6, 1837, David Abernathy, J.P.
Morris, Wm. P. to Louisa M. Davis, Dec. 21, 1837. Sol. Dec. 24, 1837, B. F. Binkley, J.P.
Geers, John B. to Catherine B. Howerton, Sep. 23, 1837, by Peter Fuqua.

Page 521
Hanks, A. J. to Matilda May, June 14, 1837. Sol. June 14, 1837, Jno. Corbitt, J.P.
Wharton, Thos. J. to Mary Edgar, June 14, 1837. Sol. June 15, 1837, Robt. Lapsley, M.G.
Cloyd, Ezekiel A. to Louisa Ann Wilson, June 12, 1837. Sol. June 22, 1837, Jno. Beard, M.G.
Laws, Anderson S. to Julia Ann Smith, June 8, 1837. Sol. June 8, 1837, Jno. Wright, J.P.
Mitchell, Geo. W. to Mary Jane Shelton, Feb. 9, 1837. Sol. Feb. 16, 1837, E. H. East, J.P.
Edmiston, Hiram to Nancy B. Davis, Feb. 9, 1837. Sol. Feb. 9, 1837, A.L.P. Green, M.G.
Olliphant, Andrew J. to Sarah C. Shelton, Feb. 11, 1837. Sol. Feb. 16, 1837, E. H. East, J.P.
Fuller, Chas. A. to Susan A. Demoville, March 6, 1837. Sol. March 8, 1837, R.B.C. Howell, M.G.
Thompson, Jno. W. to Mary Jane Whitsitt, Nov. 6, 1837. Sol. Nov. 7, 1837, Jas. Whitsitt.
Allison, Thos. J. to Tabitha M. Newsom, Nov. 6, 1837. Sol. Nov. 16, 1837, W. R. Hootin, M.G.

Page 522
Copper, Thos. A. to Martha Hall, Nov. 8, 1837. Sol. Nov. 9, 1837, J. Thos. Wheat, M.G.
Stone, Seymour to Julia A. Bass, Nov. 7, 1837. Sol. Nov. 7, 1837, Robt. A. Lapsley, M.G.
Coppage, Thos. L. to Emily Cherry, Nov. 2, 1837, by P. Fuqua.
Masson, Henry E. A. to Louisa Ann Grizzard, Dec. 6, 1837. Sol. Dec. 6, 1837, A.L.P. Green, M.G.
Graves, Richard E. to America Weigart, March 22, 1837. Sol. March 22, 1837, A.L.P. Green, M.G.
Moore, S. G. to Sarah A. L. Quinn, March 15, 1837. Sol. March 16, 1837, A.L.P. Green, M.G.

Napier, Leroy G. to Fannie H. Robertson, Aug. 26, 1837. Sol. Aug. 26, 1837, R.B.C. Howell, M.G.
Alexander, Thos. B. to Eliza J. Caldwell, March 25, 1837. Sol. April 13, 1837, Jno. Beard, M.G.
Scott, Geo. W. to Charlotte A. Steele, Aug. 31, 1837. Sol. Aug. 31, 1837, L. H. Whitaker.
Sullivan, Jas. M. to Patsey M. Holt, Sep. 1, 1837. Sol. Sep. 2, 1837, Wm. Hagans, J.P.

Page 523
McCool, Joseph to Mary Fiser, Dec. 21, 1837. Sol. Dec. 21, 1837, Chas. W. Moorman, J.P.
Jackson, Abijah H. to Julia A. Speece, Nov. 2, 1837. Sol. Nov. 2, 1837, A.L.P. Green, M.G.
Marshall, Thos. L. to Catherine Williams, Nov. 23, 1837. Sol. Nov. 23, 1837, R.B.C. Howell, M.G.
Tennison, Absolom to Lydia Castleman, March 13, 1837. Sol. March 15, 1837, Jas. Cook, J.P.
Harman, A.J.R. to Elizabeth White, Nov. 4, 1837. Sol. Nov. 10, 1837, Daniel Judd, M.G.
Wilson, James to Rebecca Bennett, April 5, 1837. Sol. April 6, 1837, John Wright, J.P.
Griffin, Jno. G. to Martha A. Watson, Nov. 15, 1837. Sol. Nov. 15, 1837, Jno. Wright, J.P.
Keeler, Archibald J. to Ellen Howard, March 14, 1837. Sol. March 14, 1837, Daniel Judd, M.G.
Stokes, L. B. to Martha J. McFarland, Dec. 11, 1837. Sol. Dec. 11, 1837, E. S. Hale.
Garvin, John to Emily Friendsley, Nov. 10, 1837. Sol. Nov. 23, 1837, Jno. Wright, J.P.

Page 524
McMurray, John M. to Mary J. Still, Feb. 22, 1837. Sol. Feb. 25, 1837, Jas. Whitsitt.
Phelps, Wm. to Jane Harris, Dec. 15, 1837, by Jas. Whitsitt.
Craddock, Benjamin to Lucy Ann Holmes, Feb. 15, 1837.
Miller, Thos. J. to Nancy J. Welburn, April 11, 1837.
Young, James to Sarah Mayo, Nov. 28, 1837.
Owen, Alford to Cynthia Goodner, Dec. 22, 1837.
Benson, Sylvanus E. to Elizabeth Marshall, Nov. 30, 1837.
Earthman, S. H. to Cicily Young, Feb. 21, 1837.
Alley, John to Margaret Reed, Dec. 11, 1837.
Lanier, Wm. G. to Paulina Stogner, Aug. 16, 1837.

Page 525
Matthews, Wm. to Christine Condon, Oct. 21, 1837.
Vick, Abner to Susan Pack, Dec. 15, 1837.
Holt, Jno. W. to Mary Condon, Oct. 24, 1837.
Hunt, Wm. C. to Elizabeth A. Ogilvie, Oct. 30, 1837.
Gower, Elisha to Sally Fowler, Feb. 8, 1837.
Tant, Richard to Mary Barnes, Dec. 8, 1837.
Gower, Edmund to Martha Small, Dec. 15, 1837.
Rollins, Wm. H. to Mary Walker, Dec. 21, 1837.

Osment, Thos. C. to Jane Vaughn, Oct. 28, 1837.
Austin, Lemuel to Emily D. Butler, Nov. 21, 1837.

Page 526
Hill, Wm. G. to Lamisa Felts, Dec. 13, 1837.

DAVIDSON COUNTY, TENNESSEE

Marriage Book II, 1838-1847

Page 1
Andrew Peterson to Elizabeth Edwards, June 25, 1838, by William Stringfellow, J.P., June 26, 1838.
Armstrong, Hugh C. to Mrs. Sarah Wilson, March 18, 1838, by Robert Boyt C. Howell, March 18, 1838.
Philip Anthony, Jr. to Athalana Waggoner, Feb. 7, 1838, by C. G. McPherson, Feb. 8, 1838.
Alley, John to Phebe Haley, Jan. 3, 1838, by P. M. Maxey, Esq., Jan. 4, 1838.
Alley, Vardeman to Martha Thomas, Dec. 12, 1838, by N. B. Butler, J.P., Dec. 13, 1838.
Allen, Felix A. to Betsey Ann Levy, Nov. 23, 1838.
Atkins, Addison L. to Nancy Coffman, Oct. 29, 1838.
Baynes, Marcus H. to Mary Ann Rowe, Jan. 16, 1838, by T. Fuquay, Jan. 16, 1838.

Page 2
David Binkley to Huldy Durard, Feb. 13, 1838.
Brown, Nicholas T. P. to Agnes P. Harris, --- 7, 1838.
Barner, Sterling M. to Sarah Jane West, Aug. 8, 1838, by J. T. Edgar, Aug. 8, 1838.
Boyle, Cornelius to Tabitha E. G. Allen, Aug. 30, 1838, by John Wright, J.P., Aug. 30, 1838.
Brumbelow, Archd. to Susanna Neely, Nov. 9, 1838.
Bostick, John H. to Catharine L. Temple, Dec. 18, 1838, by W.D.F. Sawrie, M.G., Dec. 20, 1838.
Butler, E. C. to Mary Turley, Dec. 18, 1838, by John W. Hanner, Dec. 18, 1838.
Brown, James T. to Charlott T. Hammonds, Dec. 20, 1838.
Corley, Bartlet to Letitia Hallum, Jan. 8, 1838, by W. Garrett, M.G., Jan. 8, 1838.

Page 3
Cartwright, Thomas to Elizabeth Hooper, Jan. 18, 1838.
Cooper, Thomas to Mary A. Boyd, Jan. 25, 1838, by B. M. Barnes, J.P., Jan. 25, 1838.
Conner, Amos L. to Mary Ann Beals, Feb. 2, 1838, by E. P. Connell, J.P., Jan. 4, 1838.
Clark, John A. to Jane Thompson, March 6, 1838.
Braddock, Rolla Smith to Eliza Beard, March 14, 1838, by Daniel Judd, L.E., March 15, 1838.
Cato, Robert M. to Elizabeth A. Derickson, March 24, 1838.
Cheek, Littleton R. to Elizabeth Harris, April 14, 1838.
Carper, Green to Mary Petty, April 26, 1838, by Daniel Judd, L.E., April 30, 1838.

Craddock, Elijah H. to Sarah Hulett, June 19, 1838, by Charles W. Moorman, J.P., June 20, 1838.
Corbitt, Allen T. to Mary E. Harrison, July 25, 1838.
Colby, Solon to Susan Cox, Aug. 21, 1838, by John Corbitt, J.P., Aug. 21, 1838.
Clow, Robert I. to Eveline Ball, Sep. 4, 1838, by Robert Boyt. C. Howell, Sep. 4, 1838.
Chrimp, Ezechial to Margaret Greer, Sep. 5, 1838, by S. B. Davidson, J.P., Sep. 5, 1838.
Cunningham, Jesse I. to Mary A. E. Williams, Nov. 30, 1838, by E. S. Hall, J.P., Nov. 30, 1838.
Collier, Thomas to Mary Shelton, Nov. 22, 1838.
Callaghn, Michael to Jane Roach, Nov. 20, 1838, by John Wright, J.P., Nov. 20, 1838.
Chamberlain, John B. to Rebecca Rolan, Nov. 16, 1838, by L. B. Davidson, J.P., Nov. 18, 1838.

Page 5
Carroll, William H. to Eliza H. Breathett, Nov. 5, 1838, by J. T. Edgar, Nov. 5, 1838.
Caeman, John B. to Phoebe Waddle, Nov. 2, 1838, by N. B. Butler, J.P., Nov. 2, 1838.
Cunningham, Robert to Narcissa Hamlet, Oct. 23, 1838, no return.
Couch, Peter to Ann Haley, Oct. 18, 1838, by N. B. Butler, Oct. 18, 1838.
Carlile, Wilson to Ann C. Huston, Oct. 20, 1838, by W. H. Hunt, J.P., Oct. 2, 1839 ??
Couch, George W. to Lucinda Tindal, Sep. 10, 1838, by John Wright, J.P., Sep. 10, 1838.
Driver, William to Sarah Jane Park, Jan. 12, 1838, by J. Thomas Wheat, M.G., Rec. of Cr. Ch., Jan. 13, 1838.
Dreman, David to Sarah Phillips, March 10, 1838.

Page 6
Deal, Henry to Ann M. Cole, June 15, 1838, by E. P. Connell, J.P., June 20, 1838.
Dobbs, Asa S. to Martha Smart, Oct. 19, 1838, by R.B.C. Howell, Oct. 21, 1838.
Drake, William P. to Margaret Herod, Sep. 14, 1838.
Dyer, William H. to Rhoda Dennis, Sep. 25, 1838, by John Wright, J.P., Sep. 25, 1838.
Ewing, William B. to Martha C. Graves, March 21, 1838, by A.L.P. Green, M.P., March 22, 1838.
Ewen, John H. to Susan M. Goodwin, Nov. 7, 1838, by T. Fanning, M.G., Nov. 8, 1838.
Foster, Alfred H. to Nancy Hallum, July 24, 1838.
Freas, Joel to Missouri Hughes, Feb. 2, 1838, by J. T. Edgar, Feb. 3, 1838.
Forehand, Berry Green to Matilda McDaniel, April 14, 1838, by William Roach.

Page 7
Fudge, John to Polly Parr, Aug. 29, 1838, by Wm. Shelton, J.P., Aug. 2, 1838.
Fowler, Thomas J. to Tempy Simmons, Sep. 18, 1838.
Farrell, John to Barbara Jane Hickman, Oct. 15, 1838, by Philip Lindsley, Oct. 15, 1838.
Fryer, Samuel to Juby Ann Jones, Oct. 16, 1838, by D. Ralston, J.P., Oct. 18, 1839.
Gray, John G. to Nancy Tary, Feb. 5, 1838, by B. M. Barns, J.P., Feb. 6, 1838.
Walker Goodwin to Elizabeth Manuel, Feb. 10, 1838.
Givins, Edwin L. to Margaret A. Francis, May 24, 1838, by W. Garrett, M.G., May 24, 1838.
Gower, Alexander C. to Caroline C. Smith, Aug. 22, 1838, by D. Abernathy, J.P., --- 23, 1838.
Green, James P. to Elizabeth Bevins, Sep. 12, 1838, by Daniel Judd, L.E., Sep. 12, 1838.

Page 8
Goodrick, Caleb to Angeline Bates, Sep. 25, 1838.
John J. Gower to Malvina East, Sep. 25, 1838, by R.B.C. Howell, Sep. 25, 1838.
Grooms, Benjamin to Mary Parrish, Dec. 11, 1838, by L. Garrett, Dec. --, 1838.
Gill, Micheal S. to Rhody Denton, Nov. 27, 1838, by Wm. R. Hooten, Nov. 27, 1838.
Graham, Robert to Eliza A. Folwell, Oct. 17, 1838, by J. T. Edgar, Oct. 18, 1838.
Harkreader, Sylvester to Jane Dirickson, Jan. 5, 1838, by S. S. Yarbrough, M.G., Jan. 16, 1838.
John M. Henrie to Priscilla A. Nixon, Jan. 10, 1838, by J. Thos. Wheat, M.G., Rec. of Cr. Ch.
Hancock, Dorrie A. to Laura Harris, Jan. 23, 1838, by A. T. Scruggs, M.G., Feb. 6, 1838.

Page 9
Joseph L. Homes to Sarah Buie, Feb. 27, 1838.
Harris, Thomas I. to Eliza M. Leake, March 17, 1838, by J. E. Edgar, March 20, 1838.
Henning, Joseph to Eliza Litton, March 31, 1838.
Haley, Thomas to Eliza Kelly, May 2, 1838, by John Hathaway, J.P., May 6, 1838.
Houser, Charles F. to Catharine F. Jonte, May 9, 1838, by A.L.P. Green, M.G., May 9, 1838.
Hagan, Gilbert to Caroline Sittler, May 24, 1838.
Hudnall, Thomas, Jr. to Mary Caldwell, June 19, 1838, by R. A. Lapsley, June 19,1838.
Hooten, William R. to Mary S. Berry, June 26, 1838, by Thomas Allison, Nov. 21, 1838.
Harrie, William O. to Frances A. Bartee, July 26, 1838, by A.L.P. Green, M.G., July 26, 1838.

Page 10
Hamelton, James W. to Mary E. Dunn, Aug. 8, 1838, by R. A. Lapsley, Aug. 8, 1838.

Harris, Thomas A. to Susan Austin, Sep. 1, 1838. (This license was lost).
Harris, Thomas A. to Susan Austin, Sep. 19, 1838.
Harding, George W. to Caroline F. Demoss, Sep. 28, 1838, by F. Fanning, M.G., Oct. 5, 1838.
Harrison, Joseph P. to Emely Rochell, Oct. 5, 1838, by E. S. Halls, J.P., Oct. 5, 1838.
Harris, Westley B. to Asenath Simpkins, Oct. 10, 1838, by William I. Drake, J.P., Oct. 11, 1838.
Hooper, William T. to Susan L. Lovell, Oct. 11, 1838, by John Corbett, J.P., Oct. 26, 1838.
Hanks, A. I. to Rebecca Owens, Oct. 28. 1838, by John Corbett, J.P., Oct. 28, 1838.

Page 11
Inman, Thomas J. to Nancy Ann Greer, Dec. 27, 1838, by Wm. B. Hooten, Dec. 29, 1838.
Jones, Robert H. to Joana J. Price, March 17, 1838, by A.L.P. Green, M.G., March 17, 1838.
Jones, Coleman to Tabitha Burnett, March 23, 1838.
Johnson, Parmenus to Elizabeth Greer, April 24, 1838, by William Hooven, M.G., April 24, 1838.
Jones, Spotwood A. to Jane Green, June 7, 1838, by J. W. Davis, M.G., Pastor of Christian Ch., June 7, 1838.
Joyner, Edward B. to Mary Finin, June 11, 1838, by Jno. B. McFerrin, M.G., July 10, 1838.
Johnson, A. W. to Mary E. Cheney, July 10, 1838, by J. B. McFerrin, M.G., July 10, 1838.
James, Thomas C. to Vienna H. V. Byrn, Aug. 3, 1838.

Page 12
Jones, Malon L. to Elizabeth Nelms, Aug. 7, 1838, by Thos. Stringfield, Aug. 7, 1838.
Jackson, William to Elizabeth Ferguson, Aug. 27, 1838, by T. J. Edgar, Aug. 27, 1838.
Jones, Joseph J. to Frankey Stone, Sep. 15, 1838, by Daniel Judd, L.E., Sep. 15, 1838.
Johnson, Albert to Mary Holloweay, Dec. 17, 1838.
Johnson, Allen J. to Evaline Stallings, Dec. 25, 1838.
King, Samuel B. to Mary Ann Dodson, Feb. 9,1838.
Keller, John R. to Mary Amanda Murprey, March 1, 1838, by A.L.P. Green, M.G., March 20, 1838.
Keller, Archibald J. to Mary Ann Bradley, Sep. 17, 1838, by J. Wm. Hasell Hunt, J.P., ----------.

Page 13
Kirby, Elias R. to Rachel Powell, Nov. 3, 1838, by R.B.C. Howell, Nov. 8, 1838.
Knox, James A. to Martha Ann Crockett, Nov. 8, 1838, by E. P. Connell, J.P., Nov. 29, 1838.
Koonce, John H. to Eliza Ann Rutherford, Nov. 28, 1838.
Kile, James to Minerva Jordan, Dec. 13, 1838, by W. Lowe, M.G., Dec. 13, 1838.
Lindsley, A.V.S. to Eliza M. Trimble, April 12, 1838, by Philip Lindsley, April 2, 1838.

Loving, Wm. H. to Ruth T. Fletcher, July 25, 1838, by J. T. Edgar, July 26, 1838.

Page 14

William Long to Elizabeth Gradden, Aug. 16, 1838, by Wm. Hasell Hunt, J.P., Aug. 16, 1838.

Larkins, Robt. to Lucinda Knight, Sep. 1, 1838, by Jno. Davis, J.P., Sep.2, 1838.

Lester, Wm. H. to Lucinda Ally, Oct. 11, 1838, by Wm. Hasell Hunt, J.P., Oct. 21, 1838.

Lewis, Benjamin F. to Irena Johnson, Nov. 19, 1838, by W. Lowe, M.G., Nov. 22, 1838.

Page 15

Leigh, Gilbert to Eliza Cotlort, Dec. 20, 1838, by E. B. Carpenter, Dec. 20, 1838.

Malone, Jeremiah to Lucinda Larrington, Jan. 9, 1838, by B. M. Barns, J.P., Jan. 9, 1838.

Matlock, Gabriel to Elizabeth Roberts, Jan. 11, 1838, by E. H. East, J.P., Jan. 11, 1838.

Marlin, Leonard B. to Eliza J. Guy, Jan. 11, 1838.

McCool, Westley V. to Zilpha Hullett, Jan. 30, 1838, by D. Abernathy, J.P., Jan. 1, 1838.

Mathews, Wm. H. to Mary Scruggs, Jan. 22, 1838, by D. Abernathy, J.P., Jan. 25, 1838.

Morgan, Henry J. to Martha Cleveland, March 28, 1838, by Daniel Judd, L. E., March 30, 1838.

Page 16

Madison, Thomas to Susan Mason, April 16, 1838.

Martin, Terence to Lydia Wilkinson, May 2, 1838.

McDaniel, Wm. P. to Martha E. Scantland, May 31, 1838, by Jos. M. Driver, June 1, 1838.

McGuire, Daniel to Harriet I. Cummings, June 14, 1838, by Daniel Juss, J.E., June 14, 1838.

Myers, David to Mary Ann Chatham, June 28, 1838, by Wm. Hasell Hunt, J.P., June 28, 1838.

Myers, Samuel to Julia Ann Cobbs, June 30, 1838, by Robt. Boyte C. Howell, July 1, 1838.

McClane, Wm. to Nancy Lanier, July 4, 1838, by I. B. Knowles, J.P., July 4, 1838.

McGrath, James to Mary E. Harrison, July 26, 1838, by John Wright, J.P., July 26, ----.

McNairy, Wm. H. to Elizabeth P. Duvall, Aug. 6, 1838, by J. T. Edgar, Aug. 8, 1838.

Meadors, Henderson to Elizabeth Davis, Aug. 20, 1838, by John McRobertson, Aug. 21, 1838.

Maynard, Ezekiel to Ereany Driver, Aug. 22, 1838, by J. T. Edgar, Sep. 2, 1838.

Masterson, Wm. W. to Maria G. Grundy, Sep. 2, 1838, by J. T. Edgar, Sep. 2, 1838.

Manning, Samuel C. to Mary Mayo, Sep. 4, 1838, by D. A. Abernathy, J.P., --- 6, 1838.
Morgan,Daniel P. to Susan M. Thompson, Sep. 25, 1838.
Munn, John to Mary Jane Meek, Oct. 3, 1838, by John Wright, J.P., Oct. 3, ----.
Morgan, Lewis to Martha W. Bransford, Oct. 9, 1838.

Page 18
Moore, James B. to Elizabeth Dodson, Oct. 19, 1838.
Pleasant N. Marklam to Jane Charlton, Oct. 31, 1838.
Maize, James to Malinda Johnson, Nov. 26, 1838.
Matlock, Simpson to Maria H. Shumate, Dec. 10, 1838.
Moss, David to Elizabeth Bartlett, Dec. 15, 1838, by R.B.C. Howell, Dec. 16, 1838.
McKane, Wm. to Elizabeth Sadler, Dec. 17, 1838.
MaFarlin, Anderson to Adaline Guthrie, Dec. 19, 1838.
Neunon, Balaam to Mary N. Herrin, May 23, 1838.
Micholson, Wiley B. to Roda Hill, Oct. 2, 1838, by S. B. Davidson, J.P., Oct. 2, 1838.

Page 19
Ogdon, John W. to Eliza C. White, Jan. 23, 1838.
Owens, Richard to Nancy Foster, Sep. 11, 1838.
Page, Thomas B. to Adeline Key, Aug. 4, 1838, by T. Fanning, M.G., Aug. 5, 1838.
Puckett, Lay to Susan Adcock, May 12, 1838, by D. Ralston, J.P., May 17, 1838.
Patterson, Lewis W. to Artemisia Colby, March 1, 1838, by A.L.P. Green, M.G., March 2, 1838.
Phillips, Preston D. to Amanda Appleton, May 14, 1848, by Thos. Scott, J.P., May 15, 1838.
Payne, William H. to Sarah M. Cooper, May 30, 1838, by B. M. Barnes, J.P., May 31, 1838.
John A. Pullen to Susannah E. Thompson, Aug. 6, 1838, by Thos. Scott, N.P., Aug. 16, 1838.
William Phillips to Caledonia Lucas, Aug. 30, 1838, by A.L.P. Green, M.G., Aug. 30, 1838.

Page 20
Parker, A. G. to Tennessee Mosley, Oct. 4, 1848, by W. B. Carpenter, Oct. 9, 1838.
Pate, John M. to Minerva P. Hodges, Oct. 11, 1838.
Pope, Joseph to Sarah Jane Marshall, Oct. 24, 1838.
Porter, Robert M. to Mary W. Williams, Dec. 3, 1838, by J. T. Edgar, Dec. 4, 1838.
Peles, Conrad to Mary Jane Howlett, Dec. 11, 1838, by J. T. Edgar, Dec. 11, 1838.
Quisenbury, John to Verinda Townsend, Jan. 31, 1838, by R. Weakley, J.P., Jan. 31, 1838.
Russell, Joseph to Tennessee Hower, Jan. 6, 1838, by Wm. Shelton, J.P., Jan. 9, 1838.
Rinson, Williams to Mary Thomas, Feb. 8, 1838, by Daniel Judd, M.G., March 1, 1838.
Rockwell, June V. to Margaret V. Williams, Feb. 23, 1838.

Page 21
Rowling, John to Evaline Williams, March 6, 1838, by D. Rolston, March 8, 1838.
Richards, Henry to Mary White, April 18, 1838, by J. M. David, Pastor Christian Church, April 18, 1838.
Rockwell, June V. to Margaret Ann Fowler, June 2, 1838.
Reese, Hugh to Sarah A. Drake, July 7, 1838.
Reese, Jessie to Mary Herrod, July 7, 1838.
Rains, Wm. G. to Rebecca Wright, Dec. 22, 1838, by E. M. Patterson, N.P., Dec. 24, 1838.
Ritter, Maini to Emilie Atala Ravonell, Dec. 27, 1838, by R.B.C. Howell, Dec. 27, 1838.
Rhodes, Wm. to Elizabeth Spence, Dec. 29, 1838.

Page 22
Stewart, Edward L. to Susan Simmons, Jan. 1, 1838, by William Felts, M.G., Feb. 4, 1838.
Smith, J. L. to Hannah Drake, Jan. 15, 1838.
Stull, Charles to Eliza Smith, Feb. 21, 1838, by A.L.P. Green, M.G., Feb. 22, 1838.
Spence, Joseph to Margaret Pinkerton, Feb. 28, 1838.
Stamp, Annanias G. to Jane Ramsey, March 2, 1838, by Jas. H. Cook, J.P., March 4, 1838.
Spane, George W. to Mary Treopard, March 10, 1838.
Sanders, Gabriel to Martha L. Riddick, March 15, 1838, by R.B.C. Howell, March 15, 1838.
Starkey, Samuel J. to Agnes Wright, March 23, 1838.

Page 23
Stephens, Abednego to Caroline M. Lawrence, April 3, 1838.
Stalcup, Wm. A. to Lavinia Williams, April 27, 1838.
Searcy, Wm. W. to Sarah Campbell, April 30, 1838.
Simmons, Levi C. to Martha Shivers, July 2, 1838.
Steele, John W. to Mary I. Read, July 4, 1838, by R.B.C. Howell, July 4, 1838.
Sheppard, Blanne H. to Pherby E. R. Donelson, Aug. 2, 1838.
Scruggs, George to Jane Scruggs, Sep. 17, 1838.
Smith, Henry C. to Siney Hooper, Oct. 7, 1838, by Daniel Judd, L.E., Oct. 7, 1838.
Sullivan, Lee to Ann E. Harris, Oct. 22, 1838, by J. Thos. Wheat, Re. of Cr. Ch., Oct. 22, 1838.

Page 24
Stevens, Newman to Elizabeth Mayo, Nov. 30, 1838, by P. B. Morris, Nov. 30, 1838.
Sawyers, Costen to Caroline Campbell, Dec. 1, 1838 (1828).
Snow, Anthony J. to Catherine Stratton, Dec. 12, 1838, by A.L.P. Green, M.G., Dec. 12, 1838.
Thompson, Chatin P. to Frances Clark, Feb. 21, 1838.
Thompkins, John G. to Rutha Chandler, May 28, 1838, by John Wright, J.P. May 26, 1838.

Thomas, James P. to Illinois C. Kearney, July 26, 1838, by I. B. McFerrin, M.G., July 26, 1838.
Thompson, Dela F. to Margarett Ann Whitsett, Aug. 5, 1838.

Page 25
Thompson, Wilson V. to Elizabeth Mays, Aug. 9, 1838, by Thos. Scott, J.P., Aug. 15, 1838.

Taylor, Maidson to Nancy Cryton, Oct. 18, 1838, by Daniel Mudd, L.E., Oct. 18, 1838.
Turner, James to Mary Scruggs, Dec. 24, 1838, by Chas. W. Moorman, J.P., Dec. 26, 1838.
Vaughan, Edmund W. to Matilda Johnston, Jan. 24, 1838
Whitley, Thomas H. to Rhoda Briley, Jan. 23, 1838.
White, James A. to Martha Hooberry, April 4, 1838, by H. H. Hunt, J.P., April 5, 1838.
Waggoner, Abraham to Anlla Spain, April 7, 1838, by Thos. Fuqua, April 4, 1838.

Page 26
Wood, Stancil to Louisa Grizzard, Aug. 2, 1838.
Wood, Stancil to Louisa Grizzard, Aug. 23, 1838, by W. P. Connell, J.P., Aug. 26, 1838.
Wallace, Logan D. to Eliza Smith, Sep. 17, 1838.
Wright, Wm. W. to Louisa Collins, Oct. 11, 1838.
Walker, Isaac H. to Femia Clark, Oct. 24, 1838, by O. B. Hayes, Oct. 25, 1838.
Williams, Joseph P. to Sarah Ann Pennington, Nov. 15, 1838, by J. T. Edgar, Nov. 20, 1838.
Waldron, Wm. V. to Elizabeth Everett, Nov. 28, 1838.
Yates, Townshend D. to Matilda Tomlinson, Jan. 27, 1838.
Young, Napoleon B. to Margaret E. McGavock, Feb. 11, 1838, by Chas. W. Moorman.

Page 27
Yates, David to Lucinda Smith, Aug. 17, 1838, by E. S. Hall, Aug. 17, 1838.
Yeatman, Wm. T. to Amelia Erwin, Aug. 27, 1838, by T. J. Edgar, Aug. 27, 1838.
Zumbro, Benj. F. to Elizabeth Fennemore, April 17, 1838, by Daniel Judd, L.E., April 17, 1838.
Blackwell, Thoms S. to Catharine Dickins, Nov. 29, 1838, by E. H. East, J.P., Nov. 29, 1838.
Allen, Mathew to Tennessee Walker, Jan. 28, 1839, by J. T. Edgar, Jan. 28, 1839.
Brunson, Asabel to Emily Smiley, Feb. 7, 1839, by J. T. Edgar, Feb. 7, 1839.

Page 28
Chaney, Charles J. to Sarah Ann Morgan, Dec. 12, 1839, by J. T. Edgar, Dec. 13, 1839.
Clay, Joseph W. to Sarah Fletcher, Dec. 31, 1839, by J. T. Edgar, Dec. 31, 1839.

Conlan, James W. to Catherine A. Wiert, Aug. 26, 1839, by J. T. Edgar, Aut. 27, 1839.
Franklin, Isaac to Adelicia Hayes, July 1, 1839, by J. T. Edgar, July 2, 1839.
Humphreys, West H. to Amanda Pillow, Jan. 1, 1839, by J. T. Edgar, Jan. 1, 1839.
Jackson, Thomas to Mary Keys, July 3, 1839, by J. T. Edgar, July 11, 1839.
Long, Philip W. to Susan Wills, Nov. 4, 1839, by J. T. Edgar, Nov. 4, 1839.

Page 29
Austin, Edwin to Lucinda J. Johnson, Aug. 13, 1839, by Wm. H. Hagens, J.P., Aug. 15, 1839.
Adams, John N. to Prince L. Morton, Dec. 17, 1839, by J. B. McFerrin, M.G., Dec. 18, 1839.
Allen, John W. to Sarah P. Cartwright, Dec. 11, 1839.
Almond, Thaddeus S. to Mary Ann Gordon, March 21, 1839, by D. Judd, L.E., March 31, 1839.
Bacon, James H. to Sarah Luster, May 16, 1839, by R. B. C. Howell, Pastor Baptist Church, May 16, 1839.
Bailey, Richard to Nancy Hunt, Oct. 7, 1839, by P. B. Morris, Oct. 7, 1839.
Baker, Wm. H. to Elvira Luster, Aug. 8, 1839, by P. B. Morris, J.P., Aug. 8, 1839.
Barrett, Charles to Eliza Butcher, Feb. 13, 1839, by Daniel Judd, L.E., Feb. 14, 1839.

Page 30
Barber, Elisha to Ann Patrick, Jan. 9, 1839, by N. B. Butler, J.P., Jan. 9, 1839.
Barrow, Robt. J. to Mary E. Crabb, July 11, 1839, by J. Thos. Wheat, M.G., July 11, 1839.
Beach, Andrew S. to Martha C. Thompson, July 21, 1839, by Wm. Hasell Hunt, J.P., July 22, 1839.
Belliew, William to Temperance Wolf, Nov. 27, 1839, by E. M. Patterson, J.P., Nov. 28, 1839.
Beazley, Charles to Caroline Conley, Jan 1, 1839, by John Hogan, J.P., Jan. 4, 1839.
Biggs, Leroy W. to Charlotte Gower, March 29, 1839, by Wm. Crockett, J.P., March 31, 1839.
Binkley, Jacob to Sarah Lee, April 12, 1839, by B. F. Binkley, April 28, 1839.
Brunson, Smiley to Emily Smiley, Feb. 7, 1839, by J. T. Edgar, Feb. 7, 1839.

Page 31
Blackwell, Henry to Jane Stewart, Feb. 9, 1839, by Jas. H. Cook, J.P., Feb. 11, 1839.
Bostick, James A. to Maria Z. Smith, May 20, 1839, by Jno. B. McFerrin, M.G., May 23, 1839.
Brown, Neal S. to Mary A. Trimble, Dec. 28, 1839, by Philip Lindsley, Dec. 28, 1839.
Brown, Joseph to Mary Staggs, June 20, 1839, by R. B. C. Howell, June 20, 1839.

Brown, Jas. Percy to Lezinka Campbell, April 25, 1839, by J. Thos. Wheat, Re. of Cr. Ch., April 25, 1839.
Buck, Thomas M. to Martha Hanks, Jan. 30, 1839, by W. D. T. Sawrie, M.G., Jan. 31, 1839.
Budd, Thos. L. to Eliza Jane Moffett, Nov. 9, 1839, by R. B. C. Howell, Pastor Baptist Church, Nov. 9, 1839.

Page 32
Cagle, Wm. W. to Keziah Elveritt, Jan. 5, 1839, by David Abernathy, J.P., Jan. 8, 1839.
Campbell, John T. to Emeline R. Williams, July 9, 1839, by A. L. P. Green, M.G. July 10, 1839.
Cardwell, James W. to Martha A. P. Nugent, Oct. 2, 1839, by Jno. W. Hannah, M.G., Oct. 2, 1839.
Castleman, Bery to Elizabeth Carrington, Sep. 24, 1839, by B. N. Barnes, J.P., Sep. 24, 1839.
Cato, William to Martha Peobles, Jan. 1, 1839, by Wm. Shelton, J.P., Jan. 6, 1839.
Cherry, Lewis D. to Martha McCance, Nov. 6, 1839, by E. Goodrich, J.P., Nov. 8, 1839.
Clayton, Wm. to Henrietta Woodfine, Jan. 24, 1839, by Jno. W. Hannah, Jan. 24, 1839.

Page 33
Cockrill, James Thomas to Louisa Phelps, Aug. 29, 1839, by Fountain E. Pitts, M.G., Aug. 29, 1839.
Condon, James to Ellen Adams, Feb. 22, 1839, by C. G. Macpherson, Feb. 27, 1839.
Connelly, William to Rachael Quinn, June 4, 1839, by C. G. Macpherson, June 6, 1839.
Cox, James to Martha Still, July 15, 1839, by Jas. Whitsett, July 17, 1839.
Corbitt, Nicholas P. to Frances Wills, Aug. 17, 1839, by W.D.F. Sawrie, M.G., Aug. 18, 1839.
Crawford, Andrew to Catherine O. Riley, Oct. 17, 1839, by J. Thos. Wheat, Rec. of C. Ch., Oct. 17, 1839.
Criddle, Smith to Belle Ann Bremaker, Oct. 16, 1839, by R.B.C. Howell, Pastor Baptist Ch., Oct. 16, 1839.
Crenshaw, Vincent to Ann King, Aug. 30, 1839, by Lewis Garrett, Sep. 1, 1839.

Page 34
Cooper, W. B. to Ann Litton, Jan. 17, 1839, by A.L.P. Green, M.G., Jan. 17, 1839.
Davis, Henry W. to Sally Winchester, Feb. 27, 1839, by E. S. Hall, J.P., Feb. 27, 1839
(Franklin Isaac see page 28).
Deaderick, Geo. M. to Terrissa Huffman, Dec. 26, 1839, by Wm. J. Drake, J.P., Dec. 26, 1839.
Fogg, Godfrey M. to Ellen M. Stephenson, Dec. 17, 1839, by Robert A. Lapsley, Dec. 17, 1839.
Ford, James M. to Martha D. Beard, Sep. 2, 1839, by Alexander C. Chisholm, M.G., Sep. 5, 1839.

Dryer, Alfred to Nancy McAfee, Feb. 9, 1839, by D. Ralston, J.P., Feb. 12, 1839.
Gilbert, George to Cathrine Cheek, Feb. 15, 1839, by C. Y. Hooper, J.P., Feb. 15, 1839.
Goodwin, Martin P. to Martha Williams, Aug. 11, 1839, by P. B. Morris, J.P., Aug. 11, 1839.

Page 35
Goodlet, Robert to Luvicca R. McMurray, April 25, 1839, by John W. Ogden, M.G., April 25, 1839.
Green, George W. to Amanda M. Austin, Sep. 16, 1839, by J. Thos. Wheat, Rec. of Cr. Ch., Sep. 17, 1839.
Grooms, Richard H. to Mary Wills, Dec. 24, 1839, by S. S. Yarborough, M.G., Dec. 25, 1839.
Haly, Wm. to Tennessee Berry, Sep. 8, 1839, by R. R. Barton, M.G., Sep. 8, 1839.
Haley, John to Paulina Foster, Nov. 3, 1839, by P. B. Morris, J.P., Sep. 3, 1839.
Halley, Josiah C. to Rebecca Surles, Jan. 9, 1839.
Hamilton, Mortimer to Emilene Hill, Sep. 5, 1839, by W.D.F. Sawrie, M.G., Sep. 5, 1839.
Harris, John to Mary Hayns, Sep. 27, 1839, by John McRobertson, J.P., Sep. 27, 1839

Page 36
Harper, James to Eliza Ann Luster, Aug. 7, 1839, by P. B. Morris, J.P., Aug. 7, 1839.
Harris, Archy to Mary Fielding, Aug. 3, 1839, by John Wright, J.P., Aug. 3, 1839.
Harrison, Sterling to Mary Fox, March 5, 1839, by A.L.P. Green, M.G., March 5, 1839.
Hardcastle, Philip F. to Minerva H. White, March 26, 1839, by A.L.P. Green, M.G., March 26, 1839.
Harrison, Robert to Jane Peay, March 27, 1839, by N. B. Butler, March 27, 1839.
Hartsfield, William to Susan Ewing, April 3, 1839, by Jno. W. Hannah, April 4, 1839.
Harrison, Wm. G. to Minerva Stalcup, June 13, 1839, by N. B. Butler, J.P., June 13, 1839.
Hawkins, Isham to Martha Allen, June 22, 1839, by M. B. Butler, J.P., June 23, 1839.

Page 37
Hard, Joseph F. to Virginia Parish, Dec. 24, 1839, by S. S. Yarborough, M.G., Dec. 25, 1839.
Hewgley, Jno. W. to Jane C. Whitsitt, Aug. 20, 1839, by R.B.C. Howell, Paster Baptist Church, Aug. 22, 1839.
Higginbotham, Jno. R. to Mary C. Barnes, Nov. 13, 1839, by Jno. B. McFerrin, M.G., Nov. 13, 1839.
Hinchy, John to Susan Johnson, July 24, 1839, by E. P. Connell, J.P., July 27, 1839.
Higgins, Peter to Ann Rogers, Sep. 30, 1839, by Lewis Garrett, Sep. 30, 1838.?
Hooker, James G. to Lucy Haynes, Sep. 26, 1839, by Jno. McRobertson, J.P., Sep. 27, 1839.

Hagen, Robert to Lerilda Adeline Williams, Aug. 9, 1839, by B. F. Binkley, J.P., Aug. 13, 1839.
Hughes, Andrew J. to Elizabeth H. Ball, Sep. 11, 1839, by R.B.C. Howell, Pastor Baptist Church, Sep. 11, 1839.

Page 38
Jennett, Robinson to Hester Nickens, May 21, 1839, by Jno. B. McFerrin, M.G., May 21, 1839.
Johnson, Wills to Martha McNott, March 12, 1839, by P. B. Morris, J.P., March 12, 1839.
Johnson, George A. to Martha M. King, Jan. 14, 1839, by S. B. Davidson, J.P., Jan. 17, 1839.
Johnson, Thomas H. to Ellen Ann Weaver, Nov. 27, 1839, by S. S. Yarborough, M.G., Nov. 27, 1839.
Johnson, Sydney L. to Cornelia Covington, Oct. 19, 1839, by J. T. Edgar, Noct. 20, 1839.
Jones, John T. to Sarah Caroline Ewen, Aug. 12, 1839, by R. A. Lapsley, Aug. 13, 1839.
Jones, Pinkney to Sarah Jones, July 13, 1839, by Wm. Hasell Hunt, J.P., July 13, 1839.
Keith, Henry to Eliza McCulley, Dec. 16, 1839,(no certificate).

Page 39
Kellam, Joseph to Lucy H. Allison, May 21, 1839, by Wm. Greer, J.P., May 22, 1839.
Ker, William to Sarah Knapps, Nov. 22, 1839, by P. B. Morris, J.P., Nov. 22, 1839.
Kephard (Sephard), William to Mary Ann Joslin, Sep. 23, 1839, by Caleb Rooker, Minister M.E. Ch., Oct. 24, 1839.
Kerley, William G. to Susan C. Kay, Nov. 11, 1839, by R.B.C. Howell, Pastor Baptist Church, Nov. 12, 1839.
Knight, Nicholas to Annis Moss, Dec. 18, 1839, by William R. Hooten, M.G., Dec. 24, 1839.
Knox, William to Maria Seckerson, Nov. 14, 1839.
Knight, Ephraim to Sarah Barnes, Sep. 26, 1839.
Krantz, John to Susannah Binkley, Jan. 22, 1839.

Page 40
Lane, John to Ruth F. Dunlap, Aug. 24, 1839.
Lanier, William to Caroline Sadler, Sep. 12, 1839.
Lay, John to Mary Ann Yates, April 13, 1839.
Levi, James to Janette League, May 28, 1839.
Link, John W. to Sarah King, Nov. 23, 1839.
Love, Charles J. to Julia E. L. Shrewsbury, June 5, 1839
Lovell, Holmon to Drucilla Raney, June 30, 1839.
Manning, Benj. to Mary Lee, Nov. 11, 1839.

Page 41
McAlipn, John W. to Nancy Proctor, Dec. 11, 1839.
McCool, John to Easter Bradley, July 23, 1839.
McCormack, Alfred to Susan Dorris, Nov. 8, 1839.

McKinnie, John to Martha Langston, Jan. 26, 1839.
Melvin, Andrew to Cyntha McPeake, Jan. 12, 1839.
Miles, Bedford W. to Narcissa Leeper, June 3, 1839.
Morton, Solomon E. to Tabitha J. Kimbro, Oct. 25, 1839.
Morton, Samuel to Mary Ann Fitzhugh, July 24, 1839.

Page 42
Newman, William to Flora Barrett, Aug. 24, 1839.
Parham, Isham W. to Eveline F. B. Pierce, Jan. 2, 1839.
Parks, John to Delia Bankston, July 5, 1839.
Patterson, Mark R. to Rachel T. Boyd, June 15, 1839.
Peel, Lewis to Mary Jane Watson, Nov. 4, 1839.
Pittman, Bartholemew B. to Mary E. Parish, May 9, 1839.
Pitts, Thomas to Cynthia Russell, Jan. 7, 1839.
Puckett, Cheatham to Elizabeth Beazley, Sep. 2, 1839.

Page 43
Pitts, Mukin to Mary Ann Gaulding, Dec. 30, 1839.
Ridley, James H. to Amandy R. Joslin, Sep. 18,1839.
Roberts, Bennett W. to Sarah B. Bailey, Oct. 8, 1839.
Rose, Alex to Mary A. E. Carney, June 22, 1839.
Rowlin, Jole to Pemma Beazley, July 18, 1839.
Rowlin, Joel to Lavina Williams, May 4, 1839, (no certificate).
Sanders, Thomas T. to Elizabeth Iredale, Jan. 22, 1839.
Smith, William to Rebecca A. Frazer, Oct. 31, 1839.

Page 44
Shuester, George W. to Lucy Ann Gower, March 13, 1839.
Smith, John W. to Emily J. Reed, Jan. 5, 1839.
Stuart, Edmund to Gelica Brown, Nov. 18, 1839.
Stevenson, George to Jane Halloway, Aug. 7, 1839.
Stark, John C. to Burchet Williams, May 23, 1839.
Sullivan, Edward to Nancy Brown, Aug. 23, 1839.
Sullivan, Joel to Virginia M. Willis, Aug. 5, 1839.
Scott, Charles to Elizabeth Bullus, Sep. 19, 1839.

Page 45
Swearringgean, Lemuel to Nancy B. Rains, Oct. 26, 1839.
Tarpley, Collin S. to Eliza Eastell, Sep. 24, 1839.
Taylor, Edward to Emeline Ashby, Feb. 10, 1839.
Thomas, Elisha to Eliza J. Floyd, Aug. 17, 1839.
Thompson, Wm. to Amanda Shell, Dec. 24, 1839.
Todd, Jackson to Margaret Barkley, Feb. 12, 1839.
Turman, J. M. to Mary A. Hume, April 23, 1839.
Waggoner, Wash to Eliza Fox, Oct. 24, 1839.

Page 46
Watson, Rich'd P. to Mary Camp, Aug. 27, 1839.
Weaver, Dempsey to Mary D. Johnson, April 16, 1839.
Weir, Robert to Sarah G. K. Saunders, Oct. 9, 1839.
White, A. C. to Mary Ann Ogden, Dec. 23, 1839.
Williams, McHenry to Mary Moore, Oct. 12, 1839.
Williams, George W. to Martha Ann Naves, Nov. 19, 1839.

Williams, Joseph J. to Elizabeth Peebles, April 23, 1839, May 14, 1839.
Wilkinson, James to Lydia Jane Doughty, April 29, 1839. May 29, 1839.

Page 47
Williams, Stephen to Elizabeth Roland, July 13, 1839.
Williams, Zebulon to Mary Wehrley, July 8, 1839.
Woldridge, Henry W. to Harriett Read, Sep. 3, 1839.
Young, John L. to Susan Jones, Aug. 2, 1839.
Nichol, John to E. M. Bradford, Jan. 2, 1839.
Stones, Liston to W. E. McEwen, March 22, 1839.
Wheatley, Seth to Mary Cook, April 16, 1839.
Seip, John to Eliza Martin, Oct. 17, 1839.

Page 48
Akin, John to Fatama Colly, Feb. 9, 1840.
Allen, Shadrack to Paulina Epps, July 9, 1840.
Allen, W. W. to Mary A. E. Sadler, Dec. 19, 1840.
Andrew, Alex to Mary Ann Conoway, Dec. 25, 1840.
Arthur, Wm. A. to Nancy A. Yates, Aug. 6, 1840.
Arington, George to Mary Ann Booten, Jan. 10, 1840.
Ballentine, William to Sarah Baker, June 27, 1840.
Baker, Francis to Tennessee C. Thorn, Jan. 5, 1840.

Page 49
Baker, James H. to Mariah Jones, March 7, 1840.
Baldridge, Nelson to Elizabeth Hartman, Feb. 29, 1840.
Bateman, John to Elizabeth King, Feb. 4, 1840.
Baker, B. F. to Lucy Ann Wright, May 2, 1840.
Benningfield, James W. to Elizabeth Jones, Dec. 24, 1840.
Blane, Jacob to Nancy Loyd, Sep. 8, 1840.
Bowman, Jas. to Mary Hickerson, Aug. 20, 1840.
Boyd, Milton B. to Isabel M. Dabbs, Jan. 9, 1840.

Page 50
Boyd, William P. to Catherine Waggoner, Dec. 30, 1840.
Bradford, S. to E. V. Demoss, Jan. 6, 1840.
Berry, Wm. W. to Jane Eliza White, March 10, 1840.
Brown, William to Margaret Turbeville, Nov. 10, 1840.
Brown, William P. to Elizabeth J. Hobbs, Oct. 24, 1840.
Brooks, Johnson to Elizabeth Brewer, March 21, 1840.
Bradshaw, John to Mary Jane Hickey, May 28, 1840.
Burke, Sam'l R. t- Charity Halloway, Jan. 20, 1840.
Carpenter, Wm. to Abigail Knott, May 21, 1840.

Page 51
Charlton, Willis L. to Mary S. Evans, Dec. 26, 1840.
Clay, Joshua to Eliza Still, May 16, 1840.
Clemons, William H. to Mary C. Earthman, Dec. 9, 1840.
Cleveland, H. P. to Lucinda Alderson, Jan. 1, 1840.
Cloddy, Pleasant J. to Charlotte Lazenbury, Dec. 8, 1840.
Cloyd, John W. to Sarah W. Brooks, Nov. 11, 1840.

Cloyd, William S. to Ann W. Jones, Dec. 24, 1840.
Colley, Charles to Polley Lissick, Dec. 28, 1840.
Carroll, Thos. B. to Eliza B. Ham, May 30, 1840.

Page 52
Cotton, Hiram S. to Martha Ellis, May 23, 1840.
Couch, Marshall to Amelia A. Head, Aug. 27, 1840.
Coussens, John H. to Mary Royster, Dec. 24, 1840.
Cowden, John J. to Eleanor F. Bradford, Aug. 13, 1840.
Crosway, James C. to Nancy Draper, July 16, 1840.
Cullum, Alexander to Caroline Lowry, May 30, 1840, June 14, 1840.
Cullum, Lovell H. to Martha Greer, Sep. 17, 1840.
Demoss, Jesse S. to Elvira Woodward, April 24, 1840.
Dicks, William to Mary Haymer, March 21, 1840.

Page 53
Dixon, Warren G. to Martha S. Sneed, Oct. 15, 1840.
Douglass, Lishey to Alcy Rankins, March 27, 1840.
Drake, B. C. to Mary Jane Chandler, July 21, 1840.
Dozier, William N. to Sarah Ivans, Oct. 14, 1840.
Dunavant, Pleasant to Mary Conoway, Aug. 8, 1840.
Dunn, Alfred to Sarah Ann Baker, July 11, 1840.
Duke, Green W. to Rhoda Ann Simpkins, Jan. 8, 1840.
Dunn, William A. to Lucy Woodward, April 9, 1840.
Earhart, William L. to Ann Clay, April 2, 1840.

Page 54
Edward, Balum to Rebecca Yates, Feb. 8, 1840.
Evans, Thomas W. to Mary E. Odom, Dec. 30, 1840.
Fisher, John L. to Susan J. King, Feb. 8, 1840.
Fleming, Joseph J. to Frances Gillam, Dec. 11, 1840.
Freeman, J. B. to Margaret O'Brien, April 1, 1840.
Franklin, Geo. W. to Margaret Jane McCormick, Feb. 18, 1840.
Fulghum, W. W. to Martha A. M. McQuary, Sep. 22, 1840.
Fulghum, B. F. to Caroline Ferebee, Aug. 25, 1840.
Fulghum, Thomas W. to Martha Woodward, Dec. 5, 1840.

Page 55
Gallagher, John to Lavina Russell, Nov. 10, 1840.
Gay, Edward J. to Lavina (Lavinia) Hynes, Oct. 22, 1840.
Gibson, Newsom to Elizabeth Jones, Dec. 28, 1840.
Gleaves, James T. to Sarah S. Dunaway, July 28, 1840.
Glover, James H. to Susan Bandy, Dec. 16, 1840.
Goodrich, Caleb to Martha Mason, March 10, 1840.
Granet, Peter to Sophia Mallet, Nov. 7, 1840.
Grizzard, L. H. to Elizabeth Neely, Jan. 21, 1840.
Grant, Joseph to Rhoda D. Colley, Dec. 30, 1840.

Page 56
Gunn, Lyman T. to Caroline M. Morehead, Jan. 22, 1840.
Hallum, William to Elizabeth Freeman, Sep. 29, 1840.
Ham, Mortimer R. to Martha M. Sneed, Jan. 23, 1840.

Hams, Charles G. to Susan Brown, Dec. 10, 1840.
Hayes, Zachariah T. to Martha Baker, Aug. 13, 1840.
Haynes, William F. to Nancy L. Chilcoutt (Chilcutt), Jan. 7, 1840.
Haynes, Thomas W. to Jane T. A. Buchanon, Nov. 3, 1840.
Henry, John to Maria Bloodworth, March 11, 1840.
Henry, Thomas S. to Sarah M. Anderson, Dec. 21, 1840.

Page 57
Henson, James H. to Sarah Foster, Jan. 30, 1840.
Heron, Wm. R. to Ellen Diggons, Sep. 1, 1840.
Hewlett, Taylot to Frances Mallory, Nov. 26, 1840.
Hite, Thos. H. to Martha Jane Couch, Sep. 5, 1840.
Hoffman, Thos. J. to Elizabeth L. Oldham, March 25, 1840.
Hope, James W. to Jane N. Duff, Dec. 26, 1840.
Harr, McDonald to Alvira McDonald, April 17, 1840.
Hunt, Robertson M. to Malinda Jackson, Nov. 2, 1840.
Hughes, James H. to Amanda Hartley, May 21, 1840.

Page 58
Hunt, William C. to Penelope Henderson, June 11, 1840.
Jennings, William to Maria Donelson, March 17, 1840.
Jennett, Joseph to Elizabeth Nickens, May 21, 1840.
Jenkins, William to Amanda M. Sullivant, Aug. 22, 1840.
Jenkins, Lewis to Tennessee Willis, July 29, 1840.
Joyce, Bennett A. to Sarah A. Buchanon, Oct. 5, 1840.
Jones, James P. to Mary O. Bland, Aug. 7, 1840.
Kemp, James M. to Mary Ann Halloway, Sep. 19, 1840.

Page 59
Kendrick, James H. to Sarah H. Bateman, March 16, 1840.
Kennedy, Ashly to Rebecca Abernathy, March 11, 1840.
Kreider, Emanuel J. to Mary A. Hamilton, Nov. 1, 1840.
Lampkins, Jackson to Rosanna E. Adams, Jan. 2, 1840.
Leggett, Josiah to Jane Tucker, Sep. 29, 1840.
Lenard, William to Tempy Edwards, May 16, 1840.
Lishey, Louis C. to Mary Ann Sledge, Dec. 8, 1840.
Lockhart, Mason to Amanda Malone, Feb. 13, 1840.
Martin, George F. to Martha Ann Gay, July 27, 1840.

Page 60
Mayfield, Peter P. to Mary Proctor, Oct. 19, 1840.
McClellan, Sam'l to Elizabeth E. Campbell, March 11, 1840.
McGregor, Geo. Mackenzie to Jane Maria Christian, Feb. 20, 1840.
McKay, J. D. to Maria B. Mitchell, Jan. 7, 1840.
Merritt, Theophilus to Louisa Hite, Jan. 25, 1840.
Mithcell, William to Sarah W. Foster, Aug. 12, 1840.
Milliron, Jacob to Sophia Lankford, Sep. 8, 1840.
Moore, Anthony to Frances Simpkins, Feb. 25, 1840.
Moore, William G. to Amanda Johnson, Dec. 7, 1840.

Page 61
Morris, Nathan to Delila Durarde, Nov. 16, 1840.
Morton, Elijah to Mary A. Humphreys, May 25, 1840.
Mullin, Reuben W. to Susan Bibb, July 6, 1840.
Nelson, Joseph to Clarrisa White, Jan. 5, 1840.
Nelson, Joseph to Clarrissa White, Jan. 5, 1840
Newsom, James E. to Cornelia Ann Carter, Oct. 28, 1840.
Nichol, James B. to Lodocia R. Hart, Dec. 2, 1840.
Nichols, David to Sarah Jane Simpson, April 6, 1840.
Osborn, Thomas to Mary Ann McCrory, Dec. 8, 1840.
Owens, James to Lucy Ann Dotson, Aug. 13, 1840.

Page 62
Owen, James to Amanda Owen, March 14, 1840.
Page, Egbert to Elizabeth Page, Feb. 25, 1840.
Parrish, James B. to Penelope Harman, July 15, 1840.
Parnelle, Sam'l E. to Minerva Galloway, July 18, 1840.
Percy, Charles B. to Henrietta Nichol, June 4, 1840.
Porter, Solomon to Sarah Ransom, June 11, 1840.
Read, Henry to Ann Jennett, Jan. 30, 1840.
Redmond, Henry A. to Mary White, Dec. 23, 1840.
Redman, Joseph to Nancy Cox, Oct. 15, 1840.

Page 63
Roy, Wiley to Ann Fagen, Dec. 26, 1840.
Ryman, John to Sarah Green, April 11, 1840.
Sanders, William to Margaret Bradfute, May 27, 1840.
Saunders, James to Mary Dews, April 18, 1840.
Sills, D. C. to Elizabeth Glass, March 18, 1840.
Sharpe, Benj. to Ann Morehead, July 24, 1840.
Shute, Thomas to Tennessee Demoss, Feb. 5, 1840.
Shivers, Jonas to Catherine Ferrel, May 28, 1840.
Smith, Lewis to Martha Summers, Nov. 16, 1840.

Page 64
Spain, Richard to Nancy Bivens, Dec. 7, 1840.
Spain, Littleberry K. to Sarah G. Spain, July 30, 1840.
Still, Edward J. to Theodore Ann Estes, Nov. 21, 1840.
Strait, Hiram to Hannah C. Malone, Dec. 21, 1840.
Sullivan, Franklin to Mary Robertson, Jan. 15, 1840.
Swaggard, Christopher to Emely Davis, Aug. 25, 1840.
Thompson, Shearod to Martha Ann J. Smith, Sep. 15, 1840.
Tucker, Thomas to Sarah Ann Tucker, Oct. 22, 1840.
Utley, Zebba C. to Eliza Cole, Jan. 4, 1840.
Varden, George to Mary Garland, Aug. 8, 1840.
Vaulx, Joseph to Eleanor N. R. Armstrong, Aug. 28, 1840.
Vaughn, William to Elizabeth Burk, Aug. 10, 1840.
Wallace, William E. to Elizabeth F. Young, Jan. 28, 1840.
Ware, David to Frances Thomas, April 30, 1840.
Weaver, John to Matilda Harris, June 5, 1840.
Williams, Phillip M. to Martha G. Fulghum, Nov. 24, 1840.
Wilkerson, Hansel T. to Martha Ann Buie, March 12, 1840.
White, William to Martha Phelps, Dec. 17, 1840.

Page 66
White, John to Susan Estes, June 11, 1840.
White, John J. to Mary C. Thompson, Dec. 22, 1840.
Whiteside, David to Louisa Wright, Aug. 27, 1840.
Whitsett, James to Elizabeth Woodruff, Sep. 17, 1840.
Wolf, George W. to I. Mary Baliew, Dec. 17, 1840.
Woodward, Geo. B. P. to Mary E. P. Atkin, March 12, 1840.
Zachey, Godolphus to Jane Mason, Feb. 3, 1840.

Page 67
Abernathy, James M. to Matilda Huffman, June 9, 1841.
Allen, David M. to Frances A. Pope, June 5, 1841.
Alley, Benjamine to Susan Mitchell, May 5, 1841.
Bandy, Richard C. to Eliza Grizzard, May 17, 1841.
Barry, Richard H. to Elizabeth J. Haynes, Oct. 26, 1841.
Baxter, John to Susan A. Railey, Dec. 14, 1841.
Bean, William C. to Elizabeth Burchett, Dec. 23, 1841.
Bell, Hugh H. to Prudence L. Bradford, Dec. 23, 1841.
Berry, Augustus D. to Adeline Farnham, Aug. 21, 1841.

Page 68
Bomer, William to Zibiak Freeman, Oct. 20, 1841.
Bostick, Richard W. H. to Rebecca L. Cannon, Jan. 19, 1841.
Boyd, Milton B. to Isabell M. Dabbs, Jan. 9, 1841.
Branch, John R. to Josephine J. Woods, Nov. 13, 1841.
Brinkley, Robt C. to Ann C. Overton, Oct. 18, 1841.
Brown, John G. to Martha E. Read, Nov. 25, 1841.
Brown, G. W. to Nancy Hannah, Jan. 23, 1841.
Brown, Bartlett to Temperance White, Feb. 24, 1841.
Brown, Eli to Mary Waddle, April 29, 1841.

Page 69
Buchanon, John R. to Nancy E. Hays, May 27, 1841.
Burchett, Thomas to Sarah Petty, Dec. 30, 1841.
Burke, Charles to Margaret Maynard, Oct. 24, 1841.
Butler, Edward to Ann Casey, Oct. 22, 1841.
Buts, Craven to Delilah Carter, May 15, 1841.
Capps, Robert to Sarah Fudge, June 12, 1841.
Castleman, Burrell P. to Gennette Brooks, Jan. 18, 1841.
Cerly, John B. to Lucinda Steele, Dec. 16, 1841.
Chaudoin, Reuben to Matilda Hooper, May 19, 1841.

Page 70
Camick, Charles M. to Luvica McCain, Oct. 22, 1841.
Cheatham, Edward S. to Jane Eleanor Foster, Oct. 19, 1841.
Clements, Stephen to Mary Foster, Dec. 22, 1841.
Clemmons, Eli to Nancy Rear, Jan. 23, 1841.
Cobb, James H. to Martha J. Boyce, May 21, 1841.
Cobler, Frederick to Racel (Rachel) Cobler, Nov. 29, 1841.
Collins, Enoch to Susan J. Phillips, Dec. 11, 1841.
Connelly, John W. to Angelica R. West, Sep. 15, 1841.

Cook, John F. to Caroline A. Duvall, Oct. 14, 1841.

Page 71
Corbitt, Samuel R. to Caroline Smith, Nov. 2, 1841.
Courtney, James to Mary Matthis, Aug. 16, 1841.
Cowgill, Thompson to Rebecca Hallum, June 8, 1841.
Crawford, James J. to Elizabeth T. Hogan, March 17, 1841.
Crutis, William to Eliza Ann Gower, Jan. 21, 1841.
Deal, James A. to Eliza Russell, Feb. 3, 1841.
Davis, James T. to Narcissa Moss, Jan. 14, 1841.
Denning, William to Mary Ann Cox, Nov. 2, 1841
Dillard, John to Sarah Garland, Aug. 28, 1841.

Page 72
Dillyard, Bryant to Elizabeth Garland, Dec. 18, 1841.
Dixon, Henry O. to Ann Maria Patterson, Nov. 18, 1841.
Donelson, A. J., Jr. to Sarah Melson, Feb. 3, 1841.
Downs, Thomas W. to Mary A. Phelps, July 22, 1841.
Downs, William H. to Catharine Scruggs, May 12, 1841.
Dozier, Jasper N. to Nancy Fossett, July 28, ----.
Dunaway, Drury to Mary Hoover, Dec. 13, 1841.
Dunn, Thomas to Margaret Ferebee, Jan. 4, 1841.

Page 73
Elam, James A. to Catharine M. Lingow, Nov. 3, 1841.
Earheart, Wade H. to Rebecca J. Umphreys, Sep. 21, 1841.
Ewing, Andrew to Rowena J. Williams, Sep. 9, 1841.
Fall, John T. S. to Sarah W. Bradford, Sep. 28, 1841.
Ferguson, Landus S. to Elizabeth Johnson, Sep. 9, 1841.
Fisher, Daniel to Penelope A. Williams, Sep. 14, 1841.
Fisher, Samuel to Lavinia Williams, Dec. 22, 1841.
Finney, Thomas J. to Mary A. Slatter, Nov. 8, 1841.
Judge, Simpson to Sethe Abbott, Aug. 11, 1841.

Page 74
Fulcher, William to Susan Lassater, Sep. 9, 1841.
Fuqua, Thomas to Nancy H. McLaughlin, Nov. 1, 1841.
Gerard, Wm. H. to Sarah B. Smith, Sep. 16, 1841.
Gibbs, Alexander B. to Marilla Simmons, May 13, 1841.
Gibson, Isham to Sarah Pennuel, Dec. 25, 1841.
Gillam, Edward to Amanda Porter, June 12, 1841.
Gilman, Jesse P. to Mary Jane Compton, March 15, 1841.
Glass, Robert to Margaret A. White, March 8, 1841.
Gleaves, Felix R. to Nancy F. Huggins, Jan. 8, 1841.

Page 75
Gorin, Franklin to Frances C. Boardman, July 29, 1841.
Greer, George to Martha A. Morning, Feb. 9, 1841.
Grindstead, Addison P. to Sarah E. Shumate, Feb. 3, 1841.
Hagan, James H. to Mary Ann Clark, Oct. 30, 1841.
Hale, Charles G. to Charlotte E. Napier, Sep. 6, 1841.
Hale, Thomas C. to Nancy Smith, June 15, 1841.
Hamblen, Benjamine F. to Mary F. Walker, Dec. 11, 1841.

Hampton, Benjamine to Prudy Carney, July 21, 1841.
Heatwell, John to Mary Williams, Oct. 27, 1841.

Page 76
Hedenberg, Charles J. to Mary Ellen Higginbotham, July 8, 1841.
Heron, Mathew to Emma Diggins, Oct. 14, 1841.
Herrin, George T. to Phebe J. Greer, Feb. 9, 1841.
Herring, Westley to Elizabeth Watson, Nov. 10, 1841.
Hicks, Alfred H. to Mary W. Demovelle, March 2, 1841.
Hill, Alexander to Oma Bumpass, Sep. 9, 1841.
Hite, Lebron to Celia A. Brockman, Dec. 27, 1841.
Hyde, William O. to Mary Ann Lanier, Sep. 2, 1841.
Jackson, Henry to Winney Williams, Oct. 11, 1841.

Page 77
Jenkins, George to Mary Castleman, Jan. 27, 1841.
Jefferson, John R. to Amanda M. Gillman, Jan. 6, 1841.
Jones, Benjamine F. to Jane C. Goodrich, May 10, 1841.
Johnson, William D. to Lucinda Carrington, Sep. 2, 1841.
Jones, Richard H. to Mary A. Porter, May 8, 1841.
Jordan, Jessee to Mary A. Jordan, Aug. 7, 1841.
Jourdan, Benjamine W. to Mary A. Gabwell, Dec. 14, 1841.
Kelly, Edward H. to Ann Chicks, Nov. 28, 1841.
Kimbro, John to Tabitha Burnett, Dec. 28, 1841.

Page 78
Kirkman, John to Catharine S. McNairy, Nov. 18, 1841.
Kuhnes, Francis to Mary Ann Stimple, Sep. 16, 1841.
Lee, William to Darinda Russell, Sep. 10, 1841.
Legraff, Michial to Milberry Williams, July 30, 1841.
Lindsay, Lewis to Elizab eth Everett, June 23, 1841.
Lindsey (Lindsley), Nathaniel L. to Julia M. Stevens, Oct. 18, 1841.
Lischer, George S. to Sophia Stimball, July 29, 1841.
Lenon, John J. to Elizabeth Proctor, Jan. 30, 1841.
Longinette, James to Caroline E. Logan, Sep. 27, 1841.
Lyon, Alpheus to Caroline H. Topp, Dec. 22, 1841.
Manlove, Robert C. to Susanna Hyde, Feb. 10, 1841.
Martin, Wilson D. to Martha Dean, June 30, 1841.
Massey, William to Mary Brown, Sep. 18, 1841.
May, Joel F. to Mary A. Thompson, Dec. 11, 1841.
Mayfield, Isaac W. to Lydia Deal, Sep. 25, 1841.
Mayho, Jacob D. to Nancy Lee, July 29, 1841.
McClure, William to Sarah A. Gallaher, July 24, 1841.
McCoy, William to Jane McCane, Oct. 8, 1841.

Page 80
McGehee, Benjamine F. to Mary Amanda Pennington, Sep. 27, 1841.
McLain, William A. to Mary C. Bransford, Nov. 12, 1841.
Menton, James W. to Martha Jane Chadwell, June 21, 1841.
Miller, John to Lucy Hickman, Aug. 28, 1841.
Moake, Jacob to Julina Dozier, June 23, 1841.

Moore, George W. to Emmeliza Pyrtle, July 5, 1841.
Morris, Jacob to Mary Ann Anderson, Dec. 6, 1841.
Moss, David to R. Elizabeth Vaughn, Sep. 4, 1841.
Murrey, William P. to Sarah Ann Allen, Jan. 23, 1841.

Page 81
Neely, William to Elizabeth Lowry, April 20, 1841.
Nickens, Calvin C. to Easter Murry, June 11, 1841.
Nickens, Calvin C. to Roccelany Murry, Nov. 29, 1841.
Owen, Richard to Catherine Ramer, Jan. 27, 1841.
Ogilvie, William S. to Elizabeth E. Kimbro, Nov. 11, 1840.
Overton, John to Rachel N. Harding, April 17, 1841.
Owen, Gaines to Zaravira Singletary, March 9, 1841.
Olliver, William S. to Adaline S. Marlin, Sep. 8, 1841.
Pack, B. L. to Frances G. Swinny, Dec. 7, 1841.

Page 82
Parker, Charles L. to Eliza J. Jones, Jan. 7, 1841.
Patton, Calvin to Mary Bloodworth, Aug. 26, 1841.
Patrick, Daniel D. to Elizabeth Sanford, May 27, 1841.
Peebles, C. C. to Lucretia Gower, March 29, 1841.
Pegram, John P. to Nina Ussry, Aug. 21, 1841.
Perry, Jesse to Martha Newburn, March 10, 1841.
Mitchell, Abraham H. to Tennessee C. Pritchett, June 14, 1841.
Quinn, Michael to Malinda Bailey, Jan. 19, 1841.
Ragan, William H. to Harriett Frances, April 27, 1841.

Page 83
Reno, James G. to Mary C. Glenn, Oct. 21, 1841.
Richardson, James N. T. to Emma M. Winn, Aug. 9, 1841.
Robertson, James W. to Margaret Graham, May 18, 1841.
Russell, Parean to Sarah Parr, July 5, 1841.
Sadler, William C. to Serena Deal, Oct. 23, 1841.
Sandek, Joseph to Nancy Eliza Northem, Dec. 1, 1841.
Saunders, William to Delamy Smith, June 3, 1841.
Scott, Arthur to Elizabeth McCutchen, Dec. 20, 1841.
Segraff, Michael W. to Milberry Williams, July 30, 1841.

Page 84
Sheppard, Charles to Matilda Commander, Jan. 23, 1841.
Shultz, Charles F. to Petronille Mary Tavisson, Nov. 4, 1841.
Smith, William to Nancy Meadow, March 29, 1841.
Smith, Cyrus to Dorinda Lamson, Oct. 7, 1841.
Spain, William H. to Ann Thompson, Jan. 27, 1841.
Stephens, Alphred to Ann Mariah Jackson, Aug. 30, 1841.
Stewart, Thomas H. to Mary A. M. Freeland, Oct. 14, 1841.
Steerman, Alfred to Margery Ann Holder, Jan. 11, 1841.

Page 85
Swinney, Robert to Sarah Ellis, Dec. 11, 1841.

John Swinnery to Lethia Jessup, Dec. 13, 1841.
Taylor, Jacob to Mary Ritchie, March 20, 1841.
Thomas, Joseph H. to Delany Smith, June 1, 1841.
Thomas, Sam'l E. to Rachel J. Yarnell, Sep. 28, 1841.
Trimble, Madison to Catharine Shumate, Sep. 23, 1841.
Turley, Charles A. to Virginia G. Smith, Nov. 3, 1841
Usery, Wm. M. to Sarah Ann Osborn, Sep. 7, 1841.
Veatch, Philip to Frances Jones, Feb. 9, 1841.
Vaughn, James A. to Judiana M. Cole, Sep. 15, 1841.
Waller, Rufus to Rachel McCrory, Oct. 26, 1841.
Warmack, Jesse to Mary P. Byrn, Dec. 11, 1841.
Warren, Jesse to Frances Ann Pride, Sep. 9, 1841.
Watson, Winfield S. to Sarah Ann Boyd, March 4, 1841.
Welborn, Enoch to Mary Ashbridge, March 17, 1841.
Wheeler, Benjamine to Malinda Johnson, Aug. 18, 1841.
Wilkerson, John to Martecia Hope, Oct. 18, 1841.
Williamson, Thomas N. to Olivia Connell, Sep. 4, 1841.

Page 87
Willie McCrory to Sarah McCrory, June 2, 1841.
Willis, Joseph to Mary Ann Studevant, Oct. 14, 1841.
Wilson, Thomas J. to Elizabeth Waddle, April 28, 1841.
Winchester, Geo. W. to Malvina H. Gaines, March 9, 1841.
Wing, Robert to Catharine Greer, Dec. 6, 1841.
Woods, Robert H. to Susan E. Berry, Oct. 20, 1841.
Woodward, Benjamine to Elizabeth L. Prescot, July 13, 1841.
Wright, T. J. to Mary Downs, Aug. 22, 1841.
Wright, James to Mary O'Brien, Nov. 16, 1841.

Page 88
Yandell, Jno. W. to Mildred Martin, Oct. 21, 1841.
Yeates, James to Mary E. McMurry, Jan. 14, 1841.
Young, William J. to Almeta Jones, May 20, 1841.
Zachry, Griffin G. to Lucinda Stevens, Jan. 11, 1841.
Zanone, James to Anna M. Bode, Jan. 14, 1841.

Page 89
Allen, George C. to Martha Overton, Oct. 27, 1842.
Andrews, Samuel W. to Susanna Brookman, Jan. 15, 1842.
Austin, Newton C. to Elizabeth L. Peay, Dec. 17, 1842.
Baker, Alijah to Rachael Wiles, Dec. 17, 1842.
Ballard, William to Hannah Brown, May 13, 1842.
Barnes, Benjamine to Catharine Zachary, April 20, 1842.
Banzer, George to Lousa Kuhlmann, May 16, 1842.
Baker, Leonard D. to Lamiza D. Gamer, Jan. 18, 1842.
Bailey, Cornelius to Amanda M. Duren, Jan. 1, 1842.

Page 90
Baker, James M. to Parantte True, Oct. 12, 1842.
Baker, William to Mary Jane Wilson, Dec. 7, 1842.
Beazley, William B. to Mary B. Champ, Dec. 14, 1842.
Bess, Andrew J. to Harriett Mitchell, June 1, 1842.
Bennett, Thomas to Matilda Crockett, July 20, 1842.

Bishop, John to Easter Ann Thompson, Feb. 5, 1842.
Binkley, Prestor to Eliza Ann Farmer, March 12, 1842.
Binkley, Charles to Lucinda Darrow, March 17, 1842.
Binkley, Tazwell M. to Matilda Boyd, Oct. 6, 1842.

Page 91
Blair, William to Lamiza Felts, Fec. 22, 1842.
Boyd, Robert to Rebecca Jane Campbell, Dec. 15, 1842.
Bowers, William P. to Martha S. McCaslin, May 26, 1842.
Bosley, Charles, Jr. to Martha A. Carden, March 30, 1842.
Brumet, Lerry to Elizabeth M. Clay, Aug. 25, 1842.
Brown, John to Lucinda McDaniel, Nov. 30, 1842.
Brookman, Wiliam to Elza Wyles, May 14, 1842.
Brackwell, Nowell to Penelope A. C. Brown, March 8, 1842.
Brewer, William E. to Judy Perry, May 7, 1842.

Page 92
Bryan, Wm. S. to Margaret A. Campbell, Sep. 27, 1842.
Burt, William T. to Martha A. Robertson, Dec. 8, 1842.
Burns, Michael to Margaret Filliam, March 12, 1842.
Burke, John H. to Caroline T. Vaughn, Nov. 19, 1842.
Butler, John W. to Sarah Greer Wilson, Jan. 15, 1842.
Bunton, William R. to Elizabeth Cotton, Dec. 31, 1842.
Casey, Charles S. to Mary Earthman, July 4, 1842.
Cantrell, George C. to Mary J. Davenport, May 11, 1842.
Casey, James S. to Mary D. McNish, Jan. 22, 1842.

Page 93
Carter, Francis M. to Narcissa Hannah, Sep. 10, 1842.
Champion, Henry to Catharine Singleton, June 9, 1842.
Creech, Thomas to Almanza Green, March 17, 1842.
Chadwell, John A. to Miranda E. Wright, Jan. 20, 1842.
Clark, John H. to Elizabeth Kemper, Dec. 1, 1842.
Clerdy, Patrick H. to Rachael Abernathy, Feb. 10, 1842.
Collier, Richard to Lucinda Wooldridge, April 7, 1842.
Creach, Jno. W. to Nancy Jane Bell, July 7, 1842.
Cunningham, John to Mary Cole, Jan. 8, 1842.

Page 94
Currey, Richard O. to Rachel J. Estin, May 25, 1842.
Curfman, James to Sarah Belcher, Oct. 28, 1842.
Davis, John to Celia Ann Richards, March 9, 1842.
Days, Lewis to Nancy E. Adams, March 7, 1842.
Dabbs, James to Louisa Cheek, Aug. 18, 1842.
Dabbs, Joseph W. to Mary D. Menees, Aug. 15, 1842.
Demoss, Jesse S. to Delilah Pack, May 3, 1842.
Dillahunty, Joseph S. to Elizabeth D. Burton, Nov. 29, 1842.
Dozier, Enock to Judith Gupton, Sep. 6, 1842.

Page 95
Downing, William D. V. to Nancy B. Campbell, Oct. 12, 1842.

Dozier, David to Elizabeth Demoss, Aug. 20, 1842.
Durham, George to Isabella Seat, Oct. 23, 1842.
Durard, Joseph to Nancy House, Jan. 23, 1842.
Eakin, William to Felicia Ann Grundy, July 5, 1842.
Edwards, Allison to Lavena Green, July 29, 1842.
Estes, Wm. C. to Eliza Jane Mathews, Sep. 8, 1842.
Evans, John R. to Nancy Ann Baker, Nov. 12, 1842.
Fall, Alexander to Elizabeth Horton, Oct. 20, 1842.

Page 96
Fleming, Ferguson to Frances J. McCombs, Jan. 25, 1842.
Fry, Martin to Thussey C. Crockett, Dec. 10, 1842.
Fuquay, John C. to Rebecca Cook, March 9, 1842.
Fletcher, Jermon M. to Mary Ann Hooper, Jan. 8, 1842.
Frees, Jacob W. to Margaret McBell, Jan. 24, 1842.
Ferguson, James to Elizabeth Wyatt, March 23, 1842.
Fitzhugh, James M. to Nancy Amanda Whitemore, Aug. 24, 1842.
Fullbright, Alfred to Mary Clemons, Dec. 1, 1842.
Fudge, Jacob to Elizabeth Bloodworth, July 25, 1842.

Page 97
Feilds, Edwin to Mary Ann Akin, Oct. 20, 1842.
Gallaher, William to America Whitfield, Jan. 15, 1842.
Galbreath, John H. to Martha Draper, Dec. 29, 1842.
Grant, John to Elizabeth Williams, Oct. 27, 1842.
Gardner, Edwin S. to Sarah E. Vannoy, March 17, 1842.
Gay, Seburr to Mary Surles, Aug. 30, 1842.
Goodrich, Hays to Minerva Hartman, July 19, 1842.
Goodwin, George B. to Martha A. Barnes, Feb. 2, 1842.
Green, A. M. to Mary A. E. Buchanan, July 20, 1842.

Page 98
Green, George to Matilda Richardson, Dec. 16, 1842.
Guthrie, Henry C. to Lucinda T. Reynolds, Aug. 17, 1842.
Hall, John to Elizabeth Lee, Dec. 8, 1842.
Hamilton, Gorge F. to Elizabeth O. Polk, Aug. 2, 1842.
Handy, Edward S. to Jane T. Woods, Jan. 20, 1842.
Hannah, Joseph to Mary Jane Haile, Feb. 28, 1842.
Harper, Isaac P. to Matilda Hall, May 4, 1842.
Harris, J. Geo. to Lucinda McGavock, May 3, 1842.
Harris, John H. to Mary E. Sledge, Feb. 21, 1842.

Page 99
Harris, John B. to Sarah B. Humphries, Nov. 19, 1842.
Harwood, Richard D. to Mary M. Everett, Dec. 19, 1842.
Harman, William to Isabella H. Watkins, June 13, 1842.
Hart, John to Lucy Barnett, April 14, 1842.
Hawkins, Jacob to Eliza Jane Weakley, March 28, 1842.
Heiss, John P. to Clarissa Richmond, May 27, 1842.
Holt, Joseph A. to Martha E. Lanier, Dec. 19, 1842.
Hooper, Geo. J. to Louisa C. Hooper, July 30, 1842.
Horn, William to Elizabeth Spronce, Feb. 14, 1842.

Page 100
Henderson, James to Sarah Carter, May 9, 1842.
Hill, William G. to Nancy M. Thornton, Jan. 1, 1842.
Hill, James S. to Louisa Hunt, Jan. 20, 1842.
Hoggatt, William to Milley Strange, July 25, 1842.
Howell, Zack to Lucy Mills, Aug. 19, 1842.
Hurt, John to Susan Bandy, Aug. 13, 1842.
Huffner, John to Margarett Campbell, Jan. 11, 1842.
Jenkins, Dan'l W. to Lucy A. Riley, Sep. 21, 1842.
Jenkins, James H. to Elizabeth Mathews, Sep. 22, 1842.

Page 101
Jones, Moses to Caroline Hannah, Sep. 5, 1842.
Jones, John to Jane Day, July 21, 1842.
Jones, James W. to Tabitha Barnes, June 25, 1842.
Kinley, John to Sarah Roden, Jan. 4, 1842.
Klets, Frederick to Mary Miller, Feb. 19, 1842.
Kingston, Samuel M. to Agness Pegram, May 30, 1842.
Lyon, James P. to Mary Ann Roden, Jan. 31, 1842.
Larimore, David R. to Kissiah Patterson, Jan. 5, 1842.
Lowry, Peter to Lucinda Dotson, May 7, 1842.

Page 102
Leak, James to Frances Ann Harrison, July 7, 1842.
Litton, Isaac to Rebecca C. Smith, Nov. 6, 1842.
Long, Edward to Sarah Ritch, Feb. 9, 1842.
Malone, Benjamine to Sarah Ann Adams, Oct. 18, 1842.
Mathews, Wm. B. to Celia Ann Martin, Sep. 27, 1842.
May, Joseph H. to Sidney Murry, April 2, 1842.
Mayson, Francis M. t- Anna W. Horton, Sep. 8, 1842.
McKenzie, Kenneth to Mary Marshall, June 13, 1842.
Monks, Jefferson to Fanny W. Chatham, Oct. 25, 1842.

Page 103
Morris, Peter B. to Nancy Marlin, Feb. 7, 1842.
Moody, John to Mary Alley, Jan. 4, 1842.
Murry, Berry to Harriett Murry, Oct. 3, 1842.
Noe, Ambrose D. to Elizabeth Leonard, March 4, 1842.
Nolen, Andrew to Mary Ann Osborn, June 8, 1842.
Norvell, Henry L. to Laura Sevier, Oct. 6, 1842.
Northern, Samuel to Anna Chrismon, Dec. 21, 1842.
Owen, Alfred to Mary Waters, April 26, 1842.
Peay, James to Evelina Fly, July 16, 1842.

Page 104
Park, John S. to Mary Ann Carden, March 8, 1842.
Parrish, Thomas H. to Mariah Couch, Feb. 23, 1842.
Patton, John to Catharine Holder, July 6, 1842.
Pattifer, Wm. W. to Nancy Stevenson, Nov. 16, 1842.
Peal, William to Caroline Woods, Nov. 12, 1842.
Pennington, John W. to America M. McMurry, Sep. 10, 1842.
Pennington, J. T. to Margaret Ann Sample, May 7, 1842.
Player, T. T. to Emma Yeatman, Jan. 5, 1842.

Porterfield, Robert R. to Mary D. Figures, March 22, 1842.

Page 105
Powell, Thomas to Mary Moore, March 3, 1842.
Powers, John H. to Susan W. Rives, July 20, 1842.
Quinn, William J. to Tabitha McCane, Jan. 6, 1842.
Rader, Jacob to Elizabeth Luster, Nov. 10, 1842.
Rains, Felix R. to Mary Drake, July 14, 1842.
Ray, Kindred to Elizabeth Ann Eubanks, March 14, 1842.
Ramsey, Wm. B. A. to Susan P. Washington, May 8, 1842.
Redmund, William to Susan Cox, April 14, 1842.
Reeves, Robert C. to Sarah Toombs, Dec. 21, 1842.

Page 106
Richards, Rains to Nancy F. Thompson, Jan. 11, 1842.
Roane, Francis to Elizabeth D. Jones, Oct. 18, 1842.
Roy, George W. to Margery Lazenberry, Dec. 6, 1842.
Rohrbacher, John G. to Mary Jane Barker, March 9, 1842.
Routon, Richmond to Sarah Ann Marlin, Nov. 18, 1842.
Russell, Thomas to Nancy Parkham, June 7, 1842.
Sands, Thos. T. to Elizabeth Johnson, Aug. 4, 1842.
Sawyer, Sterling B. to Martha L. Forehand, Sep. 23, 1842.
Scales, Jeremiah to Rachel G. Bosley, Aug. 14, 1842.

Page 107
Scott, William H. to Susan W. Thomas, Feb. 17, 1842.
Scott, Richard E. to Jane Bennett, Jan. 26, 1842.
Scott, Thomas W. to Adeline Tennessee Hale, July 20, 1842.
Sevier, Geo. W. to Sarah Shirley, Nov. 17, 1842.
Simpson, Washington H. to Leathey Eliza Bolton, June 23, 1842.
Simpkins, Thomas C. to Martha Wells, Feb. 14, 1842.
Sims, Boyd M. to Sarah Ann Ewing, May 11, 1842.
Shelton, Marcus L. to Sarah Noel, Dec. 1, 1842.
Shields, James to Nancy Mosley, Jan. 1, 1842.

Page 108
Shacklett, John S. to Louisa Foster, Aug. 11, 1842.
Smith, William to Isabel Simpson, Aug. 6, 1842.
Smith, Winn B. to Sarah Susan Baker, Nov. 10, 1842.
Sneed, Joseph P. to Achsah B. Harris, Oct. 12, 1842.
Sozenski, Lewis to Mary M. Stuart, June 11, 1842.
Stout, Ira A. to Sarah A. Graham, Oct. 26, 1842.
Surdevant, Benj. F. to Sarah Read, May 16, 1842.
Sweeney, Thomas G. to Julia Jones, Feb. 21, 1842.
Swiney, John G. to Mary Johnson, Feb. 21, 1842.

Page 109
Tanksley, John to Lucinda Wheeler, Jan. 5, 1842.
Terry, James to Margaret Abernathy, Oct. 31, 1842.
Thurman, Nathaniel to Mary E. Cotton, Jan. 15, 1842.
Torbitt, Granville C. to Louisa Barrow, Nov. 22, 1842.

Townsend, Wm. H. to Martha A. Kezee, Sep. 29, 1842.
Trabue, Edward to Caroline M. Campbell, Sep. 21, 1842.
Turner, Wm. C. to Sarah E. Hawkins, Aug. 10, 1842.
Turner, Janett J. T. to Martha D. Owen, March 24, 1842.
Vandyck, John H. to Elizabeth S. Smith, Jan. 24, 1842.
Veitch, Smeedes to Cornelia Ryon, March 3, 1842.
Vancourt, Alexander to Harriett O. Hinson, Dec. 9, 1842.
Walker, James A. to Susan J. Green, Aug. 11, 1842.
Walker, Thomas E. to Mary Ann Barton, Nov. 3, 1842.
Walker, John W. to Mary Gregory, Nov. 25, 1842.
Washington, George A. to Margaret A. Lewis, Sep. 13, 1842.
Warren, Jesse to Delilah Zachry, Feb. 10, 1842.
Watkins, William E., Jr. to Almira J. Cockrill, Jan. 31, 1842.
West, Wm. G. to Caroline C. Davis, Nov. 17, 1842.

Page 111
Wetherford, Josiah to Jane Alley, July 30, 1842.
Weakley, Isaac to Mary Lee, Sep. 19, 1842.
Wingo, Russell to Mary Ford, July 16, 1842.
Williams, James to Elizabeth Green, May 28, 1842.
Willis, N.B. to Rebecca E. Shaw, March 12, 1842.
Williams, Joseph to Sarah J. Page, June 18, 1842.
Williams, John to Ann Covington, Aug. 4, 1842. (No return).
Winchester, Marcus B. to Lucy Leonora McClain, Aug. 17, 1842.
Word, Fulton F. to Lucinda Buchanon, May 14, 1842.

Page 112
Wright, William W. to Nancy E. Plummer, Aug. 29, 1842.

Page 113
Abernathy, Freeman, Jr. to Elizabeth Abernathy, Dec. 26, 1842.
Allen, John W. to Eliza B. Corley, July 20, 1843.
Appleton, James to Priscilla Miles, May 29, 1843.
Armstead, Wm. B. to Robena Woods, Feb. 22, 1843.
Aydelott, J. D. to Sarah E. Grizzard, July 3, 1843.
Baker, John G. to Mary Jane Warmack, Jan. 10, 1843.
Ball, Harrison to Mary E. Alley, Dec. 15, 1843.
Bateman, John L. to Lydia Ann Read, Dec. 21, 1843.
Barnes, Wm. R. to Elizabeth Ann Wells, Oct. 19, 1843.

Page 114
Blackwell, Josiah to Betsy Hunt, Feb. 9, 1843.
Boner, James H. to Nancy Lay, Nov. 28, 1843.
Bowman, Joseph A. to Lucy Caroline White, Aug. 21, 1843.
Brady, John A. to Bedory F. Brittle, July 5, 1843.
Brownlow, John to Julia Morris, Dec. 21, 1843.
Brgan, Lewis C. to Sarah A. D. Ring, Oct. 12, 1843.
Burnham, Wm. to Martha Fields, Nov. 19, 1843.
Burnett, Henry to Jennette J. Davis, Aug. 15, 1843.

Page 115
Butler, Edward to Rebecca Gay, April 12, 1843.
Barrow, Jno. E. to Catharine S. Gingrey, Oct. 5, 1843.
Clark, Boling to Susan Travillion, Dec. 18, 1843.
Cabler, Calvin to Sarah Newburn, Aug. 26, 1843.
Cawthon, James H. to Margaret A. Patterson, Aug. 5, 1843.
Chavouse, Abraham to Eliza Weaver, July 28, 1843.
Chawning, Moses P. to Pernina T. Smiley, March 28, 1843.
Cake, John to Nancy C. Hooper, Jan. 3, 1843.
Clemon, Eli to Elizabeth Griffis, Jan. 19, 1843.

Page 116
Crockett, W.B.E.J. to Martha Jane Boyd, Jan. 11, 1843.
Chilton, James M. to Caroline M. Smith, April 29, 1843.
Cole, Bartholemeu to Amelia Witzel, April 25, 1843.
Cook, Matthew to Mary McNairy, April 24, 1843.
Collins, James B. to Martha Ann Foster, March 21, 1843.
Connell, William to Narcissa Ann Mathews, Feb. 10, 1843.
Craig, Lewis Y. to Mary E. Lowry, July 5, 1843.
Creighton, Joseph to Nancy Travillion, July 21, 1843.
Cole, John N. to Eliza Jane Walker, Oct. 31, 1843.

Page 117
Cullam, Elliston M. to Angeline Dozier, Oct. 16, 1843.
Culley, Robert to Emily Work, Oct. 27, 1843.
Cook, Ezekiel to Lucy Jones, Nov. 27, 1843.
Cox, Fountain to Zerinda Smith, Dec. 2, 1843.
Cook, John E. to Frances M. Williams, Dec. 18, 1843.
Davis, Charles to Ellen Anderson, April 26, 1843.
Duke, Mathew to Sirena West, Feb. 17, 1843.
Dunn, Wilson to Martha M. Penticost, Aug. 28, 1843.
Ducan, John H. to Almira Bankston, March 20, 1843.

Page 118
Dolway, William J. to Martha Roe, July 3, 1843.
Demumbra, Samuel to Mary Ann Rose, Dec. 29, 1843.
English, Charles G. to Martha E. Southall, Oct. 24, 1843.
Freeman, Smith to Martha R. Butler, Dec. 25, 1843.
Fisher, Joseph B. to Priscilla A. Guilleford, July 28, 1843.
French, Wm. B. to Isabella L. White, Feb. 2, 1843.
Fans, Austin R. to Louisa Simpkins, Feb. 18, 1843.
Faircloth, Wm. to Martha Ann T. Seat, May 27, 1843.
Fleming, Wm. F. to Susan Roads, Sep. 18, 1843.

Page 119
Forehand, Richard to Nancy F. Moss, Dec. 9, 1843.
Glazier, Charles to Margaret Weakley, March 1, 1843.
Goff, Andrew F. to Rebecca J. Erwin, July 1, 1843.
Goodrich, Edwin W. to Lucinda C. Stroud, Jan. 4, 1843.
Gay, Henry to Margaret Saunders, Feb. 22, 1843.
Greener, John G. to Maria Catharine Kuhn, Feb. 27, 1843.
Horn, William to Lurana R. Huffman, Feb. 28, 1843.
Hail, Wm. C. to Parscilla McQuary, Jan. 11, 1843.
Houser, John G. to Maria A. Kuhn, Jan. 30, 1843.

Page 120
Harris, Felix A. to Augusta A. Rane, April 19, 1843.
Hawkins, Rich'd to Mary C. Cabler, March 23, 1843.
Hughes, John F. to Arabella L. Gibson, March 6, 1843.
Holmes, Thos. E. to Rachael Ann Huggins, June 3, 1843.
Hamilton, William to Nancy Clark, July 4, 1843.
Hobson, Thomas to Sarah Ann Talley, July 5, 1843.
Howlett, Wm. B. to Mary Ann Wollford, July 19, 1843.
Hillsman, Charles E. to Elizabeth M. Jones, July 19, 1843.
Hargrave, Wm. H. to Eliz. L. Mitchell, Nov. 9, 1843.

Page 121
Edward S. Handy to Margaret F. Woods, Dec. 7, 1843.
Hays, Blackman to Nancy E. Blackman, Dec. 31, 1841.
Hollingsworth, Henry to Ann B. Stump, July 25, 1843.
Hill, Isaac A. to Charlotte Dozier, Nov. 25, 1843.
Hamilton, James M. to Mary L. Berry, Oct. 26, 1843.
Hartley, Geo. W. to Nancy Hooper, Sep. 2, 1843.
Hays, Charles M. to Louisa Jane Smiley, July 20, 1843.
Hatcher, Ethelbert H. to Louisa C. Graves, Aug. 31, 1843.
Hill, William to Huldah Westbrook, Sep. 28, 1843.

Page 122
Harrison, Richard P. to Mary Ann Woodward, Sep. 26, 1843.
Harrison, James W. to Angeline Ball, Sep. 21, 1843.
Hill, Robert T. to Catharine F. Stout, Sep. 21, 1843.
Jennings, Wm. R. to Cynthia Goodrich, March 1, 1843.
Joiner, Jesse to Julia Nutt, March 8, 1843.
Joseph, Isaac to Elizabeth Smith, Oct. 26, 1843.
Justice, Henry L. to Matilda Bennett, Oct. 23, 1843.
Jourdan, Warren to Agness Allison, Dec. 9, 1843.
Jones, Wm. S. to Hannah E. Dawson, Sep. 2, 1843.

Page 123
Johnson, Wm. A. to Ellen R. Hart, Oct. 30, 1843.
Kidd, Hudson A. to Martha A. Williams, Jan. 31, 1843
Keeber, Jacob to Henrietta Binkley, May 20, 1843.
Kirkpatrick, Wm. to Harriett Patterson, May 22, 1843.
Kirfman, Michael to Elizabeth Samuels, April 6, 1843.
Krantz, David to Lavina Binkley, Aug. 21, 1843.
Lambert, John W. to Sarah Jane Harrison, Dec. 4, 1843.
Langford, Wm. to Amanda Boon, April 12, 1843.
Ledbetter, Alexander to Elizabeth Stull, Feb. 9, 1843.

Page 124
Lentz, Jacob F. to Christiana Wolf, Sep. 7, 1843.
Liston, Wm. J. to Jane Vaughan, Sep. 9, 1843.
Moorman, Charles W. to Maria A. Jarratt, Feb. 28, 1843.
McCullock, Benjamine W. to Anna M. Cannon, Oct. 19, 1843.
McGavock, Hugh W. to Mary Hagen, July 25, 1843.
McPherson, Green to Elij'h Jane Cartwright, Nov. 14, 1843.
Martin, Wm. L. to Mary L. Barry, Sep. 19, 1843.

Moore, Charles W. to Julia Ann King, Feb. 1, 1843.
Mathews, Alex. R. to Tellitha Williamson, July 14, 1843.

Page 125
John Mammel to Mary Centre, March 22, 1843.
Marlin, Kinchen, Jr. to Rachael Vines, July 26, 1843.
Marshall, Gibbert to Francis Wilkinson, Feb. 21, 1843.
Marlin, Samuel C. to Jane Gunter, May 26, 1843.
Martin, Shelton to Mildried Boyd, March 25, 1843.
Moss, William to Louisa Ann Balthrop, June 12, 1843.
Medlin, Joseph to Sophronia Owen, Oct. 10, 1843.
Miles, James to Tabitha Miles, Nov. 18, 1843.
Moore, Aaron to Polly Mays, Dec. 28, 1843.

Page 126
Norpp, John to Maria L.Iredale, Nov. 19, 1843.
Nichol, Alexander to Sarah Osborne, June 19, 1843.
Newson, Samuel B. to Amelia Edmunds, May 27, 1843.
Owen, William E. to Margaret Wilson, Oct. 30, 1843.
Odell, Joseph to Sarah Ann Johnson, Jan. 11, 1843.
Olephint, Isaac N. to Martha Ann Steger, Jan. 23, 1843.
Owen, Everett to Mary F. Buchanon, July 25, 1843.
Patton, Daniel to Frances Montgomery, Jan. 4, 1843.
Price, Levi to Sarah Ferguson, March 23, 1843.

Page 127
Pigue, Robert F. to Malinda Quinn, Nov. 7, 1843.
Perry, Wm. S. to Nancy Ann Everett, Nov. 14, 1843.
Penticost, Wm. F. to Catharine Ellis, Dec. 20, 1843.
Pinkerton, James to Lydia Ann Elijh Roach, Oct. 14, 1843.
Powell, Thomas L. to Elizabeth Draper, Aug. 23, 1843.
Petway, Geo. Washington to Martha S. Gains, Aug. 9, 1843.
Patton, Yandell S. to Frances Moore, April 25, 1843.
Preston,Edward to Margaret Cole, May 18, 1843.
Ramer, Andrew to Levicy Hackney, Feb. 4, 1843.

Page 128
Robert Dempsey to Amanda H. Leonards, March 18, 1843.
Ross, Feliz G. to Nancy P. East, March 14, 1843.
Read, James to Sarah Ann Kirkpatrick, Dec. 21, 1843.
Ready, James to Martha Ann Wilson, Sep. 28, 1843.
Riley, Henderson to Susanna Kingcaid, Jan. 19, 1843.
Rassbrooks, Thomas to Annira Ham, Sep. 9, 1843.
Read, Robt. A. to Polly Ragan, Sep. 7, 1843.
Ruthland, Isaac to Minerva Buckner, Oct. 4, 1843.
Rungan, Benj. M. to Mary E. Duncan, May 31, 1843.

Page 129
Reaves, Samuel B. to Mary Ann Stewart, Dec. 23, 1843.
Reeves, Richard P. to Mary Byers, Nov. 11, 1843.
Robert, Alexis J. to Mary Ann Anna Stevens, May 16, 1843.
Reason, Kindred to Martha Ann Dew, June 17, 1843.
Riggan Asa H. to Kitty E. Greer, Feb. 10, 1843.

Stothart, Wm. F. to Mary Hannah Norvell, Aug. 9, 1843.
Simpkins, John M. to Martha Cato,March 18, 1843.
Shaw, Robert K. to Elizabeth Wilkinson, Feb. 21, 1843.
Smith, Joseph H. to Matilda Young, April 12, 1843.

Page 130
Singleton, Robert W. to Sarah Boyd, Feb. 21, 1843.
Samuel, Richard to Elizabeth Harrison, Aug. 15, 1843.
Shapley, David M. to Aureana Smith, Oct. 9, 1843.
Schulter (Schluter) Frederick A. to Ann T. Figures, Nov. 15, 1843.
Smith, Albert to Sarah Ann Tims, Dec. 27, 1843.
Simmons, Edward to Martha Ann Hooper, Feb. 6, 1843.
Stevens, Elisha to Elizabeth Simpkins, Aug. 16, 1843.
Stenett, Zebedee H. to Nancy Varden, Dec. 21, 1843.
Sullivan, Thomas to Elizabeth Perry, March 7, 1843.

Page 131
Seat, Sydney to Pannelia Owens, April 15, 1843.
Spence, Miles W. to Nancy Campbell, Dec. 18, 1843.
Terry, Oliver D. to Eliza Ann Alford, Jan. 12, 1843.
Towns, William C. to Mary Campbell, Dec. 14, 1843.
Tharepp, John to Nancy Baker, Sep. 7, 1843.
Littleton, Henry C. to Elizabeth Jane Matlock, Oct. 7, 1843.
Thomas, John F. to Sarah E. Coleman, July 11, 1843.
Tally, Thomas J. to Parmelia Butterworth, Jan. 31, 1843.
Varden, Andrew to Sarah Roads, Aug. 22, 1843.

Page 132
Vanleer, Isaac to Matilda Duff, Oct. 18, 1843.
Wright, Charles F. to Eliza M. Gillman, Dec. 5, 1843.
Woods, James A. to Elizabeth M. Campbell, March 28, 1843.
Waller, Nicholas C. to Amanda V. Tucker, Aug. 8, 1843.
Williams, Henry to Virginia Fletcher, Sep. 5, 1843.
White, Ephraim to Mary Frances Taylor, Dec. 7, 1843.
White, Hiram to Louisa F. Kimbro, May 4, 1843.
Warren, Walker to Mary Jane Tilford, March 6, 1843.
Whitfield, George W. to Wareena Spence, Oct. 24, 1843.

Page 133
Wolstenholme, Hugh to Rebecca Waggoner, Dec. 29, 1843.
Williams, W. D. to Margaret C. Wilson, Dec. 15, 1843.
Young, James M. to Elizabeth Walton, April 24, 1843.
Young, William to Frances Dews, Sep. 30, 1843.
Zachary Malchigah to Juda Jernagin, Aug. 29, 1843.
Zentzschal, Charles J. to Johanna F. Houser, Jan. 30, 1843.

Page 134 omitted.

Page 135
Haley, Nicholas S. to Almeda A. Linn, March 28, 1844.
Haley, James to Martha Young, Aug. 22, 1844.

Hall, Edward to Malinda Craig, Dec. 4, 1843.
Harff, Henry to Elizabeth F. Turner, Dec. 30, 1844.
Harp, W. to Francis Jane Richardson, Oct. 4, 1844.
Harper, John M. to Mary Jane Jones, Jan. 1, 1844.
Harris, T. B. to Mary Jane Yandle, Oct. 2, 1844.

Page 136
Harrison, Wm. B. to Ann B. Cattle, March 7, 1844.
Harwell, James F. to Susan Hagy, Sep. 16, 1844.
Henly, James to Polexancy T. Linne, Dec. 28, 1844.
Hill, Ishobod to Emeline Chappell, Dec. 21, 1844.
Hobbs, Jno. N. to Albany D. Sadler, Oct. 8, 1844.
Hogan, George M. to Louisa Binkley, March 4, 1844.
Holland, Haney H. to Amanda M. K. Webb, March 12, 1844.

Page 137
Hooper, Thomas N. to Elizabeth Shelton, Dec. 20, 1844.
Hough, Wm. to Mary Johnson, Feb. 17, 1844.
Hunt, A. M. to Mary J. Whitehead, June 27, 1844.
Hurt, Wm. C. to Mary Ann Garbra, June 4, 1844.
Hurt, F. A. to Lucy A. Fulcher, May 23, 1844.
Jackson, Wm. James to Nancy Ramer, Jan. 11, 1844.
Jackson, Calvin to Ann Eliza Bell, Sep. 23, 1844.

Page 138
Johnson, James F. to Cathenne M. Housley, Sep. 10, 1844.
Jones, Edmund to Nancy Carrington, Jan. 6, 1844.
Jones, Samuel P. to Sarah A. Wells, Nov. 4, 1844.
Jones, Thomas J. to Safrona Phelps, Dec. 18, 1844.
Jourdan, Warren to Agnes Allison, Dec. 9, 1844.
Lanier, Samuel B. to Fannie M. Fall, Feb. 8, 1844.
Larkins, Wm. T. to Clementina U. Dillahunty, March 6, 1844.

Page 139
Lattimer, A. R. to Louisa Taylor, Nov. 5, 1844.
Lincoln, George M. to Elizabeth Stockell, Dec. 12, 1844.
Lookley, James A. to Mary Ann Tate, Feb. 8, 1844.
Louis, George M. to Louiza Langford, Jan. 11, 1844.
Miles, James Y. to Louisa M. Smith, Jan. 11, 1844.
Macrery, Andrew J. to Letetia Hagan, Sep. 5, 1844.
Mason, James E. to Ann Eliza Crockett, Jan. 29, 1844.
Marlin, George W. to Martha Burnett, April 23, 1844.

Page 140
Mason, Sumner R. to Mary J. Dibble, Nov. 9, 1844.
Matlock, James to Antoinette M. Nance, Dec. 21, 1844.
Mershon, James R. to Susan M. Atwater, Oct. 15, 1844.
Mitchell, Abijah D. to Sarah Forehand, June 4, 1844.
Morgan, Irby to Julia A. Demoville, Oct. 3, 1844.
Mosby, Benjamin F. to Elizabeth Fly, Dec. 26, 1844.
Murry, Mark W. to Lucy Ann Murry, Nov. 4, 1844.

Page 141
McCutcheon, James to Maranda C. Porter, Nov. 21, 1844.
McFadden, Wm. to Martha Johnson, Dec. 19, 1844.
McGuire, John to Mary E. Earhart, April 24, 1844.
McKee, W. F. to Ann E. Brahan, Sep. 30, 1844.
McKinney, Jesse to Sarah F. Brady, Jan. 2, 1844.
McLean, Chas. G. to Temperance C. Joslin, April 2, 1844.
McLendon, James E. to Lucinda Lovell, Dec. 24, 1844.

Page 142
Nance, Wm. L. to Martha P. Castleman, Jan. 25, 1844.
Nellums, Eli to Eliza Durham, Dec. 5, 1844.
Newcomb, Hezekiah H. to Harriett E. W. Quinn, Feb. 22, 1844.
Newland, James to Mary Reasoner, July 20, 1844.
Nichol, Charles M. to Lydia T. Gallaher, Aug. 24, 1844.
Nolls, James M. to Matilda E. Gibbers, July 20, 1844.
Norman, Wm. to Temperance Cole, Sep. 16, 1844.
Norvill, Caleb C. to Jenette Gordon, April 22, 1844.

Page 143
Ogle, Spencer to Martha A. N. Harrison, July 20, 1844.
Regan, Moses to Margaret Dozier, July 30, 1844.
Raynie, George W. to Elizabeth Smith, July 22, 1844.
Reaves, Hartwell P. to Elizabeth Ann Anderson, Dec. 23, 1844.
Reading, Wm. R. to Isabella M. Williamson, Nov. 30, 1844.
Rhodes, Levin to Mary J. Edney, Jan. 8, 1844.
Riley, Henderson to Mary Ann Osborne, Oct. 5, 1844.

Page 144
Riman, Franklin to Matilda Akin, June 17, 1844.
Ritter, Jefferson W. to Mary Conley, Dec. 5, 1844.
Rucker, Thomas J. to Mary H. Frazier, May 7, 1844.
Russell, Alfred H. to Elizabeth Baird, Jan. 1, 1844.
Sadler, Wm. to Eliza Jane Burch, Jan. 15, 1844.
Sanders, Robert A. to Allison E. Doom, Dec. 12, 1844.

Page 145
Satterfield, Alexander to Elizabeth Patton, Jan. 24, 1844.
Scruggs, Wm. S. to Lucinda W. Gulleford, Jan. 14, 1845.
Scruggs, George to Frances Allen, Feb. 6, 1844.
Seay, Laban V. to Joana M. A. Cole, July 31, 1844.
Shaub, Martin L. to Catharine Caton, Dec. 29, 1844.
Simpkins, William D. to Elizabeth Cato, Jan. 6, 1844.

Page 146
Simpkins, Elias R. to Sarah Harris, Jan. 9, 1844.
Sims, John W. to Eliza Sauner, Nov. 28, 1844.
Smith, John H. to Mary Elizabeth Osborne, Feb. 2, 1844.
Smith, John J. to Eliza E. Bryant, Feb. 5, 1844.
Smith, Wm. to Jane Mayo, May 4, 1844.

Smith, Wallace to Ann Eliza Cartwright, May 23, 1844.
Smith, Wm. M. to Amelia Miles, Dec. 14, 1844.
Smith, Thomas F. to Elizabeth S. Wood, Dec. 18, 1844.

Page 147
Spane, John N. to Margaret N. Barkley, Jan. 27, 1844.
Stanfield, James to Sarah Ann Green, March 25, 1844.
Stephens, John S. to Jane Mayo, Feb. 8, 1844.
Still, Rodan to Mary Susan Ballew, June 22, 1844.
Stinnett, Benjamin to Julia Ann Edney, Dec. 21, 1844.
Stover, E. G. to Mary E. Greer, Dec. 29, 1844.
Stratton, Thos. E. to Sarah M. Morris, Nov. 6, 1844.

Page 148
Stringfellow, Wm. B. to Christina C. Hall, Jan. 26, 1844.
Swinney, Wm. G. to Mary Ann McFarland, April 18, 1844.
Waller, Levi to Elizabeth Simpkins, Feb. 10, 1844.
Wamsby, Thomas to Harriet Fletcher, April 9, 1844.
Ward, J. N. to Ellen C. Norton, Aug. 6, 1844.
Ware, David H. to Delana Huffman, Jan. 17, 1844.

Page 149
Watson, Charles T. to Emily Cook, Jan. 25, 1844.
Watts, James to Elizabeth J. Miles, June 11, 1844.
Weaver, Dempsey to Frances L. King, May 15, 1844.
Wilbern, D. N. to Mary Harman, Aug. 10, 1844.
Wing, Calvin to Mary E. Westbrooke, Oct. 12, 1844.
Williams, Robt. N. to Mary P. Ensley, July 22, 1844.
Williams, Alex R. to Amanda Harman, Sep. 11, 1844.

Page 150
Wilson, Samuel S. to Lucy Ann Marshall, Aug. 8, 1844.
Worrell, Doctor to May Seat, Jan. 18, 1844.
Worrell, Littleberg E. to Malinda C. Waggoner, April 25, 1844.

Page 151
Abernathy, Chas. H. to Nancy Crockett, Dec. 24, 1845.
Armstrong, Eli to Louisa Harrison, Feb. 1, 1845.
Baber, W. L. to Martha J. Price, Oct. 14, 1845.
Baker, Wm. H. to Feliciana Degrove, March 10, 1845.
Barnes, Luther M. to Nancy Anderson, Oct. 17, 1845.
Baugh, V. A. to Merneva Cabler, Feb. 15, 1845.
Bennett, James to Hannah Parkes, May 12, 1845.

Page 152
Bettes, Moses W. to Elizabeth B. Hope, April 17, 1845.
Bevel, Wm. H. to Mary Manning, Dec. 26, 1845.
Biggers, Wm. to Elizabeth Johnson, Jan. 2, 1845.
Billings, James J. S. to Lucinda America Nance, Nov. 4, 1845.
Binkley, Asa N. to Milly Durard, Feb. 11, 1845.
Blair, Wm. G. to Ann E. Allen, Dec. 17, 1845.

Page 153
Blair, John to Mary E. Utley, Sep. 11, 1845.
Bode,Andrew to Maria C. Gold Kamp, Feb. 1, 1845.
Bone, William to Fanniy Mayo, Feb. 1, 1845.
Boyd, William L. to Tennessee Coleman, May 7, 1845.
Brand, T. T. to Catherine Wolf, Sep. 10, 1845.
Brent, Joseph A. to Almeda W. Stanfield, Aug. 23, 1845.
Briley, William C. to Permelia Ragans, Dec. 4, 1845.

Page 154
Brown, A. V. to Cynthia Saunders, Sep. 15, 1845.
Brooks, Christopher B. to Mary Jane Pinkerton, Jan. 28, 1845.
Bruce, James M. to Sarah C. Waggoner, March 8, 1845.
Buchanan, Alexander to Margaret M. Matlock, May 31, 1845.
Burthwright, Samuel A. to Eliza Vaughn, Dec. 3, 1845.
Butler, Samuel to Mickey Earhart, July 9, 1845.
Bysor, Thomas to Lemizer Parker, April 12, 1845.

Page 155
Cabler, William D. to Louisa Harsh, May 1, 1845.
Cain, Wm. L. to Martha Ann Edmundson, Sep. 11, 1845.
Carney, Isaac T. to Mariah Boyd, April 11, 1845.
Carney, Wm. V. to Martha Copher, May 12, 1845.
Cooney, Joshua to Judy I. Demumbraum, Oct. 27, 1845.
Castleman, Robert B. to Anna E. Woods, Dec. 18, 1845.

Page 156
Chadwell, Robert to Mary Ann Burge, Jan. 22, 1845.
Charlton, Oscar to Elizabeth Greer, April 23, 1845.
Charlton, Wm. to Hannah Graham, Nov. 26, 1845.
Childress, Edward H. to Sophia C. McEwin, Sep. 24, 1845.
Chilton, Wm. O. to Ellen S. Bechnoll, Nov. 12, 1845.
Cloyd, Ezekiel to Agnes S. Campbell, Aug. 13, 1845.
Clynard, Henderson to Eliza June Wilkinson, Feb. 19, 1845.

Page 157
Cone, Colier to Elizabeth Goldin, March 10, 1845.
Conner, John to Mary Jane Turner, Aug. 27, 1845.
Conyears, Thomas to Zilpha McLendon, March 10, 1845.
Critz, James M. to Ann Eliza Scales, Oct. 15, 1845.
Currin, Robt. S. to Sophronia Williams, July 30, 1845.

Page 158
Davis, Claiborne F. to Eliza Ann Wilson, Sep. 16, 1845.
Devinny, Charles to Ann Gilliam, Sep. 15, 1845.
Dews, John to Mary Rord, Feb. 19, 1845.
Dews, William to Mary Harrison, Sep. 4, 1845.
Dickinson, Henry to Ann E. McGavock, April 28, 1845.
Dillin, Chas. R. to Julia Q. Cautes, March 15, 1845.
Donelson, Wm. to Martha J. Anderson, July 23, 1845.

Page 159
Dorris, Ira to Martha C. Elam, Nov. 27, 1845.
Dugger, Wm. D. to Ann Q. Mitchell, Jan. 7, 1845.
Durard, Lewis to Delana McCormack, Feb. 26, 1845.
Durham, James to Mary Jane Webb, July 18, 1845.

Page 160
Earthman, Feliz G. to Mary Ann Wilkinson, Aug. 6, 1845.
Edney, Wm. to Elizabeth J. Kennedy, Dec. 27, 1845.
Edwards, Lauson to Martha Hooper, April 10, 1845.
Epperson, J. H. to Mary Ann Davis, July 9, 1845.
Estes, Searcy to Milly Payne, May 19, 1845.

Page 161
Faller, Joseph to Elizabeth Old, June 5, 1845.
Ferguson, Calvin W. to Ellonnora H. Johnson, Dec. 18, 1845.
Flintoff, Thomas to Elizabeth W. Compton, March 26, 1845.
Flowers, Joshua to Eliza M. A. Daly, Sep. 18, 1845.
Fossett, William to Elizabeth Rogers, Dec. 30, 1845.
Foster, Henry W. to Martha Bland, Feb. 4, 1845.
Fowler, Thornton to Emily Stroud, June 21, 1845.

Page 162
Fulcher, Edward to Nancy Burchett, Jan. 1, 1845.
Fuqua, Jesse M. to Martha A. Whitworth, Sep. 22, 1845.
Gale, Wm. D. to Mary K. Knox, Dec. 11, 1845.
Gleaves, Albert G. to Eliza Lannahill, Oct. 9, 1845.
Goodman, Thomas to Elivira S. Compton, Dec. 30, 1845.
Goodwin, J. V. to Alsenia L. B. Gillman, Nov. 19, 1845.

Page 163
Greer, Walker T. to Catherine B. G. Charlton, Feb. 8, 1845.
Greer, Benj. K. to Lucy Cullum, Nov. 12, 1845.
Greer, Wm. M. to Nancy Jane Brown, June 10, 1845.
Grooms, R. H. to Susan V. Wills, July 13, 1845.
Gullage, Richard to Angeline Hooper, Dec. 18, 1845.

Page 164
Hardy, Thos. G. to Mary A. McLaughlin, Oct. 29, 1845.
Harris, Thomas A. to Nancy Towns, Oct. 24, 1845.
Heath, Edward to Julia Ann Fletcher, Dec. 4, 1845.
Heaton, Amos to Amy A. Harp, Feb. 12, 1845.
Hefferman, Wm. to Ellen Whipp, Feb. 1, 1845.
Henry, Wm. to Susan Hodges, Jan. 13, 1845.
Henry, Wm. P. to Corinne F. Carter, April 16, 1845.

Page 165
Hicks, Conrad to Mary Stegar, Jan. 29, 1845.
Hill, Samuel to June Brown, Feb. 3, 1845.
Holland, Noah to Martha Sadler, Aug. 15, 1845.
Hollis, Henry to Emily J. Rape, March 18, 1845.
Hooper, Alfred M. to Fanny Hooper, July 9, 1845.

Hooper, Elijah L. to Nancy A. Hall, Jan. 2, 1845.
Harwell, Logan D. to Narcissa R. Owen, Nov. 28, 1845.

Page 166
Hubbard, David to Rebecca Stoddard, July 1, 1845.
Hughes, James to Mary Ann Drake, Sep. 3, 1845.
Hunter, Henry to Margaret E. Marshall, July 1, 1845.
Hyde, Joseph H. to Mary Ann Temple, Oct. 14, 1845.

Page 167
Jackman, Woodson to Sarah Buie, Nov. 17, 1845.
Jackson, Wm. to Nancy A. Vanderville, Jan. 6, 1845.
Jackson, Henry to Sarah Ruse, Dec. 15, 1845.
Johnson, Benjamin to Caroline Austin, Oct. 7, 1845.
Johnson, Richard to Mary McFadden, Nov. 19, 1845.
Jones, Wm. to Sarah R. Hatcher, Jan. 29, 1845.
Jones, George F. to Ann Dunlap, Dec. 17, 1845.

Page 168
Jones, Squire to Tabitha Martin, March 22, 1845.
Jordan, James M. to Sarah Henderson, Sep. 23, 1845.
Joslin, Thomas to Mary H. Hooper, March 29, 1845.

Page 169
Kelly, Henry W. to Virginia Ann Phillips, July 16, 1845.
Kile, Samuel to Ann Gill, Feb. 19, 1845.
Langford, Wm. to Margaret Blanton, May 7, 1845.
Lester, George F. to Mildred A. Garner, July 23, 1845.
Litton, Abram to Julia Alice Manning, April 24, 1845.

Page 170
Lively, David F. to Susan Read, Feb. 26, 1845.
Long, Gabriel to Malinda Lea, May 30, 1845.
Lovell, James to Patsy P. Chambliss, Sep. 11, 1845.
Luster, George W. to Mary Perry, Sep. 8, 1845.
Lytle, Stephen to Elizabeth Richardson, Dec. 27, 1845.

Page 171
Mabry, Thomas J. to Sarah Ann Buchanon, Aug. 11, 1845.
Marable, James to Ann Still, Jan. 22, 1845.
Martin, C. E. H. to Cornelia F. Childress, Oct. 13, 1845.
Matthews, Henry to Susan Ray, Nov. 15, 1845.
Mason, Jno. F. to Olivia D. Zachery, March 18, 1845.
Mason, Bennett to Susan Wright, April 4, 1845.
Mays, William to Emily Harrison, June 10, 1845.

Page 172
Meacham, Wm. F. to Catharine A. Couch, Oct. 24, 1845.
Melvine, George to Mary Jane Brooks, March 1, 1845.
Minton, Andrew E. to Nancy Chadwell, March 13, 1845.
Mocksey, Nathaniel to Amanda Burgess, June 30, 1845.
Morgan, Henry to Mary Vick, Dec. 9, 1845.
Morris, Elijah to Mary Ann Alexander, March 3, 1845.

Page 173
McCain, George to Martha J. Sadler, March 1, 1845.
McRea, Hugh to Sarah E. McCall, May 28, 1845.
McCue, James to Harriet E. Spain, June 2, 1845.
McEvoy, Joseph A. to Catherine O'Connell, Nov. 22, 1845.
McNeil, Hardy to Mary P. Jones, April 9, 1845.

Page 174
Naive, James H. to Mary Harrison, Oct. 23, 1845.
Nellums, Elias to Martha A. Durham, Jan. 15, 1845.
Nicholas, Geo. to Rutha Tompkins, July 27, 1845.
Noel, Sinico A. G. to Tennessee E. Wilkinson, Aug. 27, 1845.

Page 175
Oneil, John to Elizabeth Bailey, April 10, 1845.
Owens, Andrew J. to Mary Ann Zachery, Oct. 13, 1845.
Ozement, Lewis to Matilda Griffin, March 1, 1845.
Ozment, Chas. B. to Martha C. Ward, Dec. 30, 1845.

Page 176
Page, Jesse J. to Susan H. Page, Jan. 15, 1845.
Parr, James to Mary Ann Russell, July 11, 1845.
Patton, Thos. H. to Narcissa Scruggs, April 1, 1845.
Peach, Hardin to Mary Seabery, April 4, 1845.
Pelham, Francis to Ann Eliza Moon, Feb. 1, 1845.
Pennington, Wm. R. to Fanny McMurray, Dec. 1, 1845.
Perry, John to Talitha Seat, April 10, 1845.

Page 177
Phillips, Chas. W. to Jane Crockett, Sep. 9, 1845.
Pinckerton, David to Martha Stover, Dec. 13, 1845.
Pinkerton, Wm. B. to Charity Wingo, May 12, 1845.
Plummer, James R. to Elizabeth Waller, Nov. 3, 1845.
Porterfield, John to Mary Eliza Shepard, July 3, 1845.
Powers, John H. to Mary Tombs, April 24, 1845.
Preston, Thomas W. to Nan Craighead, June 17, 1845.

Page 178
Pritchett, Sam'l to Ann Coleman, Sep. 30, 1845.
Pritchett, Wm. to Catherine Hobs, Dec. 19, 1845.
Puckett, Jesse L. to Almeda Jones, June 9, 1845.
Puckett, Anderson to Mary Adcock, Dec. 20, 1845.
Pugh, James H. to Nancy F. Waggoner, May 14, 1845.

Page 179
Reed, James to Matilda Levi, Jan. 20, 1845.
Reding, Richard H. to Catherine B. Lowe, Oct. 28, 1845.
Rice, Wm. to Mary Waters, July 22, 1845.
Ridley, John B. to Mary A. Fitzgerald, Jan. 8, 1845.
Reeves, Robert G. to Martha Ann Corbett, March 24, 1845.
Robinson, Wm. D. to Lucy A. Deadrick, Sep. 30, 1845.
Robertson, Wm. D. to Frances Yearbrough, Oct. 21, 1845.

Page 180
Rogers, John H. to Rebecca Littleton, April 11, 1845.
Roser, John to Catherine Emmett, Sep. 29, 1845.
Ruth, Robert B. to Hannah A. Murrell, Oct. 20, 1845.

Page 181
Sadler, Wm. to Eliza Jane Burch, Jan. 15, 1845.
Sample, Timothy D. to Mary Jane Buchanan, Aug. 14, 1845.
Sands, Sam'l R. B. to Rachel W. Hope, Dec. 11, 1845.
Sands, John E. to Mary A. Alexander, Dec. 23, 1845.
Schluder, Henry L. to Elizabeth R. Pigg, Oct. 21, 1845.
Scallom, James M. to Mary E. Eubanks, Dec. 18, 1845.

Page 182
Scriminger, James to Lucinda McPherson, March 22, 1845.
Seay, John to Ester Gilbert, March 30, 1845.
Shaw, Henry B. to Sarah Ann Yates, May 15, 1845.
Simmens, Edward to Sarah E. Feltz, March 25, 1845.
Sirely, David P. to Susan Read, Feb. 26, 1845.
Slack, Robert E. to Lucy J. Love, Oct. 7, 1845.
Sluder, Bright H. to Almeda Sands, Nov. 29, 1845.

Page 183
Snow, Wm. A. to Ann E. E. Slack, Oct. 4, 1845.
Staggs, Alexander to Manot J. Jenkins, Dec. 15, 1845.
Stalcup, Wm. A. to Martha Shell, Aug. 29, 1845.
Stanfield, James to Sarah Green, May 5, 1845.
Stanley, E. H. to Sarah T. James, Dec. 24, 1845.
Stewart, James to Martha G. Williams, Dec. 29, 1845.
Taunt, Kinchen to Cynthia Morgan, July 7, 1845.
Taylor, Isam to Sarah Dobson, Nov. 8, 1845.
Terrass, John M. to Lavenia R. Hitt, May 15, 1845.
Thompson, James H. to Mary Jane Devinney, Feb. 8, 1845.
Tindall, Robert to Permelia C. Colley, July 10, 1845.
Toumblinson, John P. to Eliza A. Vanhook, Sep. 21, 1845.
Towns, Fletcher to Virginia Fuqua, May 17, 1845.

Page 185
Tucker, Anderson to Lucy Foley, July 26, 1845.
Vaughan, Isham C. to Sarah Barclift, May 24, 1845.
Walker, Edward to Charlotte Fitzhugh, June 11, 1845.
Walker, Edward to Catherine Luton, Oct. 21, 1845.
Ward, Hugh to Ann World, April 19, 1845.

Page 186
Warmack, Richard to Pennia Miles, Nov. 20, 1845.
Warren, Richard W. to Martha Ann Lovell, July 6, 1845.
Whelen, Lawrence to Sarah Greenhalge, June 16, 1845.
White, George T. to Sarah Jane Stone, Sep. 11, 1845.
Whitley, Isaac to Tempe Ballew, Nov. 3, 1845.
Williams, John W. to Elizabeth Taylor, Jan. 1, 1845.
Williams, Robert W. to Catherine W. Johnson, Jan. 20, 1845.

Page 187
Wilson, Thos. J. to Angeline Stewart, July 28, 1845.
Witt, Joel D. to Sarah A. Spence, Feb. 20, 1845.
Wolf, John to Mary Denton, Dec. 31, 1845.
Wray, Henry W. to Mary Ann Brily (Briley), Dec. 10, 1845.
Wright, Wm. J. to Cynthia C. McAllister, Aug. 29, 1845.
Wright, Jacob O. to Elizabeth M. Staggs, Nov. 4, 1845.

Page 188
Zachery, Spencer to Judy Zachery, Oct. 25, 1845.

Page 189
Abernathy, Geo. W. to Mary Crockett, Dec. 19, 1846.
Achey, Peter H. to Rebecca R. Moore, May 11, 1846.
Adams, Adam G. to Susan Porterfield, May 12, 1846.
Adams, John to Sarah A. Allen, July 15, 1846.
Allen, John H. to Mary L. Whitfield, Nov. 23, 1843 (1846).

Page 190
Bailey, John M. to Artinusa T. Johnson, Dec. 15, 1846.
Barber, Sherod to Martha Tatum, July 25, 1846.
Barnes, John F. to Eliza Ann Ellis, Jan. 12, 1846.
Beasley, John W. to Nancy Sutton, Aug. 6, 1846.
Beazley, Chas. G. to Elizabeth Ozment, May 26, 1846.
Beech, Alden C. to Virginia H. Vaughn, April 9, 1846.
Bell, John to Frances Johnson, March 21, 1846.

Page 191
Bennett, Thomas to Elizabeth Harper, Feb. 26, 1846.
Berry, James to Elizabeth Pitt, Oct. 15, 1846.
Blair, John K. to Susan Smith, June 23, 1846.
Bourne, Thomas G. to Elizabeth J. Long, Nov. 24, 1846.
Boush, R. A. to Jennie M. West (Jeanie M. West), Oct. 26, 1846.
Breedlove, John to Susan Cheek, Dec. 23, 1846.

Page 192
Brennon, Luke C. to Mary E. Young, Dec. 29, 1846.
Brown, Samuel to Sarah E. Samuel, Feb. 25, 1846.
Burke, John G. to Lucy M. Moore, Dec. 30, 1846.
Byers, Wm. H. to An'd Williams, Nov. 14, 1846.

Page 193
Calcote, James L. to Elizabeth S. Overton, March 17, 1846.
Campbell, J. P. to Rebecca W. Sims, Dec. 16, 1846.
Carrey, G. W. J. to Emily D. Martin, Sep. 10, 1846.
Cartwright, James to Eliza Sutton, Jan. 30, 1846.
Cartwright, Thomas D. to Mary Ann Sudden, Nov. 28. 1846.
Chadwell, Thomas to Mary A. Childress, July 18, 1846.

Page 194
Cherry, Pierce W. to Mary Ann Gleaves, Jan. 17, 1846.

Clardy, Thomas M. to Elizabeth Lazenberry, Aug. 18, 1846.
Clark, Ben P. to Henrietta H. Morgan, May 20, 1846.
Clark, Jesse to Nancy Bowlding, Feb. 23, 1846.
Cocks, Isaac M. to Mary Ann Cunningham, March 5, 1846.
Cole, Willie W. to Gertrude McMahan, Sep. 16, 1846.
Compton, Thomas to Susan Murphy, March 30, 1846.

Page 195
Cook, Thomas to Sarah Carter, Oct. 5, 1846.
Copeland, Thomas to Jane Beazley, June 5, 1846.
Cox, George to Mary Miles, Dec. 11, 1846.
Craddock, R. S. to M. E. Holand, Sep. 30, 1846.
Creal, John B. to Mary Williams, Dec. 1, 1846.
Crocker, Benjamine F. to Elizabeth Watson, Dec. 14, 1846.
Cutter, Timothy T. to Martha J. Stalcup, Aug. 8, 1846.

Page 197
Dale, Isaac A. to Nancy F. Long, Oct. 6, 1846.
Darrow, Joseph to Chastina Henderson, Sep. 15, 1846.
Demombraum, John to Barbara Quimby, May 9, 1846.
Devinny, Charles B. to Esther Rose, Aug. 6, 1846.
Dougherty, M. L. to Maria P. Kinney, April 29, 1846.
Dozier, Enoch T. to Louisa Ann Carney, Aug. 15, 1846.

Page 198
Guston, Nathaniel to Mary Jane Hutchinson, Dec. 26, 1845.

Page 199
Eakin, A. P. to Louise P. Wright, Dec. 15, 1846.
East, Wm. A. to Elizabeth H. Searcy, May 5, 1846.
Edmunds, John to Lucinda Leach, Dec. 31, 1846.
Ellison, William B. to Ann Cannady, Dec. 26, 1846.
Etherly, Dickson L. to Susan A. Hall, May 5, 1846.
Everett, John B. to Elizabeth R. Hunt, Jan. 21, 1846.

Page 200
Faulkner, Robert P. to Mary A. Hunter, July 15, 1846.
Felts, George M. to Mary Jane Mook(Mock), May 22, 1846.
Ferguson, Edwin to Elivira S. Cantrell, Jan. 14, 1846.
Fife, James to Samira H. Hudleman, Sep. 1, 1846.
Fitzhugh, B. S. to Julia Ann Carper, Oct. 19, 1846.
Fletcher, George L. to Amanda Thomas, Feb. 19, 1846.
Flournoy, Wm. to Elizabeth M. Armstrong, Nov. 9, 1846.

Page 201
Foltz, Reuben M. to Catherine C. Geary, Jan. 28, 1846.
Fottrell, A. to Amanda Holley, Nov. 30, 1846.
Fowler, J. Smith to Maria Louise Embry, Nov. 12, 1846.
Fowlkes, Jeptha to Mariah J. Ward, Jan. 23, 1846.
Fowlkes, James C. to Nancy Wright, March 28, 1846.
Fryor, John to Lenora McAfee, Sep. 22, 1846.

Page 202
Gailbreath, Benj. A. to Jane J. Gailbreath, Oct. 8, 1846.

Garner, James to Sarah G. World, April 30, 1846.
Gatton, Wm. F. to Harriett E. Yandall, Jan. 24, 1846.
Gatton, Wm. F. to Harriett E. Yandall, May 11, 1846.
Geer, Joshua to Elizabeth Coper, June 13, 1846.
Gibbs, Richard B. to Elizabeth Simmons, Sep. 16, 1846.
Goodman, Albert G. to Lydia Ann Fitzhurh, Oct. 14, 1846.

Page 203
Goodrich, Reuben to Effie Turbeville, Dec. 17, 1846.
Goodrich, Harrison to Hettie Hartman, March 21, 1846.
Green, Enos J. to Mary A. Lawrence, April 17, 1846.
Green, Chapman S. to Elizabeth Creech, Nov. 21, 1846.
Greer, Aquilla to Martha R. Gillum, Dec. 23, 1846.
Grimes, Jesse to Martha Bradbury, June 3, 1846.

Page 204
Grizzard, Wm. P. to Mary J. Perry, Nov. 2, 1836.
Gugenheim, Mark to Sarah A. Harsh, June 29, 1846.
Gullage, John to Martha Martin, Feb. 21, 1846.
Gulledge, John J. to Caroline Dean, July 1, 1846.
Gunter, Pleasant H. to Mary June Baker, July 25, 1846.
Guinn, Andrew to Alvira Biggers, Dec. 24, 1846.

Page 205
Hager, William to Mary Caldwell, Nov. 3, 1846.
Hale, Thomas J. to Ellen M. Hollis, Dec. 29, 1846.
Haley, William to Sarah Ann Beazley, Feb. 5, 1846.
Hampton, Wm. to Sarah Moore, June 9, 1846.
Hampton, Benj. to Mary Ann Darrow, Dec. 4, 1846.
Harding, Wm. to Marion C. Roberts, Nov. 26, 1846.

Page 206
Harper, James to Elizabeth Satterfield, March 12, 1846.
Harris, John W. to Mary Waggoner, June 23, 1846.
Hawkins, James M. to Elizabeth S. Sigler, May 4, 1846.
Heath, James T. to Elizabeth Horn, May 4, 1846.
Henderson, Wm. A. to Lucretia Darrow, Dec. 4, 1846.
Henry, John to Elizabeth Shelton, April 1, 1846.

Page 207
Hicks, David to Mary Dunlap, Aug. 20, 1846.
Hill, William M. to Nancy J. Turner, Aug. 24, 1846.
Hooper, Claiburn C. to Mary Ann Mayfield, July 21, 1846.
Hope, John B. to Emeline Watson, Feb. 14, 1846.
Horn, Jackson C. to Susan A. Lowery, Sep. 14, 1846.
Hough, Thos. J. to Margaret F. Wilson, Oct. 8, 1846.
Hunt, Holbert D. to Margaret C. Hill, June 19, 1846.

Page 208
Hull, John M. to Susan G. Lanier, July 8, 1846.
Hutton, Thos. W. to Nancy W. Ferber, Sep. 15, 1846.

Page 209
Jackson, Robert C. to Mary Baker, Jan. 31, 1846.

Jackson, Wm. H. to Morgiana Napier, Sep. 10, 1846.
Johnson, Miles to Mary E. Ford, Feb. 31, 1846.
Jones, John S. to Almira Duncan, Jan. 23, 1846.
Jones, George W. to Elizabeth R. Estes, Aug. 8, 1846.
Jones, Harry to America Johnson, Sep. 14, 1846.

Page 210
Jones, James to Sarah Jane Scruggs, Dec. 19, 1846.
Jost, Thomas to Christina B. Rose, Feb. 5, 1846.
Joy, Andrew C. to Elizabeth Cannady, Aug. 17, 1846.

Page 211
Kennedy, Thomas M. to Mary Bolden, April 15, 1846.
Kezee, Sandy to Clanto Harlow, Jan. 8, 1846.
King, Edmund R. to Jane Car, March 4, 1846.
Klages, C. W. to Frances Whitzell, March 19, 1846.
Knight, Hardy to Nancy Ann Raymer, Sep. 3, 1846.

Page 212
Lambert, Mathew to Mary Ann Taylor, Dec. 22, 1846.
Lawrence, Thomas P. to Sarah Ann Vaughn, May 11, 1846.
Lee, Thomas to Mary Carrington, May 2, 1846.
Leonard, Hardin L. T. to Mary Ann Foster, April 21, 1846.
Lord, Wm. S. to Ellen D. Smith, March 11, 1846.

Page 213
Maddux, Redmond G. to Tennessee T. Robinson, April 1, 1846.
Masey, John to Sarah Fields, May 21, 1846.
Mason, E. C. to Delilah A. Park, Jan. 13, 1846.
Mays, Andrew J. to Mary Louisa Pratt, Nov. 10, 1846.
Miles, Bedford to Eliza Jane Bedford, Dec. 3, 1846.

Page 214
Miller, James F. to Sarah White, June 30, 1846.
Mills, John to Jane Abshire, Aug. 3, 1846.
Moffett, James to Elizabeth M. Richardson, Jan. 3, 1846.
Moore, Talton to Martha Akin, May 9, 1846.
Moore, Isaac W. to Nancy Young, July 30, 1846.
Morgan, Henry to Ester Ann Newland, Dec. 24, 1846.

Page 215
Morris, Isaac E. to Elizabeth Ann Richardson, Sep. 28, 1846.
Morrison, Wm. A. to Martha Ann Parrish, April 15, 1846.
Morton, Wm. E. to Margaret A. Hagan, Sep. 28, 1846.
Mosier, John to Mary Ann Harper, April 8, 1846.
Medford, Edward A. to Catherine H. Scantland, Nov. 4, 1846.
Murpo, B. S. to Elizabeth Petty, April 22, 1846.
Murray, Nicholas H. to Martha C. Bledsoe, April 27, 1846.

Page 216
McCampbell, Thomas C. to Anna Gowdy, Oct. 19, 1846.
McCormac, James to Eliza Lucas, July 13, 1846.
McCreery, Phoam R. to Mary Jane Haynes, Oct. 8, 1846.
McCullough, James M. to Mildred Yandle, Dec. 17, 1846.
McDonald, Henry B. to Julia G. Powell, Feb. 24, 1846.
McFarland, John to Fanny Gilliam, June 24, 1846.
McMurry, Presly S. to Mary Brittle, Feb. 11, 1846.

Page 217
Nellums, Elias to Martha A. Durham, Jan. 15, 1846.
Nicholas, James to Clementine C. Smith, Nov. 9, 1846.
Nowell, Hugh to Muscoga E. Worlds, April 28, 1846.

Page 218
Olifant, Franklin M. to Charlotte A. Fitzhugh, March 3, 1846.
Oliver, Wm. M. to Elizabeth Morgan, June 20, 1846.
Ott, James H. to Sarah Jane Hooper, Oct. 30, 1846.
Orton, Ray S. to Lucy Ann Wingfield, Aug. 25, 1846.
Owen, Everett to Mary M. Cowan, Sep. 25, 1846.

Page 219
Page, Wm. B. to Catherine Mosley, March 17, 1846.
Patrick, Timothy G. to Sarah Ann Powell, Aug. 3, 1846.
Patterson, Thomas M. to Mary L. S. Campbell, Feb. 19, 1846.
Patterson, John to Mary Jane Nelums, Oct. 14, 1846.
Paxson, Alfred to Julia Ann Buckley, Aug. 27, 1846.
Peacock, John to Martha Lane, July 23, 1846.

Page 220
Pegram, George to Mary Bell, July 31, 1846.
Petty, Barney W. to Emily Jane Wadel, June 26, 1846.
Phillips, Wm. to Sarah R. Hooper, April 4, 1846.
Polk, Andrew J. to Rebecca Vanlier, Jan. 9, 1846.

Page 221
Read, Enoch S. to Lority Hale, Feb. 17, 1846.
Reid, Moses to Mary Perry, May 22, 1846.
Roland, Joel to Ferbee Ann West, Dec. 4, 1846.
Russell, John M. B. to Matilda Barrett, Nov. 7, 1846.

Page 222
Sadler, Benjamine F. to Martha Frensley, Dec. 29, 1846.
Sharp, Wm., Sr. to Elizabeth Y. McMahon, April 4, 1846.
Sherrill, Robert C. to Mary J. Bell, March 21, 1846.
Simmons, James to Nancy Walker, May 25, 1846.
Simpkins, James to Elizabeth Neighbors, Aug. 29, 1846.
Simpkins, Wm. to Emily Hart, Dec. 29, 1846.

Page 223
Sledge, Nathaniel to Martha Lee, June 9, 1846.
Smiley, Robert G. to Rachel D. Boyd, Sep. 14, 1846.

Smith, Dan'l E. to Mary E. Garner, Jan. 13, 1846.
Smith, St. Clair to Charlotte Farrelle, Dec. 18, 1846.
Spain, John to Mary J. Rains, Dec. 3, 1846.
Stanley, Nathan Y. to Harreit Jonte, Sep. 10, 1846.
Steele, Solomon to Mary Ann Lytle, Dec. 24, 1846.

Page 224
Stewart, Owen C. to Caroline B. Bolton, Jan. 6, 1846.
Stewart, Sandifer J. to Nancy Hart, Dec. 23, 1846.
Story, Wm. H. to Amy Cullom, July 21, 1846.
Story, Jesse W. to Hannah Cullom, July 21, 1846.
Strange, Turner to Matilda Scruggs, Jan. 19, 1846.
Sungey, Frederick to Elizabeth Edington, Dec. 11, 1846.

Page 225
Symes, Charles to Emeline A. Robertson, Nov. 25, 1846.

Page 226
Tanksley, Dempsy to Harriet Ann Douglass, Dec. 24, 1846.
Temples, Joseph to Mary Scism, Dec. 28. 1846.
Thomas, Wm. W. to Catherine Seabery, April 2, 1846.
Thomas, Edward to Nancy Galbreath, Aug. 20, 1846.
Thomas, Micajah to Nancy Cally, Sep. 6, 1846.
Thomas, Thomas J. to Ann M. Emeerns, Nov. 11, 1846.

Page 227
Thompson, Charles A. R. to Margaret Ann Edgar, Oct. 26, 1846.
Thweat, Joseph O. to Caroline Wharton, Feb. 26, 1846.
Tooney, James to Ellenora C. Sewell, Sep. 10, 1846.
Towns, Benj. W. C. to Sarah Tompson, Oct. 31, 1846.
Tucker, Stephen P. to Harriet Smith, Jan. 12, 1846.

Page 228
Underwood, Eugene to Catherine A. Thompson, Oct. 13, 1846.
Vaughn, Asa N. to Eliza B. Moody, Nov. 9, 1846.

Page 229
Walker, Geo. W. to Elizabeth Connell, Oct. 13, 1846.
Waters, John to Ann Rawlings, Oct. 21, 1846.
Watkins, McGelne H. to Mary E. Fossett, Sep. 8, 1846.
Weaks, George D. to Margaret J. Hunter, July 15, 1846.
Webb, Edward to Susan Pike, Dec. 22, 1846.
Welch, W. H. to Mary M. Hunter, Dec. 16, 1846.
Wiemer, Geo. N. to Catherine Unlike, April 14, 1846.
Van Cleave, Wm. B. to Harriet H. Jackson, March 31, 1846.

Page 230
Williamson, H. T. to Edna H. Dozier, Nov. 18, 1846.
Wilson, Elihu to Elizabeth Stover, March 4, 1846.
Wood, Wm. to Elizabeth J. Clark, May 21, 1846.
Woods, James to Louisa Robb, Jan. 15, 1846.

Woodson, John W. to Mary J. Dibrell, Sep. 26, 1846.
Wright, Wm. W. to Mary Baker, July 28, 1846.
Wright, Richard to Elizabeth Carlisle, Aug. 25, 1846.

Page 231
Yarborough, Jefferson T. to Margaret A. Philps, July 22, 1846.

Page 232 - none.

Page 233
Adams, Sam'l A. to Mary A. L. Ogburn, April 18, 1847.
Adkins, Harvey to Julia Heath, Oct. 7, 1847.
Agen, Joseph to Delilah Parks, Feb. 25, 1847.
Allen, La Fayett W. to Louisa Jane James, June 22, 1847.

Page 234
Ballard, Wm. E. to Martha Campbell, Sep. 6, 1847.
Bass, Augustus to Susan Hamilton, May 12, 1847.
Bateman, H. S. to Martha A. White, Nov. 1, 1847.
Beazley, Thos. H. to Lorenda Cunningham, March 13, 1847.
Bedford, R. H. to Lucinda Kesee, March 16, 1847.
Bell, O. G. to Emily Horn, July 1, 1847.

Page 235
Bell, A. J. to Ellen J. A. Foster, Sep. 27, 1847.
Benton, Joseph W. to Nancy Rains, Jan. 27, 1847.
Bert, John A. L. to M. M. Griggs, May 12, 1847.
Biddle, Daniel M. to Mary Pride, Feb. 24, 1847.
Binkley, J. H. to Esther Ann Ferguson, Jan. 27, 1847.

Page 236
Birdwell, John W. to Elizabeth M. Harris, Oct. 6, 1847.
Blackwell, Blueford to Caroline Raymer, March 5, 1847.
Brackman, Herman K. to Mary Cathanne, July 29, 1847.
Branch, K. to Margaret Casey, Oct. 20, 1847.
Bransford, L. M. to Helen Anderson, Jan. 1, 1847.

Page 237
Bratcher, Farrell H. to Anna Eliza Newgent, Dec. 11, 1847.
Brittle, George W. to Melissy Dale, Aug. 25, 1847.
Brooks, Moses T., Jr. to Mary Sample, Nov. 1, 1845??
Brown, John to Elizabeth Brooks, Jan. 30, 1847.
Brown, E. H. to Ann Feribee, April 29, 1847.
Brown, John B. to Mary Dobson, May 24, 1847.

Page 238
Brown, Josiah G. to Judith Scott, Dec. 7, 1847.
Bryant, Silas to Tabitha Fogg, March 25, 1847.
Buchanon, Addison to Sarah M. Fleming, March 8, 1847.
Buchett, Wm. to Fanny Elsbery, July 8, 1847.
Butler, John E. to Harriet Earhart, Nov. 12, 1847.

Page 239
Cabler, Frederick to Elizabeth Anderson, Nov. 30, 1847.
Caldwell, John D. to Emeline Law, Sep. 9, 1847.
Campbell, Thomas A. to Louisiana Thomas, March 1, 1847.
Camlin, John to Sarah Green, Aug. 2, 1847.
Cargill, Peyton C. to Mahala Melvin, April 17, 1847.
Carney, George G. to Lucresa Mables, March 26, 1847.

Page 240
Carol, Hugh to Elizabeth Cotton, Feb. 23, 1847.
Carroll, Joseph to Malissa Starles, Jan. 16, 1847.
Cartwright, John T. to Martha Hughes, April 28, 1847.
Cartwright, Lewis to Jane Guy, June 12, 1847.
Cawthorn, Dabney to Araminta Shane, March 31, 1847.
Champ, Frank to America Gallaher, Feb. 20, 1847.

Page 241
Champ, James C. to Eliza Ann Alford, Nov. 26, 1847.
Chapman, John L. to Louisa Cheatham, June 16, 1847.
Childress, E. H. to Elmina Read, Oct. 20, 1847.
Clark, Houston to Lucinda Hannah, Feb. 18, 1847.
Clark, Jeffrey G. to Mary Murry, Sep. 6, 1847.
Clark, John H. to Mary Boyd, Oct. 18, 1847.

Page 242
Cobbs, Addison M. to Eliza Woodruff, Jan. 12, 1847.
Colby, Cyrus to Martha A. Pennington, May 29, 1847.
Collins, Thomas W. to Martha Jane Owen, March 3, 1847.
Conel, James to Rhoda Ann Simmons, Jan. 23, 1847.
Congor, Chas. H. to Mary A. Williams, April 29, 1847.
Conn, Jesse to Aneliza Reynolds, Sep. 22, 1847.

Page 243
Connelly, Owen B. to Martha Ann Plummer, Dec. 21, 1847.
Conner, Patrick to Eliza Beard, Aug. 5, 1847.
Corder, David H. to Mary S. Bowers, Oct. 18, 1847.
Crutcher, James A. to Pherebe C. McCullough, March 25, 1847.
Cox, Herman to Mary Emeline Casey, Jan. 27, 1847.

Page 244
Cox, Fuschia I. to Ann Randall, Dec. 29, 1847.
Crandell, Edwin R. to Mary Agnes Gallager, Sep. 6, 1847.
Creech, William to Mary E. Green, Sep. 18, 1847.
Crockett, Elij. S. to Elizabeth Hooper, Nov. 16, 1847.
Curry, Robert B., Jr. to Mary D. Martin, Sep. 7, 1847.
Curtis, James J. to Ellen Corbitt, Feb. 13, 1847.

Page 245
Darden, John C. to Virginia Demoville, June 1, 1847.
Demoss, Thomas to Carolyn Mays, Jan. 4, 1847.
Dews, Pinkey to Elizabeth T. Mathis, Dec. 18, 1847.
Deggons, Charles E. to Julia Page, Dec. 2, 1847.
Dodd, Allen to Lucinda Roy, Aug. 28, 1847.

Donald, John T. to Eliza M. Sevier, Aug. 23, 1847.

Page 246
Doughty, Bashrod T. to Martha Tindall, Aug. 10, 1847.
Doxey, Lewis to Amanda Miller, Nov. 11, 1847.
Dozier, George M. to Nancy A. W. Hooper, Sep. 22, 1847.
Drake, Elias C. to Lucy Cunningham, July 5, 1847.
Draper, Sam'l S. to Betsy A. Powell, Jan. 30, 1847.

Page 247
Earhart, Abner C. to Suan P. Binkley, July 21, 1847.
Elliott, Richard J. to Mary E. Stanback, Sep. 1, 1847.
Elliott, Thomas L. to Ann Barber, Dec. 22, 1847.
Ellis, Wm. W. to Susan Clark, Aug. 16, 1847.
Ellis, Travis to Mary Jane Hagan, Nov. 9, 1847.

Page 248
Faris, Alfred C. to Amanda Robertson, March 30, 1847.
Farmer, Wiley to Nancy Mosier, Feb. 22, 1847.
Faulconer, William to Catherine Winston, April 6, 1847.
Felts, Isam to Elizabeth Bennett, Sep. 9, 1847.
Fisher, John to Martha Still, April 14, 1847.

Page 249
Frensley, George W. to Elizabeth Newburn, Aug. 25, 1847.
Fry, Martin P. to Nancy Neely, Aug. 2, 1847.

Page 250
Gannaway, Archibald R. to Frances Westervent, June 22, 1847.
Gibs, Bennet H. to Sarah Balthrup, Feb. 8, 1847.
Gilchrist, Phillip P. to Sarah E. Moore, Sep. 22, 1847.
Gilchrist, Malcolm J. to Frances A. Foster, Nov. 17, 1847.
Gleaves, John Ewing to Marrilla Lorina Massey, April 5, 1847.
Gleaves, Thos. W. to Sarah G. W. Owen, Sep. 25, 1847.

Page 251
Goodlett, Robt. D. to Eliza J. H. Mathes, Sep. 6, 1847.
Goodlett, Wm. C. to Martha Ann Washington, Dec. 14, 1847.
Gorby, Lewis H. to Mary E. Horn, Sep. 15, 1847.
Gowen, Alfred to Rhoda Darows, Oct. 16, 1847.
Gower, L. T. to Rebecca Webb, Dec. 1, 1847.
Gray, William F. to Mary Jane Ninbourne, Dec. 15, 1847.

Page 252
Green, David to Adeline T. Thompson, Dec. 1, 1847.

Page 253
Halbert, John B. to Catherine M. Bostick, Sep. 9, 1847.
Hale, Jefferson to Jane Roberts, May 1, 1847.
Haley, Robt. F. to Elizabeth Powell, March 27, 1847.
Hall, Wm. to Nancy L. Allen, Aug. 4, 1847.

Hall, Joseph R. to Mary Elizabeth Bond, Nov. 13, 1847.
Hamilton, Andrew McNairy to Nancy Ellen Hooberry, July 17, 1847.

Page 254
Hannah, Green to Frances Mays, Jan. 19, 1847.
Harding, Enoch to Elizabeth Powell, April 15, 1847.
Harrison, Noah to Catherine Towns, Nov. 17, 1847.
Harrold, Cade to Sarah McCain, March 2, 1847.
Haydant, Clement to Sarah Brown, Aug. 21, 1847.

Page 255
Hegan, John to Mary W. Berry (Barry), Oct. 27, 1847.
Hitchcock, L. H. to Rachael Ann Austin, June 29, 1847.
Hollis, Wilson to Louisa Vick, Feb. 16, 1847.
Holt, James to Frances Rease, March 27, 1847.
Hogan, William to Olina Hales, Nov. 10, 1847.
Hooper, George J. to Amanda M. Alexander, June 28, 1847.

Page 256
Hooper, Jeptha to Nancy D. Garland, Aug. 9, 1847.
Horn, Thomas to Lucy Ann Mitchel, Oct. 8, 1847.
Horn, Joseph to Nancy Brown, Oct. 20, 1847.
Hume, Jno. K. to Martha E. Petway, July 31, 1847.
Hunt, Enoch J. to Lucy V. Bailey, June 16, 1847.
Hutton, T. W. to Nancy Ferebee, April 10, 1847.

Page 257
Jackson, Wm. F. to Elizabeth Wilson, June 22, 1847.
Jackson, Wm. J. to Mary Sigginfy, Nov. 5, 1847.
Jenkins, John W. to Almeda S. Wright, Nov. 13, 1847.
Johnson, John A. to Sarah Allen, June 22, 1847.
Johnson, Daniel A. to Arabella Williams, Aug. 25, 1847.
Jones, Isaac M. to Sarah A. Demoss, April 12, 1847

Page 258
Jordon, John J. to Mary E. J. Jeffreys, April 8, 1847.
Jordan, William to Julia Goodwin, Sep. 9, 1847.
Judd, J. W. to R. H. Young, Aug. 3, 1847.

Page 259
Kidd, James to Elizabeth Lockhart, Jan. 22, 1847.
Kilpatrick, T. J. to Mary Smithers, June 5, 1847.
King, John to Mary H. Phillips, June 22, 1847.
King, James to Rebecca Sullivan, July 15, 1847.
Kline, Adam to Elizabeth River, May 18, 1847.

Page 260
Knight, John A. to Sarah E. Ferguson, Aug. 25, 1847.
Knoll, Nicholas to Emma Spachour, March 3, 1847.

Page 261
Lamb, A. L. to Catherine J. Thompson, Oct. 6, 1847.
Lanier, Churchill to Martha Ann Summer, March 2, 1847.

Larkins, Robert to Helena Caladay, Dec. 21, 1847.
Lee, Clement to Charlotte Smith, July 8, 1847.
Lellyett, John to Charity B. Morris, ec. 16, 1847.
Lewis, W. P. to Helen M. Sturdevant, Nov. 2, 1847.

Page 262
Livingston, James to Mary Andrews, March 11, 1847.
Lockett, Henry C. to Helen Ann Anthony, Jan. 7, 1847.
Loftin, W. C. to Mary Hart, Oct. 12, 1847.

Page 263
Martin, Robert to Eliza L. Dickinson, July 13, 1847.
Massey, Edward to Tyronnee Bell, Oct. 25, 1847.
Matthews, Wm. H. to Jane Raymer, March 17, 1847.
Mayo, George to Rachele Jane Bone, Dec. 29, 1847.
Melvin, Philip to Mary R. Spain, Oct. 26, 1847.
Moffat, James K. to Caroline Williams, May 21, 1847.

Page 264
Montgomery, Wm. to Katherine Merritt, Dec. 30, 1847.
Moore, Samuel A. to Catharine S. Harris, July 20, 1847.
Moore, William to Sarah A. Howard, Nov. 17, 1847.
Morrison, John D. to Adelia Collier, June 14, 1847.
Moxby, Samuel to Lucy Ann Ashley, Oct. 6, 1847.

Page 265
McCormack, Wm. H. to Mary Ann Binkley, Aug. 27, 1847.
McCoy, Josiah to Parilee Goodrich, Jan. 6, 1847.
McGee, Michael to Ellen E. Byrne, Sep. 9, 1847.
McGinnis, Isaac N. to Nancy L. Johnson, March 29, 1847.
McKay, Felix G. to Jane W. Seay, Dec. 22, 1847.
McKenzie, Alexander to Mary E. Branch, Feb. 23, 1847.

Page 266
McKever, Edward to Sarah E. Hinton, Oct. 2, 1847.
McKinley, Daniel B. to Mary Bonville, Nov. 24, 1847.
McLaughlin, Wm. to Harreit Barry, Oct. 28, 1847.
McNairy, R. L. to Mary Jane Williams, June 3, 1847.

Page 267
Napier, Madison C. to Emma Louisa Davis, Jan. 21, 1847.
Norris, Isaac to Elizabeth Young, May 26, 1847.
Norvell, Hugh to Muscogo E. Worlds, April 28, 1847.

Page 268
Osborn, Joel to Martha Bland, April 29, 1847.
Otey, Paul H. to Mary Ann Bowles, March 19, 1847.
Owen, Wm. W. to Margaret G. Doom, Oct. 21, 1847.

Page 269
Page, Harvey to Rebecca Ann Parham, May 1, 1847.
Pearcy, John R. to Nancy M. Fry, Jan. 11, 1847.
Peffen, Thomas to Mary Ragan, March 15, 1847.
Pennington, John W. to Henritta Maxey, May 29, 1847.

Philips, Wm. J. to Eliza Jane Wilkerson, Feb. 24, 1847.
Poarch, John C. to Martha M. Ussery, April 10, 1847.

Page 270
Pyle, Alexander W. to Martha Jane Morris, Nov. 25, 1847.

Page 271
Reeder, Lewis to Elizabeth M. Dillard, Oct. 14, 1847.
Reeder, Isaac to Margaret L. Dillard, Oct. 25, 1847.
Rhodes, Bazil to Martha Dougherty, Nov. 27, 1847.
Rich, Wm. L. to Amanda F. Lovell, Feb. 8, 1847.
Rieves, Peter to Celeter L. Cook, Dec. 14, 1847.
Riley, Jonathan to Eliza Ann Clinard, March 15, 1847.

Page 272
Robertson, Henry to Caroline Howard, Nov. 24, 1847.
Toyster, B. S. S. to Sarah Ann Frisby, Nov. 18, 1847.
Russell, Geo. W. to Ann E. Pearcy, Jan. 27, 1847.
Russell, James S. to Evelina Hobson, Sep. 29, 1847.

Page 273
Saddler, Jarome to Susan Fentree, Sep. 1, 1847.
Sadler, James M. to Sarah Vester, July 3, 1847.
Sawyers, James G. to Mary Jane Newburn, June 10, 1847.
Sayman, Aaron to Seraphine Malang, May 6, 1847.
Scott, Alfred to Amanda Vaughan, Nov. 20, 1847.
Sears, William to Caroline Woodward, July 19, 1847.

Page 274
Seay, John, Jr. to Selina P. Wheat, Dec. 21, 1847.
Sherrill, Abel W. to Mary E. Porter, April 14, 1847.
Shucraft, George W. to Fanny Nakins, Feb. 24, 1847.
Simmons, Henry to Ann Harris, May 29, 1847.
Simpkins, Jonnathan W. to Malinda A. Linex, Dec. 11, 1847.
Sluden, A. B. to Martha Greenfield, Jan. 13, 1847.

Page 275
Smith, Samuel to Mary Trotter, April 22, 1847.
Smith, Thomas to Cany Heaton, Aug. 16, 1847.
Smith, John to Emeline McClain, Oct. 6, 1847.
Smith, Edward to Manerva Blair, Dec. 9, 1847.
Smith, Warner P. M. to Amelia A. Houser, Dec. 20, 1847.
Spruil, John A. to Catherine Cole, Dec. 18, 1847.

Page 276
Stantrough, J. Q. to Mary D. Staggs, Sep. 9, 1847.
Stanley, John A. to Margaret W. Tilford, May 13, 1847.
Starkey, Robert to Amelia O. Bryant, Nov. 3, 1847.
Stent, Robert to Mary Ann Napier, Jan. 16, 1847.
Stephens, James to Virginia Brooks, Feb. 20, 1847.
Stephens, Alfred to Sarah J. Walton, Sep. 11, 1847.

Page 277

Stephens, Thomas to Nancy Griffith, Dec. 30, 1847.
Stewart, Carter to Adell Chandler, Nov. 4, 1847.
Story, Jesse to Sarah Cartwright, Feb. 18, 1847.
Stratton, Thos. G. to Siotha P. Lingon, May 26, 1847.
Sturdevant, Wm. H. to Martha E. Bateman, Dec. 23, 1847.
Sumner, James to Angeline Shafus, Nov. 4, 1847.
Symond, Henry to Mary C. Terry, Jan. 25, 1847.

Page 278
Tally, David C. to Annamanah Boatright, March 11, 1847.
Tandy, John H. to Sarah C. Trice, Oct. 19, 1847.
Taylor, James S. to Rebecca Hendley, March 24, 1847.
Taylor, Josiah to Mary Long, May 26, 1847.
Thompson, Dela F. to Jane P. Johnson, Nov. 29, 1847.
Thornhill, Wm. to Jane Williams, May 17, 1847.

Page 279
Thornton, George L. to Harriet P. Herrin, Feb. 26, 1847.
Trotter, James M. to Colander Bennett, Oct. 28, 1847.
Turner, Edmund to Mary Moss, Dec. 20, 1847.
Tyree, Watson to Charlotte Dickinson, Jan. 23, 1847.

Page 280
Waggoner, Jno. H. to Jane C. Burnett, March 18, 1847.
Walker, James to Louisa Morgan, April 10, 1847.
Walker, Nelson to Elizabeth Hall, July 3, 1847.
Warmack, Robt. R. to Elizabeth Whiten, Aug. 11, 1847.
Warren, H. A. to Mary A. Ohilsvie, May 27, 1847.
Weaks, H. H. to Margaret E. Marshal, Feb. 16, 1847.

Page 281
Webb, Thos. R. to Sarah Ann Scruggs, April 24, 1847.
White, Aaron C. to Eliza R. Fain, April 10, 1847.
White, Lewis C. to Mary S. Chick, April 22, 1847.
Whitefield, William to Ellen Green, Nov. 6, 1847.
Whitfield, William to Emeline Carington, Feb. 19, 1847.
Willis, N. B. to Mary Ann Neely, Aug. 23, 1847.
Williams, Jno. M. to Elizabeth Boyd, Jan. 5, 1847.

Page 282
Woods, James to Penelope Porter, April 20, 1847.
Yates, David to Candis E. Burke, Jan. 23, 1847.

INDEX

(The names of JPs and clergymen are omitted)

Baird (cont.)
Willie 47
Zebulon 96
Baker, Alijah 188
Alsee 5
Andrew J. 151, 153
Ann C. 116
B. F. 180
Charity 7
Ebijah 120
Eliza 93
Elizabeth 3, 52
Francis 180
Gilbert 52
Harriet 132
Hiram 79
Humphrey 11
Isaac L. 58
James 158
James H. 180
James M. 188
Jane 80
Janette 161
Jarman 140
Jno. R. M. 129
Jno. W. 99
John 30
John G. 193
L. J. 136
Leonard D. 188
Maria G. 158
Martha 182
Mary 208, 212
Mary Jane 208
Nancy 197
Nancy Ann 190
Racel 121
Rosanna 150
Samuel 42
Sarah 22, 180
Sarah Ann 181
Sarah Susan 192
Tabitha 106
William 55, 188
Wm. 5, 111
Wm. D. 123
Wm. H. 175, 200
Balance, Joshua 3
Balch, Alfred 32, 44
Baldridge, Catherine 83
Jno. L. 133
Malinda C. 144
Mary W. 108
Nelson 180
Susan 145
Baldwin, Henry, Jr. 117
Nancy 21
Sarah 23
Wm. 87, 97
Baliew, I. Mary 184
Balim, Elizabeth 9
Ball, Angelina 195
Elizabeth H. 178
Eveline 168
Harrison 193
Israel 98
Ballame, Sally 10
Ballard, Elizabeth 129
Emily 136
Sally 37
William 188
Wm. E. 212
Ballentine, David 14
Martha 142
Mary D. 78
Nancy 31, 75
Polly 139
Sally 85, 103
Ballentine (cont.)
William 180
Zerilla 124
Ballew, Susan 200
Tempe 205
Ballou, Sarah G. 148
Ballow, Martha A. 113
Thos. W. 113
Balthrop, Louisa Ann 196
Nancy 158
Sarah 214
Balum, Edward 181
See also Edward, Balum
Bandy, Geo. 141
Richard C. 184
Susan 181, 191
Williamson B. 157, 161
Banes, Sally 52
Bang, Wm. F. 127
Bankhead, Jas. 159
Bankston, Almira 194
Delia 179
Banzer, George 188
Barber, Ann 214
Elisha 175
Sherod 206
Barclay, Shadrack 122
Barclift, Sarah 205
Sarah Ann 156
Barefield, Daniel 50
Barefoot, Elizabeth 54
Barham, John 76
Polly 37
William 45
Barker, John 35
Laban 22
Mary Jane 192
Polly 101
Rhoda M. 150
Sutton 15
Barkley, Margaret 179
Margaret N. 200
Barkly, Elizabeth 161
Barley, Thos. H. 146
Barlow, Martha 147, 148
Barnard, Joseph 143
Barner, Sterling M. 167
Barnes, Andrew J. 103
Benjamin 53, 54
Benjamine 188
Celia 28
Dempsy 36
Edy 72
Elizabeth 9, 40
James 38
Joel 28
John 61
John F. 206
Jordan 29
Lucreasy 49
Luther M. 200
Martha 97, 106
Martha A. 190
Martin 113
Mary 165
Mary C. 177
Polly 24, 39
Randal M. 97
Rebecca 33, 68
Reddeck 114
Samuel 24
Sarah 178
Tabitha 191
Thomas 70
Wm. 99
Wm. R. 193
Barnester, Celia 41
Nathaniel H. 147, 148
Barnett, Lucy 190
Mary 1
Robert 1
Barns, James 32
Barnwell, David 68
Martha 94
Barr, Hugh 12, 26
Jno. 104
Nancy 101
Sally 69
Barrett, Alexander 129
Charles 175
Elizabeth 154
Flora 179
John 133
Matilda 210
Barron, Nancy 125
Willis 24
Barrow, Jane 45
Jno. E. 194
Louisa 192
Matthew 19
Robt. J. 175
Walter 26
Washington 98
Barry, Anne 35
Elizabeth A. 146
Harreit 216
Mary A. W. 156
Mary L. 195
Mary W. 215
Richard H. 97, 184
Sarah G. M. 119
Bartee, Frances A. 169
Bartlett, Elizabeth 172
Lydia 128
Barton, Burges 54
Elizabeth 125
John 148
Mary Ann 193
Bartow, John 16
Barum, Eliza 120
Basham, James W. 137
Bashan, Biron H. 23
Bashaw, Benjamin 97
Elizabeth 80
Fanny 41
Jos. E. 140
Louisa 64
Lucinda 89
Sarah E. 131
Bashears, Jane 140
Bass, Ann 78
Augustus 212
Benjamin J. 14
Eliza 15
Jno. 119
Jno. M. 107
Julia A. 164
Kinchen C. 30
Lawrence 17
Bassford, John 6
Basye, Frances 106
Lucinda 31
Nancy 84
Bate, Amelia 25
Bateman, Charlotte 73
H. S. 212
John 180
John L. 193
Martha E. 218
Nicey 62
Sarah H. 182
Susan E. 143
Bates, Angelina 169
Robt. 127

Bates (cont.)
Wm. 79
Battle, Charity H. 70
Susan 107
Baugh, Bartly 21
V. A. 200
Bauldin, John 129
Baxter, David 11
Elizabeth 75
James 46
Jas. 58
John 184
Lucy 51, 103
Nancy 40
Nathaniel 163
Sally 74
Bay, Kennedy 6
Bayless, Lenora 8
Rachel 51
Bayless, John 53
Baynes, Marcus H. 167
Beach, Andrew S. 175
Jno. B. 98
Beals, Mary Ann 167
Bean, Armistead 89
Betsy 17
Edmund 58
Elizabeth 147
Robert 17
William C. 184
Beard, Eliza 167, 213
Martha D. 176
Richard 138
Bearden, Catherine 141
Nettie 3
Beardon, Winn 7
Beasley, Bennet H. 156
Delilah 50
James 88, 99
John 29
John W. 206
Beatty, Edward 115
Wm. 26
Beaty, Jennette 18
Jno. 98
Wm. 12
Beaver, Dishia 81
Beavers, James 61
Joel 61
Sarah 82
Beazley, Charles 175
Chas. G. 206
Elizabeth 179
Jane 207
Laban 122
Pemma 179
Sarah Ann 208
Thos. H. 212
William B. 188
Bechnoll, Ellen S. 201
Beck, Ann E. 24
Ann Eliza 26
Georgianna 101
John 20
Lavinia 75
Susannah C. 80
Beckton, Asa 29
Becton, Mary E. 3
Nancy 3
Polly 39
Sidney 9
Beddin, Maximillan 26
Bedford, Benj. W. 30, 64
Eliza Jane 209
R. H. 212
Beech, Alden C. 206
Beik, John E. 20
Belcher, Betsy 137
Sarah 189
Bell, A. J. 212
Ann Eliza 198
Catherine 7, 48
Eliza A. 57
Eliza Ann 127
Elizabeth 1, 67
Elizabeth W. 157
Frances 24, 35
Francis 23, 26
Hannah 19
Hilley 116
Hugh 63, 83
Hugh H. 184
Jane 14, 48
Jeney 64
Jno. 87, 106
John 16, 150, 206
Louisa 151
Margaret 31
Martha 74, 126
Mary 8, 164, 210
Mary E. 92
Mary J. 210
Mary W. 89
Mildred 107
Munroe 146
Nancy 62
Nancy Jane 189
Nathaniel 72
O. G. 212
Patsey 82
Patsy 60
Peggy 34
Rebecca 33, 90
Robert 8
Robt. J. 120
Sally 16, 36
Samuel 7, 34, 80
Sarah 48, 93
Thomas 37, 92
Tyronnee 216
Wm. H. 109, 147, 148
Zachriah 94
Bellamy, Isaac 13
Bellemney, Elisha 4
Belliew, William 175
Bellow, Elizabeth 17
Bellsnyder, Thomas 108
Belsher, Martha 124
Belts, Harriett 67
Benge, Patsy 10
Wm. 34
Benjamin, Thomas 4
Bennett, Colander 218
Elizabeth 6, 87, 120, 214
James 17, 200
Jane 192
Kizziah 27
Martha 87
Mary 130
Matilda 195
Nathan 33
Rebecca 165
Thomas 188, 206
Wm. 109, 164
Benningfield, James 21
James W. 180
John 31
Nancy 106
Benson, Sylvanus E. 165
Bentley, Richard 12
Bently, Richard 25
Benton, Jean 2
Joseph W. 212
Bernard, Icy Pheny 37
Bernard (cont.)
John 37
Wm. 37
Bernet, Mary 117
Berry, Augustus D. 184
Eliza 155
Isaac 9
James 206
John 85
Keziah 24
Mary L. 195
Mary S. 169
Mary W. 215
Nellie 11
Polly 4, 92
Sally 61
Susan E. 188
Tennessee 177
Wm. G. 89
Wm. W. 180
Berryal, Lewis 2
Berryhill, Mary J. 144
Bert, John A. L. 212
Bess, Andrew J. 188
Betsy Ann 164
Lydia 158
Milley 126
Best, Catherine 116
Joseph 73
Bettes, Moses W. 200
Betts, Avelena 34
Eliza 112, 137
John 35
Jonathan 29
Patsy 28
Samuel 46
Betty, John 19
Bevel, Wm. H. 200
Bevens, Charles 45
Bevins, Elizabeth 169
Bewer, Lettetia H. 124
Bibb, Adaline 129
Benjamin 32
Julia A. 125
Patsy 30
Polly 15
Sophronia 148
Susan 183
William 20
Bickly, Elizabeth 1
Biddle, Daniel M. 212
Mary 116
Sally S. 107
Bidwell, Alsia 26
Esther 17
Bigelow, Elijah 87
Biggers, Alvira 208
Wm. 200
Biggs, Alex'd 119
Jas. 99
Leroy W. 175
Margaret 155
Reuben 15
Sally 62
Bigley, Edward 68
John 134
Thos. W. 142
Billens, Harding 9
Billings, Betsy 18
Catey 13
James J. S. 200
Billingsley, John 6
Mary 6
Bilts, Selden 84
Bingham, Alexander 4
Thos. W. 130
Binkley, Absolom 68
Adam 103, 142

Binkley (cont.)
Alenida 80
Asa N. 150, 200
Burnette 145
Catherine 121
Catherine P. 135
Charles 189
Christina 28
Cinthia 49
David 66, 167
Delilah 91
Elizabeth 19
Frederick 18
George 25
Henrietta 88, 195
Henry 103, 117
Hiram 155
Hulda 136
Isaac 102
J. H. 212
Jacob 153, 175
Jane 86
Jas. 93
Jno. 80
Joanna 83
John 64
Jos. S. 134
Joseph 9
Lavina 195
Louisa 198
Mahala 113
Malinda 123
Martha 154
Mary 98
Mary Ann 216
Nancy 36
Narcissa 109
Nelly 128
Peter 120
Prestor 189
Sina 146
Suan P. 214
Susannah 178
Tazwell M. 189
Wm. 71, 133
Binns, Wm. A. 138
Bird, John 68
Moses 134
Penny 12, 26
Birdwell, Alice 24
Andrew 103
Hugh 31
Isaiaih 39
John W. 212
Polly 57
Samuel 131
Bishop, Ann 18
Elizabeth 55
John 189
Peggy 12, 25
Sarah 47
Wilmouth 52
Biter, Jane 147
John 10
Nicholas 17
Polly 36
Bivens, Nancy 183
Black, Elizabeth 7
Mitchell 2
Nancy 49
Blackamore, Harriet 6
Blackburn, Edward 16
Jno. 61
Blackman, Anna 7
Anne 40
Bennett 13
Charlotte 33
Mary J. 137
Blackman (cont.)
Nancy 56
Nancy E. 195
Blackmore, Milly 28
Nancy 24
Blackwell, Blueford 212
Henry 175
Josiah 193
Thomas S. 174
Blackwood, Hiram 78, 104
Blain, Lindsey 124
Lucinda 131
Blair, Jane 24, 26, 52
Jennie 6
John 101, 201
John K. 206
Manerva 217
Margaret 77
Martha 6
Mary 66
Nancy 75, 92
Nancy M. 57
Ralph A. 41
Sally 81
Samuel 65, 99
Sarah 28, 132
Thomas 74
William 189
Wm. G. 200
Blake, Daniel 121
John 30
Sally 24
Blakemon, James 25
Blakey, Geo. D. 114
Blanchard, Carey H. 147
Bland, Arthur 19, 56
Elizabeth 15, 160
Isaac 97
Joseph A. 110
Mahala 133
Martha 202, 216
Mary O. 182
Phoebe 27
Sally 20
Samuel L. 113
Blane, Jacob 180
Blanton, Margaret 203
Matilda 32
Bleakley, James 2
Nancy 21
Bledsoe, Jesse 139
Martha C. 209
Moses 121
Blithe, Elizabeth 4
Bloodworth, Bedford 162
Elizabeth 190
Maria 182
Mary 187
Blueford, Charlotte 61
Blurton, John 51
Boardman, Frances C. 185
Boatright, Annamanah 218
Boaz, David 99
Frances E. 144
Joshua 121
Nancy R. 122
Shadrack 87
Sarah D. 87
Bobs, Thos. 115
Bode, Andrew 201
Anna M. 188
Bodie, William 1
Boggs, Eliza 161
Boker, Mary 104
Bolden, Mary 209
Bolten, Joel 111
Bolton, Caroline B. 211
Claiborne 29
Bolton (cont.)
Leathey Eliza 192
Mary 147
Boltor, Nicholas 7
Bomer, William 184
Bond, Achsah 14
James 90
John 59
Mary Elizabeth 215
Nancy 29
Patsy 19
Shadrack 14
Bonds, Joshua 137
Nathaniel 73
Bondurant, Amanda M. 103
Jacob M. 81
Martha M. 58
Sally D. 76
Bone, Rachele Jane 216
William 201
Boner, Henry 54
James H. 193
Bonney, Ann Caroline 114
Bonville, Mary 216
Boon, Amanda 195
Bryant 47
James 44
Louise 101
Booten, Hester 108
Mary Ann 180
Polly 52
Booth, Christian 13, 26
Henry 30
Mary 59
Wm. 100, 109
Boren, James 26
Nellie 4
Borin, James 24
Bosley, Adeline T. 160
Beal 1
Charles 51
Charles, Jr. 189
Charlotte 35
Delilah 134
Elizabeth 37, 56
James R. 31
Levinie 109
Margery 158
Mariah 70
Mary 3
Polly 46
Rachel 29
Rachel G. 192
Sarah Ann 134
Bostic, Elizabeth 27
Bostick, Catherine M. 214
Hardin P. 81
James A. 175
John H. 167
Richard W. H. 184
Boswell, James 158
Bosworth, Ellen M. 153
Mary Ann 163
Wm. 48
Bourne, Thomas G. 206
Bournos, Jos. Tansea 51
Boush, R. A. 206
Bouton, Elizabeth 121
Bowen, Anne 119
Catherine 130
Mary 122
Rebecca 6
Wm. 10
Bower, Wm. P. 96
Bowers, Ann 18
Elizabeth H. 107
Jno. 5
Levina 99

Bowers (cont.)
Mary S. 213
Polly 34
Sally 81
Samuel 34
Stephen C. 96
William P. 189
Bowlding, Nancy 207
Bowles, Mary Ann 216
Bowlin, Jane 2
Mahala 113
Bowman, Jas. 180
Joseph A. 193
Boyce, Martha J. 184
Boyd, Abraham 2
Agnes 91
Clementine H. 130
Elizabeth 143, 218
George W. 37
Hannah 2, 149
James 72
Jane 92, 109
Jno. 109
John 2, 9, 28, 45
Jonathon 145
Joseph 58
Leodocia J. 124
Margaret 1, 91
Mariah 201
Martha Jane 194
Mary 2, 133, 144, 213
Mary A. 167
Matilda 189
Mildried 196
Milton B. 180, 184
Nancy 5, 149
Nicholas H. 150
Polly 22
Rachel D. 210
Rachel T. 179
Rhody 92
Richard 5, 63
Robert 163, 189
Sally 136
Sarah 7, 197
Sarah Ann 188
Sarah S. 127
Sophronia L. 97
Susan A. 144
Whitmell H. 107
William 15
William L. 201
William P. 180
Wm. 22, 144
Zaney 143
Boyle, Cornelius 167
Jno. A. 70
Sarah 135
Boyles, James 12
Nancy 102
Sarah 68
Boyt, Felix 134
James 49
Boyte, Courtney 127
Easter 88
Felix G. 144, 162
John 113
Jonathan 139
Nancy 93
Bracken, James 25
Brackett, Mary 161
Brackin, James 12
Brackman, Herman K. 212
Brackwell, Nowell 189
Bradberry, George 5
Sally 56
Bradbury, Martha 208
Bradby, Mary Jane 139
Braddock, Rolla Smith 167
Bradford, Annie B. 38
E. M. 180
Eleanor F. 181
Henry C. 45
Hugh 33
John 30
Judith L. 38
Louisa H. 142
Prudence L. 184
Robert 152
S. 180
Sarah W. 185
Sophia 55
Thomas G. 19
Bradfute, Margaret 183
Robert 108
Bradley, Easter 178
Mary Ann 170
Stephen W. 98
Bradshaw, Caroline 135
Elizabeth 31
John 180
Margaret 8
Martha 62
Mary 2
Patsy 14
Peggy 19
Polly 46
Samuel 18
Tabitha W. 121
William 18
Brady, Eliza 75
John A. 193
Jonathon 4
Polly 93
Robt. 111
Sarah F. 199
Brahan, Ann E. 199
John 14
Brailey, John 24
Branch, Chas. 94
Eliza 6
John 15
John R. 184
Julia Ann 47
K. 212
Lewis 139
Margaret 9
Martha 29
Mary E. 216
Paggy 14
Robt. 61
Wallice 65
Wilmoth 27
Brand, T. T. 201
Brandon, Thomas 29
Wm. 32
Brannen, Wm. 70
Brannon, Ann 122
John 65
Bransford, Jacob 146
L. M. 212
Martha W. 172
Mary C. 186
Brashier, Jacob 39
Bratcher, Farrell H. 212
Bratton, Thomas 14
Braughton, John 57
Bray, Wm. R. 115
Breathett, Eliza H. 168
Breeding, Tabitha 28
Breedlove, John 206
Bremaker, Belle Ann 176
Brennon, Luke C. 206
Brent, Albert H. 87
Joseph A. 201
Brewer, Eli 85
Elisha 2
Elizabeth 180
Jas. M. 130
Joseph 40
Louisa A. 157
Malinda 83
Pricilla 13
Rodham 143
William E. 189
Wm. 32, 48
Brgan, Lewis C. 193
Briant, Aggie 41
Brice, John 74
Bridgefond, Wm. 97
Bridgeforth, Ann J. 58
Bridges, John 30
Smith 134
Brient, James 6
Brierly, Robt. 60
Sarah H. 114
Briggs, Jno. 92
Brighton, Elizabeth 130
Briley, John G. 156
Mary Ann 206
Rhoda 174
Thos. B. 156
William C. 201
Brilsford, John 159
Brily, Mary Ann 206
Brim, Hannah 119
Brindley, Robt. 89
Brinkley, Alexander 72
Elizabeth 105
Hepsey 85
Robt. C. 184
Susan 143
Britt, Arthur 145
Brittain, James 64
Brittle, Bedory F. 193
George W. 212
Mary 210
Milton P. 160
Britton, Jemima 19
Brockman, Celia A. 186
Brodaway, Jimemma 80
Bromley, Neely 10
Bronson, Nancy 2
Brookman, Jane 144
Susanna 188
William 189
Brooks, Angeline 154
Ann C. 101
Anne 9
Christopher 102, 160
Christopher B. 201
Christopher M. 86
Elizabeth 212
Gennette 184
Jno. T. 156
Johnson 180
Lucy W. 99
M. D. 153
Mary Jane 203
Moses T., Jr. 212
Richard P. 102
S. 147
Sarah W. 180
Sukey 6
Virginia 217
Wm. T. 76, 161
Brother, Sarah 99
Brown, A. V. 201
Alexander Y. 50
Alfred S. 119
Ann 148

Brown (cont.)
Aris 95
Armstead 46
Bartlett 184
Bazzell 55
Benjamin F. 142
Berryman 100
Charles 32
Clary 62
David 27
E. H. 212
Eli 184
Eliza 114
Elizabeth 116
Emily 127
Ephriam 30
Frawny 18
G. W. 184
Gelica 179
Hailey 85
Hannah 188
Henry 18
Hughly 160
J. P. W. 158
James 5, 143, 156
James T. 167
Jane 75, 140
Jas. Percy 176
Jennie 7
Jesse 83, 158
Jincy 52
Jno. D. 90
Jno. E. 134
Jno. L. 77
John 37, 62, 63, 124, 127, 189, 212
John B. 20, 212
John G. 184
John M. 133
Joseph 3, 175
Joseph P. 105
Josiah G. 212
June 202
Louisa C. 129
Louise 39
Lucinda 129
Luiza V. 96
Lydia 71
Margaret 2
Mariah 112
Martin 20
Mary 35, 186
Mary E. 146
Mary L. 105
Matilda 122
Morgan W. 92
Nancy 123, 148, 179, 215
Nancy Jane 202
Nannie 147
Nathanial 60
Nathaniel 130
Neal S. 175
Nicholas T. P. 167
Penelope A. C. 189
Rachel 31
Richard B. 31
Rich'd K. 116
Robert 9, 27
Robt. 56
Sally 61
Samuel 34, 206
Sarah 215
Shadrack 10
Susan 157, 161, 182
Susan Ann 115
Thomas 1, 86, 104
Ursula 154

Brown (cont.)
Walter 138
William 180
William P. 180
Wm. 31, 144, 158, 159
Wm. B. 141
Wm. L. 105
Wm. W. 76
Zyranna 120
Brownlow, John 193
Bruce, Ezekiel 81
James M. 201
John 143
Martha P. 100
Brumaker, Frederick 149
Brumbelow, Archd. 167
Brumet, Lerry 189
Brumfield, David 110
Brumley, Jno. 96
Brumlove, Isaac 89
Brumly, Nancy 84
Brummell, Wm. 105
Brummet, Lucy 111
Brummit, Martha 77
Brunaugh, Mary P. 14
Brunch, Sarah 142
Brunson, Asabel 174
Smiley 175
Bryan, Elizabeth 65
Hardy W. 141
Harret Bryan 149
James 77
Jenny 16
Jno. T. 90
Margery Ann 106
Mary E. 30
Polly 14
Samuel 80
Sherwood 58
Wm. S. 189
Bryant, Amelia O. 217
Ann 67
Archibald H. 143
Eliza E. 199
Hannah 12, 26
Hardy S. 62
Jno. M. 118
Leathy 79
Lidia 23
Mary 1, 12, 25
Mary Ann 94
Nancy 78, 118
Nathan 18
Peggy 35
Phoebe 123
Silas 212
Wm. 97, 131
Bryn, John R. 66
Brynes, Joseph 21
Buchanan, Alexander 52, 201
Andrew 1
Celia 32
Charles 132
Elenora 32
Elizabeth 8, 15
Elizabeth N. 116
George 63
Hannah 2
James 16, 157
Jane T. 45
Jennie 1
Jno. K. 58, 150
John 2, 5, 7
Margaret 9
Margaret C. 137
Martha 1, 21
Mary 7

Buchanan (cont.)
Mary A. E. 190
Mary Jane 205
Moses R. 96
Nancy 9, 23, 25, 137, 140
Peggy 6, 28, 62
Pelly 28
Rebecca 8
Rich'd 128
Robert 16
Robt. 88, 90
Sally 20
Sarah 2
Sarah E. 139
Sarah V. 80
Thomas 3
Wm. M. 125
Buchanon, Addison 212
Jane T. A. 182
John R. 184
Lucinda 193
Mary F. 196
Sarah A. 182
Sarah Ann 203
Buchett, Wm. 212
Buchus, Hannah 59
Buck, Amelia E. 82
Ann W. 102
Caroline R. 114
Thomas M. 176
Buckler, Joseph 5
Buckley, Julia Ann 210
Buckner, James M. 110
Minerva 196
Budd, Thos. L. 176
Buel, Nancy 53
Buffington, Anderson 143
John 131
Buford, Edward 22
Henry 9
James 14
Rebecca 22
Bugg, Benjamin 89
Sam'l H. 141
Buie, Elizabeth 118
Martha Ann 183
Maryann 69
Nancy 98
Sarah 89, 169, 203
Bullard, Theophelus 70
Bullus, Elizabeth 179
Bumpass, Elizabeth Ann 122
Martha A. 161
Mary A. 161
Oma 186
Sarah 61
Washington 127
Wm. 18
Bumppass, Aloha 72
Bundy, Sophia 156
Buntin, Mary J. 162
Bujton, William R. 189
Burch, Eliza Jane 199, 205
Burchett, Elizabeth 184
Nancy 202
Thomas 184
Burge, Betsy 14
Eliza O. 110
Mary Ann 201
Pennington 128
Burges, Geo. W. 139
Burgess, A. B. 160
Amanda 203
Isabella 149
Burgis, Lorenzo D. 102

Campbell (cont.)
Margarett 191
Martha 212
Mary 3, 36, 197
Mary L. S. 210
Nancy 197
Nancy B. 189
Patrick W. 132
Peggy 71
Phillip 16
Rebecca 71
Rebecca Jane 189
Sallie A. E. 153
Sally 81
Sarah 173
Sidney 122
Sophronia W. 34
Thomas A. 213
Wm. 35, 107
Wm. P. 95
Canady, Isaac 24
Cane, Polly 9
Cannady, Ann 207
Elizabeth 209
Milburn 67
Cannon, Anna M. 195
Minos 15
Newton 30
Rebecca 49
Rebecca L. 184
Willis 46
Cantrell, Elivira S. 207
Elizabeth 128
Emeline 122
Ester 93
George C. 189
Stephen 25
Stephen, Jr. 157
Capps, Benjamin 14
Caleb 125
Eliza 110
John 133
Robert 158, 184
Sally 149
Car, Jane 209
Carden, Martha A. 189
Mary Ann 191
Carding, Allen D. 76
Cardwell, James W. 176
Cardy, Louisa 156
Carey, Pleasant 97
Cargill, Henry A. 149
Peyton C. 213
Carihan, Mary 2
Carington, Emeline 218
Carlile, Wilson 168
Carlisle, Eliza 123
Elizabeth 212
Sally 102
Carmach, Isaac 52
Carmack, Aquilla 8
Carney, Asa 108
Avelina 95
Elestus C. 88
Elijah 12, 25
Elijah M. H. 145
Ennis B. 138
George G. 213
Isaac T. 201
James 67, 78
Jno. B. G. 135
John 159
Joshua 146
Louisa Ann 207
Lucy 61
Mary A. E. 179
Mary Ann 135
Melsindy 127
Carney (cont.)
Patsy 16
Prudy 186
Vincent 21, 85
William 16
Wm. V. 201
Carol, Hugh 213
Carothers, Margaret 8
Sarah 3
Wm. 54
Carpenter, Catherine 9
Frances 73
Frederick 57
John 7
Margaret 97
Nancy 42
Polly 34
Sally 45, 65
Wm. 180
Carper, Alexander 87
Green 167
John 98
Julia Ann 207
Mary 86, 209
McCoy 120
Sampson P. 107
Susan 156
Thos. 123
Carr, Jesse D. 157
Carrey, G. W. J. 206
Carrington, Elizabeth 176
John B. 76
Lucinda 186
Nancy 198
Wm. 91
Carroll, Betsy 18
Catherine N. 134
Joseph 213
Maria 100
McWilliam 65
Nathaniel 36
Samuel 12, 25
Thos. B. 181
William H. 168
Carter, Bethiel 94
Caroline 145
Christopher 29
Corinne F. 202
Cornelia Ann 183
Danl F. 162
Delilah 184
Elizabeth 40, 123
Elizabeth A. 82
Elizabeth B. 71
Francis M. 189
Garret 113
James 17, 34
James C. 137
Jno. C. 111
John 34, 40
Nancy 15
Narcessa 48
Nelson P. 136
Paulina P. 141
Phoebe 14
Samuel J. 131
Sarah 191, 207
Sarah E. 146, 148
Sophia B. 138
Sophia D. 31
Walter O. 75
William 44
Wm. L. 15
Cartmell, Henry R. 71
Nathan 45
Cartwright, Ann Eliza 200
Cartwright (cont.)
David 43, 119
Elezette 68
Elij'h Jane 195
Eliza 121
Elizabeth 1
Emily 95
Evelina 145
Eveline A. 102
Harriet 84
Jacob 17
James 61, 206
Jefferson 120
Jeremiah J. 88
Jno. 80
Jno. H. 127
John 30, 132
John T. 213
Lewis 213
Mary A. 82
Nancy 13, 26, 31, 49
Nicy 92
Pembroke 101
Sarah 29, 218
Sarah P. 175
Talitha 115
Thermy 51
Thomas 167
Thomas D. 206
Thos. 75
Thos. M. 59
Vincent 10
Wm. 64
Caruthers, Lucinda 94
Casbear, America 133
Casey, Ann 184
Charles S. 189
Elizabeth 31
George 21
James S. 189
Margaret 212
Martin R. 130
Mary 131
Mary Emeline 213
Samuel 106
Shadrack 95
Cash, John 17
William 18
Cashaw, Rebecca 1
Cason, John 42
Lewis 14
Seth 32
Stephen 29
Casper, Catherine 39
Cassedy, Alexander A. 122
Cassellman, Anne 68
Elizabeth 67, 93
Henry 26
John 98
Martha 113
Mary 7
Rhody 73
Sally 59
Sarah 112
Senai 49
Sylvanus 16
Wm. 111
Casselman, Abraham 63
Castilio, John 8
Castleman, Amelia 33
Andrew E., Jr. 132
Benjamin 11
Bery 176
Burrell P. 184
Cynthia G. 138
David 3, 11, 156
Eliza 161
Elizabeth A. 159

Compton (cont.)
Elizabeth 84, 89
Elizabeth W. 202
Henry 36
Jno. 119
John 28
Laney 132
Mary Ann 120
Mary Jane 185
Polly 7
Rebecca 159
Richard 14
Susan L. 132
Thomas 207
Wm. 29, 61
Condon, Christine 165
James 28, 86, 176
Julian 45
Mary 165
Cone, Colier 201
Guilford 144
Conel, James 213
Conger, Peggy 63
Pernia 84
Congor, Chas. H. 213
Conlan, James W. 175
Conley, Caroline 175
Criolea 30
Mary 199
Sally 56
Conn, Jesse 213
Connell, Adie 117
Betsy 23, 27
Caroline 108
Elizabeth 211
Frances 148
Giles 125
Kitty 127
Olivia 188
Parthenia 53
Thos. J. 155
William 194
Wm. 43
Connelley, Dovey 123
Connelly, John W. 184
Lavinia 31
Owen B. 213
Peter 24, 27
Sally 19
William 176
Conner, Amos L. 167
Cornelius 128
John 16, 201
Patrick 213
Conoway, Mary 181
Mary Ann 180
Conwell, L. S. 152
Conyears, Thomas 201
Cook, Bennett 125
Celeter L. 217
Chas. 124
Elizabeth 66, 99
Emily 200
Ezekiel 194
Granville 149
Hubbard 84
James 43
James T. 73
John E. 194
John F. 185
Lewis 111
Maria 80
Mary 180
Mary Ann 159
Matthew 194
Minerva B. 110
Moses 100
Nancy T. 38
Cook (cont.)
Patsy 29
Rachel 151
Rebecca 190
Reuben 59
Sarah 67
Thomas 207
William 6
Cooke, Lettie 8
Polly 17
Thomas 30
Coon, James 12, 26
Jennie 24
Prudence 8
Shadrach 95
Sibby 28
Coonce, Areena 19
Cooney, Joshua 201
Cooper, Amelia 6
Ann L. B. 140
August 51
Chas. 60
Chas., Jr. 103
Elizabeth 43
Houston 38
James 15
John 19
Minerva 86
Nancy 112
Patsy 30, 32
Polly 6, 28
Sally 11, 12, 26
Sarah M. 172
Thomas 167
W. B. 176
Washington 127
Coots, Lavinia 28
Polly 62
Copeland, Samuel 9
Thomas 207
Coper, Elizabeth 208
Copher, Martha 201
Coppage, Thos. L. 164
Copper, Thos. A. 164
Corbett, Felix M. 162
James 81
Lucy 80
Martha Ann 204
Susannah 9
Willie B. 140
Corbit, Dempsy 108
Corbitt, Allen T. 168
Edy 93
Ellen 213
John 21
Mahala 142
Micky 153
Nicholas P. 176
Polly 13
Samuel R. 185
Wm. A. 121
Corder, David H. 213
Thos. L. 109
Corke, Celia 106
Corley, Bartlet 167
Eliza B. 193
Corn, Simon 91
Coshen, Rebeccah 70
Costello, Anne 34
Costillow, James 31
Costilo, Nancy 95
Cotlort, Eliza 171
Cotton, Allen 37
Chas. 147
Elizabeth 189, 213
Hardy 136
Hiram S. 181
Mary Ann 152
Cotton (cont.)
Mary E. 192
Precilla 51
Sarah 83
Couch, Catharine A. 203
George W. 168
Jno. A. 140
Mariah 191
Marshall 181
Martha Jane 182
Peter 168
Sarah 142
Courtney, Belizabeth 2
James 185
Micajah 150
Nehemiah 1
Coussens, John H. 181
Coverly, John 141
Covey, John 33
Covington, Ann 193
Cornelia 178
Nancy 30
Cowan, Maria E. 158
Mary M. 210
Cowden, Henry 15
James 38
John J. 181
Cowerdon, Margaret 97
Cowgill, Abner 20
Ann 81
Canzada 130
Elisha 36
Hannah 99
Martha 45
Mary 44
Moses 154
Nancy 87
Parmelia 153
Sarah 71
Theresa 156
Thompson 185
Cox, Archibald D. 148
Benjamin 126
Bray G. 122
Crosby 154
Eddy 40
Eliza 41
Elizabeth 50
Fountain 194
Fuschia I. 213
George 207
Herman 213
James 176
Keziah 37
Lorton 57
Martha Ann 56
Mary Ann 65, 185
Mary C. S. 124
Mary W. 131
Melvin G. 122
Nancy 27, 110, 183
Ruth 45
Sally 36
Susan 168, 192
Wm. 93
Wm. B. 57
Crabb, Henry 45
Jane A. 112
Mary E. 175
Ralph 48
Crabtree, Benj. 65
James 44
Craddock, Benjamin 165
Caroline C. 74
Clarissa 55
Elijah H. 168
Harriett W. 43
R. S. 207

Craddock (cont.)
Susan 129
Craig, Alexander 28, 41
David 28
James T. 153
Lewis Y. 194
Lucretia 116
Malinda 198
Sally 36
Craighead, Jno. B. 75
John B. 22
Nan 204
Crance, Polly 84
Crandell, Edwin R. 213
Cranshaw, Nicholas 16
Cravens, Abagail 31
Elizabeth 17
John 108
Tabby 55
Crawford, A. C. 160
Andrew 176
Charlotte 3
Elizabeth 38
James 5
James J. 185
Jane 38
Jane Brown 17
John 9, 67
Lydia 92
Margaret R. 10
Susannah 33
William 10
Wm. 19, 69
Creach, Jno. W. 189
Creal, John B. 207
Creech, Elizabeth 208
Thomas 189
William 213
Creel, Wm. 31
Cregan, Mary 71
Creighton, Avelina 82
Izzy 118
Joseph 194
Crenshaw, Mary H. 54
Vincent 176
Crichlow, Branker 129
Criddle, Adline 58
Edward 33
Eliza A. 64
Harriet S. 127
John 13
John, Jr. 56
Smith 176
Crisp, Elizabeth 134
Critchlow, Elizabeth G. 120
Critz, James M. 201
Sally 34
Crocker, Benjamine F. 207
Crockett, Andrew 48
Ann Eliza 198
David 86
Elij. S. 213
Elizabeth S. 159
James 74
Jane 204
Martha Ann 170
Mary 206
Matilda 188
Nancy 200
Sally 43
Sarah E. 111
Therisa 143
Thussey C. 190
W. B. E. J. 194
Crook, Bignal 69
Crooks, Jno. 126
Cropper, Wm. 6, 103
Cross, Delilah 51
James B. 137
Martin 62
Nancy 4
Nathaniel 114
Powhatan 147
Powhatton 148
Wm. E. 155
Crossweight, Ann 87
Crossy, Nichols 5
Crosway, James C. 181
Crouch, David 16
Crow, Elisha 6
Jacob 1
Nancy 1
Wm. L. 66
Crowder, Elizabeth 97
James 59
Teresy 88
Crunk, Joseph H. 155
Cruse, Samuel 53
Crutcher, Catherine 79
Elizabeth 75
Elzaline 87
Fanny 55
James A. 213
Larkin 98
Martha M. 110
Nancy 78
Patsy 44
Peggy 17
William 149
Crutchfield, Mary 34
Oliver 51
Crutchin, Saml R. 144
Crutchor, Sophia Ann 134
Crutis, William 185
Cryton, Nancy 174
Cuff, David 67
Cullam, Elliston M. 194
Culley, Robert 194
Cullom, Amy 211
Bedee 91
Hannah 211
Mary Ann 162
Wm. 143
Cullon, Tenny 71
Cullum, Alexander 181
Fanny 116
Gains F. 99
James T. 133
Jane 140
Jeremiah W. 109
Jesse P. 133
Lincy 80
Lovell H. 76, 181
Lucy 202
Culpepper, James H. 131
Cummings, Harriet I. 171
Cummins, David 63
Elizabeth 155
Henry G. 89
James 9
Wm. 44
Cunningham, Edward 132
Enoch 117
Jane 119
Jas. 90
Jesse I. 168
John 62, 189
Lorenda 212
Lucy 214
Mary Ann 109, 207
Nancy 88
Robert 168
Rosa 37
Sally 55
Cunningham (cont.)
Samuel 99
Susannah 13
Curd, Price 120
Richard D. 137
Curfman, James 189
John 85
Mary 130
Nancy 139
Wm. 114
Currell, Jas. S. 115
Curren, Anna 43
Currey, Richard O. 189
Susanna E. 128
Currin, Julia Ann 148
Mary E. 124
Robt. P. 27
Robt. S. 201
Sarah 72
Curry, Isaac 19
Margaret 5
Robert B., Jr. 213
Robt. B. 27
Curtis, Constant 47
Elizabeth 30, 38
Harriet 102
James 10
James J. 213
Jas. 98
John 60
Maria 85
Martha 110
Mary 28
Patsy 11
Peggy 4
William 9
Cutchen, Lemuel R. 93
Olly 99
Cutter, Timothy T. 207
Dabbs, Isabel M. 180
Isabell M. 184
James 189
Jno. R. 127
Joseph W. 189
Thos. C. 149
Dacus, Wm. 47
Dailey, Robert 138
Dale, Isaac A. 207
Melissy 212
Peggy 21
Daley, Elizabeth 9
Daly, Eliza M. A. 202
Dana, Russell 138
Daney, Mary 19
Dange, Enoch 5
Daniel, David 155
Edward 51
Eliza 64
Freeman R. 42
Jane 31
Julia Ann 79
Lydia 32
Martha 59
Mary 50, 70
Nancy 67
Sarah M. W. 125
Danks, Jno. W. 138
Danly, John 17
Darden, John C. 213
Dark, Chas. S. 101
Darows, Rhoda 214
Darrah, Christopher 36
Darrow, John B. 33
Joseph 86, 207
Lucinda 189
Lucretia 208
Mary Ann 208
Dascomb, Jno. 156

Dicks, William 181
Dickson, Cornelia Ann 83
Jane 21
John M. 52
Mary F. 117
William 24
Die, Betsy 18
Diffee, Wm. 117
Diggins, Emma 186
Diggons, Ellen 182
Susanna 152
DiJone, Charlotte 138
Dill, John 93
Nancy 37
Dillahunt, Delilah 123
Martha 116
Zaney 144
Dillahunty, Clementina V. 198
Elizabeth 32
Joseph S. 189
Lewis 37
Sallie L. 145
Wm. 3, 32
Dillard, Elizabeth M. 217
John 185
John B. 32
Margaret L. 217
Dillehay, Jane 154
Dillihunt, Hannah 3
Dillihunty, Polly B. 14
Dillin, Chas. R. 201
Dillingham, Polly 124
Dillon, George K. 76
James 49
Dillyard, Bryant 185
Dilworth, Thos. 50
Dimoner, John 24
Dinwidie, Catherine 114
Dirickson, Jane 169
Dismukes, Fanny 111
Geo. E. 142
Geo. R. 36
Jno. T. 56
John D. 148
Martha J. 58
Susan T. 132
Dixon, Henry O. 185
Wallace 75
Warren G. 181
Doak, John 17
Dobbs, Asa S. 168
David D. 85
Jno. R. 120
Dobson, Jane 133
Mary 212
Sarah 205
Thos. 42
Dodd, Allen 213
John 32
Robert 30
Sally 23
William 41
Dodson, Agnes 27
Archibald 158
Cynthia 47
Darky 37
Elizabeth 172
Elizabeth P. 124
Julia 101
Lucy T. 84
Martha 123
Mary 48
Mary Ann 170
Nancy 85
Polly 34
Dodson (cont.)
Presley 100
Wm. T. 127, 141
Dolway, William J. 194
Donald, John T. 214
Donaldson, James 49
Donelly, Martha 18
Donelson, A. J., Jr. 185
Andrew J. 80
Catherine 37
Clarinda 78
Elizabeth 36
Emily T. 80
Jacob D. 86
John 75, 124, 136
Lemuel 54
Lucinda O. R. 117
Maria 182
Martha H. 87
Mary 22
Mary O. 47
Mary T. 3
Pherby E. R. 173
Rachel 2, 22, 70
Sally 21
Samuel 8
Severn 63
Stephen 105
Stockley 103
Susannah 19
Thos. J. 129
William 96
Wm. 2, 70, 201
Donge, Peter 25
Donley, Margaret 76
Donly, Jane H. 77
Donnald, Nancy 70
Donnelly, Peggy 31
Rosa 46
Donoho, Scerena 63
Doom, Allison E. 199
Margaret G. 216
Dorris, Altiseer 69
Anderson 118
Catherine 139
Elizabeth D. 89
Ira 202
Margaret 17
Mary 102
Nancy 36
Nancy J. 65
Susan 178
Thomas 161
William 10
Wm. D. 94
Zilpha 146
Dortch, Jesse L. 100
Dotson, Catherine 131
Geo. C. 128
Harvey 53
Isaiah Y. 131
Limech 50
Lucinda 191
Lucy Ann 183
Marshall 127
Mary 141
Thos. 128
Doty, Edmond 12
Doudge, Peter 12
Dougal, Mary 58
Dougall, Joseph 75
Dougherty, John 37, 38
M. L. 207
Martha 217
Doughty, Bashrod T. 214
Catherine E. 135
Lydia Jane 180
Douglas, Alexander 34
Douglas (cont.)
John 6
Nancy 31
Priscilla 140
Rachel 152
Sally 22
Tempy 58
Wm. 133
Douglass, Elizabeth 44
Harriet Ann 211
Harry L. 112
Jonathan 89
Lishey 181
Mary 77
Dover, Isaac 154
Dowdy, Wm. W. 119
Dowlen, Harris 4
Dowlin, Celia 10
Downey, Benjamin 1
Elizabeth 41
Sarah W. 109
Downing, William D. V. 189
Downs, Jas. P. 42
Mary 188
Thomas W. 185
William H. 185
Wm. 48
Downsey, Wm. 50
Dowry, John 22
Doxey, Lewis 214
Dozier, Angeline 194
Ann 110
Charlotte 195
David 190
Dennis 74
Edna H. 211
Enoch T. 207
Enock 189
George M. 214
Grundy 163
Jasper N. 185
Joseph 140
Julina 186
Margaret 199
Matilda 91
Nannie B. 144
Nimrod W. 143
William N. 181
Willoughby 91, 97
Drake, Ann 138
B. C. 181
Blount W. 145
Charles A. 152
Charlotte R. 89
Eli 114
Elias C. 214
Eliza Ann 104
Eliza Jane 161
Elizabeth 24, 37, 52
Hannah 13, 173
Isaac 64, 157
James F. 97
Jane 42
Jesse 45
Jno., Jr. 49
Jonathan 21
Joshua 38
Judith A. 77
Logan 93
Margaret 144
Martha V. 84
Mary 192
Mary Ann 203
Mary J. 115
Polly 9, 62
Polly H. 33
Rachel 37

Drake (cont.)
Sally 11, 37, 56
Sarah 63
Sarah A. 173
Susan 37
Susan S. 83
Susannah 147
Temperance 39
William P. 168
Wm. J. 46
Draper, Elizabeth 196
Martha 190
Mary A. 157
Nancy 181
Sam'l S. 214
Dreman, David 168
Drenard, Martha 150
Drenen, Espy C. 141
Drennon, Mary Jane 134
Drerritt, Joseph 39
Drew, Benjamin 9
Edward 160
Eliza 90
Moses 134
Wm. 75
Drewry, Rich'd 53
Dreyfus, Isaac 159
Driver, Abner 46
Burrell 133
Ereany 171
Henry 146
Rebecca 141
William 168
Drmumbrien, Timothy 24
Drugan, James 76
Drummond, Elizabeth 100
Drury, Nancy M. 60
Dryer, Alfred 177
Ducan, John H. 194
Due, Patsy 6
Duff, Jane N. 182
Matilda 197
Robt. L. 71
Dugger, Wm. D. 202
Duke, Elizabeth 4
Green W. 181
Henry R. 133
Josiah G. 9
Macasah 9
Mathew 194
Nimrod W. 124
Philemon 5
Rebecca 128
Thos. N. 150
Wm. S. 136
Dukey, Susannah 17
Dukird, Jacob 15
Dun, Maclin 146
Stephen 18
Dunavant, Pleasant 181
Dunaway, Drury 185
Sarah S. 181
Dunbar, Susannah 84
Duncan, Alexander 93
Almira 209
Ann C. 154
Mary E. 196
Robt. P. 123
Sarah 77
Thos. A. 68
William 25
Dungee, Eliza Jane 143
Dungey, Eliza 85
Elizabeth 116, 162
Thomas 39
Wm. 162
Dunham, John 1
Joseph 2
Dunham (cont.)
Polly 8
Rebecca 5
Dunivant, Frances 34
Dunlap, Ann 203
James 122
Mary 208
Ruth F. 178
Dunn, Albert G. 81
Alfred 181
Charity 61
David 35
Eliza 94
Eliza E. G. 64
Elizabeth 1
Jesse 27
Lewis 33
Louisa 77
M. C. 9
Margaret 119
Martha A. 98
Mary E. 169
Phenia 22
Polly 59
Susan 49
Temperance 69
Thomas 185
William A. 181
Wilson 194
Dunnagen, John 33
Dunnaway, William M. 139
Dunnegan, Jas. T. 100
Dunnevant, Abram 149
Daniel 28
Joseph 110
Patsy 63
Dunneway, Elizabeth 82
Griffin J. 100
Sam. P. 121
Dunnovent, Humphrey B. 80
Dupree, James 8
Susannah 61
Durand, Milly 200
Durande, Delila 183
Durard, Huldy 167
Joseph 190
Lewis 202
Durat, John C. 39
Duratt, Sally 64
Timothy 53
Durdon, Anthony 46
Duren, Amanda M. 188
Elizabeth 23
Durham, Drusilla 137
Eliza 199
George 190
James 202
Martha A. 204, 210
Polly 19
Durrett, Lewis 39
Duvall, Caroline A. 185
Elizabeth P. 171
Dwyer, Catherine 101
Joseph 101
Dyer, Baldy 63
Cornelia J. 151
Elizabeth 11
Joel 10
Polly 114
Rhoda 150
William H. 168
Eager, Abagail 5
Eakin, A. P. 207
Absolom 40
Elinor V. 75
Minerva A. 128
Eakin (cont.)
Myra F. 74
Nancy 42
Parmelia 115
Robert H. 12
Robt. W. 26
Sally 36
William 18, 19, 190
Eakins, Absolom 45
Avelina 94
Eliza 59
Jane 57
Peggy 38
Earhart, Abner C. 214
Catherine 155
Elizabeth 119
Harriet 212
Jacob 37
John 75
Lucinda H. 128
Mahaly 49
Mary E. 199
Mickey 201
Nancy 20, 24
Nimrod 135
Patsy 125
William L. 181
Earheart, Adam 145
Wade H. 185
Earl, Austin 64
Louisa M. 81
Ralph E. W. 48
Earls, Martha 158
Earnest, Mary 114
Earthman, Elizabeth 62
Feliz G. 202
Huldah R. 90
Isaac 53
James 24
Jane 138
Jno. H. 128
John 17
Judith 130
Lewis 15
Mary 189
Mary C. 180
Nancy 16
Nelly 25
Polly 6
S. H. 165
Sally 14, 15
Eason, John G. 31
East, Addison 69
Edward H. 32
Elizabeth 150
Lucinda 16
Malvina 169
Martha 19
Nancy P. 196
Sayly 14
Wm. A. 207
Eastell, Eliza 179
Eastes, Moses 36
Sarah 151
Eastin, Wm. 22
Eastis, Barbara 90
Eastland, Maria P. 60
Thomas 44
Eastwood, Nancy 63
Eatherly, Sallie 5
Susannah 5
Eaton, John H. 30
Martha M. 88
Merilla T. 96
Ransom W. 143
Eckols, Abraham 36
Eddington, Nancy 60
Nicholas 93

Eddington (cont.)
Rhoda 45
Edds, William 30
Edgar, Elizabeth 58
Margaret Ann 211
Mary 164
Samuel 27
Edge, Jane 55
Edgert, Issabella 64
Edgin, Jno. A. 110
Edington, Elizabeth 211
Nicholas, Jr. 65
Edmiston, Alfred 92
Eliza T. 56
Hiram 164
Martha 37, 69
Samuel 8
Edmonds, Allen T. 88
Jarmett 117
Maclin B. 87
Martha 25, 54
Mary 82
Sterling 114
Edmondson, (?) 82
Esther 68
Jenette 16
Jno. 160
Joannah 61
John 7
Louise Ann 85
Margaret 7
Nancy 20, 34
Polly 24
Robt. 38
Sally 16
W. 21
William 14
Wm. 11
Edmonson, Polly 11
Edmunds, Amelia 196
John 207
Martha 12
Edmundson, Martha Ann 201
Edney, Allison 8
Dorcas 24, 26
Edmund 153
Jesse Lee 118
Julia Ann 200
Mary J. 199
Nancy 32
Newton 106
Sally 33
Wm. 202
Edward, Balum 181
See also Balum, Edward
Polly 17
Edwards, Allison 190
Elizabeth 11, 167
Hugh 137
Jacob 2
Joseph 5
Lauson 202
Patsy 24, 26
Sally 152
Tempy 182
Egbert, Eliza 99
Egnes, Jane 21
Eichbaum, Wm. A. 81
Elam, Edward 121
James A. 185
Martha C. 202
Robt. 60
Elkin, Robert 160
Ellidge, Ambrose 115
Elliott, Clary 8
Collins D. 159, 160
Elliott (cont.)
Richard J. 214
Thomas L. 214
Elliotte, Wm. 81
Ellis, Abigail 6
Azariah 160
Catharine 196
Charlotte G. 106
Eliza Ann 206
Green 149
Haley F. 162
Jesse 126
Littleton 113
Martha 181
Nancy 120
Parthena 122
Sarah 187
Thos. 164
Travis 214
William 153
Wm. F. 119, 146
Wm. W. 214
Ellison, John 64
Nancy 104
William B. 207
Elliston, Adeline I. 75
Elizabeth 60
Harriet 38
Joseph T. 4
Joseph T., Jr. 112
Mary A. E. 123
Wm. 64
Elmore, Christopher 14
Panthea 120
Wm. A. 106
Elsbery, Fanny 212
Elverby, Lucinda 121
Elveritt, Keziah 176
Embry, Maria Louise 207
Emeerns, Ann M. 211
Emmerson, Elizabeth 62
Emmett, Catherine 205
Emmons, Cyrenus 58
England, Titus 92
English, Charles G. 194
Enlow, Polly 40
Enoch, Davis 62
Enochs, Alfred 102, 162
Marie 4
Mourning 11
Robert 16
Ensley, Enoch 70
Joanna 15
Mary P. 200
Unice 89
Epperson, J. H. 202
Epps, Martha C. 143
Paulina 180
Equals, Polly 32, 39
Silas 48
Ervin, William 7
Erwin, Amelia 174
Andrew, Jr. 59
Elizabeth 33
Frances L. 140
Hugh 158
Isaac 66
Jane 45
Jas. 107, 125
John 20
Leadicia 26
Ledicia 13
Mary 129
Nancy 42
Rebecca J. 194
William 20
Espy, Robert 155
Estes, Elizabeth R. 209
Estes (cont.)
John 56, 161
Josiah 138
Lurana 138
Nancy 108
Panther 106
Robt. P. 121
Searcy 202
Susan 184
Theodore Ann 183
Wm. C. 190
Wm. W. 67
Estin, Rachel J. 189
Estis, John 8
Parthene 118
Priscy Ann 126
Etherage, John 126
Etherly, Dickson L. 207
Eubank, Ambrose 77
Nancy 26
Eubanks, Elizabeth 35
Elizabeth Ann 192
Mary E. 205
Nancy 12, 110
Polly 38
Evan, Lewis 11
Evans, Betsy 133
Daniel 2
Deal 22
Dinah 61
Eddy 17
Edith S. 143
Elizabeth 82, 104
Elizabeth K. 30
Jas. W. 84
Jno. 117
John 2, 10
John R. 190
Lorenzo D. 94
Lucy 76
Mary S. 180
Matilda 87
Nannie 146
Polly 8, 42
Robert 7, 41
Sallie 9, 18
Sally 67
Samuel 64
Thomas W. 181
William 24, 28
Wm. 26, 61, 62
Wm. H. 145
Wm. T. 108
Everett, Blake B. 158
Drusila 1
Elizabeth 174, 186
James 7
Jesse J. 64
John 9
John B. 207
Lydia 62
Mary 60
Mary M. 190
Nancy Ann 196
Simon 29
Susan 125
Thomas 120
Everitt, Comfort 2
Dolly 10
Elizabeth 11
Kincheon 123
Sarah 115
Thomas H. 15
Eves, Solomon 87
Ewell, Elizabeth 46
Ewen, John H. 168
Sarah Caroline 178
Ewing, Andrew 154, 185

Fly (cont.)
Enoch 96
Evelina 191
Jeremiah 3
Micajah 49, 85
Polly 53
Flynn, William 1
Fogg, Francis B. 75
Godfrey M. 176
Tabitha 212
Foley, Lucy 205
Foltz, Reuben M. 207
Folwell, Arabella 124
Eliza A. 169
John 33
Fonville, Jno. B. 84
Forbes, Zadach 81
Zadok 103
Ford, James M. 176
Jno. P. 126
Mary 193
Mary E. 209
Rebecca 34, 118
Sally 159
Sarah 22
Wm. 77
Forde, Sally 79
Forehand, Allen 6
Berry Green 168
Jenny 29
John 64
Martha L. 192
Pheby 60
Richard 194
Sarah 198
Forhand, Celia 149
Elizabeth 149
Forkham, Fanny 29
Fort, Beauty 8
Fortune, Susan O. 146
Fossett, Alexander 54, 82
Eliza 75
Mary E. 211
Nancy 185
William 202
Foster, Alfred H. 168
Benj. F. 148
Devid 105
Eliza 163
Elizabeth 4, 5
Ellen J. A. 212
Ephraim H. 44
Frances A. 214
Henry W. 202
Jackson 81
James 16
Jane 58
Jane Eleanor 184
Jno. L. 72
Louisa 192
Martha 103, 131
Martha Ann 194
Mary 184
Mary Ann 209
Nancy 172
Patsy 23
Paulina 177
Polly 22
Sarah 182
Sarah W. 182
Shelton 96, 115
Susan 120
Virginia W. 105
William 153
Wm. 17
Wm. S. 96
Fottrell, A. 207
Foulks, Elizabeth 142
Wm. P. 104
Fowler, Daniel 88
Elizabeth 50
J. Smith 207
Jency 60
John H. 74
Lydia 61
Malinda 144
Margaret Ann 173
Nancy 74
Pennia 51
Polly 104
Sally 47, 60, 165
Tabitha 125
Thomas J. 169
Thornton 202
Thos. J. 71
William 8
Fowlkes, James C. 207
Jeptha 207
Jno. B. 114
Mary Ann 104
Sam'l 50
Thomas 27
Fowlks, Jno. 70
Fox, Amos 158
Eliza 179
Elizabeth 142
James 27, 156
Mary 177
Foxhall, Jas. 100
Foy, James 50
Fraley, Juliet G. 30
France, Jane 60
Frances, Harriett 187
Francis, John 31
Joseph 132
Lydia 93
Macey 43
Margaret A. 169
William 23
Franklin, Elizabeth 75
Geo. W. 181
Isaac 175, 176
James 105
Milton B. 136
Washington 163
Fraser, Daniel M. 90
Frazer, Jno. 113
John 29
Rebecca A. 179
Stephen D. 142
Frazier, Elizabeth M. 129
Ephriam 108
Lucinda 108
Mary H. 199
Moses B. 58
Sally 48
Wm. 147
Frazor, Emeline M. 52
Freas, Joel 168
Frederick, Wm. M. 138
Freeland, Mary A. M. 187
Freeman, Clinton L. 160
Elizabeth 181
J. B. 181
Jas. B. 52
Lucy 90
Smith 194
Zibiak 184
Frees, Jacob W. 190
French, Wm. B. 194
Frenleyson, Richard 7
Frensley, George W. 214
Martha 210
Frensley (cont.)
Mary Jane 153
Nancy 121
Sarah R. 145
Susan C. 135
Frensly, Susanna 3
Frey, Sally 76
Friendsley, Emily 165
Frisby, Sarah Ann 217
Fry, Catherine 29, 33
Freeman 157
Martin 190
Martin P. 214
Nancy M. 216
Thomas 15
Fryer, Alfred 63
Elizabeth 72
Minerva 161
Polly Ann 81
Samuel 169
Stockley D. 142
Fryor, John 207
Fudge, Jacob 190
John 169
Nancy 91
Sarah 110, 184
Fulcher, Edward 156, 202
Lucy 91
Lucy A. 198
William 185
Fulghum, B. F. 181
Martha G. 183
Thomas W. 181
W. W. 181
Fullbright, Alfred 190
Fuller, Chas. A. 164
Judith 132
Fullmer, Jno. S. 162
Funderburk, Sally 40
Funk, Nancy 74
Fuqua, Celia 83
Elizabeth 96
Jesse 48
Jesse M. 202
Joel 74
Joshua 37
Judy 95, 108
Mary 123
Polly 61, 68
Rebecca 91
Thomas 185
Thos. 66
Virginia 205
Wm. 39
Fuquay, John C. 190
Furneville, Mary L. 43
Furney, Elizabeth 46
Furnival, Henry L. 13
Furnveel, Nancy 101
Fursman, Beulah C. 146
Fussell, John 108
Gabriel, Elinor 13, 26
Gabwell, Mary A. 186
Gaibra, Jas. S. 131
Gailbreath, Benj. A. 207
Jane J. 207
Gainer, Jesse 56
Gaines, Malvina H. 188
Sarah E. 146
Wm. W. 48
Gains, Horace 35
Martha S. 196
Galbraith, John 10
Galbrath, Mary 147
Galbreath, John H. 190
Nancy 211
Gale, Emeline 151
Wm. D. 202

Gallager, Mary Agnes 213
Gallagher, John 181
Gallaher, America 213
Lydia T. 199
Sarah A. 186
William 190
Galliher, Mary Ann 117
Galloway, Catherine 141
Minerva 183
Samuel 122
Gambal, Elizabeth 2
Gambill, Wm. H. B. 123
Gamble, Aaron 9
James 17
Lydia 9
Gambrel, Rhody 61
Gambull, John 8
Gamer, Lamiza D. 188
Gammill, James 50
Gannaway, Archibald R. 214
Gant, Lethe 131
Garbra, Mary Ann 198
Gardette, Adele 51
Gardner, Edwin S. 190
Harriett 68
Huldy 30
John S. 44
Nancy 61
Polly 9
Sally 87
Simon 60
Stephen 60
Garet, Susan 128
Garland, Charlotte 10
Dorcas 23
Elisha 32
Elizabeth 16, 72, 185
Felix 99
Jesse 38
Kitty 42
Lucy 14
Martha 76
Mary 183
Nancy 49
Nancy D. 215
Patsy 29
Polly 76
Samuel 106, 143
Sarah 28, 185
Garna, William 45
Garner, Brice M. 163
Elizabeth W. 140
James 208
John 8
Joseph 18
Mary E. 211
Mildred A. 203
Taby 82
Thos. 143
Garnet, Mary G. 138
Garrett, Catherine 109
Elizabeth A. 152
Geo. H. 128
Greenberry 131
Jacob 10
Jonathan 60
Minerva 106
Morris 6
Nannie E. 153
Patsy 29
Richard 29
Rich'd 49
Sally 20
Sarah V. 97
Winney 64
Wm. W. 110
Garrison, Geo. W. 99
Garrison (cont.)
Rebecca 45
Garter, Peggy 47
Garvin, John 165
Gates, H. F. D. 29
Jas. 114
Gatlin, John 88
Nancy 10
Nancy L. 74
Nathan 16
Polly 11
Richard 8
Susannah 8
Thomas 19
Gatton, Wm. F. 208
Gaulding, Mary Ann 179
Wallthal 151
Gay, Edward J. 181
Henry 89, 194
Martha Ann 182
Rebecca 194
Seburr 190
Gearman, Sereana 61
Geary, Catherine C. 207
Gee, Jane 115
Jno. P. 116
Joshua I. 125
Martha 97
Norvell P. 131
Polly 8
Wm. 108
Geer, Joshua 208
Geers, John B. 164
Gentry, Polly 20, 41
Sally 23
George, McClelland 20
Wm. 56
Gerard, Wm. H. 185
Germain, Elsie 62
James 62
Tristram 62
Wm. 61
Gholson, Malinda 102
Gibbers, Matilda E. 199
Gibbons, Jno. C. 30
Gibbs, Alexander B. 185
Austin 40
David 81
Elizabeth 156, 164
Jemima 140
Louisa A. 105
Richard B. 208
Thomas 54
Gibs, Bennet H. 214
Gibson, Arabella L. 195
Araminta 28
Elizabeth 6, 22
Emily 28
Isabella 7
Isham 185
Jas. M. 43
John S. 55
Joseph F. 135
Lorenzo 137
Nancy 135
Newsom 181
Polly 12, 25
Robert 18
Robt. 76, 155
Wm. 60
Gilbert, Ester 205
George 177
James 31
Thomas 37
Wilson 51
Gilchrist, Malcolm J. 214
Phillip P. 214
Gill, Ann 203
Francis 107
George 59
Michael S. 169
Thomas 39
Gillam, Edward 185
Julia 30
Gillaspey, Elizabeth 13
Gillaspie, Elizabeth 74
Gillespie, Elizabeth 26
John 10
Robt. 59
Gilliam, Ann 201
Eliza 127
Emily 122
Fanny 210
Frances 181
James 23
Mary 134
Rebecca 19
Rebecca I. 130
Sarah Ann 153
Wm. L. 148
Gilliland, Nancy 10
Gillman, Alsenia L. B. 202
Amanda M. 186
Eliza M. 197
Hannah 156
Sarah Ann 156
Gillum, Martha R. 208
Gilman, Jane 148
Jane G. 147
Jas. S. 119
Jesse P. 185
Timothy W. 42
Gilmore, John 86
Gingery, Catherine 42
Polly 14
Gingrey, Catharine S. 194
Gingrick, Barbara 14
Givins, Edwin L. 169
Glascock, E. R. 162
Glasgow, Cornelius 1
Geo. W. 123
Isaac L. 79
Jesse 149
Jno. C. 96
Lenora K. 106
Mary 78
Rutha 35
Susan 45
Wm. 88, 114
Glass, Elizabeth 183
Hannah 24, 26
John 19
Patsy 32
Peggy 33
Robert 185
Glavis, Elizabeth 63
Glazier, Charles 194
Gleason, Hannah 14
Gleaves, Albert G. 202
Betsy 39
Elizabeth 87, 137
Elizabeth T. 134
Felix R. 185
Isabella 45
James T. 181
Jas. R. 72
John 30
John Ewing 214
Martha 120
Martha Ann 114
Mary Ann 206
Mary Ann D. 128
Mary D. 8
Matthew 23

Gleaves (cont.)
Michael 32
Michael H. 128
Nancy A. 103
Sally W. 80
Sarah 157
Sophia P. 136
Thomas 4
Thos., Jr. 45
Thos. W. 214
Glenn, Mary C. 187
Glennarrey, Edward 60
Glisson, Thos. G. 83
Glover, James H. 181
Godsey, Mary Ann 52
Goff, Andrew F. 194
Goldin, Elizabeth 201
Goldsberry, Elizabeth C. 12, 25
Peggy 28
Polly 21
Goldsby, Joseph 58
Gooch, Jane 106
Goode, Mary Ann 130
Goodlet, Adam G. 132
Robert 177
Goodlett, Margaret 78
Robt. D. 214
Wm. C. 214
Goodlott, Adam G. 51
Goodman, Albert G. 208
Lidia 12, 25
Thomas 202
Goodner, Ann C. 135
Cynthia 165
Goodnough, Isiah 48
Goodrich, Caleb 181
Cynthia 195
Edmund W. 118
Edwin W. 194
Eliza S. 91
Elizabeth 108
Harrison 139, 208
Hays 190
Jane C. 186
Jas. M. 107
Lucy Ann 118
Mariah C. 83
Mary 92
Mary A. 104
Parilee 216
Polly 23, 27
Reuben 208
Robt. C. 83
Sterling W. 104
Thomas C. 163
Goodrick, Caleb 169
Goodwin, Elenor 144
George 45
George B. 190
Green B. 141
J. V. 202
John 23
Julia 215
Lavinia 27
Martin P. 177
Mary Ann 141
Michael 20
Nancy 25, 86
Polly 93
Sally 28
Sarah 22, 60
Susan M. 168
Tabitha 21
Walker 169
Wm. W. 40
Gorby, Lewis H. 214
Gordon, Caledonia 134
Gordon (cont.)
James 65, 144
Jane 68
Jenette 199
Mary Ann 175
Gorham, Thomas 7
Gorin, Franklin 185
Gorman, James O. 113
Wm. E. 119
Goss, Jno. D. 118
Gossage, Charles 21
Gotton, Nancy 59
Gowan, Minerve 84
Gowdy, Anna 210
Gowen, Alfred 214
Amanda M. 81
John 9
John J. 73
Jos. 62
Maria 105
Rhody 16
Wilford B. 91
William 7
Gower, Abel B. 107
Alexander 17
Alexander C. 169
Charlotte 175
Edmund 165
Elijah 8
Elisha 47
Elisha 165
Elishua 14
Eliza Ann 185
Elizabeth 113
Emily 118
Engley 11
Franky 67
Jane 54
Joel 134
John J. 169
Joseph 136
L. T. 214
Levinia 132
Lewis G. 104
Lorenzo D. 74
Lucretia 187
Lucy Ann 179
Martha 89
Mary 134
Minerva 146
Nancy 13, 25
Patsy 45, 114
Peggy 88
Polly 4
Prudence 4, 124
Robt. 61
Russell 93
Samuel 13, 25
William 10
Wilson 32, 60
Wm. 34
Wm. G. 32
Wm. T. 125
Gowers, Sarah 144
Gradden, Elizabeth 171
Graham, Barbara 116
Bell Ann 149
Elizabeth 71, 130
Hannah 201
James 13
Jane 84, 139
Jno. 116
Lavinia 132
Margaret 86, 187
Mary 128
Polly 93
Reuben P. 52, 77
Robert 169
Graham (cont.)
Sarah 8
Sarah A. 192
Susannah 22
Grainger, Jacob 129
Grammas, James 152
Granet, Peter 181
Grant, Elizabeth 10
Francis 142
Geo. 55
John 41, 190
Joseph 181
Mary 78
Graves, David 108
Franky 16
Henry 22
Jane B. 30
Louisa C. 195
Martha 95
Martha C. 168
Richard E. 164
Sarah W. 113
Sherrod G. 144
Susan 119
Susannah 16, 22
Gravett, Mary Jane 163
Gravis, Thos. F. 97, 126
Grawosz, Thos. F. 98
Gray, Deliverance 7
Henry W. 144
Jackson 97
Jane 87
John G. 169
Joseph 6
Lovey 87
Mary H. 123
Mason I. 131
Pierce 137
Polly 13
Serena 46
William F. 214
Young A. 11
Grayson, Henry 121
Green, A. M. 190
Abraham 5
Alex'd L. P. 123
Almanza 189
Anne 36
Asa 6
Chapman S. 208
David 214
Elizabeth 23, 140, 193
Ellen 218
Enos J. 208
Gardner 140
George 190
George W. 177
Hansel 129
Henry 2, 144
Hiram 128
Isiah D. 55
James 5, 101
James H. 122
James M. 151
James P. 169
Jane 170
Jas. H. 144
Jas. W. 133
Jno. B. 114
Jonathan 131
L. S. S. 147
Lavena 190
Littleton 10
Lucretia 140
Martha 55
Mary 31
Mary E. 213
Myra 67

Haines (cont.)
Charles 156
Harriet 40
Hainey, Samuel 27
Hainson, Thos. T. 125
Halbert, John B. 214
Haldeman, Jno. 88
Hale, Adeline Tennessee 192
Charles G. 185
Jefferson 214
Lority 210
Thomas C. 185
Thomas J. 208
Hales, Olina 215
Haley, Ann 137, 168
Elizabeth 141
James 197
John 177
Nicholas S. 197
Phebe 167
Robt. F. 214
Thomas 169
William 208
Hall, Allen A. 105, 126
Anestine 162
Ann 113
Chas. M. 23, 39
Christina C. 200
Edward 198
Elisha 68
Elisha S. 21
Elishu S. 92
Eliza 54
Elizabeth 72, 218
Elizabeth A. 159, 160
Emily E. 137
George 6
Henry 124, 137
James 25
Jno. 134
John 190
John B. 38
Joseph R. 215
Lucy 36
Martha 52, 164
Mary 159
Mary Ann 138
Matilda 190
Nancy 42
Nancy A. 203
Polly 62
Richard 162
Robt. B. 123
Sam'l S. 154
Sarah 29, 142
Sophia W. 135
Susan A. 207
Tabitha 15
Theodorich 117
Theodrich 145
Wm. 214
Wm. M. 151
Hallahar, Sarah Ann 133
Halley, Josiah C. 177
Halliday, Alex'd 71
Halloway, Charity 180
Jane 179
Mary Ann 182
Hallum, Letitia 167
Nancy 168
Rebecca 185
William 181
Hallums, Jane 68
Hally, John 162
Halsey, Sally 20
Halstead, Parmer 7
Haly, Wm. 177
Ham, Annira 196
Elijah 75
Eliza B. 181
Mary 120
Mildred 44
Mortimer R. 181
Hamblen, Benjamine F. 185
Mary Ann 155
Hambrick, Jerry 154
Hamelton, James W. 169
Hamilson, Margaret 32
Hamilton, Absolom 99
Andrew McNairy 215
Elizabeth 102
Geo. T. 80
Gorge F. 190
Hamadither 150
James D. 10
James M. 195
Jane 29
Jas. 95
John 7, 63
Martha O. 163
Mary A. 182
Mortimer 177
Susan 212
Thos. 54
William 194
Wm. H. 23
Hamlet, Narcissa 168
Sally 6
Hammer, Daniel 62
Hammon, Elizabeth 91
Hammond, Eli 62
Hammonds, Charlott T. 167
Hampton, Anthony 3
Benj. 208
Benjamine 186
Elizabeth 5
Nancy 20
Wm. 208
Hams, Charles G. 182
Hancock, Dorrie A. 169
Handoin, Jno. W. 105
Handy, Edward S. 190, 195
Hanes, Elizabeth 4
Haney, Fanny 119
Samuel 6
Hanks, A. I. 170
A. J. 164
Jackson 150
Joshua 50
Martha 176
Nancy 61
Richard 32
Hannah, Annie 18
Benj. F. 63
Caroline 191
Eliza 75
Green 215
Jas. H. 38
John 40
Joseph 190
Lucinda 213
Nancy 184
Narcissa 189
Patsy 34
Sallie 11
Susannah 11
Wm. 38
Hannum, Washington L. 18
Hans, Eliza M. 44
Hard, Joseph F. 177
Hardcastle, Philip F. 177
Hardeman, Eleazer 4
Franklin 142
Harder, Marinda 115
Hardgrave, Johnston 74
Sally 96
Hardgrove, Lewis 43
Skelton 33
Hardiman, Nancy 1
Hardin, Amanda P. 75
Howard D. 22
Wm. 19
Harding, David M. 38
Elizabeth V. 95
Enoch 215
George W. 170
Giles 18, 33
Job 144
John 13, 22
Judith 17
Margaret 105
Patsy 11
Polly 13, 14
Rachel N. 187
Sally 25, 57
Thos. 56
Wm. 115, 208
Wm. G. 111
Hardy, Levinia 42
Nancy 49
Sally 56
Thomas 31
Thos. G. 202
Wm. 36, 114
Harff, Henry 198
Hargrave, John 24
Wm. H. 195
Hargrove, John 26
Katy 9
Sallie 9
Sally 4
Harkin, Ann 6
Harkreader, Jacob 20
Sylvester 169
Harley, Jacob 25
Harlin, Joshua 1
Matilda 36
Harlow, Clanto 209
Levi 126
Maria 48
Harman, A. J. R. 165
Amanda 200
Jefferson 110
Margaret 108
Mary 200
Penelope 183
Rachel 10
William 190
Harmon, Hardiman 53
John 85
Rich'd 129
Sarah 129
Thomas 8
Thos. R. 77
Harn, Minerva W. 115
Harness, Jno. 126
Richard 8
Harney, Geo. W. 62
Janey 21
Perry 98
Harnley, Margaret O. 56
Harp, Amy A. 202
W. 198
Harpe, Nathaniel 90
Harper, Bretain 29
Elizabeth 206

Harper (cont.)
Isaac P. 190
James 177, 208
John M. 198
Mary Ann 209
Mary C. 138
Nancy 23
Patsy 43
Priscilla 113
Sally 49
Sterling J. S. 114
Wm. 97
Harr, McDonald 182
Harral, Cadar 35
Harrie, William O. 169
Harrin, Abimelech 14
Harrington, Abijah 1
Whitmell 91
Harris, Achsah B. 192
Agnes P. 167
Agness 13
Alcey 22
Alfred M. 30
Allen P. 161
Ann 136, 217
Ann E. 173
Archy 177
Asa 36
Catharine S. 216
David P. 132
Eliza 150
Elizabeth 98, 113, 167
Elizabeth M. 212
Ethelrel 66
Felix A. 195
Fleming 113
Gideon 110
Howell 66, 92
Howell G. 33
Isaac 16
J. Geo. 190
James 50, 126, 144
James H. 112
Jane 165
Jno. B. 163
Jno. L. 91
Jno. P. 156
John 3, 177
John B. 161, 190
John H. 190
John W. 208
Laura 169
Levina 55
Littleberry 90
Louisa 157
Louise 120
Margaret 147
Martha W. 160
Mary 4, 20
Matilda 183
Matthew 38, 129
Michael 12, 25
Parmenia 23
Polly 43, 74
Prescilla 66
Rebecca 46
Rebecca N. 50
Robt. B. 110
Roxina 151
Sally 6, 12, 25, 43, 72
Sam'l B. 62
Sarah 143, 158, 199
Sarah E. 57
Susannah 19, 36
T. B. 198
Thomas A. 170, 202
Thomas I. 169
Harris (cont.)
Thomas K. 15
Wallace 37
Westley B. 170
William 28
Willie 14
Wm. 49, 90, 112, 113, 130, 146
Wm. H. 159
Harrison, Caleb G. 161
Eliza B. 133
Elizabeth 197
Emily 69, 203
Frances Ann 191
James W. 195
Jno. E. 110
John 12, 25, 39
Joseph P. 170
Lidia 4
Louisa 141, 200
Martha A. N. 199
Mary 201, 204
Mary Ann 152
Mary E. 168, 171
Nancy 139
Noah 215
Peggy 33
Richard P. 195
Robert 177
Rolla 147
Sally 13, 121
Sarah Jane 195
Sterling 177
Thomas 13, 144
Thos. B. 152
William 23, 27
Wm. 153
Wm. B. 198
Wm. G. 177
Wm. H. 114
Zachriah 30
Harrod, Barnebeth 3
Thos. 53
Harrold, Cade 215
Harsh, Louisa 201
Sarah A. 208
Hart, Charles 24, 26
Elinor H. 83
Eliza T. 152
Ellen R. 195
Emily 210
Jane I. 142
Jesse 151
Jno. H. 163
John 41, 190
Joseph 2
Lodocia R. 183
Mark 61
Mary 216
Micajah 122
Nancy 211
R. W. 20
Richard 19
Wm. D. 135
Hartgrave, Susannah 4
Hartley, Amanda 182
Eliza A. 151, 154
Geo. W. 195
Hartman, Andrew 83
Elizabeth 180
Hettie 208
James 150
Martha 150
Mary 35
Minerva 190
Sarah 117
Hartmen, Peggy 47
Hartsfield, William 177
Harvey, Finey 55
Mary 18
Susan 76
Weltha 89
Willie 36
Harwell, Frederick 49, 110
James F. 198
Logan D. 203
Harwood, Catherine 19
Elizabeth 35
John 65
Mary 96
Peggy 11
Richard D. 190
Sarah 50
Susan 18
Wm. 5
Hastie, Bridget 71
Hatcher, Elijah 100
Ethelbert H. 195
Sarah R. 203
Hathaway, Ann 58
Wm. 58
Hawkins, Isham 177
Jacob 190
James 42
James M. 208
Julia 116
Nathan 157
Rich'd 195
Robt. 107
Sarah E. 193
Willis M. 140
Haws, Kitty 92
Hawthorne, Catherine 73
Hay, Barbara 37
David P. 14
Joseph W. 18
Haydant, Clement 215
Hayes, Adelicia 175
Anna 63
Celia 12
Charles 11
Chas. 7
David 69
Esther 53
George 135
James 10
John 69
Nancy 8
Rachel 20
Sarah 25
Wm. 67
Zachariah T. 182
Haymer, Mary 181
Haynes, Aaron 119
Catherine 122
Elizabeth 148
Elizabeth J. 184
Lucy 177
Mary Jane 210
Robert S. 106
Stephen 42
Thomas W. 182
William F. 182
Hayns, Mary 177
Hays, Ann 157
Ann C. 132
Anna 62
Balaam 19
Barbara 28
Blackman 84, 89, 195
Charles M. 195
David 59
Henry 41
Issabella 134
Jane 7

Hays (cont.)
Jno. C. 64
Lucy 19
Mary 35
Mary P. 149
Nancy 43
Nancy E. 184
Patsy T. 27
Robt. 99
Sally 14
Stockley D. 27
Tabitha 73
William 44
Haythorn, William 1
Haywood, Eliza 64
Harriet 20
Martha M. 51
Thos. 45
Hazelings, Wm. 126
Hazlerig, Martha 126
Head, Amelia A. 181
Ann 94
Heard, Stephen 15
Hearn, Ann 148
Ebenezer 138
Heath, Alcey 156
Edward 202
James T. 208
Julia 212
Heaton, Amos 202
Cany 217
Elizabeth 32
Enoch 1, 10
Lucinda 42
Mary 59, 104
Polly 3
Prudence 73
Sally 5, 12, 26
Susan 69
Thomas 1
Heatwell, John 186
Heckling, Polly 11
Hedenberg, Charles J. 186
Hedgepath, Sally 54
Hedspeth, Milly 30
Hefferman, Wm. 202
Hegan, John 215
Heiss, John P. 190
Helbourne, Nancy 44
Helburn, Docas 22
Hellums, Minerva 141
Patsy 55
Hemphill, William 5
Henderson, Chastina 307
James 191
Penelope 182
Rebecca 3
Robert 18
Sarah 203
Wm. A. 208
Hendley, Rebecca 218
Henly, James 198
Henning, Joseph 169
Henrie, John M. 169
Henry, Alexander 34
Harriet 144
Hugh 63
John 95, 182, 208
Thomas S. 182
Wm. 202
Wm. P. 202
Henson, James H. 182
Wm. 33
Herbert, Rosanna 102
Vincent 44
Herbison, John 32
Herculus, Sally 10
Herd, George 70
Herman, Duncan N. 155
Herndon, Joseph 61
Herod, Margaret 168
Heron, Mathew 186
Wm. R. 182
Herren, Joseph 72
Herrin, Chas. J. 161
George T. 186
Harriet P. 218
Mary N. 172
Sarah 90
Herring, Beverly 40, 146
Solomon 29
Westley 186
William 27
Wm. 23
Herrod, Mary 173
Herron, Bannistine E. 119
Hester, David 122
Mary 158
Hewgley, Elvira 115
Jno. W. 177
Hewitt, Ann E. 92
Caroline C. 116
Emily D. 46
Hazael 60
Matilda R. 55
Hewlett, George 30
Marie A. 163
Martha A. T. 113
Taylot 182
William 148
Wm. 147
Hewsom, Ann E. 65
Heyl, Lewis J. 138
Hibdon, Andy 163
Hickenbottom, Wm. 22
Hickerson, Anne 27
Mary 180
Warner 147
Hickey, Calvin M. 129
Caroline J. 146
Mary Jane 180
Hicklance, Betsy 24
Hickman, Barbara Jane 169
Betsy 8
Jane 11
John P. 36
Lucy 186
Susannah N. 24
Hicks, Alfred H. 186
Conrad 202
David 208
Edward D. 116
Gensy 67
John C. 31
Marvell 56
William 10
Hiett, Granthom 113
Higdon, James 8
Higginbotham, Jno. R. 177
Mary Ellen 186
Reubin 36
Wm. 161
Higgins, Margaret 54
Peter 177
Polly 53
William 25
Wm. H. 101
Hight, C. (Doctor) 150
Hightower, Richard 2
Hiland, Geo. W. 114
Henry I. 76
Hiland (cont.)
Joseph B. 75
Hill, Alexander 186
Alianna 114
Ann C. 69
Daniel B. 126
Darcus 60
Elizabeth 31, 48, 72, 101
Emilene 177
Isaac 141
Isaac A. 195
Ishobod 198
James 3
James J. 72
James S. 114, 191
Jas. S. 162
Jno. M. 79
Jno. T. 101
John 24, 26, 151
John H. 131
Lucinda 45
Marcus R. 117
Margaret C. 208
Mary Jane 141
Nancy 47
Robert 141
Robert T. 195
Robt. S. 87
Roda 172
Samuel 156, 202
Sarah P. 107
Thomas 5, 31
William 195
William G. 191
William M. 208
Williams 142
Wm. 31, 113
Wm. G. 166
Wm. W. 95, 154
Hillburn, Ambrose 29
Sally 24
Hillsman, Charles E. 195
Hilton, Daniel 3
Hinchy, John 177
Hiney, Jacob 60
Hinkle, Elizabeth 44
Peter 92
Hinson, Harriett O. 193
Hinton, Elizabeth A. 75
Harrison B. 122, 163
Jeremiah 7
Jno. J. 68
Sarah Ann 109
Sarah E. 216
Wm. M. 58
Hise, Elijah 130
Hitchcock, L. H. 215
Hite, Henry 122
Hiram 82
Horatio 142
Lebron 186
Louisa 182
Mary Ann 132
Robt. C. 160
Samuel 78, 112
Thos. H. 182
Hitt, James S. 88
Lavenia R. 205
Hixon, Elijah 2
Hobbs, Collin S. 51
Edward 69
Elizabeth 68
Elizabeth J. 180
Jno. N. 198
Julia 130
Littleberry 39
Mary 18

Hopper (cont.)
Classie 121
Elizabeth 59
John 57
Sarah 115
Thomas 26, 90
Winney R. 104
Wm. 13
Horn, Berry 74
Caroline 156
Charlotte 50
Elizabeth 151, 208
Emily 212
Henry 93
Jackson C. 208
Joseph 115, 215
Lewis 88
Littleton 153
Louisa 157
Mary E. 214
Matthew 78
Sarah 17
Stephen H. 97
Thomas 215
William 190, 194
Wm. H. 42
Horney, Perry 147
Horton, Anna W. 191
Elizabeth 190
Ellen D. 162
Jas. W. 36
Jennette 32
Kitty 33
Nancy G. 31
Rachel 5
Robinson 121
Wm. D. 79
Hosford, John 85
Hoskins, Robt. T. 144
Hough, Thos. J. 208
Wm. 198
Hous, Elizabeth 112
House, Ambrose 135
Eliza 57
Jacob 79
Jesse 34
Joseph 24, 26
Laurahanny 133
Nancy 190
Ruhama 130
Winnie 143
Housely, Stephen T. 91
Houser, Amelia A. 217
Charles F. 169
Johanna F. 197
John G. 194
Housley, Cathenne M. 198
Houton, Daniel 51
Hoven, Mary 99
How, Lucinda 116
Howard, Caroline 217
Elizabeth C. 110
Ellen 165
James 118
Mimmecan H. 130
Sarah A. 216
Howell, Elizabeth 3
James 47
Margaret 104
Peggy 6
Samuel 35
Willie 14
Zack 191
Hower, Tennessee 172
Howerton, Catherine B. 164
P. 157
Howerton (cont.)
Prithey P. 154
Howington, James W. 152
Willis 68
Howlett, Addison B. 156
Ann M. 107
Dorinda T. 118
Florida 149
Isaac 31
Jane 98, 156
Mary Jane 172
Stockley H. 110
Susan 141
Wm. B. 195
Hows, Brinkley 142
John 163
Lovahanna 131
Rasa 140
Howsley, Alexander 52
Hubbard, David 203
Hubbell, Wm. T. 90
Hubble, Lucretia 111
Hubbs, Barri 49
Huddleston, Baldwin 3
Hudgins, John 65
Nancy 43
Pharvale 40
Hudleman, Samira H. 207
Hudnall, Elizabeth 152
Thomas, Jr. 169
Thos. 152
Hudson, Adam B. 8
Cindarilla 15
Hepsee 8
Jane 21
Jno. T. 78
Joseph 130
Martha P. 74
Mary 108
Polly 21
Richard 139
Wesley 14
Wm. 1
Wm. G. 151
Huff, John 105, 137
Huffman, Delana 200
Elizabeth 38
George 58
Lurana R. 194
Matilda 184
Solomon 104
Terrissa 176
Wm. 82
Huffner, John 191
Huggins, Chas. 62
Elizabeth 54
Francis M. 154
Issabella 129
Jno. 81
Jonathan 57
Margaret 162
Nancy F. 185
Priscilla 73
Robt. 88
Sally 20
Hugh, Haffy 150
Hughes, Andrew J. 178
Champness 14, 55, 78
James 203
James H. 182
John 56
John F. 195
Judith 2, 6
Lynch 115
Martha 213
Matilda 77
Missouri 168
Nancy 23
Hughes (cont.)
Narcissa 158
Oliver 146
Patsy 7
Sally 45
Sarah 117, 129
Wm. 46
Hughs, Claiborne W. 132
Matilda 111
Hugle, Mary 17
Huie, Richard 72
William 29
Huison, Philip 62
Hulett, Sarah 168
Hull, John M. 208
Hullett, Zilpha 171
Hume, Alfred 142
Eliza M. 147
Fountain 111
Jane W. 112
Jno. K. 215
Mary A. 179
Humerithhouse, Mary 126
Humphrey, Wilson 73
Humphreys, Mary A. 183
Patsy 58
Samuel 155
West H. 175
Humphries, Daniel 35
Patsy 73
Reuben 99
Sarah B. 190
Willie J. 46
Wm. 91
Humphrys, Julius 152
Hunt, A. M. 198
Betsy 193
Elizabeth R. 207
Enoch J. 215
Holbert D. 208
Louisa 191
Mary Ann 143
Mary S. 3
Matthew 7
Nancy 175
Robertson M. 182
Sion 5
Theodoric 22
Tilman S. 119
William C. 182
Wm. C. 165
Hunter, David 17
Henry 203
Isaac 73
Jacob 147
Jno. T. 74
Manuel 19
Margaret J. 211
Mary A. 207
Mary M. 211
Matthew R. 88
Peggy 67
Polly 21
Sally 21, 53
Huntsinger, Jacob 95
Hupp, Philip 6
Hurt, Benjamin 67
Charity 41
Elizabeth 64
F. A. 198
Floyd 27
Henry 49
Jno. 113
John 191
Judy 47
Martha 98
Phillips 20
Prudence 90

Hurt (cont.)
Sarah 82
Sarah Ann 116
William 40
Wm. 107, 112
Wm. C. 198
Huston, Ann C. 168
John 30
Sarah 20
Hutchens, Mary 3
Hutchings, Lemuel 22
Rachel D. 13
Hutchinson, Mary Jane 207
Sally 102
Susannah 34
Hutchison, Wm. 90
Hutson, Robt. 74
Hutton, Charles 14
Charles P. 22
Mary 22
Mary G. 149
Samuel 35
T. W. 215
Thos. W. 208
Wm. B. 116
Wm. D. 137
Hyde, Benjamin 23
Caroline L. 157
Charlotte G. 89
Edmond 35
Edmund 107
Elibeth H. 151
Henry 62
John 62
Jordon 83
Joseph H. 203
Maria W. 76
Mary D. 109, 145
Polly 10
Rebecca 9
Richard 35
Sally 11
Susanna 186
Tazewell 37, 104
William O. 186
Hynes, Andrew 42
Lavina 181
Lavinia 181
Margaret 154
Ichmon, Meranda 128
Ingram, Henry 21
Sally 66
Inman, Elizabeth 17, 78
Katie 30
Lazarus 65
Mary 69
Matilda 160
Pricilla 18
Thomas J. 170
Innman, Polly 24, 27
Insel, Thomas 91
Inyard, Rosetta 107
Irby, Fanny 31
Levica 111
Iredale, Elizabeth 179
Jane M. 163
Maria L. 196
Sarah B. 48
Iredell, Mary Ann 32
Irley, Annie C. 30
Irwin, David 44
James 141
Jas. 134
Nancy 74
Isham, Strong 84
Ivans, Sarah 181
Ivey, Isaac 124
Jencey 81
John 19
Wilson 132
Ivy, Frederick 11
Jabe, James 29
Jackman, Woodson 203
Jackson, Abijah H. 165
Abner 94
Abraham 46, 82
Alexander 30
Andrew 2
Ann 76
Ann Mariah 187
Anne 5
Betsy 9
Burrel 98
Calvin 198
Daniel B. 105
Dyer 60
Elizabeth 103, 120, 130
Hardy 85
Harriet H. 211
Henry 20, 186, 203
Jacob D. 95
James 18
Jane 112
Jas. 136
Jno. T. 118
John 5
Judith 94
Kindred 88
Levin E. 160
Lucas 96
Malinda 182
Mary 94
Mary W. 94
Matthew 35, 82
Nancy 82, 137
Polly 14, 50
Rachel 5
Robert C. 208
Sally 14, 22, 43
Samuel 75
Sarah 90, 128
Susannah 25
Thomas 11, 175
Warren 106
Washington 122
Wiley 105
William 26, 170
Wm. 12, 14, 38, 96, 135, 203
Wm. F. 215
Wm. H. 209
Wm. J. 215
Wm. James 198
Wm. O. 132
Woodson 94
James, Amos 17
Ann 76, 142
Joshua 21
Louisa Jane 212
Lyman 83
Margaret 14
McAlister 4
Patsy 68
Rhoda 38
Sarah T. 205
Smith 52
Thomas 4, 18
Thomas C. 170
Thos. H. 119
William 40
Wm. 62, 80
Jameson, James 17
Jamison, David S. 82
Jamison (cont.)
Rich'd 127
Jarnegan, Carey 132
Jarnett, Nathan G. 152
Jarratt, Maria A. 195
Jefferies, Stephen 143
Jefferson, Anne S. 126
Eliza 71
Frances A. 125
Henry 77
John R. 186
Lydia 132
Sarah 71
Thos. 53
Thos. B. 95
Jeffreys, Mary E. J. 215
Jeffries, Henry 138
Jelton, Jane R. W. 127
Jenkins, Dan'l W. 191
George 144, 186
Hiram 17
James H. 191
John W. 215
Lewis 182
Manot J. 205
Robt. 119
William 182
Jennett, Ann 183
Harvey 92
Joseph 182
Robinson 178
Jennings, Ann E. 105
Emeline 110
Isaac 141
Isaac R. 135
Mary S. 154, 157
Rebecca 155
William 17, 182
Wm. R. 195
Jent, James N. 158
Jernagin, Juda 197
Jessup, Lethia 188
Wm. 110
Jewell, Joseph 54
Mary Elizabeth 83
Wm. C. 74
Job, Andrew 44
Robert 41
Jobe, Mary 31
Jobes, Wm. 83
John, Diamond 41
Johns, Elizabeth 7
Joel 111
John 19
Judith 29
Louisa S. 80
Nancy 37
Patsy 50
Sally 62
Sarah H. 132
Wm. 50
Johnson, A. W. 170
Albert 170
Allen J. 170
Amanda 100, 182
America 209
Anderson 100
Andrew M. 41
Ann L. 162
Artinusa T. 206
Benjamin 203
Catherine W. 205
Celia 163
Daniel A. 215
Drusilla 117
Eliza W. 155
Elizabeth 135, 185, 192, 200

Johnson (cont.)
Ellonnora H. 202
Esquire 125
Exum 14
Frances 150, 206
Fredonia 138
George A. 178
George J. 132
Irena 171
Isaac 101
Isham 139
James 97
James F. 198
Jane 105, 152
Jane P. 218
Jas. 114
Jesse 79
Jno. 128
John 28
John A. 215
John W. 163
Joseph 109
Joseph H. 107
Judith 47
Lewis 112
Louisa 118
Lucinda J. 175
Malinda 172, 188
Margaret 104
Martha 117, 163, 199
Mary 192, 198
Mary D. 179
Miles 209
Nancy 142
Nancy L. 216
Nimrod 115
Parmenus 170
Polly 91, 98
Rachel 156
Richard 203
Robert 146
Sally 81, 130
Sarah Ann 196
Susan 177
Sydney L. 178
Tabitha 151
Thomas H. 178
Ursula 12
William D. 186
Wills 178
Wm. 133
Wm. A. 195
Wm. H. 136
Wm. J. 115
Johnston, Abraham 6
Anthony W. 73
Barbara 38
Bettie 5
Burrell P. 112
Casey 39
Charity 7
Charles 28
Elenor 72
Elizabeth 1, 6, 18, 57, 108
Fanny 30, 77
Gabriella 16
Hannah 72
James 62, 143
Jane 123
Jas. 78
Jennie 2
John 3, 4, 28, 55, 77
John L. 146
Joseph 4
Lucinda 37
Lucinda L. 155
Johnston (cont.)
Martha 61
Mary T. 64
Matilda 174
Matthew 11, 15
Miles 91
Nancy 7, 50, 58, 63
Parmelia 79
Patsy 30
Polly 9, 22
Rich'd 56
Robert 24
Rosanna 26
Rosannah 12
Sally 19, 62, 92
Sarah 3
Sophia 49
Stephen 22
Susan 58
Susannah 43
Tabitha 44
Joiner, Jesse 195
Susannah 31
Wm. 131
Jonas, James 66
Jones, Alexander 38
Almeda 204
Almeta 188
Ann 94
Ann W. 181
Aquilla 8
Benj. B. 51
Benjamine F. 186
Betsy 24, 26
Caleb 76, 147
Catherine 154, 163
Catherine E. 40
Charlotte 20
Chas. A. 133
Coleman 170
Daniel 149
Dempsey 31
Dorothy 21
Edmund 198
Eliza 41, 63, 129, 153
Eliza J. 187
Elizabeth 8, 16, 39, 68, 74, 84, 180, 181
Elizabeth D. 192
Elizabeth M. 195
Elizabeth W. 144
Esther 148
Fanny 27, 123
Frances 188
George F. 203
George W. 209
Harriet 153
Harry 209
Holloway 145
Isaac 24, 26
Isaac M. 215
James 209
James P. 182
James W. 191
Jane 21, 91
Jarvis 22
Jas. C. 110
Jefferson 156
Joel L. 143
Jno. 116
Jno. H. 98
John 19, 30, 191
John N. S. 64
John S. 209
John T. 178
Joseph J. 170
Joseph W. 106
Jones (cont.)
Juby Ann 169
Judith 18
Julia 153, 192
Lewis 57, 150
Lucy 194
Malon L. 170
Maria 77
Mariah 180
Martha 20, 128
Martha Ann 77
Martha S. R. 67
Mary 158
Mary Jane 198
Mary P. 204
Moses 191
Nancy 57
Nancy E. 148
Nancy S. 124
Olley 22
Pinkney 178
Polly 23, 69
Rebecca 56
Redding B. 46
Richard H. 186
Robert H. 170
Sally 39, 90
Sally A. 23
Samuel P. 198
Sarah 95, 178
Shadrack 10
Sion 152
Solomon 20
Spotwood A. 170
Squire 203
Susan 180
Susannah 45
Tempo 7
Thomas 96, 148
Thomas J. 198
William 33
Willie 64
Wm. 15, 203
Wm. S. 195
Jonte, Catharine F. 169
Harreit 211
Jordan, Avelina 53
Elizabeth 107
James M. 203
Jessee 186
Lavinia 38
Lucy F. 142
Mary 65
Mary A. 186
Minerva 170
Norfleet 105
Sally 71
William 215
Jordon, Benjamin 39
John J. 215
Sally 101
Joseph, Isaac 195
Joslin, Amandy R. 179
Burgess 28
Daniel 23, 65
Dinah 48
Elizabeth 17, 22
Gabriel 9
James 30
Lavinia 39
Mary Ann 178
Nancy 62
Nancy B. 148
Nannie B. 147
Richard 39
Temperance C. 199
Thomas 203
Wm. 22

Levy (cont.)
William 44
Lewallen, Mary 54
Lewis, Ambrose G. 49
Archibald 62
Bede 50
Benjamin F. 171
Charlotte 58
Eliza W. 61
Elizabeth B. 97
George 32
John 43
Margaret 31
Margaret A. 193
Mary Louisa 83
Mary W. 32
Miriam 48
Myra E. 30
Nathan 95
Sallie 9
Samuel 31
Sarah T. 5
Seth 1
Utility W. 138
W. P. 216
Washington 99
Wm. 82
Wm. B. 31
Wm. C. 59
Lie, Judith 19
Lightfoot, Henry 72
Thos. 5
Lile, Daniel 11
Henry 61
Lucinda 57
Polly 57
Sophia 93
Liles, Deborah 8
Malachi 9
Mary 21
Robert 17
Linch, Arren 130
James 10
Linck, Joseph 75
Lincoln, George M. 198
Lindsay, Lewis 186
Lindsey, Nathaniel L. 186
Lindsley, A. V. S. 170
Nathaniel L. 186
Linex, Malinda A. 217
Lingon, Siotha P. 218
Lingow, Catharine M. 185
Link, Francis 84
John W. 178
Levica 46
Mary 72
Linn, Almeda A. 197
Joseph 17
Linne, Polexancy T. 198
Linton, Alson 29
James 76
Joannah 68
Kizziah 20
Nancy 106
Polly 11
Samuel 45
Silas 56
Wm. 83
Lischer, George S. 186
Lishey, Louis C. 182
Lisle, George W. 9
Lissick, Polley 181
Liston, Wm. J. 195
Little, Belinda 89
Elizabeth 69
Jno. C. 137
Little (cont.)
John 50
Joseph H. 42
Nancy 94, 115
Neal 31
Sarah 62, 85
Littleberry, Williams 28
Littlepage, Frances 23
Littleton, Henry C. 197
Rebecca 205
Litton, Abram 203
Ann 156, 176
Benjamin 86
Eliza 169
Elizabeth 153
Isaac 191
Margaret R. 81
Susan 101
Littrell, Elizabeth 66
Lively, David F. 203
Livingston, Addell A. 136
James 216
Polly 52
Wm. 150
Lloyd, Winney 57
Lock, Jno. W. 47
Joseph 59
Lucreasa 57
Rebecca 41
Sally 67
Lockby, Nancy 156
Lockett, Henry C. 216
Lucy 10
Lockhart, Elizabeth 215
Mason 182
Loften, Wm. B. 80
Loftin, Elizabeth 43
Jeremiah 3
Martha Ann 75
Mary 122
Susannah 33
Tempe 134
Thomas 19
W. C. 216
Lofton, Nathaniel 74
Logan, Caroline E. 186
Elizabeth 120
Jane 95
Jno. 117
Margaret 101
Martha 114
Mary 100, 137
Thomas 86
Logue, Carnes 34
Charlotte 66
David 113
Elenor 40
Josiah 32
Ruth 4
Lomax, Alfred 39
London, Lucinda D. 59
Long, Edward 191
Elenor P. 149
Eliza 153
Elizabeth J. 206
Gabriel 203
James 42
John 4, 158
Mary 218
Milly 158
Nancy F. 207
Philip W. 175
Polly 13, 25, 41
Thos. 101
William 171
Wm. 72
Longinette, James 186
Lookley, James A. 198
Lord, Wm. S. 209
Louis, George M. 198
Louther, George 102
Love, Charles J. 178
David B. 33
Eliza M. 112
Frances 94
Henry J. 79
James 71
Jane E. 94
Jane N. 79
Jno. T. 143
Joseph 22, 157
Lucy J. 205
Mary 1
Nancy 14
Polly 24
Rhody B. 79
Wm. 116
Lovel, James 61
Lovell, Amanda F. 217
Benjamin P. 133
Caroline 122
Chas. G. 157
Eliza W. 148
Elizabeth 90
Emelia 100
Holman R. 148
Holmon 178
James 203
Jane 19
Jno. H. 162
John M. 21
Lucinda 199
Martha Ann 205
Nancy 22, 140
Napoleon B. 161
Polly 53
Robert 28
Sally 51
Susan L. 170
Wm. 22, 49, 83
Wm. H. 133
Loving, Catherine 63
Gabriel 149
Jane D. 112
Wm. H. 171
Lovitt, Fanny 13, 25
John 30
Low, Albert P. 82
Elenor 8
Lauretta 85
Marvel 4
Lowe, Alexander 144
Catherine B. 204
Elizabeth 36
Gertrude 45
Hannah 59
Lewis 146
Neri 129
Nevi 129
Richard 20
Sally 40
Tennessee 124
Lowery, Susan A. 208
Lowrey, Turner 43
Lowry, Caroline 181
Elizabeth 187
Mary E. 194
Melitea 27
Peter 191
Loyd, James 48
Nancy 180
Patsy 20
Loyons, Jno. B. 44
Lucas, Abel 46

Mason (cont.)
Jane 184
Jno. F. 203
Martha 181
Ramsey 41
Sumner R. 198
Susan 171
Thomas 47
Massey, Edward 216
Marrilla Lorina 214
Thos. 91
William 186
Masson, Henry E. A. 164
Masterson, Thos. G. 141
Wm. W. 171
Mathes, Alexander R. 108
Allen 4
Eliza J. H. 214
Mathews, Alex. R. 196
Edward 72
Elisha 55
Eliza Jane 190
Elizabeth 59, 191
Narcissa Ann 194
Wm. B. 191
Wm. H. 171
Mathias, Rachael 47
Mathis, Allen 84
Elizabeth T. 213
Evelina 52
Henry 157
James D. 118
Matlock, Elizabeth Jane 197
Gabriel 171
James 198
John 61
Lavine 71
Margaret M. 201
Mary 156
Nicholas 88
Sarah 83
Simpson 172
Matsel, Henry 66
Matterson, Joel 125
Matthes, Elizabeth 51
Matthews, Alexander 112
Ann W. 93, 103
Anne 17
Dudly 17
Henry 203
Howard 152
James G. 118
John G. 148
Wm. 165
Wm. H. 216
Matthias, Stephen 72
Thomas 160
Matthis, Mary 185
Maury, Abraham P. 88
Maxey, Henritta 216
Jane 145
John 44
Powhatton W. 130
Sarah 89
Maxwell, Elizabeth 79
Jennett 71
Jno. 117
Mary 102
May, James 17
James F. 141
Joel F. 186
John 5, 10, 11
Joseph H. 191
Margaret J. 161
Mary L. 97
May (cont.)
Matilda 164
Nancy 19
Nathaniel 14
Mayers, Peter 23
Mayfield, Elizabeth 79
Isaac 10, 122
Isaac W. 186
Jas. S. 134
Jno. W. 114
Linas 19
Mary Ann 208
Nancy 114
Peter 143
Peter P. 182
Polly 1
Samuel 16
Sutherlin S. 106
Mayho, Jacob D. 186
Maynard, Emeline 146
Ezekiel 171
Margaret 184
Rich'd 65
Maynor, Pleasant 101, 163
Mayo, Benjamin 153
Eliza Ann 142
Elizabeth 173
Fanniy 201
George 216
Jane 199, 200
Mary 172
Sarah 165
Susan 157
Mays, Agnis 119
Amy 15
Andrew J. 209
Carolyn 213
Elizabeth 71, 174
Frances 215
John 48
Joseph 120
Judy 33
Minerva H. 143
Nancy 39
Polly 48, 196
Tabitha 41
William 203
Wm. W. 51
Wright 111
Mayson, Francis M. 191
McAdams, James 12, 26
Jesse 74
McAfee, Lenora 207
Moses 8, 63
Nancy 177
Thomas 92
McAlipn, John W. 178
McAlister, (?) 13
John 3
Mary 7
McAllister, Cynthia C. 206
George 31
James 15, 68
John 25, 37
June 17
McArter, James 24
McBell, Margaret 190
McBride, Evelina E. 104
James 27
John 138
Joseph 24
Mary C. 109
Priscilla 54
Sam 3
McCabe, Wm. 146
McCain, George 204
John 18, 93
Luvica 184
Robert 39
Sarah 215
McCall, Alexander 83
Sarah E. 204
Wm. 126
McCallister, Wilson 64
McCallum, Mary 34
McCampbell, Isaac N. 148
Thomas C. 210
McCance, Elenezer W. 66
Martha 176
Matthew 2
McCane, Jane 186
Tabitha 192
McCanless, Catherine 48
McCann, Jane 12, 26
McCarmack, Elizabeth 72
Polly 25
McCarter, James 26
McCarty, John 6
McCasland, Caroline L. 138
Elizabeth 67
Isaac 43
John 32
McCaslin, Andrew 18
Martha S. 189
Ruthie 38
Sallie 34
McCauley, Isabella 121
McClain, Emeline 217
Lucy Leonora 193
McClane, Wm. 171
McClean, Elvira 88
McClellan, Sam'l 182
McClenden, Jesse 73
McClendon, Clark 94
McClening, Jane 17
McClich, William 2
McClure, Jno. S. 73
John 75
William 9, 186
McCollouch, Alexander 63
McCollum, Jno. D. 126
Polly 45
McComb, Charles 38
McCombs, Baptist 108
Frances J. 190
Gabriel 108
West 32
McConnell, Ann 103
Jno. P. 12, 25
McCool, John 178
Joseph 165
Westley V. 171
McCoold, Ann 149
McCord, Mary 113
McCormac, James 210
McCormach, Grace 91
McCormack, Alfred 178
Azillah 131
Berry 116
Delana 202
Polly 12
Rachel 78
Richard 22
Rule 47
Wm. 27
Wm. H. 216
McCormick, Elizabeth 5
Margaret Jane 181
McCoy, Daniel 31
Dan'l 56
Elizabeth 19
Josiah 216

McCoy (cont.)
Miles 80, 87
William 186
McCrary, Jane 156
McCreary, Andrew 11
McCreery, Phoam R. 210
McCrory, Agnes 156
Charles 79
Cynthia 119
Hugh 15
Jno. 90
Mary 105
Mary Ann 183
Rachel 188
Robt. E. 140
Sarah 188
Thomas 32
Willie 188
Zilpha 72
McCue, James 204
McCueston, Robt. 61
McCulley, Eliza 178
Wm. 147
McCullock, Benjamine W. 195
McCullough, James M. 210
Pherebe C. 213
McCully, James 71
Sarah 79
McCutchem, James 61
McCutchen, Elizabeth 187
Gazzel 8
James 7
Jane R. 85
John 6
Mary J. 4
Patrick 8
Samuel 7
McCutcheon, Elenor 93
Elizabeth 67
James 199
Mary 111
Patrick 99
McCutchin, Mary J. 145
McDaniel, Alexander 24
Amandy 95
Chloe 37
Elizabeth 153
Esther 87
George 152
Harriet 156
John 62
Lucinda 96, 158, 189
Matilda 168
Nancy 115
Polly 149
Sally 100
William 34
Wm. P. 171
McDonald, Alexander 138
Alvira 182
Henry B. 210
James 43
McDonelson, Milberry 82
McDowell, Jane 44
Samuel 92
McElleya, Margaret 6
McElroy, John 46
McElwain, Anna 30
Elizabeth 114
Polly 31
McEvoy, Joseph A. 204
McEwen, Elizabeth 45
Elizabeth C. 150
McEwen (cont.)
Margaret D. 149
W. E. 180
McEwin, Felix G. 110
Sophia C. 201
McEwing, Margaret 151
Mary Ann 100
McFadden, Mary 203
Ralph S. 45
Wm. 199
McFaddin, Ann C. 138
Aseneth 41
Barnett 69
Mary 80
Polly 20
Rebecca 54
Susannah 64
McFarland, Betsy 23, 27
John 210
Martha J. 165
Mary Ann 200
Rachel 12, 26
Robert P. 57
Sarah 155
McFarlin, Joseph 23
Thomas 98
McFaugh, Susannah 2
McFerrin, James 19
John B. 135
Nancy 10
McGaugh, Aggie 33
Cena 38
Giney 30
John 7, 11
Sarah 4
Thomas 11
Wm. 61
McGaughey, Abner 27
McGavock, Ann E. 201
David 137
Frances 75
Hugh W. 195
Jacob 53
James 14
Jno. 56, 75
Lucinda 190
Margaret E. 174
Margaret K. 141
Randall 28
Randall, Jr. 48
Sarah 80
McGee, Michael 216
McGehee, Benjamine F. 186
McGihee, Geo. W. 89
McGinnis, Augustus 152
Isaac N. 216
Polly 78
McGlendon, Mary 72
McGoldrick, Edward P. 129
McGowen, F. H. Milissa 153
McGrath, James 171
McGraw, Elijah 102
George 96
Jacob 61
Jno. C. 128
McGregar, Geo. Mackenzie 182
McGrigger, Jno. 82
McGuffey, Rebecca 133
McGuin, Elizabeth 149
McGuines, James 112
McGuinnis, Elsey 110
McGuire, Daniel 171
Delilah 85
Elizabeth 33
McGuire (cont.)
John 199
Mary Jane 109
McIlwain, John 55
Wm. 117
McIntire, Benj. 39
James 86
Robert 49
McIntosh, Daniel 52
McIntyre, Mary 162
McIver, Evander 89
Jno. 136
McKain, Elisha 147
Sally 30
McKane, Wm. 172
McKay, Alexander 6
Almyra 116
David 12, 25
Felix G. 216
Frances 25
J. D. 182
John 10
Lydia 31
Rebecca 12, 25
McKee, W. F. 199
McKenzie, Alexander 216
Kenneth 191
McKever, Edward 216
McKiernan, Bernard 27
McKinley, Daniel B. 216
McKinney, Caleb 140
Jane 1
Jesse 199
John, Jr. 8
Margaret 63
Wm. C. 92
McKinnie, John 179
McKnight, Erwin 130
John 7
Nancy 2
Thos. W. 106
Wm. W. 112
McLain, William A. 186
McLane, George 7
McLaughlin, Henry 6
James 51, 86
Mary A. 202
Nancy H. 185
Saml. B. 21
Wm. 216
Wm. H. 46
McLean, A. Andrews 157
Chas. D. 125
Chas. G. 199
McLemon, John C. 36
McLemore, Mary A. 139
McLendon, Dennis 61
James E. 199
Polly 62
Thos. J. 162
Zilpha 201
McLure, Wm. 68
McMahan, Gertrude 207
McMahon, Elizabeth Y. 210
Morgan 158
Richard 36
Wm. 109
McMannis, Samuel 45
McMillin, William 27
McMillon, Polly 35
McMorn, Elizabeth 10
McMurray, Fanny 204
John M. 165
Luvicca R. 177
Sarah L. 160
McMurrey, Amanda 157
McMurry, America M. 191
Evarilla 150

Montgomery, Elizabeth
31
Frances 196
Hamilton 51
Lottie 21
Wm. 216
Moody, Cynthia 42
Eliza B. 211
John 191
Marilla 32
Moses 61
Phoebe 20
Tabitha 46
Mook, Mary Jane 207
Moon, Ann Eliza 203
Sally 17
Sarah Ann 154
Moonfield, N. E. T.
155
Moore, Aaron 196
Adeline 119
Affie 143
Alexander 3
Alfred 124
Amos 7, 70
Annie 25
Anthony 182
Catherine P. 138
Celia Ann 102
Charles W. 196
David 20
Elizabeth 49, 140
Elizabeth W. 50
Ezekiel 21
Frances 89, 196
George W. 187
Gilman 104
Hannah 7
Harriett A. 108
Isaac W. 209
Isham 68
Isham M. L. 77
James 15
James B. 92, 172
James D. 127
Jane 123
Jas. R. 152
Jeremich 7
John 85
Judith 21
Lucy M. 206
Mahala 40
Mancy G. 51
Margaret 7
Martha D. 68
Mary 179, 192
Matilda S. 105
Nancy 25
Nathan W. 54
Polly 2, 15
Rebecca R. 206
Robert 17
Robert L. 127
S. G. 164
Samuel 21
Samuel A. 216
Sarah 208
Sarah E. 214
Sepressa 89
Summerset 61
Susannah 126
Tabitha W. 56
Talton 209
Thomas 120
William 30, 216
William G. 182
Wm. 2
Moorefield, Mary 105
Mooreman, Chas. W. 100
Moorhouse, Lucretia C.
90
Mooring, Lucy 41
Moorman, Charles W. 195
Morehead, Ann 183
Caroline M. 181
Geo. 157
Moreland, Edward 65
Moreman, Polly 42, 69
Morgan, Benjamin 106
Betsy A. 30
Cynthia 205
Daniel P. 172
Elizabeth 10, 210
Elizabeth K. 159
F. H. 154, 157
George 31
Henrietta H. 207
Henry 203, 209
Henry J. 171
Irby 198
Isaac 11
James 142
John 6, 119
Lewis 162, 172
Louisa 218
Mary Ann 99
Rufus M. 153
Sarah Ann 174
Sophy 139
Thos. 97
Thos. R. 92
Wm. C. 28
Morment, Mary Ann 114
Mornan, Elvira 12
Morning, Martha A. 185
Morris, Andrew 62
Celia 18
Charity B. 216
Chloe 29
Cynthia 83
Delilah 28
Elijah 203
Eliza 33
Elizabeth 6, 35, 51
Emily 118
Frances 9
Huldah I. 133
Isaac 89, 160
Isaac E. 88, 209
Isiah 35
Jacob 187
John 68
John J. 7
Joseph 83
Josiah H. 119
Julia 193
Julisa 103
Lemuel 24, 26
Lucinda 128
Luraney 61
Martha 86, 106, 114
Martha Jane 217
Matilda 48
Martin 34
Matthews 9
Micajah 18
Mildred B. 23
Nancy 10, 32, 155
Nathan 183
Patience 102
Peter B. 191
Polly 54
Robt. 129
Sally 24, 90
Samuel 23, 27
Sarah 149
Morris (cont.)
Sarah M. 200
Susan 95
Susannah 14
Tabitha 120
Thomas 28
William 18
Wm. P. 164
Morrison, Andrew 161
John D. 216
Wm. A. 209
Morriss, Simeon 4
Morrow, John 153
Morton, Allen 136
Barzillai G. 104
Caroline 139
Elijah 183
Elisha 41
James 12, 25
Louisa R. 136
Peggy 160
Polly 49
Prince L. 175
Samuel 98, 179
Sarah 146
Silas 36
Solomon E. 179
Wm. E. 209
Mosby, Benjamin F. 198
James C. 130
Wm. T. 132, 146
Moseley, James 83
Mosely, John 59
Moses, Henley 95
James 28, 35
Mary 124
Mosier, David 87
John 209
Nancy 214
Mosley, Catherine 210
Japtha 31
John 34
Mary 27
Nancy 192
Tennessee 172
Thos. D. 135
Moss, Anne 96
Annis 178
Benjamin 13, 25
David 172, 187
Jane 79, 118
Jennie 25
Mary 162, 218
Mary Jane 73
Nancy 42, 104
Nancy F. 194
Narcissa 185
Rebecca 66
William 196
Motherel, Catherine 63
Jane 34
Mothershed, Elizabeth 36
Esther 32
Mouldings, James 13
Moulton, Catherine 106
Sally 14
Moxby, Samuel 216
Moxey, Margaret E. 98
Mulherin, Betsy 10
Mulherrin, Chas. 18, 133
Mullen, Agatha 102
Jno. 80
Louisa 4
Lurena 116
Mary 102
Reuben W. 148
Wm. 3
Mullin, Henry 92

Mullin (cont.)
Jane 73
Jno. B. 97
Reuben W. 183
Solomon 128
Susannah 61
Thos. 123
Mullins, Rebeccah 96
Mulloy, Martha 10
Mumford, M. A. M. 146
Marshall B. 31
Sarah W. 110
Elitha S. 89
Mungle, Pheley 58
Munn, John 172
Munroe, William 32
Murdoch, Wm. 82
Murdock, Wm. 73
Murfit, Samuel 87
Murphy, Emeline 144
Geo. W. 136
George 20
Jas. 131
Mariah 90
Martha 128
Susan 207
Wm. 13
Murpo, B. S. 209
Wm. B. 162
Murprey, Mary Amanda 170
Murray, Nicholas H. 209
William 12, 25
Murrell, Elizabeth J. 89
Hannah A. 205
James M. 134
Jas. D. 55
Susannah 44
William 12
Murrey, Joshua 121
Robt. 100
Thomas 6
William P. 187
Murry, Berry 191
Easter 187
Harriett 191
Jenny 18
John M. 50
Lucy Ann 198
Margaret 85
Mark W. 98, 198
Mary 213
Roccelany 186
Sidney 191
Temperance 98
William 2
Wm. 1
Musgrove, Edward F. 107
Mary M. 123
Mussellman, Abraham 95
Myers, Adam 13, 26
Cynthia 94
David 171
Jacob 94
Mary 12
Peter 27
Rachel 118
Samuel 171
Naive, James H. 204
Nakins, Fanny 217
Nall, Catherine 43
Nancanon, John 7
Nance, Antoinette M. 198
Elizabeth 93
Elizabeth V. 126
Nance (cont.)
Lucinda America 200
Martha F. 118
Sicily M. 134
Susan 106
Wm. L. 199
Nanney, Wm. 115
Nanny, Elizabeth 141
Napier, Charlotte 160
Charlotte E. 185
Leroy G. 165
Levina 74
Lucinda 93
Madison C. 216
Martha C. 3
Mary Ann 217
Morgiana 209
Nash, Fereby 142
John 142
Thomas 17
William 8
Wm. 92
Naves, Martha Ann 179
Nay, Elizabeth 32
Neal, Ralph 117
Richard P. 114
Samuel 109
Turner 52
Neeley, Peggy 144
Neely, Elisha 142
Elizabeth 16, 181
Geo. W. 125
Haddassar 154
Jacob 120
James 4
Jean 94
Jennie 3
Joshua 126
Margaret 7
Mary Ann 218
Nancy 214
Polly 59
Rhoda 157
Rhoda L. 152
Samuel 59, 62, 124
Samuel B. 90
Sophia 62
Susanna 167
Thos. B. 142
William 6, 187
Wm. 57
Neiblet, Henry 70
Neighbors, Elizabeth 210
Neily, William 1
Neilums, Eli 199
Nellums, Elias 204, 210
Nelms, Elizabeth 170
Martha 161
Nelson, Anne 20
Benjamin 103
Chas. B. 16
Frances 141
Humphrey 14, 22
James B. 26
John 44
Joseph 183
Matthew 104
Moses 23, 27
Nancy 18
Nichols 66
Peggy 70
Polly 39
Robert 1
William 13
Nelums, Mary Jane 210
Nesbit, Rebecca 10
Nesbitt, Jeremiah 61
Nesset, Grizzel 11
Neugent, Emeline 139
Neunon, Balaam 172
Nevins, Isaac 17
John 22, 148
New, Martin 95
Newberry, James 137
Newbitt, Elizabeth 61
Newburn, Elizabeth 214
Martha 187
Mary Jane 217
Sarah 194
Newby, James 141
Newcom, Thomas 26
Newcomb, Hezekiah H. 199
Nancy 28
Thomas 24
Newell, Celia 16
Hugh F. 69
McNairy 109
Sally 79
Thos. H. 139
Newgent, Anna Eliza 212
Newland, Ester Ann 209
James 199
Jesse 37
John 57
Wm. 108
Newman, Alice 17
Anne 44
Mary 105
Nathan 24
William 179
Newsom, Caroline 60
Catherine W. 100
Elizabeth 19, 131
Frances 54
Herbert 57
James 67
James E. 183
Joseph 161
Mary H. 102
Nancy 12, 25
Peggy 19
Susan 47
Tabitha M. 164
William 25
Wm. 132, 144
Wm. E. 76
Newsome, Rhoda 41
Newson, Jane 38
Samuel B. 196
Newton, Lytle 133
Nancy 16
Robert 33
Susan 51
Wm. 34
Nice, Martha 91
Nichelson, Sally 113
Nichol, Alexander 196
Alfred 34
Charles M. 199
Elenor R. 150
Henrietta 183
James B. 183
Jane 158
Jno. W. 66
John 29, 100, 180
Margaret 34
Nicholas, Angeline 35
Elemilech 38
Geo. 204
James 210
Jordan 38
Nennette 34
Nichols, David 183
Jane E. 95
Keziah 13

Nichols (cont.)
Mary W. 66
Nancy 8, 74
Ruthy 109
Susannah 21
Nicholson, Ann 107, 153
Caroline 124
Elijah 85
Henry 90
John 39
Jonathan 40
Margaret 147
Margery 12, 25
Margery M. 27
Mary 42
Wm. 32
Nickens, Calvin C. 187
Elizabeth 182
Hester 178
Nimmo, Wesley G. 35
Ninbourne, Mary Jane 214
Nix, James 56
James E. 150
Nixon, Priscilla A. 169
William 28
Noaks, Chas. H. 102
Noble, Mark 5
Mary 140
Noe, Ambrose D. 191
Noel, Catherine P. 140
Mary 129
Sarah 192
Sinico A. G. 204
Zacharriah 24
Noell, Elizabeth G. 88
Mildred C. 85
Reuben 108
Sally 108
Zachriah 26
Nolen, Abram 4
Andrew 191
Noles, Ann Tennessee 119
Butler 35
Martha 72
Nolls, James M. 199
Norfleet, Perry 42
Norman, Frances 118
Henry 138
John 62
Joshua 90
Nathan 28
Tennessee 152
Wm. 199
Norment, Elizabeth 103
Norpp, John 196
Norris, Isaac 216
James 24
Northem, Nancy Eliza 187
Northern, Samuel 58, 191
William 24
Norton, Elizabeth 20, 162
Ellen C. 200
Joseph 10
Martha 57
Thomas 35
Norvell, Caleb C. 134
Emeline R. 154
Henry L. 191
Hugh 216
Joseph 73
Martha 113
Norvell (cont.)
Mary Hannah 197
Moses 35
Norvelle, Mary 74
Norvill, Caleb C. 199
Norwood, Elizabeth 103
Thos. 107
Nowell, Hugh 210
Nowland, Ann 2
Nugent, Delitha B. 162
Martha A. P. 176
Nunnley, Lawson H. 81
Nutt, Julia 195
Oakford, Martha C. 163
Oats, Charity 150
O'Briant, James 112
O'Brien, Margaret 181
Mary 188
Sophia 150
O'Brient, John 93
O Bryant, Anna 97
OBryant, Rebecca 60
Wm. 59
O'Connell, Catherine 204
O'Dair, Stephen 7
Odear, Darky 62
Odell, Joseph 196
Thos. J. 149
Odom, Harris H. 75
Mary E. 181
Wm. 109
O'Donnelly, Henry 42
O'Donnely, James 53
Ogburn, Mary A. L. 212
Ogden, Mary Ann 179
Ogdon, John W. 172
Ogelvie, Frances 62
Ogilsvie, Wm. 10
Ogilvie, Elizabeth A. 165
Nancy 22
William 32
William S. 187
Ogle, Spencer 199
Oglesby, Polly 18
Sallie 4
Ohilsvie, Mary A. 218
Okelleywood, James 23
Old, Elizabeth 202
Michael 25
Oldham, Chas. 47
Elizabeth 79
Elizabeth L. 182
Martha M. 57
Sarah W. 56
Susan 49
Olephint, Isaac N. 196
Olifant, Franklin M. 210
James 7
Oliphant, Henry 141
Samuel 86
Thos. J. 94
Oliver, Anne 42
Enoch 25
Eunice 29
Frederick 4
Jno. C. 117
Joanna 62
Mary 118
Minerva 28
Parmelia 79
Rebecca 21
Robert 25
Rosanna 4
Wm. M. 210
Olliphant, Andrew J. 164
Olliver, William S. 187
Omps, Benjamin 80
Oneal, Mitchel 2
Mitchell 2, 6
Oneil, John 204
Oneill, Asa 81
Ord, Margaret H. 148
O'Rielly, James C. 111
Orr, John 11
Wm. 54
Orten, Jane 111
Orton, Joseph 14
Polly 75
Ray S. 210
Rich'd 62
Samuel R. 151
Wm. 61
Osborn, Alfred M. 44
Ichabod 8
Joel 216
Mary 119
Mary Ann 191
Sarah Ann 188
Thomas 183
Osborne, Mary Ann 199
Mary Elizabeth 199
Sarah 196
Thompson 71
Thos. H. 145
Osbourne, Kitty 59
Osburn, Harriett 70
Lucy 69
Osmar, Wm. 15
Osment, Alfred 73
Granberry 81
Harriet 159
Thos. C. 166
Osmon, Polly 20
Osmore, Elizabeth 56
Osteen, Gabriel 19
Ostrander, Matthew 64
Otey, Paul H. 216
Ott, James H. 210
Overall, Elizabeth 5
Nancy 6
Sophia E. 71
Overby, Isabella 83
Patsy 81
Overton, Ann C. 184
Elizabeth S. 206
John 187
Martha 188
Mary G. 147
Patrick Henry 78
Owen, Alford 165
Alfred 191
Amanda 183
Arney 106
Campbell W. 154
Edmond, Jr. 47
Edmund 42
Elisha 81
Elizabeth 122
Emily A. 136
Everett 196, 210
Frederick 15
Frederick, Sr. 126
Gaines 187
Henry 30
Jabez 35
James 54, 183
Jane 27
Jas. G. 85
Jno. W. 87
John 79
Lucinda 98
Lucy 27
Martha D. 193

Payne (cont.)
Squire 11
William 2
William H. 172
Payton, Jno. W. 62
Payzer, Elizabeth 58
Mary Making 57
Peach, Hardin 204
Josephine 114
Peacock, John 210
Peak, Simmons 162
Peal, Nancy 65
William 191
Pearce, Margaret 65
Pearcy, Ann E. 217
John R. 216
Pearl, Dyer 78
Pearsons, Julia Ann 141
Pease, Jno. B. 163
Peay, Elizabeth L. 188
Geo. 50
James 191
Jane 177
Thomas 88
Peck, Elizabeth 22, 75
Jno. 127
Nathaniel 39
Peebles, C. C. 187
Catherine 46
Cordy 23
Elizabeth 180
Jane 151
Maria 100
Martha 34
Mary 66
Nancy 31
Peek, Wm. 137
Peel, Lewis 179
Mary Ann 120
Peelar, Hazlewood W. 95
Peffen, Thomas 216
Pegram, Agness 191
Edward 159
Elizabeth 140
George 91, 210
Glenn 137
Jane 164
John P. 187
Patsy 111
Roger 125
Sally 104
Wm. 119
Peles, Conrad 172
Pelham, Francis 204
Pembleton, Wm. 132
Pen, Almyra 152
Penington, Graves 16
Penn, Marry Ann 48
Pennington, Graves 58
J. T. 191
Jno. W. 124
John W. 191, 216
Martha A. 213
Mary Amanda 186
Robt. 39
Sarah Ann 174
Wm. R. 204
Pennuel, Sarah 185
Penticost, Martha M. 194
Wm. F. 196
Penuel, Alanson 135
Peobles, Martha 176
People, Yeaho 37
Peoples, Nancy 133
Perch, Henry 62
Louisa 113
Percy, Charles B. 183
Perkins, Artemessa 97
Charity 69
James 13
James M. 128
James W. 56
Joseph W. 150
Leah P. 30
Nancy 49
Nicholas P. 43
Sally 13, 22
Samuel 13, 96
Sophia Ann 70
William 28
Perkinson, Jackman 32
Perodean, Paul 45
Perry, Allen M. 115
Burrell, Jr. 134
Charlotte 50
Eliza E. 136
Elizabeth 197
Ellender 84
Francis S. 32
Hugh 3
Jesse 187
John 7, 204
Judy 189
Lenora 4
Littleton 93
Mary 203, 210
Mary J. 208
Nancy 23
Noah 33
Polly 13
Rachel 42
Robert 149
Simpson 29
Thomas 123
Wm. S. 196
Peters, Thomas 128
Peterson, Andrew 167
Pettus, Stephen 28
Petty, Barney W. 210
Elizabeth 124, 209
Isaac H. 145
Jas. H. 139
Mahala S. 163
Mary 167
Sarah 184
Petway, Geo. Washington 196
Jno. S. 134
Martha E. 215
William 18
Wm. 146
Pew, Adeline 155
Peyton, George Y. 9
Polly 30
Phelan, Druey 134
Richard 26
Phelps, Annie 25
Cassander 65
Charlotte 65
Clarissa 92
Easter 77
John 36
Josiah 23
Louisa 176
Luticia 96
Martha 183
Mary A. 185
Miles B. 133
Nancy 10
Rachel 32
Safrona 198
Silas M., Jr. 129
Wm. 165
Phelts, Lucy 15
Phenix, Eliza 81
Phenix (cont.)
Henry 3
Jane A. 124
Philan, Richard 24
Philips, Asa R. 156
Catherine 132
Delilah 86
Eliza 87
Elizabeth 81
Joseph 85
Lucy Ann 117
Rebecca 78
Sally 77
Wm. J. 217
Phillips, Ann 40
Betsy 74
Catherine 159
Chas. W. 204
David 55
Eleanor 4
Eliza F. 141
Elizabeth 55
Geo. W. 159
Jas. 141
Jesse H. 161
Joel 115
John 20
Lina 62
Margaret T. 33
Mark 54
Mary B. 155
Mary H. 215
Patsy 23
Polly 34
Preston D. 172
Sally 24, 55
Sarah 2, 168
Susan J. 184
Thomas 144
Virginia Ann 203
William 172
Wm. 210
Wm. H. 79
Wm. J. 161
Philps, Margaret A. 212
Phinehus, Thomas 12
Phipps, Caroline 137
Eldridge N. 49
Elizabeth 35
Eveline E. 137
Martha 47
Robt. W. 84
Sarah M. 48
Susan 72
Phips, Lenia 72
Pickard, Allen 129
Geo. W. 118
Pickering, Wm. 66
Pickett, Wm. 52
Pickle, Louisa 133
Robert 48
Pierce, Catherine 85
Chas. R. 87
Elizabeth 17, 75
Eveline F. B. 179
Isaac 21, 69
James 67
Jeremiah 30
John 44
Merit 23
Nancy 40
Phillip 28
Polly 31
Richard J. 153
Sally 57
Sarah 139
Spencer 75
Susan 68

Pierson, Isham 51
Pigg, Dicey C. 99
Elizabeth R. 205
Nelson W. G. 102
Pierce P. 78
Robert F. 135
Sally 13
Pigue, Robert F. 196
Pike, Emma C. 149
John 153
Josiah 116
Susan 211
Piland, Sarah 92
Pilant, Frances 147
Pilcher, Lucinda 111
Mason 111
Merritt S. 125
Piles, Susannah 16
Pilkington, Wm. B. 120
Pillow, Amanda 175
Elizabeth 2
Gideon 11
Polly 9
Rachel 88
Urcella 8
Vincint 42
Pillows, Mary 134
Pinckerton, David 204
Piniham, John 146
Piniham, Linsey 146
Pinkard, Edward W. 109
Pinkerton, Ann 151
David 16, 28
Eliza 135
James 37, 196
John 93
Joseph 65
Margaret 129, 173
Mary Jane 201
Wm. B. 204
Pinkley, Betsy 12
Pinkly, Betsy 26
Pinkston, James 33
Mishek 32
Pipkin, Enas 18
Phillip 2, 14
Stewart 71
Pipkins, Mary Z. 3
Pirtle, Elizabeth 19
George 25
Patsy 30
Sally 13
Pitman, Henry H. 76
Pitt, Elizabeth 206
Pittman, Bartholemew B. 179
Pitts, Barnabas 92
Burrell 112
Jesse B. 91
Mukin 179
Thomas 179
Pitzer, Wm. 64
Platts, John 54
Player, T. T. 191
Plummer, Caroline 47
Hillary C. 81
James R. 204
Martha Ann 213
Nancy E. 193
Poarch, Jno. C. 156
John C. 217
Poindexter, Wm. G. 151
Polk, Andrew J. 210
Elizabeth O. 190
Jno. T. 145
Pomprey, Jonathan 18
Pope, Ann 103
Elizabeth D. 133
Pope (cont.)
Frances A. 184
John 82
Joseph 172
Sarah 121
Porch, Henry 123
Isaac 25
Martha Ann 150
Porter, Amanda 185
David 10, 11
Eliza 66
Ellen 149
George 35
Henry 137
James 129
James B. 21
Jane 11, 36
Jane Eliza 96
Jas. A. 98
John 4, 69
Joseph 7
Joseph Y. 149
Lydia 35, 84
Maranda C. 199
Mary A. 186
Mary E. 217
Mary M. 101
Mathew 46
Matilda 55
Milley 90
Penelope 218
Rebecca 130
Robert M. 172
Solomon 116, 183
Thomas 12, 26
Porterfield, Elizabeth 160
John 204
Robert R. 192
Susan 206
Portloch, Wm. 75
Posey, Thos. 116
Postlethwaight, Jno., Jr. 132
Postly, Samuel 45
Poston, Alex. R. 160
Potter, James O. 151
Powell, Barton P. 138
Benj. R. 90
Betsy A. 214
Catherine 105
Edmund L. 145
Elizabeth 214, 215
Elizabeth M. 65
James 11
Jane 127
Julia G. 210
Lucinda M. 87
Mary 104
Nancy 5
Polly 15
Rachel 170
Sarah 78, 126
Sarah Ann 210
Seymons 150
Thomas 34, 192
Thomas L. 196
Power, Jno. F. 155
Powers, Jane 30
John H. 192, 204
Poyzer, Mary M. 127
Pratt, Ephriam 2
Mary Louisa 209
Nancy C. 151
Susan E. 155
Prescot, Elizabeth L. 188
Preston, Edward 196
Preston (cont.)
Thomas W. 204
Price, Aquilla 81
Dorcas 155
Harriet 82
Jenny 6
Joana J. 170
John 71
Levi 196
Martha 156
Martha J. 200
Mary Ann 162
Nancy 37
Priscilla 14
Ruth 21
Sally 21
Samuela 136
Prickley, Anne 73
Pride, Frances Ann 188
Mary 212
Shelton 28
Priestly, Sarah Ann E. 98
Prim, Abraham 18
Lorenzo D. 124
Prissie, Thomas 8
Pritchard, Benjamin 100
Mary 99
Wm. 127
Pritchett, Annie 85
Benjamin 68
Chloe 27
Elizabeth 41
James 20
Jno. S. 81
Mary 122
Milley 88
Nancy 81
Peggy 56
Robert 38
Sally 24, 106
Sam'l 204
Tennessee C. 187
Wm. 204
Pritchitt, Jno. C. 161
Nancy 19
Probart, Sarah 95
Probast, Almyra A. 135
Wm. G. 19
Proctor, Elizabeth 186
Martha 132, 143
Mary 182
Nancy 179
Provine, John 132
Pruett, Peggy 61
Pryor, Laura L. 20
Susannah 27
Puckering, Mariah 90
Puckett, Anderson 204
Cheatham 179
Douglas, Jr. 69, 81
Ethelrid 153
Jesse L. 204
Jones 121
Jordon 138
Lay 172
Mary 108
Nancy 63
Pugh, Diana 145
Hannah 35, 82
Henry H. 123
James H. 204
John 79
Polly 76
Sally 50
Sarah 145
Pugsley, Caroline 137
Pullen, John A. 172

Pulleu, Nancy 137
Pulliam, Washington 43
Pulling, Nancy Ann 57
Purdy, John 145
Putman, James R. 70
Putney, Martha W. 30
Pyle, Alexander W. 217
Pyles, Mary 25
Smith 155
Pyron, Chas. S. 152
Jno. C. 151
Pyrtle, Emmeliza 187
Quesenbury, Wm. M. 17
Questenberry, Mary 121
Questinberry, Elmira 111
Quilling, Nancy 5
Quimby, Barbara 207
Burwell 13
Caswell K. 121
Tennessee 138
Quinn, A. L. 164
Harriett E. W. 199
Lott 101
Louisa E. 157
Malinda 196
Matthew H. 38, 73
Michael 187
Rachael 176
William J. 192
Quinton, Allen 97
Quisenberry, Louisa 123
Mary A. 163
John 172
Rader, Jacob 192
Radford, Jasper S. 104
John 100
Ragan, Mary 216
Polly 196
Susan 153
Susannah 30
Thomas 29
William H. 187
Ragans, Permelia 201
Ragin, Nancy 22
Railey, Susan A. 184
Raimer, Adam 2
Eva 2
George 108
Rainey, Elizabeth 133
Jesse G. 92
Silas 57
William 137
Wm. 134
Rains, Barbara 28
Charlotte M. 138
Christiana 26, 107
Christianna 24, 92
Elizabeth 9
Elizabeth H. 90
Felix R. 159, 192
Hance H. 137
Jno. 62
Martha 7
Mary 70
Mary E. H. 159
Mary J. 211
Nancy 29, 212
Nancy B. 179
Polly 91
Sarah 101
Susannah 13
Ursula 91
Wilford H. 105
William 8
Wm. G. 173
Raison, Jacob 68
Ralston, Catherine 132
James 21
Joseph 3
William 137
Ramer, Andrew 196
Catherine 187
Geo. 138
Geo., Sr. 124
Henry 131
Nancy 198
Ramond, Nicholas 17
Ramsey, Elizabeth M. 31
Jane 173
Susan 31, 110
Wm., Jr. 55
Wm. B. A. 192
Ramsy, Hannah 1
Randal, Cordelia 97
Susan 113
Randall, Ann 213
Aquilla 78
Elizabeth 39
Exit 51
Presly M. 72
Sally 83
Randolph, Greeberry 89
Jas. 129
Lewis 146
Rane, Augusta A. 195
Raney, Drucilla 178
James 23
Ranier, Jno. 101
Rankins, Alcy 181
Eliza 126
Ransom, Ann 133
Sarah 183
Rape, Amelia 50
Augustus 38
Daniel 100
Emily J. 202
Franky 84
Henry 22
Jacob 35
John 59
Nancy 41
Peter 33, 40
Susannah 94
Rappe, Elizabeth 35
Rasberry, Geo. 50
Thomas 136
William 23
Raspberry, Mary 153
Rassbrooks, Thomas 196
Ratcliff, Benjamin 5
Ravonell, Emilie Atala 173
Rawling, Nancy 146
Rawlings, Ann 211
Anne 129
Edward G. 70
Jas. S. 13
Martha M. 131
Rawlins, Lucy I. 131
Ray, Henry D. 106
Jenny 12
Jinnie 26
Kindred 192
Lucinda 157
Sally 30
Susan 203
William 8
Raybourn, Samuel S. 115
Rayburn, Jno. K. 103
Rayman, Harriet 72
Raymer, Caroline 212
Henry 54
Jane 216
Nancy Ann 209
Raymer (cont.)
Susan 65
Raymond, Sarah 130
Raynie, George W. 199
Rayworth, Egbert A. 124
Reace, Mary J. 140
Read, Cain 91
David 76, 156
Eliza J. 115
Elizabeth C. 81
Elmina 213
Enoch S. 210
Guillford 87
Harriett 180
Henry 22, 183
Isabella 100
James 196
Joel 138
Lydia Ann 193
Martha E. 184
Mary I. 173
Matthew 114
Nancy 96
Olivia F. 110
Robt. A. 196
Sarah 192
Susan 203, 205
Theodorick 58
Reader, Jacob 1
Reading, Wm. R. 199
Ready, James 196
Reams, Rowland 19
Rear, Hamblin 85
Nancy 184
Reardon, Thomas 16
Rease, Frances 215
Reason, Kindred 196
Peter 96
Reasoner, Mary 199
Peter 101
Reaves, Ann 81
Anne 18
Burwell 103
Edmund 13
Ellender 60
Franky 112
Hannah 44, 50
Hartwell P. 199
Hetty 98
Isabell 4
James 4, 77
John 98
Jonathon 12, 26
Jordon 62
Levithia 114
Lottie 77
Mary 20
Nancy 37, 55, 110, 111
Peter 136
Priscilla 112
Samuel B. 196
Sarah W. 102
Thos. 80
Timothy 68
William 14
Reavis, James 24
Rece, Elisha 6
Redd, John P. 164
Parm B. 135
Reddick, Jno. 133
Prudence 141
Reddin, Maximillian 24
Redding, Augustus 44
Hulda 59
Iredale 55
Nancy 132
Reddish, Polly 57
Reding, Richard H. 204

Robertson (cont.)
Jas. R. 49
Jesse 145
John McNairy 43
Lavinia 20
Louisa M. 137
Lucinda 124
M. C. C. 57, 82
Martha A. 147, 148, 189
Martha E. 92
Mary 183
Mary E. 153
Nancy 22
Patsy 18
Patty 5
Peyton 57
Polly 24, 26, 62
Reddick 21
Rhoda 28
Robert A. 33
Robt. A. 29
Sally 9, 10, 29
Susannah 49
Virginia 161
Wm. B. 13, 26
Wm. D. 204
Wm. E. 90
Robinson, J. B. 163
James C. 101
John 140
Polly 30, 95
Tennessee T. 209
William P. 21
Wm. D. 204
Rochell, Emely 170
Rockwell, June V. 172, 173
Roden, Jane 121
Mary Ann 191
Sarah 191
Roses, Ephey 6
Rodgers, Elizabeth L. 72
Elizabeth M. 44
Mary 141
Patsy 5
Roe, Martha 194
Rogers, Ann 177
Benjamin 132
Elizabeth 202
Feliz 35
George 36
Isom 8
John H. 205
Mary D. 41
Peter 13
Sally 28
Sarah 33
Sarah R. 109
Simon 1
William 15
Wm. 121
Rohrbacher, John G. 192
Rolan, Rebecca 168
Roland, Elizabeth 180
Joel 210
Sallie 11
Roler, John 154
Roller, John 158
Rollings, Henry 98
Rollins, Wm. H. 165
Rolston, David 84
Geo. 51
Rooker, Caleb 48
Roper, George 13
Rord, Mary 201
Rordine, Francis 1
Roscoe, Peyton 153
Sarah A. 164
Rose, Alex 179
Christina B. 209
Esther 207
Mary Ann 194
Roseberry, Robert 2
Rosenbaum, Jno. 109
Roser, John 205
Ross, Daniel 3
Feliz G. 196
John 28
Sarah 61
Rosser, David 151
Roundtree, Thomas 81
Rounswell, Amos 1
Rountree, Nathaniel 99
Routon, Richmond 192
Rowe, Mary Ann 167
Rowland, Balam 44
Delilah 88
Elizabeth 134
Joseph 85
Nancy 19
Wm. 88
Rowlin, Joel 179
Jole 179
Rowling, John 173
Roy, George W. 192
Lucinda 213
Wiley 183
Royster, Lucy 159
Mary 181
Sarah M. 56
Rucker, Benjamin 150
Benjamin A. 131
Jonathan 24
Lucinda 16
Thomas J. 199
Rucks, James 96
Malvina H. 159
Rudd, James 12, 26
Rule, Polly 100
Susannah 15
Ruleman, Jacob 95
Rumoner, John 32
Rundalls, Elizabeth 156
Rundell, Peggy 34
Rungan, Benj. M. 196
Runkle, Elizabeth L. 88
Sarah 83
Runner, Nancy 42
Rupard, John 101
Ruse, Sarah 203
Rush, John 33
Nelly 15
Russell, Alfred H. 199
Cynthia 179
Darinda 186
Elizabeth 15
Elizabeth G. 106
Ferbe 17
Ferrebee 68
Geo. W. 217
Hiram 77
James 23, 154
James S. 217
John M. B. 210
Joseph 172
Lavina 181
Lucinda 145
Malvira 91
Mary 115
Mary Ann 204
Mills 105
Miriam 154
Russell (cont.)
Nancy 31, 35
Parean 187
Patsy 77
Peggy 50
Polly 38
Sally 14
Sarah 151
Sophronia 133
Stephen 93
Thomas 11, 58, 192
William 11, 15
Ruth, Robert B. 205
Rutherford, Catherine W. 59
Eliza Ann 170
Eviline 84
James 1
Robt. H. 52
Thos. 3
Ruthland, Isaac 196
Rutland, Wm. B. 94
Rutledge, Emma P. 121
Frederick 86
Henrietta 86
Henry A. 124
Mary 75
Thos. 133
Ryall, Thos. C. 163
Ryman, John 183
Ryon, Cornelia 193
Saddler, Jarome 217
Sadler, Albany D. 198
Benjamine F. 210
Burrell B. 151
Caroline 178
Edith 53
Elizabeth 172
James M. 217
Jeremiah 49
John G. 94
Martha 202
Martha J. 204
Mary A. E. 180
Polly 24, 26
Thomas 15, 52
William C. 187
Wm. 199, 205
Saffarans, David 120
Sager, Sally 13
Sailors, Jno. 157
Dane 24
Sally, Panky 18
Salsberry, Tansy 15
Saluder, Elizabeth 64
Sample, Eliza 29
James 24, 26
Margaret Ann 191
Mary 32, 212
Peggy 5
Sarah 83
Thomas 84
Timothy D. 205
Wm. 31
Sampley, Joseph 155
Sampson, Agnes P. 86
Ann 140
Caroline M. 106
Martha E. 33
Mary H. 63
Narcissa M. 84
Samuel, Addison L. 161
Richard 197
Sarah E. 206
Samuels, Elizabeth 195
Sandek, Joseph 187
Sander, Martha 124
Sanders, Chas. 129

Shaffer (cont.)
Elizabeth 8
Josiah 19
Maria G. 83
Richard 2
Sarah 163
Shafus, Angeline 218
Shain, Sarah 21
Shall, Ephriam P. 123
Jacob 76
Sally 56
Shandoin, Emeline 105
Shane, Andrew 55
Araminta 213
James 133
Nancy 29
Patience 11
Rhody 56
Shannon, Easther 21
George 4
Joseph 6
Mary Ann 77
Samuel 63
Thos. S. 42
Shapard, Wm. B. 87
Shapley, David M. 197
Shappel, Elizabeth 10
Shares, Jenny 38
Sharlock, John 4
Sharp, Ambrose 55
Darcus 69
Jane 12
Jas. G. 106
Jno. M. 83
Wm., Sr. 210
Sharpe, Benj. 183
Shaub, Martin L. 199
Shaw, Barbary 68
Elizabeth 30
Ella 21
Fanny 90
George 96
Henry B. 205
James L. 115
Kiziah 29
Margaret 134
Mary 15
Mary Ann 142
Patsy 32
Prissilla 15
Ralph 36
Rebecca E. 193
Robert K. 197
Sally 17, 130
Sarah 76
William 23
Wm. 27, 71
Shearon, Thos. W. 124
Sheers, Delia 36
Shegog, Phebe 153
Shelby, Ann M. 98
Carter 139
Priscilla 121
Rachel 106
Shelhorn, Elizabeth 123
Shell, Amanda 179
Janisha 101
Martha 205
Shelter, Phil 127
Shelton, Betsy 41
Elizabeth 29, 198, 208
Franklin 111
Jesse 156
John 35
Lucy H. 75
Marcus L. 192
Shelton (cont.)
Maria 24
Mary 105, 168
Mary Jane 164
Mary P. 130
Nancy 111
Robt. W. 121
Sarah C. 164
Washington G. 90
Wm. 54
Wm. H. 163
Shepard, Mary Eliza 204
Shephard, Mary 135
Shepherd, Mary 131
Thomas 128
Sheppard, Blanne H. 173
Charles 187
Sherley, David 53
Sherrill, Abel W. 217
Robert C. 210
Sherwood, Catherine 11
Shewell, Thos. 117
Shields, Catherine 159
James 192
John 38
Nancy H. 30
Wm. 119
Ship, Elizabeth 17
Shirley, Sarah 192
Shirly, Mary Ann 157
Shivers, Asa 99
Elizabeth 106
Emiline 145
James 17
John C. 146
Jonas 67, 183
Lydia 34
Martha 173
Mary 153
Noah 120
Penny 20
Polly 29
Rebeccah 94
Sarah 107
Telpha 37
Shoat, Jacob 91
Sarah 7
Shons, Betsy 23
Shores, Nancy 19
Short, Arsenia 28
Thomas 21
Wesley 149
Shouse, John 5
Joseph 28
Shrague, Lucretia O. 158
Shrewsbury, Julia E. L. 178
Shucraft, George W. 217
Shuester, George W. 179
Shule, Andrew W. 129
Christiana 128
Jas. C. 85
Shull, John 161
Shultz, Charles F. 187
Shumate, (?) 4
Catharine 188
Elizabeth 121
J. J. D. R. 159
Maria H. 172
Sarah E. 185
Willis L. 30
Shute, Elizabeth 3, 78
Jno. A. 136
John 3
Lee 119
Lydia 9
Shute (cont.)
Margery 1
Martha 135
Philip C. 125
Rachel 29
Susannah 13
Thomas 183
William 5, 28
Sidebottom, Polly 54
Siecrist, Mary 5
Sigginfy, Mary 215
Sights, Betsy 19
Sigler, Elizabeth S. 208
Silbird, William 149
Sills, D. C. 183
Joseph 158
Simmens, Edward 205
Simmon, Dan'l 135
Simmons, Charles 5
Chas. 70
Edward 31, 197
Eliza 65
Elizabeth 41, 144, 162, 193, 208
Ephriam 82
Henry 217
Jackson 143
James 120, 210
Jesse 85
John 24
Levi C. 173
Marilla 185
Nancy 115, 156
Patsy 49
Rhoda Ann 213
Susan 173
Susannah 15
Tempy 169
Simonton, Jno. D. 28
Simpkins, Asenath 170
Elias R. 199
Elizabeth 197, 200
Frances 182
James 210
John M. 197
Jonnathan W. 217
Jos. 40
Louisa 194
Martha A. 136
Orman Allen 37
Rhoda Ann 181
Thomas 28
Thomas C. 192
William D. 199
Wm. 210
Simpson, Betsy 61
David 64
Elias H. 103
Elizabeth 91
Isabel 192
Jno. S. 117
Louisa 7
Robert 28
Sally 34
Sarah Jane 183
Thomas 5
Washington H. 192
Wm. 136
Sims, Boyd M. 192
Elizabeth 52
Eveline R. 162
James 15
Jno. W. 104
John W. 199
Mary 107
Rebecca W. 206
Walter 99
Wm. P. 115

Sinclair, Laury 73
Singletary, Elizabeth 13
Elsie 36
Esther 15
Nancy 19
Peggy 36
Zaravira 187
Singleton, Ander J. 164
Catharine 189
Edward 30
Lucinda 117, 145
Milley A. 149
Robert W. 197
Singltray, Nancy 79
Sirely, David P. 205
Sirles, Elizabeth 150
Sirls, Henrietta 155
Mary 139
Site, Rebecca 14
Sittler, Caroline 169
Skeggs, Thos. L. 134
Skelley, Mary 143
Skelly, John 35
Nancy 13
Skiles, Jas. R. 57
Skillem, Zippora 125
Skinner, Henry 7
Slabaugh, Nancy 22
Slack, Ann E. E. 205
Robert E. 205
Slaton, Nancy 7
Slatter, Mary A. 185
Slaughter, Francis 45
Mary H. 28
Sarah C. 47
Slavens, Nancy 47
Slaybrooks, Levy 20
Slayton, Seward 1
Sledge, Mary Ann 182
Mary E. 190
Nathaniel 210
Sluden, A. B. 217
Sluder, Aaron B. 140
Bright H. 205
Martha 73
Sludor, Henry 62
John 62
Small, Cynthia 99
Daniel 3
Martha 165
Samuel 49
Smart, Bennett W. 68
Martha 168
Smelser, Michael 20
Smiley, Catherine 141
Emily 174, 175
Louisa Jane 195
Pernina T. 194
Rachel 112
Robert 28
Robert G. 210
Thos. T. 154
Smith, Abner 91
Abraham 105
Abraham H. 65
Albert 197
Alexander 9
Andrew 54
Aureana 197
Bartholomew 10
Benjamin 28, 84
Benjamin D. 127
Betsy 23
Burton 142
Butler 90
Cadie 27
Calvin M. 94
Smith (cont.)
Caroline 185
Caroline C. 169
Caroline M. 194
Catherine 95
Celia 27
Charlotte 216
Clementine C. 210
Cyrus 187
Daniel 68
Dan'l E. 211
David 8
Davidson M. 154
Delamy 187
Delany 188
Drury 23
Ebenezer 11
Edmund B. 96
Edward 217
Edwin 15, 40
Elijah 116
Eliza 173, 174
Elizabeth 8, 22, 23, 37, 54, 90, 96, 129, 152, 195, 199
Elizabeth C. 6
Elizabeth S. 193
Elizabeth W. 57
Ellen D. 209
Ezekiel 88
Francis 14
Geo. W. 126
Guy 28, 43
Hannah 3
Harriet 211
Henry C. 173
Issabella L. 152
J. L. 173
Jackson 140
Jacob C. 34
James 79
Jane 20, 88
Jane E. 125
Jason 110
Jennie 15
Jesse 31
Jno. B. 124
Jno. H. 139
Jno. P. 156
Joel 52, 77, 137
Joel M. 73
Joel R. 60
John 149, 217
John H. 36, 199
John J. 199
John W. 179
Joseph 59
Joseph H. 197
Joshua 18
Judith 11
Julia Ann 164
Lewis 183
Louisa M. 198
Lucinda 23, 174
Lucindy 93
Lucy Ann 124
Major L. 96
Maria 161
Maria Z. 175
Martha 119
Martha Ann J. 183
Mary 1, 8, 74, 215
Mary Ann 105
Mary E. 142, 158
Mary M. 28
Matilda 39
McDaniel 145
Metilda 104
Smith (cont.)
Moses 3
Nancy 2, 3, 37, 139, 185
Nancy A. 85
Nancy C. 108
Nelly 70
Partheny 52
Patsy 54
Pleasant 159
Polly 29, 40, 61
Ralph P. 107
Rebecca 7
Rebecca C. 191
Richard 119
Rich'd 126
Robert 3, 108
Roberts 4
Ruth 3
Sallie 3, 4
Sally 4, 25, 54, 103
Sam 22
Samuel 139, 217
Sarah 48, 60, 104
Sarah B. 185
Sarah E. 160
Sarah H. 138
Sarah R. 147, 148
Sidney 83, 132
St. Clair 211
Susan 102, 139, 206
Susannah 13, 38
Thomas 65, 151, 217
Thomas F. 200
Thos. 45, 127, 142
Thos. C. 55
Thos. S. 70
Virginia G. 188
Wallace 200
Warner P. M. 217
William 2, 5, 10, 179, 187, 192
Willie 121
Winn B. 192
Wm. 3, 13, 83, 103, 133, 143, 157, 199, 200
Wyley 154
Wynne B. 150
Zerinda 194
Zillah W. 126
Smithwick, Edward 72
Smothers, Jno. 11
Mary 10
Nelly 17
Sneed, Alexander E. 144
Catherine H. N. 32
Eliza 67
Geo. W. 80
Gilley Ann 151
Joseph P. 192
Martha M. 181
Martha S. 181
Mary 109
Mary D. 80
Matilda 88
Sarah S. 108
Susan 97, 126
William 15, 18
Wm. T. 120
Snell, Rosseau S. 137
Snow, Anthony J. 173
Davie 14
Hannah A. 118
Mary A. 141
Susan 111
Wm. A. 205
Snowden, Samuel B. 112

Walker (cont.)
Rebecca 13, 27
Sally 31
Sarah 116
Serena T. 110
Tandy 10
Tennessee 174
Thomas E. 193
Wesley 13, 25
Wm. 126, 155, 156
Wall, Burgess 13
Eliza Ann 90
Wallace, Benj. R. B. 121
Eaton 77
Edwin R. 83
Elizabeth 87
Harriett 76
Hartwell H. 81
Jas. B. 74
Jno. M. 160
Logan D. 174
Reubin 34
William E. 183
Wm. P. 93, 131
Wm. W. 156
Waller, Edith 139, 145
Elenor 9
Elizabeth 131, 204
Fanny 126
Harriet M. 137
Ketturah 160
Leanna 100
Levi 200
Nicholas C. 197
Polly 1
Rufus 188
Sallie 33
Sarah 88, 106
Walls, George 6
Walltrip, Mary 143
Walsh, Hency C. 103
Walters, George 47
Walton, David H. 99
Elizabeth 197
Josiah 31
Olly 98
Sarah J. 217
Wamsby, Thomas 200
Waner, Lucy H. 116
Ward, Albert G. 158
Benjamin 91
Elizabeth 23
Fleming 40
Frederick 3
Hugh 205
J. N. 200
John H. 162
Mariah J. 207
Martha C. 204
Pleasant 14
Sally 15
Wm. B. 125
Wm. L. 78
Ware, David 183
David H. 200
John 14
Wm. K. 105
Warmach, Henry H. 85
Thos. 104
Wm. 92, 121
Warmack, Edward 140
Jesse 188
Mary Jane 193
Richard 135, 205
Robt. R. 218
Wm. 17
Warmath, Mary 159
Thomas 138
Warmoth, Martha S. 129
Sarah 95
Warner, Edw'd W. 144
Wm. S. 145
Warren, H. A. 218
Jesse 188, 193
Noble 59
Richard W. 205
Thomas 78
Walker 197
Washington, George A. 193
Gilbert G. 71
Gray 11
Jas. G. 94
Martha Ann 214
Mary E. 73
Susan P. 192
Thomas 119
Wm. L. 105
Wasson, Sarah 88
Waters, Catherine 42
Delia 27
George W. 15
John 78, 211
Lydia 20
Maria 31
Marianna C. 27
Mary 191, 204
Perry 138
Thos. J. 102
William 32
Wates, Agnes 149
Watkins, Geo. P. 125
Icypheny 114
Irean 126
Isabella H. 190
Jacob 35
Jane 49
Joseph P. 23
Martha 33
McGelne H. 211
Micajah 37
Nancy B. 31
Nancy H. 136
Noel 3
Peggy 33
Polly 41, 62
Sally 12, 26, 41
Samuel 34
Sibella T. 104
Thomas 101
William E., Jr. 193
Wm. E. 31, 55
Watson, Charles T. 200
David 40, 68
Elizabeth 186, 207
Emeline 208
James 57
Jas. R. 83
John 12, 25
Jonathan 77
Letitia 65
Martha A. 165
Mary Jane 179
Mary M. 28
Nancy A. 92
Nancy J. 19
Polly 34
Rich'd P. 179
Sarah 146
Winfield S. 188
Wm. P. 137
Watts, Hance H. 118
James 200
Jesse B. 103
Sarah 8
Thomas 24,26
Watts (cont.)
Winnie 4
Waugh, John 14
Way, Ann 90
Wayne, Wm. 147
Weakley, Eliza Jane 190
Elizabeth M. 100
Fanny 51
Isaac 4, 193
Jane B. 77
Margaret 194
Narcissa 36
Polly 14
Weaks, George D. 211
H. H. 218
Weatherly, Wm. 46
Weaver, Dempsey 179, 200
Eliza 194
Elizabeth 35
Ellen Ann 178
John 35, 183
Jonathan W. 84
Margaret 149
Nancy 113
Orrin D. 42
Reuben 70
Seaborn J. 72
Williamson 73
Webb, Amanda M. K. 198
Edward 211
James 12, 25
John D. 21
Kendal 58, 150
Mary Jane 202
N. E. 155
Rebecca 214
Sallie 4
Thos. R. 218
Webber, John 51
Webster, Daniel 130
Weeks, Henry 93
Robt. 92
Wegle, Henry 4
Wehrley, Dane 142
Daniel 78
Mary 180
Weigart, America 164
Weir, Robert 179
William 31
Welborn, Enoch 188
Welbourne, Enoch 80
Welburn, Nancy J. 158, 165
Welch, Eliza 150
Thomas 75
W. H. 211
Wells, Barbary 97
Elizabeth Ann 193
Haney 21
Hiram 68
Josiah 23
Martha 192
Nancy 21
Polly 25
Sarah A. 198
Sarah P. 125
Thomas 87
Wendel, Polly 9
Rachel 3
West, Angelica R. 184
Ferbee Ann 210
Hannah 17
Harriet R. 35
Jeanie M. 206
Jennie M. 206
Lidia 33
Mathias S. 100
Polly 32

William, Gleaves 20
Williamison, Rebecca
67
Williams, (?) 77
Alex R. 200
Alsee 22
Amelia 151
Amelia Ann 156
An'd 206
Anna 13
Anne 67
Arabella 215
Benjamin 151
Benjamin W. 107
Betsy 18
Burchet 179
Caroline 125, 216
Catherine 24, 165
Christopher 57
Christopher C. 95
Claiborne 4
David 121, 135
Dicey 76
Elisha 34, 124
Eliza 39
Elizabeth 16, 18,
114, 190
Emeline 110
Emeline R. 176
Elmon W. 151
Eunice 8
Evaline 173
Fannie E. 159
Frances M. 194
Gardner 91
George W. 179
Harriet N. 142
Helena 131
Henry 197
Isaiah F. 33
James 82, 193
Jane 218
Jane L. 153
Jane R. 126
Jas. 85
Jas. B. 80
Jeremiah 36
Jno. M. 218
Jno. S. 40
Jno. T. 111
John 12, 23, 25, 36,
62, 193
John W. 205
Jordan E. 87
Jos. N. 34
Joseph 193
Joseph J. 180
Joseph P. 174
Lavina 179
Lavinia 173, 185
Lemuel 70, 119
Leonard 90
Lerilda Adeline 178
Lewis 65, 138
Lucinda 106
Margaret 35
Margaret V. 172
Maria Ann 43
Martha 136, 177
Martha A. 195
Martha C. 139
Martha G. 205
Martha J. 159, 160
Mary 134, 186, 207
Mary A. 213
Mary A. E. 168
Mary Jane 216
Mary W. 172
Williams (cont.)
McHenry 179
Milberry 186, 187
Milbrey H. 125
Nancy 1, 80, 98, 142
Nancy A. 127
Nancy L. E. 33
Nathan A. 86
Oliver 8
Penelope A. 185
Phillip M. 183
Plummer 147, 148
Polly 3, 42
Priscilla B. 65
Rebecca 44, 61, 152
Rebecca P. 132
Rhoda 35
Richard 5
Robert 36
Robert W. 205
Robt. J. 107
Robt. N. 200
Rowena J. 185
Sally 40, 87
Simon 16
Solomon 31
Sophia 50
Sophronia 201
Stephen 180
Susan 118
Susanna 143
Susannah 21, 50
Tellepe 34
Thomas 10, 37
Thos. 56
Tildy 70
Turner 43
Virie 105
W. D. 197
William 6, 24, 48
William S. 71
Willie 118
Willoughby 74
Winney 186
Wm. 52, 60
Wm. A. 116
Wm. H. 117
Wm. S. 66
Zebulon 180
Zippo 104
Williamson, Adams 37
Benj. S. 57
Catherine 20
Elizabeth A. C. 125
Geo. 51
H. T. 211
Harriet 123
Henry G. 115
Isabella M. 199
James D. 72
Jane 9, 123
Jno. L. 123
John, Jr. 24, 26
Marry J. 4
Martha 89
Nancy 148
Peggy 16
Rebecca 100
Robt. T. 123
Sally 29, 70
Sarah 16, 97
Tellitha 196
Thomas 16
Thomas N. 188
Wm. 46
Wm. W. 35
Willis, Amos 29
Catherine 104
Willis (cont.)
Jno. 116
Joseph 188
N. B. 193, 218
Nancy 23
Susan B. 163
Susannah B. 128
Tennessee 182
Virginia M. 179
Walter 104
Wm. 32
Willocks, Thomas 1
Wills, Andrew L. 115
Benjamin 56
David 54
Elizabeth 120
Frances 176
Mary 94, 177
Mary E. 54
Rebecca 37
Susan 175
Susan P. 107
Susan V. 202
Wilmoth, Jane 133
Wilson, Agnes 36
Agness 87
Benj. W. 75
Caroline 133
Catherine C. 142
Dicy 154
Elenor 8
Elihu 211
Elijah 101
Elisha 82
Eliza Ann 201
Elizabeth 215
Geo. 130
George 152
James 12, 53, 165
Jenny 16
Jno. H. 124
Jno. W. 100
Joel 28
John 2, 157
John G. 21
Joseph 91, 117
Louisa Ann 164
Luke 143
Mahala 93
Margaret 196
Margaret C. 197
Margaret F. 208
Martha 131
Martha Ann 196
Mary 8
Mary Jane 188
Mathew 59
Matilda J. 160
Methursy 99
Nancy 99
Nancy A. 150
Nicholas 33
Oliver H. 119
Patsy 102
Polly 14
Robt. 48, 131
Sally 53, 76
Samuel S. 200
Sarah (Mrs.) 167
Sarah Greer 189
Susannah 41
Thomas J. 188
Thos. J. 206
Walter 104
William 10, 17
Wm. T. 124
Winburn, Wm. M. 109
Winchester, Geo. W. 188

Winchester (cont.)
Jabez 95
Marcus B. 193
Margaret 101
Sally 176
Susan 113
V. P. 136
Windel, Juliet A. D. 25
Winfrey, Thos. A. 120
Valintine 29
Wing, Calvin 200
Robert 188
Wingfield, Lucy Ann 210
Maria 112
Wingo, Charity 78, 204
Roland 86
Russell 193
Ruth 134
Winn, Edmond 69
Emma M. 187
Winstead, Mason 21
Patsy 4
Wm. C. 47
Winston, Catherine 214
John J. 58
Prissy M. 164
William 28
Winters, Wm. 55
Wise, Henry A. 105
James 120
Wisiner, Wm. 6
Wisner, Nelly 18
Sallie 17
Wistion, Frances 135
Witcher, Mary 121
Witherald, James 35
Witherly, Isaac 62
Witherspoon, John 3, 16
Witt, Charlotte R. 49
George C. 35
Joel D. 206
Witty, Jno. C. 135
Witzel, Amelia 194
Woldridge, Henry W. 180
Wolf, Catherine 68, 201
Christiana 195
Elizabeth 128
George W. 33, 184
James 106
John 206
Philip 9
Polly 123
Rebecca 156
Temperance 175
Wolford, Mary Ann 195
Wolstenholme, Hugh 197
Womble, Elizabeth 105
Wood, Agnes G. 58
David S. 143
Edward G. 162
Eliza 72
Elizabeth S. 200
Fleming P. 56
Frances 12
John H. 10
Johnson 121
Judidah 94
Robert 48
Rosanna B. 99
Samuel L. 33
Sarah 145
Stancil 174
Staneel 89
Stephen 79
Thos. J. 144
Wm. 211
Woodard, Elizabeth 112, 151
Eveline 163
Martha B. 106
Mary 3
Rebecca 70
Thomas 86
Woodcock, Jno. 78
Wooden, Sophia 6
Woodfin, Ryland H. 103, 149
Silas 78
Susan M. 33
Woodfine, Henrietta 176
Woodfolk, Wm. W. 162
Woodfork, Patsy 54
Woodlin, Cassandra 143
Wm. 69
Woodruff, Dolly 45
Eliza 213
Elizabeth 184
Nancy 20
Patsy 32
Woodrum, Jacob 9
Woods, Adine A. 150
Alexander H. 42
Anna E. 201
Caroline 191
Edward 52
Eli L. 118
Elizabeth 154, 158
Elspa 31
Emeline 98
Harriet 154
James 211, 218
James, Jr. 159
James A. 197
Jane T. 190
Josephine J. 184
Margaret F. 195
Robena 193
Robert H. 188
Sarah 77
Woodson, John W. 212
Wm. 124
Woodward, Benj. 65
Benjamine 188
Caroline 217
Cynthia 119
Edmund 40
Elvira 181
Evelin 161
Geo. B. P. 184
Geo. P. 146
Henry 8
James 70
Jeremiah 20
Lucy 181
Lucy Ann 127
Martha 20, 181
Mary Ann 195
Wooldridge, Lucinda 189
Woolridge, Josiah 13
Wooten, Daniel 41
Sarah 66
Wooton, Emile W. 108
Word, Fulton F. 193
Rebecca 151
Work, Andrew 145
Elizabeth 123
Emily 194
Ester 42
Jane 95
John F. 148
Joseph A. 137
Nancy 67, 84
Polly 43
Rebecca 93
Work (cont.)
Robert 135, 138
Robt. 97
Sally M. 44
Samuel 89
World, Ann 205
Sarah G. 208
Worlds, Muscoga E. 210
Muscogo E. 216
Worley, Isaiah 34
Wormach, Mathew 86
Worrell, (?) (Doctor) 200
Littleberg E. 200
Wortham, John 19
Wozencraft, Oliver M. 163
Wray, Elizabeth 54, 99
Harriet A. 92
Henry W. 206
James 129
Jane 160
John 12, 26
Mary 79
Savannah 27
Susannah 23
Wm. 55
Wren, Rebecca 83
Sally 28, 142
Wm. 35
Wrenn, Elizabeth 46
George 33
Peggy 57
Wright, Aaron 128
Abraham 39
Adam 61
Agnes 173
Almeda S. 215
Anne 78
Benjamin 57
Betsy 33, 134
Charles 27
Charles F. 197
Cynthia M. 137
Elijah 36
Elizabeth 27, 49, 59, 113
Geo. P. 78
George 27, 49
Gilley 59
H. M. 156
Jacob O. 206
James 41, 188
James W. 125
Jane 113, 143
Jane H. 53
Jas. W. 111
Jennie 28
Jesse 161
Jno. 137
Jno. A. 125
Jno. B. 67
John 47, 63, 89, 143
John M. 14
Jonathon 115
Joseph 31
Louisa 184
Louise P. 207
Lucinda 139
Lucinda S. 100
Lucy 59, 97
Lucy Ann 180
Margaret 16, 74
Martha 161
Mary 162
Miranda E. 189
Nancy 36, 111, 207
Olive 83

ADDITIONS